DEVINE RULE

IN SASKATCHEWAN

DEVINE RULE
IN SASKATCHEWAN

A DECADE OF
HOPE AND HARDSHIP

Lesley Biggs and Mark Stobbe, Editors

FIFTH HOUSE PUBLISHERS
Saskatoon, Saskatchewan

Design: Robert Grey, Apex Graphics
Cover Photo: The *Star Phoenix*

Canadian Cataloguing in Publication Data

Main entry under title:

Devine rule in Saskatchewan

Includes bibliographical references
ISBN 0–920079–72–5

1. Saskatchewan – Politics and government – 1982– *
2. Saskatchewan – Economic policy. 3. Saskatchewan – Social policy.
I. Biggs, Lesley. II. Stobbe, Mark.
FC3527.2.D5 1991 971.24'03 C91–097009 2
F1072.D5 1991

This book has been published with the assistance of The Canada Council.

The authors have generously volunteered their time and donated their royalties to the Saskatchewan Association on Human Rights.

1 2 3 4 5 6 93 92 91

Fifth House Publishers
620 Duchess St.
Saskatoon, Saskatchewan   S7K 0R1

Printed in Canada

CONTENTS

ACKNOWLEDGEMENTS

A book of this type is a collective effort. We can mention only some of the people who have made it possible.

A special thanks must go to the authors for the essays in this book. Neo-conservatives will argue that people's only motivation is cash. This book proves them wrong. When we asked these authors to contribute a chapter, every one of them did so without asking about terms of payment. We are still not sure if they realized what they were getting themselves into. Each contributor spent several hundred hours on his or her chapter. They were subjected to late-night telephone calls, demands for yet further documentation, and impossible deadlines that were (almost always) met. Finally, when the book was completed, it was proposed that their royalties be donated to the Saskatchewan Association on Human Rights. Without exception, they agreed. Thay were motivated by a love of their province and community rather than personal gain. One of the greatest pleasures of putting this book together was having the opportunity to work with this group of people.

A great many other people also contributed to this book. To be honest, we do not know how many. Over the past two years, dozens if not hundreds of people have said, "Oh, by the way, so-and-so was in to see me researching a chapter in your book." At times it seemed as if the entire province was at work on the project. A partial list of the people who provided research assistance or editorial comment on chapters includes: Craig Dotson, Joan Feather, Martin d'Entremont, Gerry MacPherson, Tim Shoulak, Laurie Stone, Gerry Aldridge, Aina Kagis, Garnet Dishaw, Pam Hanna, Don Anderson, Pat Atkinson, Bob Todd, Deb Hartung, Eric Cline, Marie Warner, Don Kerr, Kerry Westcott, Gloria Bourke, Jim Sutherland, Greg Trew, Keith Bell, Herman Rolfes, Marni Allison, Linda McCann, Pat Stuart, and Bill Troupe. A special thanks goes to Kathy Tunnicliffe for typing many of the chapters, and to Lana Hornridge for undertaking the tedious task of verifying and standardizing endnotes.

We would like to express special appreciation for the work of Beth Smillie and Gerry Sperling.

Finally we would like to thank our parents Pam Sturgess and William Bigggs and John and Margaret Stobbe. Without their love and support we would never have been able to undertake a project such as this book.

AN EXAMINATION OF THE CONSERVATIVE YEARS, 1982-1990

by Lesley Biggs and Mark Stobbe

For a week rumours had been swirling around the province of Saskatchewan.

Two weeks before the 1990 session of the legislature was scheduled to be called back, Premier Grant Devine had requested free television air time to make a major, emergency announcement. He and his staff refused to divulge the contents of the speech.

When the cameras began to roll, the province saw a tired and sombre premier. He began with an outline of the province's economic position.

> We all know this province has been rocked by one economic challenge after another in recent years. Throughout this time, which has included years of high interest rates, bankruptcies, drought, low commodity prices, and subsidy wars, we've all struggled to reconcile two competing factors of hope and hardship . . .

The situation was now desperate, said the premier. "All of these factors amount to the world declaring economic war on Saskatchewan and our way of life."

After he had set the stage, Devine began making the policy announcements. One by one, the popular, vote-grabbing programs from the 1982 and 1986 election campaigns were eliminated or cut back. The first to go was one of the cornerstones of the 1986 campaign. The Home Improvement Program, which offered matching grants of up to $1,500 and 6% interest on loans of up to $10,000, was cancelled effective midnight that night. The next program to be pared was one of the two key planks of the 1982 victory. The interest rate for the Mortgage Protection Plan was increased from 9¾% to 10¾%. Then came the announcement that must have been the hardest for the premier to make:

You know when I was first elected Premier in 1982, I said Saskatchewan people would not have to pay provincial tax on gasoline as long as I was Premier. Tonight, I have to tell you that I can no longer deliver on that promise. To do so under the current situation of hardship would be nothing more than a personal, partisan, face-saving charade.[1]

For the beleaguered premier, the election night of 26 April 1982 must have seemed like a distant memory. Then, 2,871 days earlier, he had been swept to power with the largest legislative majority in Saskatchewan's history. The new government had won 57 seats. The once invincible NDP had its caucus slashed from 44 members to 7. Of the NDP cabinet, only Allan Blakeney and two cabinet ministers had survived.

Now, in 1990, Devine was being forced to admit that the province could not afford to continue the programs that had won him this overwhelming victory.

The mood of the Conservative party in 1982 was confident, expansive, and optimistic. On election night, the celebrating Conservatives in Devine's home riding of Estevan had originally booked a basement room at the Derrick Hotel for the celebration. Shortly before election day, it became clear that the 200-person capacity of the hotel hall would not be enough. The Estevan Curling Club was hastily booked, and 700 exuberant supporters turned out to celebrate.

Devine expressed hope for the future: "The good old province of Saskatchewan is not going to be the same anymore. We're not going to be seventh or eighth any more. We're going to be No. 1." Dismissing questions about the cost of his election promises, Devine flatly stated, "They're very down-to-earth, common sense promises. The resource wealth is there. We're going to start passing the benefits onto the people."[2]

The good humour and confidence of Devine and his supporters had been demonstrated the night before the election. Devine, along with his family and staff, had dined at the Prairie Stonehouse Inn at the village of Halbrite near Estevan. The restaurant's owners produced a white porcelain chamber pot filled with champagne. If Devine lost, they warned him that the "victory mug" would be filled with something else the next time he dined at their restaurant. Everyone in Devine's party took a turn from the mug.[3] Eight years later, the restaurant was closed and its owners had left town.

When Grant Devine became premier, he and his supporters believed that the future belonged to Saskatchewan. Campaigning on the slogan "There's so much more we can be," the Conservatives argued that the socialist CCF and NDP governments had stifled economic development and opportunity. With a Conservative government, this would change. Capital investment would flood the province. The entrepreneurial spirit of Saskatchewan people would be freed from the yoke of government restriction. The result would be prosperity for all and wealth for the entrepreneurs. In the new Saskatchewan, the role of government would be to keep out of the way of the entrepreneurs, and to pass out the money that would flow in from the booming economy.

Devine and his supporters believed in the market with an enthusiasm that was contagious and a naivety that was touching. Upon taking office, the Tories proclaimed that Saskatchewan was "Open for Business," and waited for the economic boom. It never materialized. Instead, the expensive promises which gave Devine electoral victory helped create a budget deficit that had reached crisis proportions by the end of the 1980s.

During Devine's first term, the government retained its optimism that unrestricted free enterprise would lead to a capitalist nirvana. From 1982 to 1986, the Devine government lacked ideological clarity in its programs. In addition to its enthusiastic celebration of free enterprise, it rewrote labour legislation in favour of employers and showered private companies (particularly in the resource sector) with tax breaks and royalty cuts. However, there were no wholesale cuts to social programs. Growth of crown corporations was curtailed, but there was no dramatic sale of public assets. Government expenditures rose rapidly as the Conservatives proved that support for free enterprise was not incompatible with free spending. When combined with a reduction in oil royalty rates and abolition of the consumption tax on gasoline, the result was a rapidly climbing governmental deficit, a new development after 11 years of balanced or surplus NDP budgets.

The Conservatives campaigned on an optimistic platform in the 1986 election. The government claimed that the economy was being diversified and that the province was prosperous. All that was needed was more time for an unrestricted market to work its magic.

The year 1986 was a turning point for the Devine government. The election was won, but only by the narrowest margin. The NDP garnered more votes than did the Conservatives, but lost enough close races to allow the Tories to form the government. Two thousand more votes for the NDP, distributed properly, would have changed the outcome of the election. Most observers attributed the Conservative victory to the last-minute promise of $1-billion in farm aid from the federal Conservative government of Brian Mulroney.

Perhaps the most disturbing trend for the government was that it lost the constituencies in which the benefits of its economic strategy showed the most results. In Prince Albert, the sale of the crown-owned pulp mill to the American multi-national timber giant Weyerhaeuser had brought with it the construction of a new paper mill. The voters of Prince Albert responded by voting out both Conservative MLAs representing the city. In North Battleford, government grants and tax credits had attracted a bacon processing plant, a facility to manufacture recreational vehicles, and an overhead-door manufacturing plant. For his efforts, the minister of economic development was unceremoniously turfed out of office. Voters in the constituencies closest to the government's economic development strategy had rejected it.

The year 1986 also marked the beginning of a severe downturn in the Saskatchewan economy. The prices of both oil and wheat collapsed. The government, already burdened by a debt it had run up when times were relatively good, was restricted in its ability to respond to these economic problems generated by market developments beyond Saskatchewan's borders. The government's problems were aggravated by drought. As the sky filled with clouds of dust, the highways filled with moving vans of people heading for Alberta, British Columbia, and Ontario.

The Conservatives responded to the twin problems of electoral unpopularity and economic crisis by sharpening their ideological focus. The attempts to please all groups in the province were dropped. The government became far more explicit in expounding a right wing, neo-conservative philosophy. Social programs were cut. Civil servants were given their layoff notices. Crown corporations were placed on the auction block. Politics became polarized and bitter.

It quickly became clear, however, that the attempt to implement an ideologically consistent neo-conservative agenda in Saskatchewan would meet with substantive opposition. The first major battle came in the spring of 1987 when the government announced a series of cuts to social programs. In June, the largest demonstration in the history of Saskatchewan arrived at the legislature. A series of petitions protesting cuts in the health care system garnered over 100,000 signatures. The government's popularity plummeted.

Devine attempted a political recovery in 1988 and 1989 through a strategy of clarifying his ideological position even further. From Britain, he imported an aggressive privatization strategy. The government sought to actively mobilize public opinion in favour of free enterprise through the sell-off of Crown corporations and through contracting out government services. For a time, it appeared as if his strategy was working. Then Devine broke his word and attempted to sell off a major public utility, Sask Energy, the corporation which distributes natural gas to Saskatchewan homes and businesses. As the NDP caucus boycotted the legislature, the opposition mobilized. Devine was forced to capitulate. The attempt to shape public opinion in favour of the market had met with disaster.

The privatization battle destroyed the Devine government's ideological consistency. Since then, the government has fitfully alternated between promising to listen, to consult, to follow public opinion, and launching efforts to reclaim the initiative in creating a neo-conservative agenda in Saskatchewan. Initiatives were announced and then forgotten. The government was in disarray as it alternatively attempted to win back popularity through deeds or through consulting and listening. To date, very little has worked for the troubled premier and his government.

Devine Rule in Saskatchewan outlines the way in which the government of Grant Devine has performed after receiving (at least initially) the largest political mandate in Saskatchewan history. Each essay examines the government's record in a selected policy area. In total, the book is a report card on the Conservative government's attempt to transform Saskatchewan.

Lesley Biggs and Mark Stobbe

CHAPTER 1

POLITICAL CONSERVATISM AND FISCAL IRRESPONSIBILITY

by Mark Stobbe

The provincial deficit has become one of the key political issues in Saskatchewan during the Devine decade.

Deficit financing in Saskatchewan broke with the political traditions of the province. In the 1930s, Saskatchewan had flirted with bankruptcy, but since the 1940s, all governments in the province have been fiscally conservative. The Douglas CCF government brought down a series of surplus budgets, and by 1962 had succeeded in paying off the accumulated debt that it had inherited in 1944. Lloyd's CCF, Thatcher's Liberal, and Blakeney's NDP governments all upheld the thrifty house-holder's maxim of "don't spend more than you have." This fiscal conservativeness resulted in a string of balanced or surplus budgets in 36 of 38 years.

The tradition ended abruptly when the Devine Conservatives took office. Since that time, the provincial government has had nine consecutive deficit budgets. The accumulated debt has totalled over $4.3 billion dollars, and by the fiscal year of 1990–91, the province estimated that it would be paying $493 million in interest charges (see Table 1.1). This budget item has become the third largest in the provincial budget, and has imposed severe restrictions on the government's ability to respond to the political and economic events of the day.

The Devine government's attitude toward deficit spending can be divided into two phases. These coincide with its two terms in office.

The first phase was characterised by optimism. Building on the 1982 campaign slogan of "there is so much more we can be," the government dismissed the long-term consequences of the budget, and argued that the long-term strength of the Saskatchewan economy ensured that the debt was easily manageable. In his November 1982 budget address, Finance Minister Bob Andrew announced that Saskatchewan would have its first deficit in 38 years. This, he said, was the fault of his predecessors. However, there was no cause for alarm. "This is a minimized and manageable deficit, which has been directly translated into assistance for the people of this province," Andrew declared.[1] Four years into the government's mandate, the new Finance Minister, Gary Lane, acknowledged that the deficit and the accumulating debt were beginning to cause some concern, but that "we are not prepared to fight the deficit on the backs of seniors, farmers and small business." Further, Lane argued that the deficit was simply cyclical and that a balanced budget would be achieved within five years.[2]

Less than a year later, following the 1986 election, Lane was singing a different song. The province, he said, was in a state of fiscal crisis. "If the provincial deficit had been caused by a temporary downturn in the economy, our deficit would not be of concern . . . however, it is now clear that Saskatchewan's deficit is not a short-term phenomenon and, as such, it threatens the economic and financial well-being of our province."[3] These words ushered in the second phase of the political treatment of the deficit. The growing debt became the centrepiece of the government's political rhetoric. Harsh medicine was now needed to cure a potentially terminal illness. "Dealing with the deficit" became the Devine mantra used to justify program cuts, restrictions in funding, or old-fashioned meanness.

When attempting to explain how a Conservative government became the most fiscally irresponsible in Saskatchewan's history, the Devine government abdicates responsibility. The deficit is the result of a combination of the effects of 11 years of NDP rule, and of forces beyond the control of any government, including drought, low prices for such commodities as oil, potash, and uranium, and an international price war in grains. Premier Devine has even gone so far as to state that the world has "declared war" on Saskatchewan. Members of the government thus argue that the deficit is not their fault, and that they are struggling valiantly to make the best of an impossible situation.

There is no doubt that world markets have not been kind to Saskatchewan products during the last half of the 1980s. The government argues that a downturn in commodity markets caused the deficit. However, these markets remained relatively strong until well into 1986. Despite this, by the end of the 1985–86 fiscal year, the province had an accumulated debt of over $1.5 billion. The majority of the debt accumulated since that time has simply been interest charges being rolled over. Saskatchewan's fiscal crisis existed before the economic conditions that the government uses to explain the existence of the crisis. The government's explanation needs further examination.

THE SOURCES OF SASKATCHEWAN'S DEFICIT

During the 1982 election campaign, Devine's Conservatives ran a campaign that centred on an idea that was easily conveyed to voters: cash in the pocket. The candidates' policy handbook was called *Pocketbook Politics*, and outlined measures by which a Progressive Conservative government would provide immediate increases in disposable income for the common voter. The two key promises were a mortgage protection plan and the abolition of the gas tax, applied at the retail level.

The 1982 election coincided with soaring interest rates. The monetary policy of the Bank of Canada was to create a recession in order to lower the inflation rate. Homeowners forced to renegotiate their mortgages were faced with the prospect of interest rates in excess of 20%. As a result, many feared that they would lose their homes. The more fortunate were scrambling to come up with enough cash to meet mortgage payments that had suddenly doubled. Devine's Conservatives tapped this reservoir of fear and anger. Promising a mortgage protection plan that would subsidize interest payments in excess of 13¼%, the Conservatives ran ads with the simple message: "It means more of your money stays in your pocket." [4]

Devine was also promising cheap gasoline; the pump tax on gasoline would be abolished immediately. The ads trumpeted: "Save 40 cents/gallon –8.00/tankful. Vote Progressive Conservative." Devine's figures were challenged by groups ranging from the NDP to Shell Canada to the Canadian Petroleum Association, who argued that the pump tax actually was only 29 cents per gallon. The facts did not get in the way of Devine's campaign, as he insisted that "it amounts to 40 cents a gallon. That's exactly what it is and don't let anyone tell you different." [5] The voters of Saskatchewan ignored the quibbling over numbers. Cheap gas was cheap gas.

Combined with an attack on the NDP for being out-of-touch and uncaring, these two promises formed the basis of the Conservatives' 1982 election campaign. They worked so well that by the end of the campaign, Devine was bragging that he still had promises left over. Plans to promise universal day care, free telephones for seniors, improved water quality, double laning of the Trans-Canada Highway, and a comprehensive waste-management system were all shelved because of the success of the

17

campaign.[6] A 10% cut in personal income tax and the elimination of the sales tax were promised, but were not featured prominently in the Conservative advertising.

There was, however, one significant promise that was made with even less fanfare than the elimination of the sales tax or the reduction in personal income tax. This was a promise to change the oil royalty structure. During the 1970s, the NDP government had moved to capture a significant portion of the revenue generated by rising oil prices. This effort to capture the economic rent from oil production had been a constant preoccupation of the Blakeney government.[7] By 1981, the government was receiving 64.9% of the value of production in taxes and royalties. In the fiscal year of 1981–82, this amounted to $532,712,000, or 20% of the government's revenue.[8] For Devine and his Conservative colleagues, the capture of this economic rent from oil simply served to discourage the industry. Speaking at a rally in the oil-producing district near Lloydminster, Devine promised modifications in the royalty structure "because nobody makes any money if you stop working, if the oil isn't flowing and people aren't working . . . The government doesn't make any money, the people don't make any money and you close down and leave. The potential here in this part of the province for oil productivity is fantastic and we're fools if we don't take advantage of it."[9] The promise to lower oil royalties was made publicly in the oil-producing regions of Lloydminster and Estevan, and no doubt privately in corporate boardrooms. During the campaign stops in the rest of the province, Devine preferred to talk about abolishing the pump tax for consumers.

It was never clear during the election campaign just where the money would come from to implement the campaign promises being made. The mortgage program was estimated to cost $35 million. The promises for tax reductions were far more expensive. The abolition of the gas tax would cost the government $110 million per year. In 1982–83, the sales tax was projected to bring in $358 million and individual income tax was projected at $597 million. The cost of eliminating the sales tax and reducing personal income tax by 10% would therefore have been $418 million. The cost of the promised oil royalty reductions was never spelled out. In short, the Conservatives were promising tax cuts to individuals totalling $528 million as well as unspecified cuts to oil royalty rates, while at the same time, Devine was promising that there would be no cuts to health care, education, or other social programs. The closest the soon-to-be premier ever came to explaining the economics of these proposals was to state that they would be paid for by not buying Norcanair (the NDP had proposed to purchase the regional airline for a price of $60 million). The seeds of the deficit were thus sown during the 1982 election campaign.

Upon taking office in April 1982, the new government almost immediately implemented the mortgage protection plan, abolished the gas tax, and restructured oil royalty rates. The promises to abolish the sales tax and reduce personal income taxes were quietly dropped. With the exception of these policy changes, the new Conservative government largely followed the budget for 1982–83 that the NDP government had introduced prior to the election. However, the policy changes introduced by the new government necessitated a mid-year financial statement which projected Saskatchewan's first deficit budget in close to four decades. Finance Minister Andrew blamed the situation on the previous NDP government.

The two most fiscally significant policy decisions made by the new government both revolved around fossil fuels. Indeed, in a real sense, the story of Saskatchewan's fiscal crisis begins and ends with hydrocarbons. Had it not been for policy changes regarding pricing of these fuels at both the production and consumption ends of the cycle, Saskatchewan would still have a balanced provincial budget.

Let us begin by examining energy consumption taxes. As promised in the election campaign, the gasoline pump tax was removed. Revenue from the fuel tax dropped from $120,686,000 in the 1981–82 fiscal year to $15,046,007 in the 1982–83 fiscal year and $13,592,540 in 1983–84. The majority of the remaining revenue came from taxes on aviation fuel and on diesel fuel used by railway locomotives. In the first budget following the 1986 election, a 7 cent per litre tax on gasoline was imposed. Saskatchewan residents were to collect receipts, submit these to the government, and receive rebates. These rebates would be issued for fuel consumed by individuals for their own personal use, and for fuel used by farmers and primary producers of renewable resources. Other business, commercial, or government users would not be eligible for the rebate. With this change, revenue from the fuel tax increased from $31,541,000 in 1986–87 to $161,168,000 in 1987–88. In 1989, the "rebatable fuel tax" was increased from 7 cents per litre to 10 cents. Then, two weeks before the legislature reconvened for the 1990 spring session, Devine made a special television appearance. He noted that he had promised in 1982 that "Saskatchewan people would not have to pay provincial tax on gasoline as long as I was Premier," but that "I can no longer deliver on that promise." The fuel tax rebate was abolished completely, effective back to 1 January 1990. Only half of the rebate would be paid for fuel purchased in 1989. Thus, eight years after Devine abolished the fuel tax, Saskatchewan residents were paying 10 cents per litre, compared with 6.6 cents prior to its abolition. Projected revenue for 1990–91 from this tax is $206,000,000, or $85 million more than in the fiscal year before the tax was abolished.

Revenue forgone as a result of the abolition of the fuel tax and the later rebate programs was substantial. Based on the 1982 tax rate of 6.6 cents per litre and gasoline consumption for the 1982 to 1987 period, the outright abolition of the fuel tax cost the provincial treasury approximately $590 million. The subsequent rebate programs to individuals cost a further $145 million.[10] A total of $735 million in revenue was thus forgone because of the Devine government's fuel tax promises. Since this resulted in deficit financing, the true cost of the policy must also include the resulting interest charges. If this is factored in, the 1982 election promise of cheap gasoline accounts for over $1 billion of the Saskatchewan government's accumulated deficit.

The changes to the royalty structure for oil companies have been less publicized and more expensive than the changes to the consumer gasoline tax.

During the summer of 1982, the Saskatchewan cabinet hammered out the details of a new royalty structure for the oil industry. The most important features of the new policy, which was implemented in July 1982, were to be a reduction in the royalty rates for existing production, and a three-year royalty-free period for production from new wells. According to then-Energy Minister Colin Thatcher, the changes were opposed in cabinet and caucus by Gary Lane. However, "those who had any connection with the oil industry were all supportive."[11]

The 1982 changes to the oil royalty rates, and subsequent changes in 1986 and 1990, led to a dramatic decrease in the share of the value of oil production being captured by the provincial treasury. Table 1.2 outlines trends in Saskatchewan oil production and taxation during this period. In 1981, the province received $532 million in royalties on production valued at $821 million. By 1989, the provincial government was receiving royalties of $254 million on production valued at $1.17 billion. The province's share of the value of production dropped from 64.9% to 21.7%.

It is impossible to determine with exact precision what the changes in oil royalties cost Saskatchewan. The royalty structure has an impact on production. So do federal energy policies, international prices, the activities of OPEC, wars in the Middle East, and the weather. In 1981, 7,409,000 cubic metres of oil were pumped in Saskatchewan. This amount increased steadily until 1988, when 12,242,000 cubic metres were being produced. In 1989, production dropped to 10,989,000 cubic metres. There can be no question that the Devine government's policy of giving much of this oil away for free and taxing the remainder at reduced rates contributed to the increase in production. Indeed, Thatcher argued the royalty holiday cost the province nothing since it would not receive any revenue if the oil was left in the ground.[12] To the extent that the oil companies increased production because the government was giving away the oil for free, this argument is correct. It is also short-sighted in the extreme. Oil is a finite, non-renewable resource. If left in the ground, it increases in value. While giving oil away may not result in any immediate drop in revenue, in the medium and long-term the province has given away a nonrenewable resource without receiving any compensation in return. Further, by making the production from new wells royalty-free, the government encourages oil companies to artificially shift production from old wells to new ones. This creates a few drilling jobs, but makes no long-term economic sense. The royalty structure encourages waste and inefficiency by giving an incentive to producers to restrict output from existing wells while drilling new wells in the same field. Finally, the government's argument that the new royalty structure was cost-neutral neglects the lowering of rates for production from existing wells. A lowering of these rates represents a direct loss of government revenue.

Thatcher argued that the new royalty schedule would either be cost-neutral or would increase revenues to the government because it would spur an offsetting increase in production. In assessing the cost of the changes to the royalty structure, an extreme assumption would be that the royalty rates would have no impact on the production decisions of the oil companies, and that world price and consumer demand would determine the level of production. The potential and forgone revenue columns in Table 1.2 are based on these assumptions. That is, if the 1981 rate of taxation had remained constant and oil production and prices had remained as they actually were, the potential revenue is what the Saskatchewan government would have received in royalties, and the forgone revenue represents the difference between the potential and the actual revenue. With this assumption, the calculation of the cost of the Devine government's changes to oil royalties totals $3,897,610,000 from 1982 to 1989. This comes very close to equalling the entire accumulated provincial deficit for this period. Given that this revenue shortfall was met by government borrowing, the resulting interest charges add dramatically to the cost of the royalty changes.

In the real world, the actual cost of the changes in the oil royalty rates lies somewhere between the government's claims of cost neutrality and costing based on the assumption that production was unaffected by royalty rates. During the 1980s, the oil industry was extremely volatile. Prices increased steadily until 1985, and then dropped by 50% in 1986. Since then, the trend has been a gradual recovery in prices. In Saskatchewan, the situation was complicated by the rise and fall of the federal National Energy Policy. In 1983, the federal government agreed that prices for oil produced in Saskatchewan and Alberta would move toward world prices. This resulted in a large increase in the price paid to producers. Drilling activity in Saskatchewan parallels world oil prices. Drilling (including natural gas wells) peaked in 1985 with 3,851 wells drilled; with the collapse in prices, drilling dropped to 1,079 wells in 1986. By 1988, 2,082 wells were drilled.[13] The pattern of drilling in Saskatchewan follows the world price more closely than it does the provincial royalty structure.

In its political pronouncements, the government claimed full credit for increases in oil production in Saskatchewan. For example, in his 1984 budget speech, Finance Minister Bob Andrew noted that his government had "taken steps to revitalize our oil industry by introducing royalty holidays." The result, he modestly claimed, was an "enormous success" and the policy had "resulted in the most significant increase in oil activity in Saskatchewan history."[14] These wildly optimistic forecasts contrast somewhat with the analysis by the government's employees in the Department of Energy and Mines. Only three months before Andrew's bombastic claims in the budget speech, the government was telling the National Energy Board that it anticipated oil production would rise by 13% between 1983 and 1994. After 1994, production was projected to drop. The Department of Energy and Mines noted that the "provision of world prices and more favourable royalty and tax treatment has largely been responsible for the increased drilling activity."[15] In actual fact, Saskatchewan oil production initially increased more than projected, but peaked in 1988 rather than in 1994.

In effect, the royalties represent the price at which the people of the province, as the owners of the resource, collectively sell crude oil to the oil companies. There can be many different objectives of an oil royalty schedule. During the 1970s, the Blakeney government set this price at a level designed to maximize revenues to the provincial treasury. With the election of the Devine Conservatives in 1982, this philosophy changed. As John Reid, deputy minister for the Department of Energy and Mines noted in 1990, the government's goal was to "establish a regime that encourages conservation and production rather than just maximizing royalty revenue." [16] While there is some inherent contradiction in a policy seeking to encourage both production and conservation, Reid succinctly captured the essence of the policy change. Increasing the volume of production rather than revenues to the owners of the resource became the guiding imperative of the government. The oil companies were the beneficiaries of this change in mandate. The citizens of Saskatchewan were the losers.

The changes to the oil royalty schedule were the most significant fiscal decision made by the Devine government. While the exact cost of this decision will never be known, the economic reporting service *Sask-Trends Monitor* concluded in 1990 that "even with the declining prices, had the royalty and taxation levels remained at their earlier levels, the current provincial debt of $4 billion would simply not exist."[17]

Had the Devine government done nothing differently except avoid implementing its policies on gasoline consumption taxes and oil royalties, Saskatchewan would have a balanced budget and no deficit. However, there were of course many other decisions made on both the revenue and expenditure side of the ledger that had impacts on the fiscal position of the province.

TAXATION IN SASKATCHEWAN DURING THE 1980S

During the tenure of the Devine government, revenues to the government increased substantially. In the fiscal year 1981–82, the last full year of the NDP administration, total revenue to the provincial government amounted to $2,663,702,686.[18] By the fiscal year 1990–91, total revenue was estimated to reach a record $4,235,200,000.[19] During this nine-year period, revenues thus increased by $1,571,497,314, or 59%.

Table 1.3 presents the figures for the fiscal years 1981–82, 1986–87, and 1990–91 and outlines the changes in the major sources of revenue for the Saskatchewan government. A comparison of the trends during Devine's two terms in office can thus be made.

During Devine's first term, total annual revenue to the province increased by only $137 million, or 5.15%. This stable revenue picture, however, masks significant shifts in the sources of revenues. Oil royalties dropped by $319 million, and revenue from the gasoline consumption tax dropped by $89 million. These revenue shortfalls were offset by increases in almost every other revenue category. In dollar terms, the most significant increase was in transfer payments from the federal government, which increased by $264 million, or 49%. In percentage terms, the largest increases were in liquor (186%) and tobacco (157%) revenues. Instead of being eliminated as promised in the 1982 election, revenue from the sales tax increased by $39 million or 12%. Revenue from individual income tax increased by $180 million or 35%.

During Devine's second term, the government moved to deal with the deficit it had created in its first term by increasing its revenue. From the fiscal year 1986–87 to 1990–91, total annual revenue is projected to increase by $1.477 billion dollars, or 53%. During the second term, oil royalties increased by a modest $29 million, or 14%, from four years earlier. It is important to remember, however, that revenue from oil royalties is projected to be $290 million lower than nine years earlier, even though the value of production will be higher. In the second term, increases in federal transfer payments were once again the largest source of additional revenue, rising by $319 million or 40%. Revenue from individual income taxes rose by $204 million or 30%, and revenue from the sales tax rose by $173 million, or 49%. In percentage terms, the largest increase in revenues comes from the consumption tax on gasoline, which increased by 553%, or $174 million.

Table 1.4 outlines the share contributed to the provincial budget by selected revenue sources in 1981–82 and the projections for 1990–91. The most dramatic change is in oil royalties. At the beginning of the decade, oil royalties accounted for 20% of the provincial budget. By the end of the Devine decade, this figure had dropped to 5.7%. Consistent with this drop in collection of revenue from resources, revenue from sale and lease of provincial lands dropped from 0.7% to 0.3%. Corporate income tax also declined marginally in importance, dropping from 3.5% to 2.8%.

As the revenue share from resources declined, the federal government picked up an ever-increasing share of the cost of running Saskatchewan.

In addition, taxes and charges to individuals increased in importance. By the end of the 1980s, the government of Saskatchewan collected more of its revenue from the sale of liquor than from collecting corporate income tax.

Not included in Table 1.4 is revenue from the sale of crown corporations and government assets. In 1988–89, the government collected no revenue from the Crown Investments Corporation (CIC), which is the holding company for Saskatchewan's crown corporations. The government projected that it would receive $200 million in 1989–90 and $310 million in 1990–91 from the CIC.[20] The transfers from the CIC represent 4.9% of the government's projected revenue for 1989–90 and 7.2% for 1990–91. In presenting their respective budgets, neither Gary Lane nor Lorne Hepworth made any acknowledgment of this sudden new source of revenue. Since the transfers from the CIC coincide with the government's privatization campaigns, it is likely that this $510 million represents proceeds from the sale of government assets. The Devine government thus is winding up its second term by funding current expenditures through the sale of assets. This financial strategy is like selling a car to buy gasoline. It is viable only as long as assets remain to sell.

The Devine government's taxation policies have resulted in a decrease in the revenue share from natural resources, an increasing reliance upon federal transfer payments, and an increased share of revenue coming from individuals rather than corporations. The impact of this policy worsens when we turn our attention to the changes within revenue categories. By way of example, let us consider changes in the income tax structure in Saskatchewan.

As noted earlier, during the 1982 election, the Devine Conservatives promised to cut individual income tax rates by 10%. Despite this promise, the Saskatchewan government has increased personal income taxes at a greater rate than there was growth in incomes. Expressed in current dollars, from 1981 to 1989 there was a 57% increase in personal income in Saskatchewan,[21] and an increase of 75% in revenue from individual income tax.[22] During this time, the percentage of total personal income paid out in provincial income tax rose from 4.62% to 5.16%. This increase in the effective rate of taxation was achieved primarily through the implementation of the "flat tax." This tax, applied at a uniform rate on a person's net income, was implemented at a rate of 1% in 1985. It was increased to 1.5% in 1987 and to 2% in 1988. The flat tax has regressive effects since it is applied prior to the calculation of deductions or credits for such things as dependent children, tuition fees, or charitable donations.

While the government was introducing the regressive "flat tax" which placed a disproportionate burden on low- and middle-income earners, it was also introducing a series of tax shelters for those with money to invest. Beginning in his 1984 budget, Finance Minister Bob Andrew created a series of tax credit programs collectively described as the Saskatchewan Tax Initiative Program. The stated purpose of these tax credit programs was to encourage investment in Saskatchewan enterprise by providing tax credits for approved investments. For example, those investing in a registered "venture capital corporation" would receive a tax credit amounting to 30% of their investment under the Venture Capital Program. Those purchasing shares in Saskatchewan corporations would also receive a 30% tax credit on the money invested. From their inception in 1984 until 1990, a total of $114.5 million in tax revenue was forgone as a result of these programs. The peak year was 1986, when $32 million in investment tax credits were issued.[23] In 1989, the most visible of the tax credit programs, the Venture Capital Program, was transformed into a program dispensing cash grants to investors rather than tax credits. The old program, said the Finance Department, led to distortions in investment patterns around "tax time." It was hoped that "cash grants will encourage the development of more projects throughout the year."[24]

The Devine government has never published any detailed analysis of the actual effect of its tax credit programs on the level of investment, employment, or economic development. However, by March of 1989, 184 venture capital corporations had been formed for a total investment of $75 million. Of this, investors were eligible for $22.5 million in tax credits. Tax credits averaging $5,489 from this one program alone were received by 4,100 people in Saskatchewan.

In summary, during Devine's first term in office, overall revenues were relatively stable. A huge drop in revenue from oil companies and consumers of gasoline was offset by increases in federal transfer payments and taxes on individuals. During the second term, in the face of a growing fiscal crisis, the government moved to increase its revenue. While the tax break to consumers of gasoline was reversed, the oil companies continued to be taxed at the reduced rate established in the first term. Federal transfer payments and income and consumption taxes to individuals were the primary sources of additional revenue. The taxation policies tended to be regressive, with the relatively wealthy being the beneficiary of a series of tax-avoidance schemes. The middle- and lower-income groups experienced substantive increases in their taxation levels.

The deficits run up by the Saskatchewan government were thus achieved in the face of increased taxation of ordinary Saskatchewan residents. We now turn our attention to the expenditure side of the government ledger.

SPENDING SPREES AND FISCAL RESTRAINT

In 1981–82, the last full year of the NDP administration, the government of Saskatchewan spent a total of $2,407,838,669.[25] Nine years later, projected expenditure was budgeted at $4,641,345,000.[26] During two terms in office, expenditures increased by 92.8%. This was substantively higher than both the rate of inflation and the increase in government revenues.

While the revenue side of the ledger was characterized by a small increase in total revenues during Devine's first term and large increases in the second, the expenditure side of the ledger featured the opposite pattern. During Devine's first term, expenditures increased by $1,624,822,000, or 67.5%. During the second term, the growth in expenditures was only $608,684,000, or 15%. Half of the second-term expenditure increase was consumed by debt-servicing charges. Actual expenditure on government programs and services increased by only $305,606,000, or 7.6% during Devine's second term. This was substantively below the rate of inflation during this period. Inevitably, the second term was characterized by program and service cuts and stringent restraint measures.

Government spending could thus be described as a first-term party and a second-term hangover. There were also shifts in what the government chose to spend money on.

The largest area of growth in government expenditures was in interest costs to service the government debt. In 1981–82, interest charges accounted for 1.8% of government expenditures, and were offset by interest earnings. By 1990–91, interest charges were projected to consume 10.63% of all government expenditure. For the Saskatchewan government to present a balanced budget in that year, it would have to collect close to half a billion dollars more in taxes than it spent on programs and services. This amounts to $500 for every man, woman, and child in the province. If the Devine government had not accumulated Saskatchewan's debt, the provincial government would have had a budget surplus of $145,234,000 in 1989–90, and would be projected to have a surplus of $130,255,000 in 1990–91. Instead of being in this pleasant position, the past fiscal policies of the Devine government have created a massive debt and interest charges that are growing exponentially. Consequently, severe restrictions are imposed on the ability of both the Devine government and any future governments to deliver programs and services to the people of Saskatchewan.

During Devine's first term, the program categories that received the largest relative increase in spending were programs and services aimed at promoting economic development, and programs and services to agriculture and rural development. Agencies assisting industry spent $85 million in 1981–82. By 1984–85, this spending had increased to $180,209,000. The departments' share of the provincial budget increased from 3.54% to 5.47%. After 1984–85, expenditures in this area stabilized in dollar terms, and declined slightly as a proportion of the provincial budget. Spending on agricultural and rural programs was increased from $120 million in 1981–82 to a peak of $398 million in the 1986–87 election year. The share of the provincial budget received by these programs increased from 4.97% to 9.88%. After the 1986 election was over, spending on agriculture declined in terms of both dollars and budget share. By 1990–91, this spending was projected to total $320 million, or 6.89% of the provincial budget.

The increase in the share of the provincial budget devoted to these two program areas, and to interest charges, was offset primarily by spending restraint in highway construction and maintenance and in programs and services to urban municipalities and residents. The share of the provincial budget spent on roads declined from 7.82% in 1981–82 to 5.54% in 1986–87. This decline continued during Devine's second term. By 1990–91, spending on roads was projected to account for 5.01% of provincial expenditures. Programs and services directed toward urban areas were cut even more dramatically. In 1981–82, this portion of the provincial budget accounted for $158 million, or 6.54% of total spending. By 1986–87, this had dropped to $91 million, or 2.36% of total expenditures. The trend continued during the second term. In 1990–91, this program category was projected to receive $92 million, or 1.98% of total expenditure.

The most significant shifts in overall spending consisted of a redirection of funds from urban programs to assistance to business and support for agriculture. The ideological priorities of the Devine government are also reflected in smaller-line items of expenditure. For example, in 1981–82, the province spent almost $20 million on jails and correctional facilities.

By 1990–91, these expenditures were projected to surpass $47 million, for a 233% increase. During this same period, funding to the Saskatchewan Legal Aid Commission was increased by 43%, funding to the Human Rights Commission increased by only 17%, and funding for the Native court-workers program was terminated completely.

In addition to the actual funding shifts, there were paper changes. There were constant shifts of program line items from department to department and agency to agency. While some of these transfers, such as the reassigning of nursing home and home care expenditures from the Department of Social Services to the Department of Health made administrative sense, other transfers appeared to have resulted from political considerations. The government wanted to argue that it had increased spending on politically popular programs, and cut spending on unpopular ones. The quickest way of accomplishing this was to transfer spending from one department to another. For example, the Department of Social Services was stripped of numerous functions. In addition to the transfer of programs to the Department of Health, responsibility for correctional facilities was transferred to the Department of Justice. Ironically, responsibility for legal aid was transferred from Justice to Social Services.

In terms of the amount of money being shuffled, the most significant device used to optimize the political advantage of government spending was the abolition of the Department of Supply and Services, and its replacement by the Saskatchewan Property Management Corporation (SPMC). Supply and Services had acted as a central agency responsible for providing other departments and agencies with office space, supplies, and other services. These functions were assumed by the SPMC in 1987. The corporation then billed other departments for rent and services. The new arrangement had two advantages for the government. First, as a crown corporation, SPMC was subjected to a lower degree of scrutiny by the provincial auditor and legislature than was the Department of Supply and Services. Second, the new arrangement allowed the government to, on paper, cut expenditures on "bureaucracy" and increase it for more politically advantageous purposes such as "health care." Thus, in the 1987–88 budget, payments to the SPMC by the Department of Health were budgeted at $10,716,700.[27] In a time of severe fiscal restraint, the use of the SPMC allowed the government to claim this money as an increase of expenditure on health care. The fact that the same money had been spent the year before by the Department of Supply and Services was ignored in the government's pronouncements on its commitment to the health of Saskatchewan citizens.

With the possible exception of the Department of Social Services, the branch of government that was stripped of the most expenditure line items was the Executive Council, whose budget covers expenditures by cabinet. Consequently, it offers a tempting target for political opponents of the government. Cuts in the budget allocation for the Executive Council allow the government to claim that it is spending less money on "itself." The most politically expedient shift of expenditure away from the Executive Council occurred in the restraint budget for the 1987–88 fiscal year. Cabinet ministers' salaries were transferred from the vote for the Executive Council to the departments for which the ministers were responsible. This transfer of slightly over $600,000 in the ministers salaries' allowed the government to claim that it was exercising restraint on itself as well as on programs and services. The Saskatchewan Bureau of Statistics was removed from the vote of the Executive Council in the 1986–87 budget. After a short stay as part of the spending of the Saskatchewan Library, this agency soon became part of the Department of Education. Thus, spending "by the cabinet" was cut while spending "on education" was increased correspondingly.

Most of the changes in funding allocations during Devine's first term could be plausibly justified in terms of appropriate administrative responsibility. After the passage of the Government Organization Act immediately after the 1986 election, the government gave itself the power to transfer expenditure from one department to another without taking the matter to the legislature. Shifts in expenditures began to occur with greater frequency. In many cases, there appears to be no administrative reason for the transfers. In all cases, however, there was a political rationale as the government shifted expenditures to departments favoured by voters.

THE POLITICS OF A FISCAL CRISIS

When Grant Devine and his Conservatives were running for election in 1982, confidence in the province abounded. When the government took office, it cut gasoline consumption taxes and oil royalties. These revenue losses were offset by increases in federal transfer payments and income taxes. However, when the losses of oil-based revenue were combined with a failure to adjust expenditures, the result was an immediate and growing deficit. Devine inherited a balanced budget. During his first term, total revenues increased by 5.15% while expenditures increased by 59%. The result was that by the time the bills for the 1986 election promises came due, the government had accumulated a debt approaching $3 billion.

In its second term, the Devine government belatedly discovered fiscal responsibility. During this term, revenues increased by 59% while expenditures increased by only 15%. Half of the increase in expenditures was due to increased debt-servicing costs. With its first-term actions the Devine government had created a monster it could not control. The interest on the debt continually added to the province's overall debt. By the end of the second term, the government was achieving substantial operating surpluses. Despite this, the accumulated debt inexorably continued to grow. As interest charges were rolled over, despite the harsh restraint in program spending, the province got deeper and deeper into debt. Desperate for revenue, the government was even forced to reverse the major plank of its 1982 election victory and re-impose the gasoline consumption tax. However, while it has attempted to control the deficit by restraining spending and increasing taxes to individuals, the government has steadfastly avoided moving to increase its share of revenue from oil production. Tax cuts to consumers of gasoline could be abandoned in hard times, but those to the oil companies were deemed to be sacrosanct.

The fiscal crisis faced by the Saskatchewan government was compounded by the downturn in resource and agricultural markets after 1986. For the government, the economic disadvantages were offset by the political advantage of the downturn providing a justification for the deficit, and for the harsh measures being used to control it. The Devine government created the largest debt in Saskatchewan's history during a time when the province was still relatively prosperous. It then entered the economic downturn burdened with soaring interest charges and with restricted room for manoeuvring to deal with the economy.

There are two explanations for the Devine government's fiscal irresponsibility during its first term. The first and more charitable explanation is incompetence. The government was new, inexperienced, and genuinely enthusiastic about the economic prospects for the province once the marketplace was unfettered. Like a teenager with a new job and credit card, the government could have been lured into a financial crisis by the combination of easy credit and unrealistic dreams for the future.

The second possible explanation is less charitable. This is that the government intentionally and consciously created a deficit during its first term in order to provide the political justification for implementing its true agenda during its second term. It is difficult to persuade voters to agree to cuts in social programs when the government has money. If the government is bankrupt, however, cutbacks can be justified on the grounds that they are unpleasant but necessary. The presence of a large debt also has the added political advantage of making it difficult for any succeeding government to reverse the Conservative agenda. Burdened with interest charges exceeding a half billion dollars per year, any future government will have its ability to rebuild Saskatchewan's social service system greatly hindered.

Regardless of whether the government of Grant Devine ran up Saskatchewan's debt consciously or unconsciously, regardless of whether it was the result of incompetence or malevolence, there is one inescapable result. Saskatchewan citizens will be paying for the fiscal policies of the 1980s for decades.

HUMAN RIGHTS AND THE PC GOVERNMENT

by Peter Millard

B ecause those who have power tend to use it against people who have none, and because it is natural to be afraid of anyone different from oneself, most abuses of human rights are directed to the weak in society and to those who differ from the majority—in other words to the disadvantaged and to minorities. Consequently, a society that cares about human rights enacts legislation to protect actual and potential victims, and monitors itself for attitudes and actions that tend to perpetuate inequalities. It can be said that the best gauge of a society's spiritual health is the degree of concern for the welfare of its minorities.

At the time the Progressive Conservative Party came to power (1982), Saskatchewan had a reputation as a dynamic place for human rights. In 1972, the provincial government had passed human rights legislation which contained a Human Rights Code, and established the Saskatchewan Human Rights Commission (SHRC) to enforce the code. The SHRC was, compared with similar bodies in Canada, extraordinarily progressive. It fought, and won, two landmark cases—for wheelchair access in a Regina theatre, and against prohibition of Seeing Eye dogs in a Saskatoon hospital. Indeed, in the case of the University of Saskatchewan and a homosexual graduate student, the SHRC pushed the legislation somewhat beyond the then understood limit when it attempted to claim that "sex" in the provincial legislation included "sexual orientation" as a prohibited ground of discrimination. (The commission abandoned the case when the university was awarded an injunction against the decision.) A citizen's group called the Saskatchewan Association for Human Rights (SAHR) was active in monitoring abuses and in pressuring government for improvements in the legislation. SAHR enjoyed close cooperative relations with the SHRC.

When the Conservatives first came to power, there was a certain amount of trepidation on the part of those active in human rights. With chilling thoroughness the government set about rooting out from official positions those who were not of their party and viewpoint. It was assumed that progressive organizations would also suffer and that regressive ideas would be given prominence.

To begin with, however, this did not happen. On the contrary, early in Devine's administration there was a heartening sign that he was interested in protecting human rights. In December 1982, Lloyd Hampton, a government backbencher, made racist remarks before a legislative committee reviewing the budget estimates for the SHRC. Natives were not reliable as workers, he said, "because of incompetence and a hangover." What was more, when immigrant families move in with all their relatives, the value of homes goes down, and "the aroma floats across the fence." Premier Devine's reaction was swift and sharp. He removed Hampton from all legislative committees and assured the House that "The member's views do not represent those of the government." [1] It was not only human rights activists who were relieved at Devine's action. The *Star Phoenix* (Saskatoon) summed up the feelings of many people when, in an editorial, it commended the premier for his decisiveness and went on to say:

> When the Conservatives were swept to power last April there were concerns that the government's overwhelming majority combined with the rather extreme views of a few caucus members might lead to reactionary elements within the provincial administration.
> The handling of the Hampton affair indicates Devine is capable of reining in his forces and demanding from them the common sense and moderate approach to government which the vast majority of Saskatchewan residents favour. [2]

Another encouraging fact was that Human Rights Commissioner Ken Norman, known for both progressive views and his association with the NDP, was not fired. He was allowed to remain in office until his term expired, and his successor, Ron Kruzeniski, was a credible appointment. In the following three or four years, although there were one or two inflammatory statements from within the caucus, the government made no official attacks on the human rights of minorities in Saskatchewan or on the organizations which had been established to protect these rights.

All this changed, and changed dramatically, after the Tories were reelected in 1986. From then on, leaders of government were responsible for a series of attacks on human rights, both verbal and practical. These were sometimes of the crudest kind. This shift in policy did not go unnoticed by political commentator Dale Eisler. In an article in the *Leader Post* (Regina), Eisler speculated on the reasons behind the change. The Tories, he said, were elected on a populist wave in 1982 with a populist agenda. During their first term there was little ideological consistency. By the second term, however, with a massive $3-billion deficit, the stage was set for the Tories "to confront their conservative ideology." There was furious debate within the administration, with cabinet meetings almost every day, to determine the direction of policy. The vociferous right wing of the party won out. The result, said Eisler, was plain to see:

> The government is advancing aggressively on its privatization strategy, deficit reduction has become a cornerstone of fiscal policy, and there is a consistent emphasis on self-reliance in social programs. *But perhaps more importantly, religious-moral issues have become a bigger part of the political equation for the Tories.*[3] (Emphasis added.)

A brief examination of the government's record in the various areas of concern in human rights reveals the effects of the victory of the reactionaries.

The picture since the 1986 election is not totally bleak. Groups concerned with the rights of the handicapped are fairly satisfied with the government's actions. In late 1988, the premier announced that the Saskatchewan Human Rights Code would be amended to include protection for people with a mental disability. This brought Saskatchewan into line with most other provinces. It also adopted the new Uniform Building and Accessibility Standards Act. Grants and easy-term loans were offered to modify homes to make them more accessible to disabled persons. The system of group homes for the mentally handicapped was dramatically expanded. The government added to all this by implementing an affirmative action program for government employees.

What the government did to improve the position of the disabled minority, however, was counterbalanced by other actions which hurt them. It announced the closing of the school for the deaf in Saskatoon; reduced funding for supportive groups like the Saskatchewan Voice of the Handicapped; and seriously hurt many disabled people when it implemented the prescription drug plan fees. Even so, on balance, the government's record in the area of support for the disabled is commendable.

The government's positive contribution to human rights in its second term begins and ends with its efforts on behalf of the disabled. The rest is a depressing record of cuts, support of repressive groups, and open insults.

We can begin with the poor. At the time the Tories came to power, the minimum wage was $4.25, with three increases of 25 cents each scheduled to come in at six-month intervals. The new administration cancelled the projected increases. In 1985 the minimum wage was raised to $4.50 (in time for the election) where it remained, despite the relentless rise in inflation, until a slight increase in November 1989 (also in time for an election).

Welfare recipients have been hardest hit. Marginal cuts to assistance in current dollars have resulted in a real reduction of about 45% when inflation is taken into account. It is not a coincidence that the Regina Food Bank delivered five times as much food in 1985 as in 1983, and that a shocking 53% of the clients were children.[4] Grant Schmidt, minister of social services, has displayed little sympathy for the plight of those on welfare. His wife, he said, could easily manage on the amount given by welfare. With shrewd budgeting, helped out by gardening, welfare recipients could do quite well, assuming they did not spend their welfare cheques on beer and bingo. As for the alleged shortage of jobs, Schmidt pointed out that many "foreigners" were working in hotels – the implication being presumably, that Canadians were "too picky" about their employment.[5]

The government did not stop there. Schmidt's predecessor as social services minister, Gordon Dirks, cut assistance benefits for single assistance recipients who were categorized as employable. A Human Rights Commission board of inquiry and the Saskatchewan Court of Appeal eventually ruled that this constituted discrimination on the basis of marital status, and was therefore in violation of the Human Rights Code. Schmidt, who had taken over social services following Dirk's personal defeat in the 1986 election, responded by removing the discrimination by cutting benefits to married recipients. He also cut funds for transportation from welfare cheques and, in April 1989, he introduced a rule requiring families with at least one nonworking "employable" adult to pick up the welfare cheque in person. The purpose of the later requirement could only be to achieve a psychological effect since there was no discernible practical reason for it. Schmidt also asked the public to inform him of any welfare abuses they knew about, effectively inviting citizens to spy upon each other.

If the Tory administration's attitude to the poor is questionable, in the matter of racism, their record is worse. The premier's reproof of Lloyd Hampton for his racist comments in 1982 was anomalous. Grant Schmidt's reference to foreigners working in hotels, although relatively mild, is revealing. It indicates a racist mind set: white, middle class, and exclusionist. One cannot imagine Schmidt would think that a person from Britain, for instance, could be in such a job. It does not seem to have occurred to him that in order to be employed in Canada at all, the worker must be a landed immigrant and consequently on the way to becoming a full Canadian citizen.

A similar disclosure of attitude could be seen in a remark that Grant Devine made during a discussion of public health and AIDS. Once AIDS got on to the reserves, he said, it would be "hell on wheels." [6] Such terminology is hardly appropriate from the premier.

The clearest, and most serious, indication of the government's attitude to Native issues, however, was demonstrated by its response to the call for a public inquiry into the lack of support services for Indian and Metis youth in Saskatchewan. In a letter to the premier dated 6 March 1989, the Saskatchewan Coalition Against Racism (SCAR) called on the government for such an inquiry. The immediate reason for their action was the death of Marlon Pippin, a 17-year-old Indian youth who died in a confrontation with Regina City Police on 1 February 1989. A brief dated 15 September, presented by SCAR to the SHRC, provided the facts. SCAR saw Pippin's tragic death as yet one more result of a wretched social environment for Native youth. The suicide rate among such people, the brief pointed out, is 7.4 times higher than the national average (Pippin himself had attempted suicide three times). The brief also pointed out that 66% of children in the care of the Department of Social Services are aboriginal, yet there is no special recognition of this fact in the provincial programming. Of the 128 foster homes in Saskatoon, only nine are operated by aboriginal people. Sixty-five percent of males and almost 90% of the females in the provincial correctional centres are of Indian or Metis ancestry. Morbidity levels for Native youth are considerably higher than for their non-aboriginal counterparts. The lack of adequate housing, sewer and water facilities, and garbage disposal on the reserves, is partly responsible. There is almost no attempt by the city police forces to implement affirmative action, just as there seems little practical recognition of the fact that by the year 2000 46% of the students in Saskatchewan schools will be of Indian or Metis origin. SCAR's request for a broad-based inquiry was supported by about 20 public groups.

Shortly after Pippin's death, the Saskatchewan Association on Human Rights called for a more specialized inquiry. The association pointed out that Pippin's inquest had been limited in scope. SAHR argued that an investigation into the circumstances surrounding the tragedy was in order, especially since Pippin's family did not have a lawyer at the inquest.

The government's response, delivered by Social Services Minister Grant Schmidt, was immediate and definite. "I see no need at this time to second-guess juries or coroner's inquests," he said. "If there is no evidence, I'm not going to start spinning around and pointing my finger at the established institutions that have served us for eighty-five years . . . To allege that all of the authorities in Saskatchewan practise racism is irresponsible." Schmidt then found a device to evade responsibility for government action. "I cannot lead the native community," he declared, "nor can the government. The native community has to develop the leaders who will lead them to the promised land and we will help them on the way." [7] In other words, as far as the social services minister is concerned, Native people are not residents of Saskatchewan in the ordinary way, but a group apart.

Grant Schmidt also used a familiar tactic in denying the calls for an inquiry. He claimed that the groups calling for it were "predominantly offshoots of the NDP in some shape or form." Consequently, "what you have here is a political dispute and not a genuine dispute about the concern for people." He held to this convenient fiction even when reporters pointed out to him that one of the approximately 20 groups in question was a Roman Catholic church.

Grant Schmidt's response to the request for the inquiry provoked some strong words. The *Leader Post* began an editorial by stating that "Grant Schmidt is at it again – showing that he has about as much sensitivity as a stone wall." The editorial went on to remark that "If the rejection was galling, so was the accompanying rationale," and strongly criticized the minister for shifting the responsibility for action onto the Natives themselves. [8]

The most egregious example of the government's contempt for individual liberties, however, is found in its attitude to gay and lesbian rights. The first broadside came from Grant Schmidt in October 1987. Schmidt gave his views in a private interview with CBC reporter Bob Nixon who later played the tape to other reporters. Employers had the right to bar homosexuals, Schmidt said. Gay men and lesbians would not be allowed to adopt children. He doubted that homosexuals could be Christians. In expanding his views on the employment of homosexuals, Schmidt drew an analogy between homosexuality and crime: "If somebody believes that stealing is not morally wrong, then I would think employers should have the right to dismiss people who they think disagree with their opinion that stealing is . . . morally wrong," he explained. When he was asked why he thought homosexuals were unstable, Schmidt dodged the question. "Why don't you go out and find out for yourself?" he retorted. "Everybody knows the answer to that question." [9]

Five months later the government was at it again. The occasion was Svend Robinson's public announcement that he was gay. This open, indeed proud, statement by a prominent member of Parliament made headlines across the country. The media was quick to seek Grant Devine's reaction. The response was what by now everyone had come to expect—vintage Saskatchewan Tory. Devine supported Robinson's decision to be truthful, but "it's like you say you love the sinner, but hate the sin" he explained. [10] He made it clear that he considered homosexuality an unacceptable "lifestyle," and regretted that Robinson was giving homosexuality some credibility. "I don't want my children thinking this is a reasonable, normal thing to do," he said. Following Grant Schmidt's lead in linking homosexuality and crime, Devine went on to deliver his now famous analogy between homosexuals and bank robbers. "If somebody stood up and said, 'Well, I rob banks,' [I'd say] 'Well, it's a good thing you told me. But, I'm not going to encourage you because I don't think that people should think it's a good idea that you, as a Member of Parliament, can go around and rob banks.'" [11] This astonishing farrago of muddled nonsense was duly published across the nation.

While many people were appalled at Devine's attitude, one man was delighted. Paul Cameron is an American ultra-right psychologist who has conducted a virulent campaign against gay men and lesbians. Censured by two professional associations, [12] singled out by a Texas judge for his fraud and misrepresentation in a court hearing dealing with sodomy laws, [13] described by a prominent sociologist as a disgrace to his profession, [14] Cameron uses a combination of misinformation and inflammatory rhetoric to inspire hatred against gay people. One of his many anti-gay pamphlets, for instance, is entitled "What Homosexuals do (It's more than merely disgusting)." The opening sentences give a taste of what is to follow:

Throughout recorded history, all civilizations and major religions have discriminated against homosexuality. In Puritan New England, conviction of a homosexual act was a capital offense. Thomas Jefferson believed that homosexuality "should be punished, if a man, by castration, if a woman, by cutting through the cartilage of her nose a hole of one-half inch in diameter at least." [15]

When Cameron arrived at the Saskatoon airport on his second visit, customs officials seized pamphlets like these on the grounds that they were hate literature. They were returned to him after officials learned that only "visible minorities" were protected under the Criminal Code provisions. [16]

For this man, AIDS is a godsend. His major theme is the extreme danger posed to decent people and their children by the malicious homosexuals. In one article, he comes within a hair's breadth of calling for the extermination of gay people. [17]

If Cameron made his remarks about any other minority group in Canada, he would of course be charged in short order with disseminating hatred. But gays are not protected under either the Criminal Code or the Saskatchewan Human Rights Code, and so the extreme right was free to welcome him to the province. Cameron was conducted around the legislature by Vonda Kosloski, the very vocal director of an organization called the Committee to Protect the Family, and by a Roman Catholic priest from Elrose, Mike McCarthy. Kosloski's group has views similar to those of Gay Caswell's Victorious Women. At the legislature, Cameron was able to meet and talk with members of the P.C. caucus.

Cameron seized delightedly on Devine's comments about gays and bank robbers. The premier was "right on target . . . On average, homosexuals engage in much more socially disruptive activity than heterosexuals." He then cited statistics from one of his own surveys to back up his claim. Psychologists in Saskatoon described Cameron's claims as "off the wall," "just not true," and "really crazy," but this did not prevent the *Star Phoenix* from giving the article front page prominence, accompanied by a photograph of the premier as a sort of imprimatur. [18]

The next contribution to the debate on the subject of homosexuality came from Grant Schmidt. In April 1989, the federal Human Rights Commission ruled that a government agency discriminated against an employee when it refused him bereavement leave to attend the funeral of his male partner's father. In effect, the ruling meant that for certain legislation a gay couple could be considered a family. Such a thing, Schmidt declared grandly, is "contrary to the rules of Allah, God, the Great Spirit, and I've always put the rules of God before the rules of men." He then rejected the ruling as far as Saskatchewan was concerned. "This is a ruling of a federal commission, it isn't a ruling by anyone elected to govern Canada," and consequently it would not affect the legislation in Saskatchewan.[19] There cannot be many examples, in a democratic country, of a cabinet minister openly expressing such contempt for a responsible adjudicatory body.

■　　　　■　　　　■

The government's shift to the right had consequences not only for the individual disadvantaged groups, but also for the various organizations concerned with minority rights.

In the spring of 1987 the office of ombudsman seemed to be threatened. Grant Schmidt, with his genius for missing the point, suggested during a debate in the legislature that there might be no need for an ombudsman because MLAs should be able to handle problems people have dealing with government. In fact, the ombudsman's office was allowed to remain. When the incumbent's term expired, a prominent Conservative lawyer from the premier's home riding of Estevan was appointed to the position. The government broke tradition in not securing unanimous consent in the legislature for the appointment.

The Human Rights Commission also suffered. In August 1986, its Prince Albert office was closed. The north of the province, with its large Native population, would be less efficiently served. In July 1987, the commission's funding was cut by a crippling 25%. There was a slight increase in 1989. The Saskatchewan Association on Human Rights, a citizen's group, was treated even worse. In May 1987, it was told that after 15 years of funding it was no longer eligible for provincial grants.

Other progressive groups felt the squeeze. Planned Parenthood Saskatoon Centre was forced to seek non-government funds in 1984, and by 1986 was talking of having to close. The Department of Health cut off funding in 1987—a 45% reduction in budgeted revenue. The attack was matched by the federal funding agency and by the City of Saskatoon, both of which cut funding dramatically. The centre has since remained operating, albeit at a reduced level of service.[20]

Money for anti-abortion organizations was initially increased handsomely on the other hand. In 1983–84, for example, Saskatchewan Pro-Life received government funding for the first time. It received $60,000 versus Planned Parenthood Saskatchewan's $55,530. In the 1987–88 budget, the government announced that it was cutting off funding to "both sides of the abortion debate." This display of impartiality provided the justification for ending Planned Parenthood's funding. However, the action ignored the fundamental difference between Planned Parenthood and Saskatchewan Pro-Life. Planned Parenthood is a service group that provides birth control counselling. It has a pro-choice policy, but promotion of this policy is not the reason for its existence. Saskatchewan Pro-Life, on the other hand, is a group devoted solely to advocating a political position on the abortion issue. Following the government's widely publicized "even handed" funding cut, the Pro-Life association quietly obtained funding under the Saskatchewan Works program. This is a wage subsidy program enabling employers to hire welfare recipients.

The government's support of nonprogressive groups was not limited to cash. Senior Tories made a habit of appearing at events sponsored by groups dedicated to an extreme conservative agenda, a habit that carried important implications for human rights.

A headline in the *Melfort Journal* for May 1989, for instance, tells the story: "HIGH PROFILE SPEAKER LENDS MORAL SUPPORT TO MOVEMENT." Grant Devine and his wife Chantal were guests of honour at an anti-abortion banquet. His speech there provides an example of the premier's habitual mixing of religion and politics. An abiding faith in God, it appears, gave Devine "direction and balance" in a rapidly changing society, and he confessed: "I do not believe I could do half the things I do without that belief." Abortion was indisputably wrong in his view, and he told the assembled Christians that "I believe you are on the right track." [21]

In fall 1987, Chantal Devine and Grant Schmidt were guests at a more remarkable event. Ex-MLA Gay Caswell, having left REAL Women, was the leading spirit behind a splinter organization calling itself Victorious Women of Canada. This group held a weekend founding convention and a tape of part of the proceedings has been marketed. What the tape has preserved is a self-righteous hodgepodge, fulsome in its sentimentality, astounding in its lack of analysis. The word "family" appears over and over again like some sort of incantation, and there are frequent appeals to "principles," "integrity," "morality," and "ethics," with never an attempt to define what they mean. The name of God is invoked constantly. [22] The speakers and audience saw themselves as defenders of a society besieged by malicious, evil forces made up of communists, feminists, and homosexuals. They took for granted that moral rectitude was indistinguishable from their own narrow, antichoice, antifeminist, and homophobic agenda.

The key speaker at the banquet was Alberta MP Alex Kindy. He delivered a rambling, predictable New Right speech, attacking peace groups, calling for a military buildup, and criticizing Canada's opposition to the South African government. He deplored his own federal party's laxness on homosexuality as well as its softness on abortion and its support of feminist groups.

During the proceedings, Chantal Devine received a prize and delivered a speech extolling the Family and her husband. At a particularly climactic point, Grant Schmidt was given the first annual award for protecting the family. The award seemed to be a reward for his refusal to allow homosexuals to adopt (not that any homosexual couple had asked to do so). In his acceptance speech, Schmidt acknowledged the existence of other religions in the province, but insisted that Saskatchewan was still predominantly Christian and that consequently "Christian" values must prevail. [23]

■   ■   ■

The rhetoric employed by the government has been very effective. Devine and Schmidt mention God in just about every speech they make. They are careful to create the impression that they are led by a higher authority in all their actions and beliefs. This blasphemy, for blasphemy it undoubtedly is, gives them a distinct strategic advantage. Most people, after all, are not given to analysis, and are comforted by the frequent allusions to God. Also, it makes opposition more difficult. It places opponents at a psychological disadvantage because they will seem to be opposing God Himself when they attack these servants of the Almighty. The rightwing groups that the government supports utilize the same tactic. For example, the name of God was invoked over and over again at the founding dinner of Victorious Women. Not only is God on their side, according to them, but so is patriotism – the guests piously sang "O Canada" at the beginning of the evening and "God Save the Queen" at the end. They were convinced that they were standing on guard for Canada and Christianity.

Such an appropriation of religion has several effects in addition to those just mentioned and quite apart from the desecration of true religion that it represents. First, it alienates that large section of the population that is not Christian—Jews, Moslems, atheists, agnostics (reasonable Christians, too, for that matter), and so on. It leaves the distinct impression that unless one subscribes to a particular religion, one is outside the mainstream as far as the government is concerned.

Second, it causes the government to take a side in some controversial matters where it ought to remain neutral. This creates a further sense of alienation for those who do not subscribe to the same beliefs. Several examples of religious bias have already been shown, but to these one could add such events as the appointment of Chris Gerrard to the newly created directorship of private schools. Gerrard is a fundamentalist of extreme conviction and is well known for his fights to cancel city taxes on the Christian Centre Academy and to institute the American-based accelerated Christian education program. He also headed the provincial association of independent church schools, a group that wants public funding of private schools. Even the normally quiescent *Star Phoenix* was roused by this appointment. An editorial began: "It sounded like a lobbyist's dream come true . . ." and ended by saying: "The public interest is also best served by assuring that the separation of school and church remains clear. Creation of this private school post and the credentials of the director may call both these areas into question." [24]

An even more extraordinary example of favouring a religious group is seen in Bill 9, which opens the way for private adoption agencies. The sum of $106,000 was provided for a Saskatoon agency called Christian Counselling Service to help it with its adoption activities. The agency's executive director, Bruce Pringle, explained that "The majority of young women coming to us will want their child placed in a Christian home . . . so the agency will likely try to limit itself to prospective parents who are Christian." He also said, "The agency counsels against abortions and if mothers can be convinced to continue with their pregnancies, that will help to fulfil the needs of waiting parents." [25] Bill 9 makes it possible for members of a religious denomination to set up an adoption agency and be given large sums of money provided by taxpayers, many of whom do not agree with the religion and principles espoused by the agency.

The last, and perhaps most dangerous effect of mixing religion and politics, is rather more subtle. It results in a strange kind of transference in the mind of the legislator. If you believe that you are acting according to the dictates of a divine will, then you need not feel immediately responsible for those actions. The belief bestows a licence, an arrogance, that is not merely repulsive but downright dangerous. History provides all too many examples of what happens when an individual in power abandons rational analysis and objective self-awareness in order to follow what he thinks is a higher authority. The controlling effect of rationality once removed, the way is open for the escape of whatever ambitions and prejudices swarm, hidden, beneath the surface. And all in the name of the Lord.

One effect of Devine's shift to the extreme right and his mingling of religion and politics was shrewdly noted by columnist Dale Eisler. Referring to the claim of Paul Cameron that homosexuals are more likely to commit crimes than heterosexuals, he cited the "understandable" reaction of an official from the Human Rights Commission: "I'm almost speechless, I've never heard of such a thing." Eisler contrasted this to the response from Justice Minister Bob Andrew who remarked laconically: "It might be strong stuff, but I'm not excited by it. There is always a polarization on issues like this." Andrew repeated his belief that there was no need to change the Saskatchewan Human Rights Code to include protection for gay men and lesbians. Eisler ended his article with a significant remark: "As it turns out, the reaction by Andrew was itself reflective of what has happened to the Tories. At one time, he was considered the voice of moderation in the PC caucus." [26]

Moderate members of Devine's cabinet felt constrained under the new regime; ordinary citizens became nervous. The wave of firings early in the government's first term acted as a stern lesson to those outside the party and gave special power to the government's threats of further firings. This, together with the cuts in funding of various agencies, became a tool for frightening people into silence. I was present at a meeting called to found a group protesting the government's human rights policies, when it was virtually impossible to find a female spokesperson. No fewer than six women who were approached refused on the grounds that they were connected with an organization that depended on public funding. They were scared at what might happen to these funds if they took a public stand. One woman employed by a federal agency finally agreed to consult her supervisor on the matter. Without a moment's hesitation the supervisor told her that if she became identified with the protest group, funding for the agency would be seriously endangered. What was more, if she ever left her job she could give up any hope of finding another government position. The fear among professional people spilled over into the general public. One welfare recipient, for instance, who was interviewed by the *Star Phoenix* at the time of restrictions on welfare payments, asked that her name not be published "for fear of repercussions." [27]

Another characteristic of the government's discourse on human rights has been muddle. Grant Devine is not the most articulate of people at the best of times, but his pronouncements on human rights have been particularly confused. For example, take a close look at his remarks on homosexuals and bank robbers (cited above). As a piece of prose it is an extraordinary tangle, with shifting (and slippery) syntax. The main point emerges not as the result of a clear argument, but is slipped in loosely. Exactly the same thing happens with Grant Schmidt's remarks on the employer's right to fire a homosexual. They are worth repeating to illustrate the point. "If somebody believes that stealing is not morally wrong, then I would think employers should have the right to dismiss people who they think disagree with their opinion that stealing is . . . morally wrong." Now, what Schmidt is trying to say does not, of course, make sense logically, because: a) it is not a question of belief in the morality or immorality of homosexuality but of *being* homosexual; b) homosexuality and stealing are not analogous; and c) homosexuality or homosexual acts are not morally wrong. But – and here is the essential point – the very opaqueness of Schmidt's syntax works to conceal the fact that he is talking nonsense. In other words, if his sentence was clear, the falsity of his thinking would be much more obvious. Schmidt's muddle gives him another tactical advantage. In order to refute him, it is necessary to untangle what he has been saying. If you try to carry out such analysis in public debate you soon lose your audience. In particular, Schmidt's target audience (i.e., prejudiced people) finds it easy to dismiss such "nit-picking" and happily feeds on the muddy, rambling language that Schmidt and Devine employ. It provokes not a considered response, but an automatic, emotional gut reaction.

It is difficult to know to what extent the leaders of the PC government are aware of what they are doing. No doubt they actually believe that they are on the side of Christian truth and morality. Disturbing as it is to contemplate, they perhaps think that their frighteningly mangled thinking makes sense. But at some level, even if only partly conscious, they must know that they are employing a religion and a rhetoric for dubious political purposes. They have seen in the examples of President Reagan and Prime Minister Thatcher how effective such tactics can be, and have tried, in their much crasser way, to emulate those two politicians. Cruel and selfish policies, as well as intolerance of minorities, are paraded in the guise of religion and right thinking.

Whatever the degree of Devine's and Schmidt's own consciousness of what they are doing, the fact is that because of them the level of public debate on human rights in Saskatchewan has sunk depressingly low. In happier days, outrageous views such as Devine and Schmidt have uttered would be expressed only by a few mavericks on the fringes of society. In most cases they would be ignored as being beneath notice. But when the highest officials in the province utter those opinions, they must be taken notice of. The very fact that they are debated at all gives them a kind of credibility. There is an almost irresistible temptation to resort to the same distorted rhetoric that the extreme right uses, to fight fire with fire. Calm, reasonable discussion seems no longer possible.

■　　　■　　　■

It is clear that during the Tory term of office the cause of human rights in Saskatchewan has seriously suffered. It is not merely that the government has done nothing to improve human rights (with the one exception of the legislation helping the handicapped) but that leaders of government have worked actively against human rights. This is what they have achieved. Saskatchewan is now a place where many people have learned to fear the government, and have been cowed into silence. It is a place where, when debate on human rights does take place, the voice of moderation is considered weak and is derided. It is a place where anyone not of a certain class, colour, race, and religion may feel excluded, and where gay men and lesbians are publicly insulted by the highest officers of the province.

Most serious of all, Saskatchewan is now a place where intolerance is normal, expected and, indeed, respectable. Leaders of government have made no attempt at impartiality, but have allied themselves in a deliberately public way with repressive groups and with a narrow, inhumane, version of Christianity. Inevitably, the moral climate of a province is powerfully affected by the attitudes and public pronouncements of its chief ministers. Consequently, those in favour of human rights feel embattled, on the defensive, while others feel free, at last, to impose their restrictive beliefs and intolerant views on others. This is the exact reverse of the situation

47

that existed when the P.C. government first came into power.

In human rights matters, the voices most frequently heard have been those of Premier Devine and Minister of Social Services and Human Resources, Labour, and Employment Grant Schmidt. Both have been guilty of provocatively intolerant statements, but Grant Schmidt has been considerably more crass than the premier. The contrast leads some observers to think that Grant Devine is fairly reasonable and that, somehow, Grant Schmidt is an *enfant terrible* for whom no one is responsible. It needs to be said clearly and unequivocally that the premier is solely responsible for the human rights situation as it now exists in Saskatchewan. Following the usual New Right practice, he consciously, as a matter of policy, appointed to the ministry of social services a man whose aim was not to support the portfolio, but to undermine it. He was entirely aware, at all times, of everything Grant Schmidt said and did, and indeed on more than one public occasion he has commended Schmidt for what he was pleased to call his outspokenness. In any case, Devine has shown himself on occasion to be capable of terminology as offensive as that used habitually by Grant Schmidt. Apart from all this, obviously the premier is responsible for the conduct of his ministers. In the area of human rights, Grant Devine has left a shameful legacy.

PARLIAMENTARY DEMOCRACY IN SASKATCHEWAN, 1982–1989

by Merrilee Rasmussen and Howard Leeson

Our constitution makers did not want what they saw as the tempestuous currents of popular democracy, which had wreaked such damage on revolutionary France and the United States, set loose on the good colonies of the north. They wanted something quieter, more discrete, good for the merchant and for the banker, for the lawyer and, perhaps, for the farmer, but not likely to go to anyone's head. The brief experience of the 1830s was enough—we were inoculated against any further outbreaks of the disease.

Parliamentary government, then, was not meant to engage the citizenry in political affairs. It was not to function, as Pericles in his Funeral Oration had claimed for Athens, as a school for democracy. Nor were citizens who placed their private interests over public affairs to be disdained, as in that city-state. Quite the contrary. The assumption was that, aside from voting, the electorate would allow the party politicians to get on with the job which had been so tersely defined as "peace, order and good government." The same assumption held good at the provincial level, confined though it was to matters of "a merely local or private nature." Nowhere in the B.N.A. Act do the Canadian people appear as political subjects in their own right.[1]

Philip Resnick's view of parliamentary democracy is not shared by all. His work is permeated with the idea that popular sovereignty is a utopian concept. Nonetheless, he raises fundamental questions about how democratic our Parliaments (federal and provincial) really are. If by democracy we mean full and equal participation in social decision making, our parliamentary institutions fail miserably to meet that standard. Few would argue that we have more than an occasional passing acquaintance with such a heady arrangement. If, however, we mean the right to be informed on issues and decisions, and to eventually pass judgement on those who make the decisions, then Parliaments fare somewhat better.

As van Loon and Whittington have stated, "Parliament functions as a communications link, informing the public of impending decisions prior to legitimating their passage." [2] If we accept the argument that this function is democratic and important, then any removal of Parliament's ability to function is a serious assault on democracy. Put another way, the removal of the power of Parliament to debate and decide important questions is the removal of a fundamental democratic right for all of us.

In Saskatchewan, there has been a lively history of political debate, and even livelier sessions of the legislature. This can be traced to the clash of ideologies which has dominated political life in the province since 1944 and to the history of citizen participation which has permeated prairie life since early European settlement. Until recently, this attitude has been entrenched in the Saskatchewan legislature. For example, when Lieutenant-Governor Bastedo, on his own initiative, reserved legislation respecting oil royalties in 1961, the Liberal opposition critic asked the CCF government to return the bill in question to the legislature. She was incensed by his action and assured the government that the legislature would pass the bill unanimously. There was no doubt that everyone thought the legislature ought to be supreme.

However, such attitudes depend greatly on the broader socialization process, and on the particular attitudes to these institutional arrangements held by key individuals like the premier. If the executive branch has little understanding of the role of the legislature, or worse, views the legislature as simply an opposition forum, great damage can be done to the democratic process.

PARLIAMENTARY DEMOCRACY

Parliament is an institution comprising many individuals, officers, procedures, traditions, and concepts. In a legalistic sense, Parliament consists of very specific constituent parts which are constitutionally enumerated. The relationship between these parts determines a Parliament's political complexion. The particular manifestation of a Parliament at any specific point in time and place is a direct result of the struggle for power that takes place between the legislative and executive branches of government.

A primary foundation of the Westminster parliamentary model from which Saskatchewan's legislature is derived is the Bill of Rights of 1688. The Bill of Rights is an English statute that marks the culmination of the long struggle between the King and Parliament known as the Glorious Revolution. Two fundamental parliamentary principles are enshrined in that statute: the Crown may not spend money without the prior approval of Parliament; and the Crown is subject to the rule of law; that is, it has no power to suspend the operation of laws enacted by Parliament. (Remember, however, that in law, Parliament is the Crown/executive acting *together with* the Legislative Assembly. In Saskatchewan, as in other Canadian jurisdictions, the legislature is the Legislative Assembly acting by and with the advice and consent of the lieutenant-governor.[3])

It seems odd to invoke, in Saskatchewan, the authority of a statute in support of a proposition of law asserted on the other side of the globe more than 300 years ago. However, the Bill of Rights forms part of the received law of Canada and is still in force here.[4] These long-established underpinnings of our parliamentary system of government are the foundation upon which the superstructure of parliamentary democracy has been constructed.

In Saskatchewan since the assumption of power by the Devine administration in 1982, this struggle between legislative and executive has boiled over on a number of specific occasions. The relationship between the legislative and executive branches of government – and, therefore, the nature of Parliament in this province – has been subtly changed. In many instances, these changes have directly undermined parliamentary institutions and thus parliamentary democracy in Saskatchewan.

THE 1982 ELECTION CAMPAIGN

Removal of the provincial tax on gasoline was a key promise of the opposition Progressive Conservative Party in its bid for election in 1982. Party leader Grant Devine announced that a Conservative government would remove the gas tax on the day after it was sworn into office, whether it was necessary to pass a statute or a regulation or even to recall the legislature. This statement illustrates that from the outset, the Progressive Conservatives had a basic misunderstanding of the inner workings of government; it also betrays a lack of awareness of the existence of limitations on executive power.

This naiveté was not surprising. Only 15 of 57 Conservative MLAs elected in 1982 had previously served in the Legislative Assembly. A Parliament tends to evolve slowly over time as small numbers of members come and go after each election, learning and passing on the various traditions and practices of the institution. The election results in 1982 produced the potential for a dramatic split with the past. The new premier, Grant Devine, was one of the many who had no prior experience as an MLA.

The practical difficulty with the promise to remove the gas tax was that the tax was levied by a statute enacted by the legislature (The Fuel Petroleum Products Act, R.S.S. 1978, c. F–23). The gas tax could, therefore, be removed only if the legislature repealed the act that imposed the tax. The executive had no legal authority to suspend the operation of the law that the legislature had enacted. Ultimately, on the suggestion of the legislative counsel and law clerk, the "remission" provisions of The Department of Finance Act were relied upon to pass a regulation (made by cabinet, the executive government) exempting almost all users of fuel petroleum products from the liability to pay tax. This authority is without doubt legally questionable; but its utilization is in stark contrast to the original plan which rested upon the invocation of a royal prerogative more suitable to an absolute monarchy than a modern parliamentary democracy.

SPECIAL WARRANTS

The government's fiscal year ends on 31 March and usually the new budget and the detailed estimates on which it is based are presented to the legislature prior to that time. In Saskatchewan in 1987 that didn't happen. More significantly, there was no indication that the government was planning to recall the legislature in the near future so that it could happen. In the meantime, however, government expenditures continued. These expenditures were met through the use of special warrants.

The executive is required to obtain prior approval for its expenditures from the legislature. A special warrant is an exception to that requirement, provided by statute, by which expenditures can be approved by a cabinet directive under very specific and limited circumstances.[5] Special warrants are commonly used in all Canadian jurisdictions to provide for any shortfall between the estimates of expenditures that are approved at the beginning of a fiscal year and the actual expenditures that are required by the end of the fiscal year. They are also used to provide for programs of assistance necessitated by unforeseen natural disasters such as flood, drought, or storm. The important difference in Saskatchewan in 1987 was that special warrants were being used at the *beginning* of the fiscal year to finance *ordinary* expenditures.

Because the situation was unusual, the leader of the opposition requested a formal opinion from the legislature's legislative council and law clerk on the constitutionality and legality of the government's actions: is the executive government bound by constitutional convention to present a budget and estimates to the legislature prior to the beginning of the fiscal year to which they relate and, in any case, was the government's use of special warrants in the particular circumstances of 1987 legal?

In discussing these two issues – convention and law – the facts about the ways in which special warrants have actually been used in Saskatchewan are significant. Following the traditions of the Saskatchewan legislature, it was unlikely that a special warrant would have been possible at the beginning of a fiscal year because the House would normally have been sitting at that time and special warrants cannot be used while the House is actually sitting.

On investigation this hypothesis is borne out. Only on four occasions in Saskatchewan history prior to 1987 had the legislature not been sitting at the beginning of the fiscal year. There were thus only these four times at which the 1987 situation could possibly have been duplicated; none of them saw special warrants used in the same way as in 1987.[6]

While these facts can be used to demonstrate evidence of a convention, they also point to the history out of which any convention must have developed. This history determines not just the convention, but also the meaning to be attached to the statutory provision that provides the legislative authority under which the special warrants were issued. The practices surrounding the use of special warrants are a consequence of the fact that their use is an exercise of the major crown prerogative that Parliament fought to achieve effective control over – spending power. The special warrant power in Saskatchewan and elsewhere in Canada is modeled on amendments to legislation that were first enacted as a result of illegal government spending necessitated by the Fenian raids in 1866.[7] Considering the dramatic circumstances out of which the special warrant has evolved legislatively, it is reasonable to construe the special warrant authority in a narrow fashion. Obviously, the legislature should approve executive expenditures if the legislature is available, because the special warrant power was not enacted with the objective of handing back the spending power to the crown. Accordingly, the statutory provision authorizing special warrants which permitted them to be issued in cases of expenditures that were "not foreseen or provided for or insufficiently provided for" cannot be interpreted so as to permit the government to decline to ask the legislature for any appropriation to provide for the expenditures it will inevitably incur, and then provide for them itself by special warrant.

The opinion provided by the legislative counsel and law clerk concluded that although a convention requiring government to present a budget and estimates prior to the beginning of a fiscal year might not exist, the use of special warrants to finance ongoing ordinary expenditure in the circumstances of 1987 was illegal. Shortly after this opinion was made public, Premier Devine announced that the assembly would resume sitting on 17 June 1987. Shortly after that, a budget and estimates were presented to the legislature for its approval.

But while the events of 1987 represent a major attack by the executive on the legislative, it is also instructive to examine the use of special warrants in 1982–83, the first year of the Devine administration. In 1982, a budget and estimates were presented to the legislature on 18 March, but the government which presented them was defeated at the polls in a general election held on 26 April. The new administration reconvened the legislature on 16 June. Between the time when the legislature was dissolved until the official return to the writ of election, there was no legislature in existence. The special warrant was the only method available for financing government expenditures. It is precisely to deal with this kind of special situation that the special warrant exists. It should also be remembered that these special warrants were issued with reference to a budget and estimates that *had* been presented to the previous legislature, even though the government that had presented them had been defeated. Interestingly, although the legislature sat several times throughout the 1982–83 fiscal year, interim supply bills—that is, the prior approval of the legislature on an interim basis pending completion of the legislature's review of the estimates—were never enacted. They were avoided by the simple expedient of scheduling special warrants throughout 1982–83 to obviate the legal difficulties of the legislation authorizing their use (that is, that special warrants were not available while the legislature was sitting). The spirit of the requirement, based on the idea that it is the legislature that *should* approve expenditures, was ignored.

The use of special warrants in 1982–83 is an aberration that might be explainable by virtue of the fact that it was a transitional period during which a novice administration was in control. The immediate return in the next fiscal year to the previously established norm lends credence to this view. It suggests that the Devine administration's use of special warrants in this technically "correct" manner was inappropriate, even in its own view.

INTERFERENCE WITH OFFICIALS OF THE LEGISLATURE

The controversy in 1987 over the use of special warrants also produced another new phenomenon in Saskatchewan politics: a direct attack by the executive on an official of the legislature. This phenomenon was repeated two years later in the context of another controversial issue concerning the executive's fiscal accountability to the legislature. These attacks took the form of slandering the professional ability, competence, impartiality, and integrity of the officials in question.

On 24 June 1987 the Speaker of the Saskatchewan legislature made an important ruling on a matter of parliamentary privilege which arose out of negative comments made by the minister of justice outside the House about the credibility, competence, and impartiality of the legislative counsel and law clerk. The remarks were made to the press by the minister upon his learning of the content of counsel's opinion concerning the government's use of special warrants. Portions of the Speaker's ruling, as recorded in the "Votes and Proceedings" for that day, are as follows:

> With regard to the role of the Legislative Counsel and Law Clerk, it is her role and duty to advise the Chair and all Members equally and impartially. It is the duty of the Legislative Counsel and Law Clerk to offer opinions when requested from any Member of the Legislative Assembly and once that opinion is given, it is beyond the control of the Law Clerk as to how it is used. It is then the responsibility of the Member to act in such a way as to protect the independent status of the officer of the Assembly.
> . . . [I]t is clear that any action which may tend to deter a parliamentary office from doing his/her duty may be considered to be a breach of the privileges of parliament. It is vital, if parliament is to get fair and impartial advice from its officers, that these officers must be defended from intimidation while conducting their duties. Critical comments attacking the competence of and credibility of an individual can be construed as a form of obstruction. I do feel that the remarks made by the Minister may have harmed the credibility of the Legislative Counsel and the Law Clerk and may have drawn into question her capacity to serve the Legislative Assembly. While

a Member may disagree with a particular legal opinion, in this case the Minister's remarks may have gone beyond the bounds of fair comment. Because the officer's capacity to carry out her function may be inhibited, I find that this matter is of sufficient concern to merit consideration by the Assembly. I find that a *prima facie* of privilege has been established and I leave the matter in the hands of the Assembly.[8]

The minister of justice consequently apologized to the House for his actions. The apology was accepted with a resolution that confirmed the Speaker's position that the minister's remarks constituted a breach of the privileges of the assembly. The ruling and the resolution establish a precedent recognizing the importance of the ability of legislative officials to function without executive interference. It is both interesting and unfortunate that this demonstration of support by and for the institution was necessitated by the actions of one of its members.

But this particular manifestation of executive interference was not entirely new. The office of the legislative counsel and the law clerk had existed in Saskatchewan from 1905 until 1985 as an autonomous agency attached to the legislature. It drafted all legislation whether government or opposition, public or private. In 1985, cabinet decided that it wished to control the drafting of government legislation from within the Department of Justice. It purported to transfer staff and budget to that department through the use of Orders in Council issued pursuant to The Legislative Assembly and Executive Council Act which granted this power to cabinet in relation to the "executive government." The proper course of action was for the government to establish a drafting activity and positions within the Department of Justice and to fill those positions. It would then be for the legislature to reassess the budget and staff needs of the legislative counsel and law clerk in the face of declining demands for service. Instead, cabinet moved legislative staff into executive positions unilaterally through the use of its "transfer OC." Concerns of affected staff were met with anger and personal intimidation. The complaints were consequently dropped.

In 1989, the provincial auditor became the target of government attack. The auditor is also an independent official of the legislature. His function is to review government expenditures to ensure that they have been made in accordance with the prior approval given by the legislature. On 17 May 1989 the provincial auditor tabled his report to the legislature for the year ended 31 March 1988. In his report, the provincial auditor stated that he was unable to effectively carry out his role of watching over the public purse on behalf of the Legislative Assembly because he did not have enough information. Again, the reaction of the minister of justice was to slander the provincial auditor, both personally and professionally. (The minister appeared to have learned one lesson from his experience two years earlier. This time, he confined his adverse remarks to his answers during question period in the House.[9] He was thus immune from civil prosecution and spared himself the additional ignominy of a written apology to the official in question.)

A number of events had caused the provincial auditor to deliver his unprecedented report to the legislature. There was an increasing tendency to use crown corporations as instruments to effect government policies and to remove their financial affairs from the scrutiny of the provincial auditor by appointing private sector auditors. According to the provincial auditor, in 1987 he saw 90% of the expenditures from the public purse; in 1989 he saw 50%. While private sector auditors do produce audit reports which are then provided to the provincial auditor, he was denied information upon which to determine the reliability of those reports. Private auditors serve their clients, the crown corporations which they audit; the provincial auditor must serve *his* client, the Saskatchewan legislature. The interests of the two do not necessarily coincide. The provincial auditor's other concern related to the control of his budget. Clearly, the resources made available for the auditor to perform his function will determine how well he can do his job. At present, his budget is determined by the executive and represents another conflict of interest.

INTEGRITY OF PARLIAMENTARY PRIVILEGES

In 1984 the Devine administration provoked the first bell-ringing episode in the Saskatchewan legislature because it refused to deal seriously with an allegation of an opposition MLA of "breach of privilege." Privilege is that special body of parliamentary law that protects MLAs in their ability to function as members. Most notable is an MLA's absolute freedom of speech with regard to anything said within the course of parliamentary proceedings. This aspect of privilege is based on an acceptance of the principle that an MLA must be able to speak freely in the legislature without regard to whether or not the words spoken might be slanderous. The public interest is more effectively served by the granting of the freedom than by making MLAs liable to civil action.

On 25 April 1984, Ned Shillington, a member of the Saskatchewan Legislative Assembly, rose in the House on a point of privilege. Mr. Shillington had been served with a statement of claim (the document which initiates a civil court action) claiming damages on behalf of the plaintiffs for the "publication of an injurious falsehood." The claim was based on remarks and allegations Mr. Shillington had made in the legislature concerning the plaintiffs while questioning the government about the sale of a particular government property. The statement of claim was accompanied by a letter from the plaintiff's solicitor demanding a satisfactory settlement within 14 days or the matter would be vigorously pursued in the courts.

Mr. Shillington contended that this clearly constituted a breach of the privileges of the legislature protecting freedom of speech and a contravention of particular provisions of The Legislative Assembly and Executive Council Act. He called upon the Speaker to find that a "prima facie case of privilege" had been established and expressed his intention that, if it were, he would move a resolution to refer the matter to the Legislative Assembly's Committee on Privileges and Elections. Procedurally, it is the function of the Speaker to determine that an issue of privilege exists. It is then up to the assembly to determine what to do about it. The Speaker deferred his ruling until the following day, at which time he ruled that a prima facie case of privilege was indeed established. Mr. Shillington then moved his motion.

Bob Andrew, then government house leader, sought to amend the motion. The amendment asserted the existence of the privilege and called upon the plaintiffs' solicitor to apologize to the Legislative Assembly by sending a letter to the Speaker. Gary Lane, then minister of justice, spoke in support of the amendment and intimated that the issue of the existence of the privilege was one to be determined by the ordinary courts, and not by the Legislative Assembly in constituting *itself* as a court in accordance with statutory authority. This proposed course of action was seen by Mr. Shillington as too weak to adequately assert and protect the privileges of the House. When the vote on this disputed amendment was called and a recorded vote was demanded, the division bells rang from 3:40 P.M. on 26 April until 5:40 P.M. on 1 May 1984. Nothing happened in the House during that time, but the battle raged on in the press and in the back rooms.

The issues involved in this situation are subtle and complex. While it is no doubt difficult for individuals to hear their names mentioned in the course of debate in the legislature, "it is axiomatic that the practice of this right of free public discussions of public affairs, notwithstanding its incidental mischiefs, is the breath of life for parliamentary institutions." [10] In this particular case, the opposition took the position that it is the responsibility of the Legislative Assembly to be vigilant in asserting and guarding its privileges. The government's position suggested that once a person runs through the door of the court house, the matter is, by virtue of that fact alone, brought under the jurisdiction of the ordinary courts and somehow placed beyond the reach of the legislature.

This position exhibits both a lack of understanding of the sub judice convention [11] and a misunderstanding of the respective roles of the legislative and judicial arms of government. If the provisions of The Legislative Assembly and Executive Council Act which permit the assembly to constitute itself a court are to have any meaning at all, they must be applicable to this situation. This is not to say that the assembly should or could interfere with the internal workings of Her Majesty's Court of Queen's Bench for Saskatchewan. However, the assembly is not precluded from sitting *itself* as a court in order to adjudicate any issues that may be properly brought before it, just as a civil court is not precluded from hearing an action for damages because a criminal action arising out of the same incident may be pending in another court. It would be open to the assembly to call any persons before it, to conduct a hearing into the matter of the breach of its privileges, and to punish any persons that might be found guilty of such a breach. This avenue was not available to the Court of Queen's Bench. If, and when, the matter came up for trial, the court would be required to dismiss it as unfounded, since, as a matter of law, the words spoken by the defendant as set out in the plaintiffs' statement of claim were not actionable. To put it another way, even if all the matters alleged by the plaintiffs were conceded, they disclosed no cause of action known to the law. Thus, for the assembly to act in this situation would not interfere with the judiciary.

The subtlety of this point was lost in the public discussion of the issue. But nevertheless, on 1 May 1984, the issue was resolved by the passage of another amendment to the original motion pointing out that the lawsuit had been discontinued and a letter of apology received by the Speaker. [12]

The rather cavalier dismissal of the privilege issue by the Devine administration in this incident demonstrates its lack of concern for the integrity of the assembly and the necessity for members of the executive to be aware of and prepared to assert the privileges of the assembly in appropriate circumstances.

EXECUTIVE GOVERNMENT REORGANIZATION

In 1983, the Devine administration undertook its first major reorganization of executive government. It accomplished this in the usual way: introducing legislation in the legislature to amend and repeal existing statutes that establish various government departments and agencies. This can be a mammoth legislative task. In the 1983 reorganization, 10 new acts were enacted to create new departments and agencies, four existing department acts were amended, three acts were repealed, and two "consequential" acts were enacted to make consequential amendments (mostly to names of departments, ministers, and agencies) to 159 other statutes. This volume of work precipitated a search for an easier way to accomplish reorganization in the future.

That easier way was established by The Government Organization Act. The act permits cabinet to "determine the organization of the executive government and of its various departments" and specifically provides authority to establish, disestablish, continue, or vary any department, determine the objects or purposes of any department, and determine or change the name of any department. All of these powers may be exercised regardless of any specific legislative statement to the contrary elsewhere and of any contrary notion that might exist at common law. Thus cabinet is permitted to restructure the executive government at will, outside the legislature.

Cabinet's powers in this respect are exercised, for the most part, in the form of instruments called "regulations." The important feature of regulations is the requirement that they be centrally filed and officially published in order to have effect. A regulation that establishes a department has the same legal effect as a statute. A regulation that disestablishes a department that was originally established by a statute clearly declares the demise of the disestablished department, but does not actually repeal the statute by which the department was created. Many provisions of departments' acts predating the enactment of The Government Organization Act have been superseded or supplanted by general provisions applicable to all departments and contained in the latter statute. These provisions, while not repealed, are not legally effective. The practical effect of executive government reorganization by cabinet order is the confusion created by the fact that the words of the statute will not necessarily represent the legal reality.

To complicate the matter further, The Government Organization Act also authorizes the making of Orders in Council (again, cabinet orders) to assign or transfer any power, duty, or function conferred or imposed by law on any department to any minister or other department, along with portions of the public service and related appropriations. An act effecting consequential amendments has now been enacted to make the many specific changes to the whole of the statute law that the first round of government reorganization under the enabling statute has dictated. But it took 18 months for this to occur, and not all of the complex legal issues raised by the methodology have been clarified. Furthermore, there is no legal method of compelling the executive to bring forward this type of amendment in the future as other reorganizations occur.

It is now a simple matter for cabinet to effect a reorganization quickly, behind closed doors, and to present it to the legislature as a fait accompli or not at all. It is thus difficult to effectively scrutinize government expenditures or to compare expenditures from one year to another. On a simpler more mundane level, it may now be difficult even to know who to contact in government in relation to any question or concern arising under legislation.

In October 1989, a new problem with government organization by cabinet order arose. A cabinet shuffle had been effected on 3 October, and with it a minor government reorganization that saw the creation of several new government departments and agencies. On 17 October, a series of special warrants were issued purporting to authorize funds for these departments and agencies to the end of the 1989–90 fiscal year. Of course, when the budget and estimates were presented to the legislature in March 1989, these departments and agencies did not exist. Consequently, they were not–and could not be–included in the budget and estimates or in the 1989–90 Appropriation Acts passed by the legislature. Formerly, this would not have been possible, since the reorganization could not have been effected without the legislature passing several statutes to do it. It should be noted that authority does exist in The Government Organization Act to transfer the funds that the legislature has approved from one department to another. However, this transfer power does not permit the creation of "new money." [13]

CLOSURE

On Monday, 7 August 1989 (a statutory holiday in Saskatchewan known as "Saskatchewan Day") the Devine administration invoked closure in the Saskatchewan legislature. While closure is not unique to Saskatchewan in Canada, it is not a frequent parliamentary event. It was the first time closure had been invoked in Saskatchewan.

The precipitating issue was debate on The Potash Corporation of Saskatchewan Reorganization Act. The NDP opposition was conducting a vigorous attack on privatization in general, and on the proposed sale of the potash corporation in particular. The potash privatization debate was significant both because it provoked debate on the part of the NDP opposition, and because it did *not* provoke any debate from the government in support of its initiative. In fact, Premier Devine did not speak to the issue at all.

After weeks of debate and an opposition filibuster that appeared to have no end, the government introduced an ad hoc and unilateral amendment to the rules of the legislature to limit debate on the potash bill in all its stages. The usual rules require three readings and clause by clause scrutiny in the Committee of the Whole. In the case of this particular bill, this process could require as many as 22 individual motions, 21 of which are debatable. Each MLA is permitted to speak once to each motion and for as long as he or she wishes. The motion to limit debate permitted only two days to complete second reading and Committee of the Whole review and two hours for third reading. Closure was invoked on this motion, rather than on each of the motions that would have been required in the usual course of events. It was a clever solution to a situation the government saw as being a difficult problem. But although clever, it is a solution that directly contradicts the concept of Parliament as a forum in which discussion forces the executive to publicly declare and debate its positions. The executive must govern not simply by virtue of holding a majority of seats in a representative assembly, but by the persuasive authority of the "rightness" of its positions when held up to public scrutiny. Closure stops discussion and invokes the authority of power.

REGULATIONS ACT

In 1989, a new Regulations Act was introduced and enacted. Proclaimed effective 1 April 1990, it has the effect of altering the definition of the term "regulation" so that when a statute says that something is to be done "by regulation," it must be; and if the statute doesn't use the magic word, it won't be. Determining what is and what is not a regulation is thus a simple matter.

This question is significant because powers exercised through the enactment of regulations are, as a consequence, evidenced by a legal document whose validity depends upon its being filed in a central registry and officially published. Previously, "regulations" were powers that were "of a legislative nature," the precise determination of which was controllable by the courts in at least a quasi-objective (that is, nonpartisan) fashion.

Arguably, of course, the legislature retains direct control over determining what is and what is not a regulation by virtue of the fact that it enacts the statutes in which the magic word is or is not used. This position assumes that the legislature will be aware of the nature of the powers that the executive proposes to exercise pursuant to the authority granted. In fact, this is rarely true. The move to the new definition of "regulation" comes at the same time that legislation is more and more becoming a simple framework providing wide and general authority to the executive to do whatever it wishes. One is drawn to the conclusion that this is not power given away, but power given back.

ELECTORAL BOUNDARIES

In 1988, The Electoral Boundaries Commission Act, which replaces the former Constituency Boundaries Act, was enacted. Its goal is to establish a methodology for determining the boundaries of provincial constituencies which will be seen by the electorate to be objective and fair. Significant alterations in the preexisting procedure were affected by the new law.

First, the independent commission established to draw the boundaries within the parameters set by the act removed the clerk of the Legislative Assembly as one of its three members and replaced him with the chief electoral officer. The chief electoral officer, while certainly knowledgeable about the election process, is a servant of the executive rather than the legislature. In Saskatchewan the position has always been a partisan appointment. The clerk, however, is accountable to the legislature and enjoys a certain tenurelike security of office which permits him the independence necessary to function as an impartial member of a boundaries commission.

Second, The Electoral Boundaries Commission Act itself establishes not only the total number of provincial constituencies, but also the number of seats that must be created in rural Saskatchewan and the number of seats that must be created in each of the cities. Furthermore, urban constituencies are strictly contained by the municipal boundaries of the cities in which they are located. All of this coincides with an urban/rural split in the Saskatchewan electorate in which the Progressive Conservative Party tends to enjoy rural support, and the NDP urban support. Rural seats are statutorily set at 35; urban seats at 29, regardless of population. Thus, even before the commission begins its work, the outcome of a general election is stacked in favour of the party which is primarily based in rural Saskatchewan and the value of a vote in the cities of Saskatchewan is worth less than the value of a vote in the country. The principle of "one person; one vote" is a fundamental underpinning of representative democracies and equality of the vote is a corollary notion. Interfering with the commission's ability to draw boundaries which attempt to adhere as closely as possible to this principle interferes with a basic democratic right.

As if to emphasize the suspicious nature of this new legislation, its enactment was also preceded by unusual events. The former Constituency Boundaries Commission Act required the establishment of a commission at specifically described times. A commission should have been established (by cabinet order) prior to 31 January 1987, but the period of time permitted for its establishment was extended, also by cabinet order and for no apparent reason. That extended time expired before a commission was reluctantly set up, but the commission was not provided with any staff or resources to do its work. At least some members of the commission were concerned that the commission would be expected to produce a report dictated by the government. Fortunately or unfortunately, before that issue came to a head, the new legislation was enacted and the old commission was removed.

ANSWERING QUESTIONS IN THE LEGISLATURE

Question period is a portion of the parliamentary day that is set aside for members to ask questions of cabinet ministers. It is predicated on the notion that ministers are accountable to the legislature for the activities of the departments and agencies for which they are responsible. Question period is not a time for debate between government and opposition, but a time for the backbenches to quiz the front. Obviously, the opposition endeavours to bring to public attention matters that will tend to embarrass the government. Just as obviously, cabinet ministers endeavour to avoid the traps that are set for them.

In recent years there has been a significant trend developing in the conduct of question period in Saskatchewan: for the most part, ministers simply don't answer the questions put to them. On the one hand, the ministers avoid admitting or conceding any fact asserted by an opposition member, perhaps in the belief that they will not thus be led down any garden paths. On the other hand, ministers more frequently answer the question they wish to answer rather than the question that is asked. The result, of course, is to whittle away at the notion that the executive is accountable to the legislature. It is simply another sign of the disrespect for parliamentary institutions shown by this executive and corresponds to the government's handling of orders for return.

"Orders for return" are orders made by the Legislative Assembly and directed to the government to table in the legislature the information described in the order. The government, with its majority, is able to make or amend proposals for orders for return to correspond with the information it is prepared to release. Even though all outstanding returns that have been ordered were issued on this basis, the government is still two years behind in tabling the information that has been ordered.

CONCLUSION

Democracy is served when a legislature is allowed maximum ability to scrutinize cabinet decisions and inform the public about them. This usually means that a clash of ideologies and analyses between the governing party and the opposition will emerge. Such an exchange in our society is usually healthy. It is clear, however, that during the two terms of office of the present government, the Saskatchewan legislature has been increasingly unable to perform this vital function.

The Devine administration displays a consistent tendency to equate "legally correct" with "right," a tendency that leads to an emphasis on the letter of the law, not its spirit, and an inability to understand the nature of tradition and convention in the parliamentary process.

Parliament is a delicate balance. Its continued relevance, its continued legitimacy, rests upon its ability to separate "government" from "power." The executive carries the burden of ensuring that this happens, and must recognize that simply possessing a majority of the seats in a Legislative Assembly does not give it licence to do whatever it likes.

CULTIVATING THE CORPORATE AGENDA

by Terry Pugh

A couple of farmers were sharing a coffee in the Rosetown co-op one morning in mid-August 1989. A dry stretch (which started at the end of May) had aided them in harvesting an early but not altogether bountiful crop.

"So are you finished?" asked one farmer.

"Yeah," replied the other acidly. "In more ways than one."

While the 1980s marked a difficult decade for farmers around the world, Saskatchewan producers could be forgiven for thinking they bore the brunt of the crisis.

Approximately 1,000 Saskatchewan farm families have been forced off the land every year since 1981–victims of a variety of factors that combined to render their operations "nonviable." High interest rates, low commodity prices, large debt loads, falling land values and drought all contributed to an ongoing crisis in rural Saskatchewan. But as some of the more astute philosophers in small-town coffee rows were inclined to point out, federal and provincial government policies may have had the biggest negative impact of all.

Saskatchewan's status as an agriculturally based province is still intact, despite numerous attempts by provincial governments to "diversify" the economy through industrial incentives and other corporate tax breaks. And, just as farming retains its status as the "backbone" of the economy, rural communities continue to be seen as the "heart" of the Saskatchewan identity. Culturally, Saskatchewan has been slower than other provinces to alienate itself from its rural roots. This fact is not lost on political parties, whether they constitute the government, the official opposition, or merely inhabit the margins of the electoral arena.

Indeed, one of the foremost propagandists of idealized rural life is

Premier Grant Devine. He exploits the fact that he is the only Canadian premier with a valid Canadian Wheat Board permit book. Depending on his audience, he alternately trumpets and downplays his Ph.D. in agricultural economics. When he is talking to bankers and federal government representatives, his academic credentials are prominently displayed. When he's talking to farmers in rural communities, on the other hand, "folksy" homilies pepper his speeches, reassuring the audience that he's really just a country boy at heart. When the premier is absent from his office in the legislature during seeding and harvest periods, the image is effectively conveyed that he is "in touch" with the harsh but ultimately cleansing and character-building realities of life down on the farm.

Grant Devine shares two other things with a sizeable percentage of Saskatchewan farmers: he has an off-farm job that helps pay the bills, and his farm is in financial trouble.

According to the Economic Council of Canada (ECC), approximately 22% of the "marginal farms" in the prairie region were "part-time," with the operator working off the farm; an additional 10% of the "commercial" farms also relied heavily on off-farm wages.[1] Unlike the premier, however, most of the people driving school buses or working in gas stations, nursing homes, and truck-stop cafes don't rake in high salaries or benefit from tax-free perks. For them, the family farm is more than an expensive hobby; it is the centre of their existence. It defines their identities, their culture, and their role in society. The off-farm income which they earn is used to prop up their farm operation, which in turn effectively subsidizes the production of food. Unfortunately, it also results in the continuing tendency of governments, economists, and corporations to undervalue the economic contributions of family farms.

Grant Devine is a farmer. Even with the off-farm job of running the provincial government, the crisis in the farming sector has reached the point where he is forced to admit that "the revenue just isn't there. You can have an average crop and you still can't make your payments. When I have an average crop, I'm 50 per cent short in cash flow to make the payments."[2] The plight of the Devine farm is a personal tragedy for the premier. The failure of his government to deal with the causes of the farm crisis ensures that this tragedy will be repeated in thousands of farm homes across the province.

CREDIT CARD POLITICS

Many political observers believe Grant Devine has staked the future of his party on voters in rural areas. They suggest Devine has exploited a "rural/urban split," relied on support in "traditional" conservative areas, and bolstered his prospects for the next election through changes to electoral boundaries that give proportionately greater weight to rural votes.

Besides appealing directly to rural voters with his "country-boy" image, Devine has also not hesitated to cultivate a split between urban and rural people by blaming urban workers and social assistance recipients for the province's economic troubles.

At first glance, Saskatchewan politics during the 1980s makes little sense. The agricultural sector is in a state of crisis. Mounting debt, unmanageable interest charges, high input costs, and depressed prices have combined to force farmers off the land in record numbers. The majority of Saskatchewan farmers have seen their economic situation, their communities' infrastructure, and their quality of life deteriorate during the last decade. Ironically, the government whose policies have contributed to this crisis relies on rural voters for political survival.

Superficially, it seems that farmers should oppose an administration that has clearly pursued an agenda hostile to family farmers. However, the reasons for Devine's success in rural constituencies are readily apparent. His party is particularly good at exploiting the fact that there are a lot of cash-starved farmers and small businesses in rural Saskatchewan. Any scheme that promises to help pay the bills is a recipe for electoral victory. Additionally, Devine's "friend-of-the-farmer" image has been carefully cultivated. Millions of dollars have been funnelled into various agriculturally-based programs since 1982.

In the 1982 election campaign, the Tories rode to power not only on the strength of the Farm Purchase Program's promise of subsidized interest rates, but also on a pledge to eliminate the 7 cent per litre provincial sales tax on gasoline. Voters were enticed by the prospect of retaining more of their hard-earned income in their own pockets.

In Devine's Saskatchewan, farmers have come to expect a bumper cash crop during election years. Leading up to the 1986 election, all farmers received a $25 per acre low interest "production loan." Hog producers received the hog incentive cash advance of $25 per hog. Those in the livestock business received the livestock facilities tax credit worth a total of $1.75 million per year. The farmers oil royalty refund was implemented to give each farmer an average rebate of $650. In the final days of the 1986 election campaign, a desperate Devine received a promise of an even $1 billion for the special Canadian grains payment from the federal government. In the end, $415 million of this was divided up among Saskatchewan farmers, with the balance being spread among farmers in other provinces.[3] The NDP estimated that each farmer received, on average, $37,000 in cash and low-interest loans.

The trend continued. In 1988, in the midst of the federal election campaign, the federal government came through with a promise of Canadian crop drought assistance; $400 million was earmarked for Saskatchewan. In the 1990 provincial budget, Finance Minister Lorne Hepworth offered to subsidize operating loans of up to $12.50 per acre at an interest rate of 10¾%. In total, $525 million was expected to be loaned out.[4] In the end, only 13,371 of Saskatchewan's 60,000 farmers applied for the operating loan. Of these, 517 had their applications rejected. Only $156.9 million of the projected $525 million was loaned out.[5] Hepworth and Devine also promised to ask the federal government for more assistance. A federal grant of $5 per acre was eventually secured.

All these promises were aimed at satisfying the immediate needs of cash-hungry farmers and vote-hungry politicians. However, while many producers received short-term benefits, their financial health either remained the same or deteriorated over the long term. As the federal and provincial governments' long-term agricultural programs took effect, farmers became more and more desperate, and thus more susceptible to being bribed with promises of immediate cash.

As Saskatchewan's financial situation deteriorated, the price offered for the farmers' vote declined. For example, in the budget immediately prior to the 1986 election, farmers were offered loans of up to $25 per acre at 6% interest. There was no similar program through the nonelection years of 1987, 1988, or 1989. By 1990, however, an election year once again coincided with the discovery of the need for immediate help to plant the crop. This time farmers could only qualify for half the loan level and at much higher interest rates than had been granted four years earlier. The plight of farmers was worse in 1990 than in 1986, but the government's estimate of the cost of their vote had plummeted in step with grain prices.

There were two other sides to the dispensing of cash aid to farmers. First, it was accompanied by a cut in services to farmers. In 1987 alone, the Devine government: cut the grants for veterinarian travel and clinics; cancelled the perennial weed control program; eliminated the pest control program; cancelled the soil- and feed-testing grants; terminated funding for agricultural fairs; reduced funding to 4-H clubs; and reduced the funding for the Prairie Agricultural Machinery Institute. Election-year cash payouts to individuals were accompanied by cuts to rural infrastructure and services.

Second, individual farmers were not the only recipients of government largesse. Corporate agribusiness also received its share. Included in the list of beneficiaries were meat packing firms such as Gainers, Intercontinental Packers, and Canada Packers for plant expansion; CARGILL grain for a new fertilizer plant; and Ag-West Biotech for research and development.

While assistance is given to both farmers and agribusinesses, the money to producers is almost always "conditional" aid that seldom stays in their pockets very long and is distributed at politically opportune times. Money to the corporate sector is not dependent on election timing, and ends up padding profit figures and strengthening market domination. In the Tories' overall agenda, aid to the "agrifood sector" is designed to enhance the competitiveness of agribusiness corporations and to encourage the "globalization" of the food system through freer trade. This agenda has little room for family farmers.

Statistics compiled by the federal and provincial departments of agriculture indicate that the only sectors of the farm population experiencing growth are the corporate "super-farms" with gross sales of over $500,000 annually, and the ranks of "part-time" farmers who subsidize their operations through off-farm employment. The largest proportion of the farm population, the "full-time" family farmers, who provided the bulk of the Tories' political base in the country in the 1980s, have seen a rapidly accelerating decline in farm numbers and land holdings during the Devine administration's tenure.

There are many contradictions between the platforms espoused by the Conservatives during election campaigns and the actual conditions that have evolved during their terms of office. In the election of 1982, for example, the Tories stressed the concept of individual farmland ownership as the cornerstone of their campaign in rural Saskatchewan. The perceived evils of the crown-administered Saskatchewan Land Bank, established in the early 1970s by the NDP government, were stressed throughout the months leading up to the election. To be a tenant farmer, even one with a secure lease and an ability to transfer that lease to the next generation, was seen as alien to the spirit and character of rural people. To eliminate the evil of lease-hold farming, the Tories pledged to replace the Land Bank with the "Farm Purchase Program." Under this plan, farmers took out loans from lending institutions at guaranteed interest rates of 8% in the first five years and 12% in the second five years. Farmers were given rebates by the government for the difference between the interest rate charged by the lender and the guaranteed rate.

A total of 5,905 farmers took advantage of this program during the first five years of its operation. By 1987, a total of $617 million in loans had qualified for the subsidy. The average rebate to each farmer (which in turn was passed on to the lending institution) amounted to $3,512.[6] The main beneficiaries of this program, however, were the major lending institutions, which were able to expand their loan portfolios and collect interest at the prevailing high rates.

One of the advantages of the Land Bank was the fact that young and beginning farmers did not incur huge mortgages as a result of land purchases. The elimination of the Land Bank resulted in an increase in farm debt. It also failed to achieve its stated objective of reducing the number of farmers who leased the land they farmed. Seven years after the dismantling of the Land Bank, the number of farmers in Saskatchewan actually owning their own land has decreased markedly, while the percentage of producers renting land from private corporations, other individuals, and the provincial government has mushroomed. The number of farmers with total ownership over their land fell from 34,135 in 1981 to 29,416 in 1986. In 1981, the level of farmland ownership was 66.1% involving 43.3 million acres of land. By 1986, the percentage of farmland ownership had declined to 62.1%, involving 40.8 million acres.[7] Since 1984, roughly 2.5 million acres of land have changed from ownership status to rented land. This amounts to about 2.5 times the total amount of land held by the Land Bank prior to 1982. The Farm Purchase Program also contained an implied promise to increase the number of young and beginning farmers in the province, but the number of producers under the age of 35 has shrunk since 1982.

THE DISAPPEARING FAMILY FARM

There were 19 formal farm bankruptcies in Saskatchewan in 1981. In 1988, there were 112. For every formal bankruptcy, it is estimated that seven farmers are forced out "voluntarily" through quit claims, liquidations, or seizure of assets by creditors. In 1981, this province had 67,318 census farms. By 1986, that number had fallen to 63,431. At present, the number hovers around the 60,000 mark. The farm population declined from 187,163 in 1981 to 168,505 in 1986. The number of primary elevators shrank from 1,805 in 1981 to 898 in 1986. Between 1976 and 1981, the rate of disappearance of farms in Saskatchewan was 5.1%. Between 1981 and 1986, the rate of attrition accelerated to 5.8%. The average acreage of farms rose by 5.5% between 1976 and 1981, and by 6.4% between 1981 and 1986. [8]

More revealing than the number and size of census farms, however, are the statistics regarding "marginal, commercial and corporate" farms. According to the Economic Council of Canada, "marginal" and "commercial" farms each experienced a 15% drop in numbers from 1971 to 1986, while "corporate" operations "actually increased in numbers." In the ECC's view, "marginal" farm operations are those that have sales of less than $20,000 per year, "commercial" farms have sales of less than $150,000 per year, and "corporate" enterprises have sales of over $500,000 per year.

According to the ECC study, roughly 38% of all farms in the prairie region are marginal, while 60% are primarily family-owned and -operated commercial farms. Only about 2% of prairie farms are corporate operations (with 1.5% family-owned and 0.5% owned by "others").

The ECC predicts that by the year 2000, marginal farmers will be producing only 10% of the region's agricultural output, while the top 2%, the corporate farms, will produce about 20%. The dwindling number of family-owned and -operated commercial farms will still account for the bulk of production (roughly 70%) as their average acreage and productivity increases. A further 15% decline in farm numbers, almost exclusively from the ranks of the full-time marginal and commercial farmers, is also predicted for the coming decade. The ECC expects increases in the number of corporate and part-time farm operations, and an overall 40% increase in farm commodity output by the year 2000. [9]

While the right-wing economists at the ECC applaud these trends as indicative of "productivity improvement," and advocate "facilitating" marginal farmers out of agriculture, the dominance of fewer, larger, more capital-intensive farm units and processing facilities ultimately leads to a widening income gap. Evidence of this trend can be seen when net farm income statistics are contrasted with profit figures for multinational agribusiness corporations. In 1986, when grain prices were at record low levels, CARGILL Grain Ltd. of Minneapolis reported its highest profit in 12 years — a 66% increase over a year earlier. Its profit rose from $246.4 million in 1985 to $409.5 million in 1986.[10] In 1989, as farm incomes plummeted in the wake of the worst prairie drought since the 1930s, CARGILL's Canadian subsidiary posted sales of $1.5 billion and a profit of $5.6 million.[11] This profit was reached even though CARGILL spent $70 million in capital projects across the country that year: $55 million on a high-tech beef processing facility at High River, Alberta; $2 million upgrading western elevators; and an unspecified amount for the purchase of the retail fertilizer division of Cyanamid Canada.

CARGILL is gearing up to be the dominant meat packer in western Canada with its High River plant. The High River plant employs nonunion labour and has the capacity to butcher 15,000 head of cattle every week, which would make it the largest slaughtering facility in the country. Analysts suggest cattle prices paid to farmers will drop dramatically once CARGILL attains its monopoly in the market, just as prices in the United States have declined with the emergence of three packing companies (CARGILL, Con-Agra, and IBP) in control of virtually the entire market.

A proposed $435-million CARGILL fertilizer plant announced in May 1989 by Grant Devine is slated to be built with generous assistance from the provincial government. CARGILL, the government, and an unspecified financial institution will invest $65 million, $64 million, and $1 million respectively. The government also intends to guarantee bank loans for the remaining $305 million.

Profits for major agricultural lending institutions have also climbed considerably despite the farm crisis. In the 1989 fiscal year, Canada's six major banks recorded $1.979 billion in profits, even after setting aside $3 billion in reserves against shaky Third World loans.[12] The Toronto Dominion profit was $695 million; the Royal Bank reported $529 million; the Canadian Imperial Bank of Commerce was next with $450 million; the Bank of Nova Scotia followed with $222 million; the Bank of Montreal was in fifth place with $51 million; and the National Bank reported $32 million in profit. While these profit figures for agribusinesses are taken as evidence of continuing growth and prosperity in the agricultural industry, they mask the reality of depression in rural communities across Saskatchewan.

A study prepared by the Christian Farm Crisis Action Committee (CFCAC) in the fall of 1988 illustrated in concrete terms the economic and social impact that the loss of 15 farm families has on a small town. In a hamlet of 125 farmers, a loss of 15 producers represents a 12% drop in population. According to the CFCAC, this figure is typical of the rate of rural depopulation currently underway. While production levels would likely not decline, the money those 15 displaced farmers previously earned from off-farm jobs would no longer be spent in the community. This would amount to a probable loss of around $172,000 per year for the community. Add to this the loss of spouses' off-farm wages and the loss of family allowances and other social payments, and the community would forgo roughly $244,000 in purchases. Local financial institutions would experience a drop in revenue due to the closing of those 15 farmers' accounts, and other local businesses would experience a decline of about $225,000 as a result of their shrinking market.

The bottom line is that "outside revenue no longer being brought into the community amounts to $133,000" and "total expense dollars no longer available to the local businesses amounts to $770,000."

Assuming those 15 families were made up of 62 people, with 32 being school-age children, the CFCAC suggests two teaching positions would be phased out, with a resulting payroll loss to the community of about $60,000. Two more families (of the laid-off teachers) would then be forced to move away from the community. A combined loss of sales from the displaced farmers and teachers ($770,000 plus $60,000 equals $830,000) would mean the loss of at least one retail store, resulting in yet another two families being obliged to leave. Once people move away from a small town, it is unlikely they will return to retire there. The CFCAC puts the loss of pension revenue for the community at about $267,000 annually. The decline in tax base for the municipality would be about $20,000; and demand for health, social, recreational, and other services would be reduced. In addition, people who remain in the town would find it increasingly difficult to effectively run community-oriented volunteer organizations which contribute so much to the quality of life in rural towns.[13]

FARM INCOME AND DEBT

Farm income is the critical factor in the economic and social health of Saskatchewan, since all sectors of the provincial economy are heavily dependent on agriculture. In 1981, realized net farm income for Saskatchewan farmers peaked at $1.14 billion. By 1986, the province's realized net farm income was only $767,038,000. By 1987, it had risen slightly to $921,253, with 53% of that actually coming from off-farm income. After rising to $1.079 billion in 1988 (primarily due to payments under the

Special Canadian Grains Program and other federal stabilization plans), net farm income fell again in 1989 to an estimated $686,600,000.[14] In 1990, realized net farm income in Saskatchewan is expected to be only $364.7 million. When expenses and depreciation are taken into account, the province's farmers will actually experience a loss of $9.4 million – the first time expenses exceeded income since 1933, the worst year of the Great Depression[15] (see Table 4.1).

Despite an increase in overall farm cash receipts from $4 billion in 1981 to $4.455 billion in 1989, Saskatchewan farmers actually found their purchasing power declining. When adjusted to the Farm Input Price Index, farm cash receipts declined from $4 billion to about $3.78 billion. When adjusted to the Consumer Price Index, the decline in purchasing power was "even more startling: from $4 billion to $3.295 billion." In real terms, "farmers have lost over $1 billion during the past seven years."[16]

In its first issue of the 1990s, *The Western Producer* compared farm production costs and commodity prices in 1980 and 1989. The figures illustrate why overall farm incomes are declining for the majority of producers. Grains covered under the Western Grain Stabilization Act were worth 43% less at the end of the 1980s than they were at the beginning of the decade. Gross grain receipts dropped from $6.4 billion in 1980 to $5.3 billion in 1989, while production expenses rose from $1.8 billion to $2.8 billion. This caused prairie grain farmers' cash flow to be 41% lower at the end of the decade.

The price of No. 1 CW Red Spring Wheat was $222.12 in 1980–81; in 1988–89 it will likely be about $195. In 1980, it cost an average of $37 per acre to plant wheat in central Saskatchewan; by 1989, the cost had risen to an average of $45 per acre. Once that wheat had made it to the elevator, farmers had to pay the freight to get it to export position. In 1980, under the statutory Crow's Nest Pass rate, farmers paid $4.85 per tonne. The Crow was abolished in 1983. Farmers are now paying an average of $9 per tonne to ship grain by rail.[17]

The debt burden carried by Saskatchewan farm families continues to rise as incomes fall (see Table 4.2). In 1983, total farm debt in this province was $4.435 billion; by 1987 it had increased to $5.78 billion. Provincial government policies directly contributed to the increase in farm debt on two occasions. From 1982 to 1984, the Farm Purchase Program encouraged young farmers to borrow from the chartered banks. This program is partially responsible for the $277-million increase in debt owed to the banks during this two-year period. In addition, the level of debt held by provincial lending agencies jumped substantially from $293,950,000 in 1985 to $1,423,158,000 in 1986. This increase in provincial farm debt was largely attributable to the one-time $25 per acre production loan program, instituted just prior to the 1986 election. The average debt load per farm works out to about $150,000. The Economic Council of Canada puts the number of Saskatchewan farms in financial difficulty at 28%.[18]

Younger farmers have been hit hardest by the farm crisis of the 1980s: "Every second farmer under the age of 35 was in financial difficulty, whether working full-time or part-time, independently or as a partner. Roughly every fifth or sixth farmer in this group was in a nonviable financial situation."[19] Devine's Conservatives had begun the 1980s attacking the NDP's Land Bank Program, and promised to ensure that young farmers could buy land immediately. By the end of the decade, these young farmers were collapsing under the weight of the resulting debt.

Given the burgeoning level of farm debt, it is not surprising that financial institutions' farmland holdings have grown rapidly since 1982. The Royal Bank, a major source of agricultural credit in the province, tripled its agricultural land holdings in the 12 months prior to the end of October 1988. By the beginning of 1989, it held 120,000 acres in Saskatchewan. The Farm Credit Corporation, a federally owned crown agency, held title to 420,000 acres across the country in January 1989, with much of that in Saskatchewan. By mid-1989, it was estimated FCC held 620,000 acres, with the bulk of that having been repossessed over a two-year period from April 1987 to April 1989. Financial institutions may hold as much as 1.5 million acres of farmland across the three Prairie provinces.[20]

Farmland values have also tumbled. Land values fell 40% between 1984 and 1988 in Saskatchewan. In 1981, the total value of farm capital in the province was $31.4 billion. By 1986, the value had fallen to $29.6 billion.[21] Farmers who had borrowed from lending institutions on the strength of their land values suddenly found themselves overextended in their lines of credit, and were vulnerable to foreclosure and seizure actions by their creditors.

FORECLOSURES INCREASE

At a farm crisis meeting in Middle Lake, Saskatchewan, on 10 August 1989, one of the most keenly read documents that circulated among the more than 200 farm men and women in attendance was a list of foreclosure notices issued for each rural municipality in the province. Compiled by the federal Farm Debt Review Board (FDRB) in the spring, the list illustrated just how widespread the farm financial crisis had become. It listed the number of farmers in each RM who had filed for a stay of proceedings under Sections 16 and 20 of the Farm Debt Review Act, and the number of foreclosure notices received by the FDRB from creditors. Altogether, over 10,000 farmers had received foreclosure notices, with a further 3,500 filing under Sections 16 and 20 of the Farm Debt Review Act.

According to the FDRB document, many rural municipalities had well over half the farmers within their boundaries receiving foreclosure notices. In some cases, it was as high as two-thirds or greater. Mass meetings across the province in the fall and winter of 1989 repeatedly called for a moratorium on farm foreclosures and restructuring of the nearly $6 billion in provincial farm debt to allow families to remain on the land.

A revised list compiled by the FDRB dated July 1989 indicated that the total number of foreclosure notices which came before both the FDRB and the Farm Land Security Board (FLSB) was 5,968. However, the FDRB noted that approximately 100 farmers in the midst of foreclosure proceedings were not included because of problems in identifying which RM their residence was in. The list also failed to take into account "the significant number of farmers who have settled their financial difficulties on their own and who have not employed the services of either" the FDRB or FLSB. [22]

WHO WINS, WHO LOSES?

Despite millions of dollars in aid to the agricultural sector between 1982 and 1989, the trend toward a widening split within the farming community is accelerating. Family farms, once the dominant class in Saskatchewan, will likely disappear at an increasing rate throughout the 1990s unless substantial policy changes are implemented by provincial and federal governments. With the demise of the family farm, the ranks of the corporate-style "super-farms" are likely to increase, as is their share of commodity production. Also expected to increase in numbers are the so-called "part-time" farms, which in many instances are actually full-time farms in which one or both spouses also work at full- or part-time jobs as a way of subsidizing their operation.

The income gap between the corporate-style farms and the marginal operations is indicative of a growing class division within Saskatchewan's rural areas. Communities, in the end, will experience a deterioration in the quality of life, as "successful" farmers increasingly identify not with their neighbours, but with the corporate sector. For these large-scale farmers, farming as "a way of life" will give way to farming "as a business," and a narrow, profit-oriented style will be pursued, regardless of environmental and social consequences.

The economic and political power of multinational agribusiness corporations will also continue to grow if current trends remain unchecked. The wholesale embrace of the concept of "free trade" in agricultural produce within a global market by both the provincial and federal governments has put increasing pressure on farmers in Saskatchewan, and in Canada as a whole. Not only are producers feeling the negative consequences of the Canada-US Free Trade Agreement, but they are also being hit with unfavourable trade rulings emerging from the General Agreement on Tariffs and Trade (GATT). In both these trade arenas, the avowed objective of negotiators from all countries involved, including Canada, is to "lower trade barriers" and eliminate "trade-distorting subsidies" to agricultural producers.

The push for free trade is based on the concept of "comparative advantage" among producing countries, which suggests that farmers in any given country should only produce commodities which cannot be raised cheaper somewhere else. In the emerging globalized economy, food is treated as just another commodity, and the idea of self-sufficiency in the most basic of human needs is dismissed by governments as irrelevant.

But while governments negotiate trade pacts, it is the corporate sector which benefits from those agreements. A handful of multinational corporations dominate the global trade in grains, meat, and processed foods. The dismantling of "nontariff barriers" (aimed at protecting a country's farmers from the unbridled excesses of the market economy) will primarily benefit corporations, since they will be able to manipulate investments, markets, and supplies on a global basis. Corporations are able to achieve maximum profit when they are in a position to procure cheap raw materials (crops and livestock) from farmers, and operate with cheap labour. As a result, farmers and workers become increasingly exploited as the corporate sector gains greater economic leverage in the global market. This is a process which has been underway for decades, but which has accelerated tremendously in the 1970s and 1980s, in no small part due to the encouragement of successive federal governments. In 1970, a

79

Task Force Report on Agriculture spelled out clearly the direction the Canadian government wanted to see farm policy take. The agricultural sector was to be guided by the imperatives of the market, and marginal farmers were to be eliminated. In 1981, another document known as the "Agri-Food Strategy" updated the task force report but retained the same basic pro-corporate direction. The most recent update, entitled "Growing Together," was released in November 1989 by federal Agriculture Minister Don Mazankowski.

In Canada, the targets of international trade agreements include such institutions as the Canadian Wheat Board, the Canadian Dairy Commission, and other orderly marketing agencies which offer some income protection to producers. Other policies, such as grain transportation payments under the Western Grain Transportation Act, have also come under fire as being of a "trade-distorting" nature. Even such things as stabilization payments and crop insurance have been called into question by trade negotiators for the United States.

Significantly, subsidies to the corporate sector are rarely examined under the same microscope as payments to farmers, even though they constitute a far greater expenditure by governments. The American "Export Enhancement Program" which began in 1985 has provided billions of dollars in export subsidies to multinational grain companies while at the same time working to depress the world price of grain paid to farmers. Despite the obvious "trade-distorting" character of the Export Enhancement Program, it has not been discontinued because it has proved beneficial in furthering the interests of the corporate sector.

Farm policy is more than a series of ad hoc loans disbursed to farmers in the heat of an election campaign with the aim of garnering the maximum number of votes. It is, in the final analysis, an overall agenda which benefits some players in the food system at the expense of others.

The trends evident in Saskatchewan for the better part of the past decade illustrate that while the majority of farmers have seen their net worth, farm income, standard of living, and quality of life decline, agribusiness companies and a minority of large producers have profited. This has occurred not in spite of the Devine government's "assistance" programs, but because of them. Although the government's farm policy superficially appears to benefit farm families, closer analysis reveals it is aimed at promoting the interests of "super-farms" and large-scale agribusinesses.

THE SELLING OF SASKATCHEWAN

by Mark Stobbe

L ong considered a beachhead of social democracy in North America, in the 1980s Saskatchewan suddenly became home to one of the most aggressive free enterprise governments in Canada's history. After winning the 1982 election, Grant Devine and his government inherited a province with a long history of political solutions to economic problems and a degree of public ownership that were unmatched in North America. Public enterprise had been used as a tool for regional development, to provide utility service, and to capture resource revenue for use within the province. Two waves of the development of publicly owned corporations had created a high degree of state enterprise that was unmatched on the continent.

The first wave of public ownership occurred under the Douglas/Lloyd CCF government, which was in power from 1944 to 1964 and concentrated on the creation of public utilities. Electrical generation and distribution and natural gas distribution were controlled by SaskPower. The province's telephone system was controlled by SaskTel. Saskatchewan Government Insurance (SGI) had a monopoly on basic automobile insurance, and was a dominant force in general property insurance in the province. Public ownership of utilities is by no means unique in Canada, and most economists concede that there are advantages to public ownership in the case of natural monopolies such as electrical distribution and telephones.[1] What made Saskatchewan unique is that it was, and is, the only jurisdiction in North America that featured public ownership of the complete range of utilities as well as insurance.

In addition to the utility sector, the CCF government also created a number of publicly owned small resource, service, and manufacturing enterprises. Of these, the most important that still existed by 1982 were: the Saskatchewan Transportation Company (STC), which offered bus service within the province; Sask Minerals, which ran two sodium sulphate mines in Chaplin and Fox Valley and a peat moss operation in Carrot River; Saskatchewan Forest Products, which operated sawmills in locations such as Hudson Bay, Big River, and Meadow Lake; the Saskatchewan Government Printing Company; and the Saskatchewan Economic Development Corporation (SEDCO), which provided financing to Saskatchewan businesses.

The second wave of expansion of public ownership was conducted by the Blakeney NDP government, which was in power from 1971 until its defeat by the Conservatives in 1982. It featured a major expansion into resource companies. The Blakeney government created major crown corporations which, by 1982, owned significant portions of the province's oil (Sask Oil), potash (PCS), and uranium (SMDC) industries. In 1980, the government also purchased the province's only pulp mill, located at Prince Albert, and formed the Prince Albert Pulp Company (PAPCO). Sask Comp was established to consolidate computer facilities for the government.[2]

In addition to these crown corporations, the Saskatchewan government also had equity positions in a number of major and minor corporations. These included Intercontinental Packers, S.E.D. Systems (one of the pioneers of Saskatchewan's high-tech industry), Interprovincial Pipe and Steel Company (IPSCO), and Prairie Malt (a barley malting plant based in Biggar). As a rule, these equity investments occurred when Saskatchewan companies required capital infusions for expansion or survival.

Thus, when the Devine government took office in 1982, it surveyed a province in which the government owned all or part of the only meat packing plant, the only steel mill, the only pulp mill, its leading high-tech firm, all utilities, insurance, a bus company, and major portions of the oil, potash, forestry, and uranium industries. Given this level of public ownership and the ideological orientation of the new government, it was inevitable that Devine and his ministers would look for ways to put private enterprise into the driver's seat.

Privatization can be summarized as any policy of government which transfers assets or activity from public ownership and control to private hands. This can occur in a number of ways, including: the sale of assets either to a single purchaser or through a share offering; the contracting out of services or activities formerly provided "in house"; the withdrawal of publicly provided services which come to be offered in the marketplace by privately owned providers; and the removal of legislative public monopolies to allow private firms to compete with public ones.[3]

The implications of privatization go beyond simply changing the service-delivery mechanism, selling off some assets, or contracting out some services for reasons of convenience or corruption. The ideologically motivated privatization campaigns that have occurred in Britain, British Columbia, and Saskatchewan are part of an attempt to change fundamentally and permanently the role of the state, and the way control over resource allocation is exercised. The proponents of privatization see it as a means of converting the political process into a market process. The ballot box is replaced by the buck both in determining what productive and allocational decisions are made, and in legitimizing this process.[4] Its proponents envision nothing less than a "complete social revolution"[5] in which the clock will be turned back to the mystical days when there was no welfare state, no public ownership, and no restrictions on property rights or consumer sovereignty.

The Devine government reached this hard-core, ideologically driven perspective on privatization gradually. To be sure, its members always considered themselves "free enterprisers," and their preference for private over public enterprise was never a secret. As Colin Thatcher, the government's first energy minister states in his memoirs, the government "was highly business orientated and made no bones about it . . . We had to demonstrate that we're ready and open for business and this was a new era in Saskatchewan. 'Open for business' was Grant Devine's slogan and he wanted to spread the message far and wide."[6] The crown corporations were viewed as havens for socialists and looked upon with suspicion and hostility. However, the new government initially contented itself with purging crown corporation ranks of those who were ideologically impure. Its commitment to private enterprise initially took the form of homilies, exhortations, and tax breaks rather than a wholesale dismantling of publicly owned enterprises.[7]

During its first term in office, the government did privatize a few agencies and corporations. In 1983 and 1984 the government dismantled the Department of Highways road-building capacity and contracted out this activity. In 1983, 157 departmental employees were laid off, and another 237 received pink slips in 1984. According to then highways minister Jim Garner, "These lay offs are a move from socialism to freedom for the employees who will now have the opportunity to work for the private sector."[8] In May 1984, the government held a massive public auction in which 400 pieces of road building equipment were put on the block. This equipment, with a replacement value estimated at $40 million, fetched $6 million.[9]

In 1984, the government privatized its court-reporting service through contracting out with former employees.

In 1982, SaskPower sold a drag line used for strip mining coal to Manalta Coal of Alberta for $45 million. The government guaranteed the loan which Manalta took out to buy the drag line, and contracted to lease it back. Two years later, the Poplar River Coal Mine used to provide coal for the Coronach power plant was also sold to Manalta Coal. Although SPC had evaluated the mine as being worth $129 million, it was sold for $102 million. Of this, the government lent Manalta $89 million. SaskPower signed a long term contract for the purchase of coal produced at this mine.

In January 1986, the government issued a share offering in the crown oil company, Sask Oil. This share offering raised $110 million, of which $75 million was returned to the province and $35 million was retained by Sask Oil. This first share offering in the corporation reduced the government's equity position in the company to 58%.

Later in 1986, the Prince Albert Pulp Company (PAPCO) was sold to the American lumber multinational, Weyerhaeuser, for a stated price of $248 million. This price was subsequently reduced to $236 million following the 1986 provincial election. The deal was a good one for Weyerhaeuser. In addition to the pulp mill, the company received PAPCO's forestry operations (7.5 million acres of timber rights), a chemical plant in Saskatoon, and a sawmill and woodland operation in Big River. The sales agreement also committed the province to building 32 kilometres per year of forest-access roads for Weyerhaeuser, exempted the company from weight restrictions or road bans imposed on provincial roads, and gave the company the right to "close or restrict" access to any road within its forest area. Weyerhaeuser was promised that aboriginal land claims would not affect areas within its forest area. The province guaranteed that it would not approve any attempt by the City of Saskatoon to annex the area where the Saskatoon chemical plant was located should annexation result in an increase in electrical rates (the City of Saskatoon operates its own electrical distribution system). The chemical plant was removed from the authority of the Meewasin Valley Authority, which is responsible for regulating development along the shores of the South Saskatchewan River in and around Saskatoon. Financing the deal was easy for

Weyerhaeuser. There was no down payment, and the province issued a debenture with an 8.5% interest rate payable over 30 years. However, the corporation is not required to make any payments in years when its return on its Saskatchewan operations are under 12%.[10]

The Devine government entered the 1986 election touting this deal as being a good one for two reasons. First, as part of the sales agreement, Weyerhaeuser promised to build a paper mill in Prince Albert. It received an $83-million provincial loan guarantee in order to finance this project. As a result, the government was able to claim that the sale of PAPCO would lead directly to job creation. Secondly, PAPCO had lost money for three of the four previous years. The government ran a series of election ads claiming that the company had cost taxpayers $91,000 per day, and that the sale ended this expense. These claims overlooked both the effects of management on the company (it had been profitable while publicly owned under an NDP government) and the cyclical nature of the pulp industry. The 1986 sale coincided with a trough in the pulp and paper market. The following year there was an increase in demand and prices, which ensured that the Prince Albert mill would have been profitable whether in public or private hands.[11]

The PAPCO deal is noteworthy for a number of reasons. It was both the largest and the last privatization initiative in the Devine government's first term. It also occurred before the government began to import expert advice on the political nuances of privatization, and to explicitly imitate the British model for privatization. It was a sale of a prominent corporation to a single, foreign buyer for terms which could be perceived as being a sweetheart deal. According to Oliver Letwin, a former advisor to Margaret Thatcher and head of the International Privatization Unit of N.M. Rothschild, "on its own, as a single method, I think it [single buyer sales] would prove a political disaster."[12] After losing both of the Prince Albert constituencies in the 1986 election, the Devine government was in the mood to hear how it could create a privatization campaign guaranteed by the experts to make long-term political success inevitable.

THE PRIVATIZATION MANIA BEGINS

The Devine Conservatives came out of the 1986 election bruised, battered, and shaken. Although winning a healthy majority of seats, they had survived by the narrowest of margins. The NDP had gained more overall votes, winning by huge margins in many urban ridings while losing a lot of close ones in rural areas. Two thousand votes to the NDP, distributed properly, would have changed the result. Most observers agreed that the only thing that had saved Devine was the last-minute federal promise of a billion-dollar agricultural aid package.

Probably most disturbing to the government was the rejection of its economic policies in constituencies which had ostensibly benefited the most from them. The sale of PAPCO, and the resulting promise of new jobs in a paper mill, did not prevent voters in both Prince Albert ridings from defeating the Conservative incumbents. In North Battleford, tax breaks and grants had lured three new major employers to the city in the year prior to the election. The voters responded by turfing out the Conservative cabinet minister who was running on this record of accomplishment.

The jubilation of re-election was therefore short lived. The government members had to say goodbye to (or find jobs for) a lot of their friends. They had narrowly won an election that, had they been left to their own devices, they probably would have lost. Their economic strategy had been rejected by voters in the areas where it had been, by the Conservatives' standards, most successful. Added to this was a major fiscal crisis. It would soon have to be revealed that the annual deficit for the province had been underestimated by $800 million.[13]

In the spring of 1987, the government responded to its fiscal crisis with a series of dramatic spending cuts. Included in this was the contracting out of the children's dental plan to dentists in private practice. This initiative entailed the sudden firing of 411 dental workers, almost all of whom were women and almost all of whom lived and worked in rural areas.[14] These cuts were extremely unpopular. While the government plummeted in the polls, over 100,000 Saskatchewan residents signed petitions protesting various service cuts, and the largest demonstration in the history of the province was organized at the legislative building.

These were the circumstances in which the government was offered a way out of its difficulties. Devine and his colleagues were promised that not only could they actively promote private enterprise, but that they could become popular by doing so. The religion offering this salvation was privatization, its patron saint was Margaret Thatcher, and its high priests were a handful of right-wing economists working out of groups such as the Fraser Institute of Vancouver, the Adam Smith Institute of London, England, and the Reason Foundation of California.

The big revival meeting was held at the Bayshore Hotel in Vancouver in July 1987. Organized by the Fraser Institute, the high-priced, three-day conference on privatization brought together the high priests of privatization, representatives from banks and investment houses, and government officials from Canadian jurisdictions who had something to sell and the itch to make a deal.

The Saskatchewan government sent more people to this conference than did any other government in Canada. Included were the Minister Responsible for SGI, her assistant, and the vice-president for Finance of the corporation; the premier's principal secretary; both the chair and the president of the Crown Management Board; a policy analyst for the Saskatchewan Executive Council; the president of the Saskatchewan Housing Corporation; and the chairman of the board of the Potash Corporation of Saskatchewan. Also attending was an employee of the Policy Secretariat who would later become the first research director of Saskatchewan's own version of the Fraser Institute, the Institute for Saskatchewan Enterprise. [15]

The Saskatchewan delegation got what they came for. They heard the gospel of privatization and became believers. They also made contact with a group of British privateers who would play a key role in shaping Saskatchewan's privatization program.

The message at the Fraser Institute conference was simple and, for conservatives, appealing. It was that privatization could be the method whereby not only the role of the state would be reduced and opportunities for private enterprise expanded, but also the political sociology of a country or province could be fundamentally changed. Undertaken properly, privatization would destroy the base of support for socialism, and actively create a conservative constituency. The role model was Thatcher's Britain, where according to the high priest of privatization, Madsen Pirie, "no intellectual battle was won. We didn't win the argument first. We privatized first and used the success of privatization to win the argument . . . We didn't get public opinion until after it was done." [16] Privatization, said Pirie, was the key to Thatcher's modern-day record of three successive majority governments. The Saskatchewan delegation applauded vigorously.

According to the privatization experts, the key to making privatization politically popular was to spread the benefits as widely as possible. Sale of crown corporations to single buyers should be avoided in most cases. Instead the corporations should be sold through the issuing of share offerings or employee buy outs. Where possible, employees should be given the opportunity to purchase shares at nominal prices. A portion of any share offering should be reserved for small Saskatchewan investors. These were to be marketed aggressively in major advertising campaigns. Share prices should be low enough that a rise in their value would be almost inevitable. This would give large numbers of voters a taste of success in the stock market, give them a profit on the privatization deal, and allow the government to point to the rise in share values as proof of the superiority of private over public enterprise. Objections to the privatization deal should be anticipated and addressed in the enabling legislation or terms of the deal.[17]

Two of the speakers at the Fraser Institute conference played a particularly important role in Saskatchewan. Madsen Pirie, the president of the Adam Smith Institute and a former advisor to Margaret Thatcher, travelled to Saskatchewan in the fall of 1987 to address a supper meeting organized by a Regina businessman and the National Citizens' Coalition. Over 1,000 Saskatchewan government and business leaders turned out to hear the gospel of privatization from its most enthusiastic salesperson.

Oliver Letwin, a former member of Thatcher's Policy Unit on Privatization, a defeated Conservative candidate for the House of Commons, and the head of Rothschild's International Privatization Unit, spent even more time in Saskatchewan. He was hired by the government on a consultant's contract paying $22,000 per month to help formulate its privatization program.[18] While in the province, he made public sales pitches to groups such as the Conservative Party annual convention and the Chamber of Commerce. Letwin's intellectual signature was firmly stamped on the government's emerging program and on some of the complicated deals that were put together.[19]

By the beginning of 1988, the government was geared up to launch its campaign. Devine began suggesting that all crown corporations except the utilities would be available for sale. In January 1988, he shuffled his cabinet. The shuffle featured the creation of a new department, Public Participation. Heading this new department was veteran minister Graham Taylor, who was also given responsibility for SGI. The insurance corporation was slated to be among the first sold.[20]

Taylor said that the responsibilities of the new department would be to examine all aspects of government operation to determine where "public participation" could be encouraged through contracting out, the sale of assets, share issues, employee buy outs, and the issuing of "participation bonds" in crown corporations. Action was promised "in the next two week period." [21]

While 1988 was billed by the government as the year of privatization, its program actually was a little slow developing. During the spring session of the legislature, it introduced an omnibus privatization bill, Bill 55, The Public Participation Act. This legislation died on the order paper following an NDP filibuster. In the meantime, Taylor held a series of day-long, by invitation only, consultative meetings throughout the province. The meetings were followed up with local newsletters containing at least one article stating that people at the meeting had voiced their support for privatization. However, the credibility of this consultative process suffered a blow when a comparison of the newsletters describing different meetings showed an amazing uniformity, right down to the pictures of the meetings and quotes from participants. [22]

While the government was stumbling slightly with the political sales job, its supporters were mobilizing to mount the propaganda campaign in earnest. During the summer of 1988, letters were sent to a select group in the business and academic community suggesting that they attend a lunch meeting at Regina's exclusive Assiniboia Club if they saw the need for an "independent" group that would study the impact of privatization. The meeting was chaired by George Hill, the president of SaskPower and a former president of the Saskatchewan Conservatives. [23] Out of the meeting came the Institute for Saskatchewan Enterprise (ISE), an ostensibly neutral think tank devoted to analyzing the economic effects of privatization.

The Saskatchewan Enterprise Institute has a board of directors dominated by businessmen, accountants, and commerce professors. The lone woman is Eva Lee, the former dean of the now defunct College of Home Economics at the University of Saskatchewan, and later the president of the province's technical school system. The chair of the board is IPSCO president Roger Phillips.

The institute's facade of political neutrality did not last long. In his public statements, Phillips made it clear that the benefits of privatization were seen as a given. It was the task of the institute to provide supporting facts. As its first research director, the institute hired Morley Evans, who has close links with California's Reason Foundation. Evans could also speak firsthand about the benefits of privatization, since he had obtained his Ph.D. in economics from a private American university, Union Graduate School of Ohio, which had awarded his degree despite having no faculty members trained in economics. The tuition fee for a Union Graduate School Ph.D. is $13,000. Its work requirements are attending 35 days of seminars and "peer meetings" and completing a "project demonstrating excellence." Acceptable projects for the Ph.D. include such things as "outstanding creations in poetry" and "a documented project of social change."[24]

The Institute for Saskatchewan Enterprise has contributed to the privatization debate through the publication of a report on PCS and an appearance before the Barber Commission on the sale of SaskEnergy. It favoured the sale of both crown corporations.

The ISE's major effort was the organization of an "International Privatization Symposium" held in May 1990. The speaker's list was a "who's who" of privatization enthusiasts from Britain, the United States, and Canada.[25] However, despite the high-profile speaker's list, the symposium was a failure. Attendance reached only a quarter of pre-symposium predictions, and the gathering was plagued by organizational mistakes such as the failure to provide translation facilities for the multilanguage international event.[26] While the provincial government officially had nothing to do with the affair, it did host an opening reception complete with the choral group from the RCMP training depot singing a song composed in honour of the occasion.

Throughout 1988, the process of privatization was moving along. The government turned over to private hands a number of minor operations ranging from the White Track Ski Hill to the Moose Jaw Wild Animal Park, and contracted out some data-entry work at the Department of Finance. Saskatchewan Government Printing was sold to an employee-owned company, Printco Graphics Incorporated. The employee group purchased $189,000 worth of tax-deductible shares. They also received a loan for 30% of the $1.5-million purchase price, and a six-year guarantee of government work.[27]

The more significant privatization initiatives in 1988 were the creation of the Westbridge computer corporation, the sale of Sask Minerals, the sale of a government-owned sawmill in Meadow Lake, the reorganization of SMDC to prepare it for privatization, and a complicated deal between SaskPower and Sask Oil.

Westbridge was created through a merger of: the government's computer crown corporation, Sask Comp; the data terminals and data centre for SaskTel; Mercury Group Graphics, a Saskatoon printing company; and

Leasecorp Western, a leasing company specializing in financing computer purchases. The government initially held 67.1% of the new Westbridge Corporation. This share was reduced in a subsequent share offering. Westbridge launched an aggressive expansion program. During its first year of operation, the newly created corporation purchased a software firm (Management Systems Ltd.), a chain of office supply stores (Superior Business Systems), and another computer-leasing firm (Leasecorp). Leasecorp owner Leonard McCurty was hired as the new president of Westbridge. The goal was to create a computer company capable of delivering a full range of services to business and government clients.[28] The growth of Westbridge was assisted by a $150-million, long-term contract to provide computer services to SaskPower and the departments of finance, health, social services, highways, and agriculture.[29] These contracts have prompted Saskatchewan's provincial auditor to express concern about the security of these departments' data files and programs.[30] In addition, SaskPower quietly offered 3,000 of its employees interest-free loans repayable through payroll deductions if they purchased personal home computers from Westbridge.[31]

The growth of Westbridge was held up by the government as a prime example of the success of their privatization program. However, in 1990 the corporation suddenly experienced difficulties. In the fiscal year ending on 31 March 1990, Westbridge declared a $7.1 million loss. Share prices dropped from $15 per share to $4.50.[32] Superior Business Machines was sold for a $1.2-million loss only seven months after it had been bought.[33] Mercury Group Graphics, one of the original Westbridge components, was also sold at a loss. The NDP tabled documents in the legislature showing that Westbridge paid much more than the assigned value for the privately owned components of the company when it was created. Westbridge had paid $4.9 million to receive Mercury Group's assets possessing an assigned value of $2.4 million. The computer company paid $20.5 million for the assets of three companies controlled by soon-to-be Westbridge President Len McCurty. These companies had a book value totalling $104,000.[34]

The government did not talk much about another 1988 initiative, the sale of Sask Minerals in March. Its sodium sulphate division went to Kam Kotia Mines Ltd., a subsidiary of Dickenson Mines, while the peat moss division was sold to Premier CDN. This asset sale to single buyers could have been written up as a "how not to proceed" case study by privatization proponents. Although Privatization Minister Graham Taylor had promised just a few months earlier that there would be consultation prior to any deals, consultation with workers and municipal officials in the affected towns meant meetings to inform them that an agreement had been reached.[35] The corporation was sold, without tender, to two out-of-province corporations. Finally, there were controversies about the price paid for the corporation. In announcing the sale, the government stated that it had received $12.5 million from Kam Kotia and $3.4 million from Premier CDN. The deal periodically surfaced in the media when the NDP opposition revealed that four months before the sale, Premier CDN had gone to the stock market to raise money for its purchase of the peat moss operation. The prospectus stated that the sale price would be $3.8 million. A year later, it was revealed that Kam Kotia had in fact paid only $12.1 million, or $400,000 lower than the announced price, for its portion of the company. Fuel was added to the fire when Sask Minerals' last annual report was released. This showed that the book value of the corporation was $5.1 million higher than the sale price. Devine and Taylor responded by insisting that the province had made a good deal, and by refusing to release the appraisal done before the sale.[36]

While the sale of Sask Minerals violated the experts' every rule on privatization, the sale in June of the sawmill in Meadow Lake was a showpiece of the new program. The sawmill was sold to NorSask Forest Products Inc. for $6 million. NorSask was owned equally by two companies, one composed of employees and management at the mill, and the other of 10 Indian bands in the area. In addition to giving ownership to these local stakeholder groups, this privatization project was accompanied by an announcement that the new arrangement would make it possible for other companies to build an $80-million pulp mill and an $11.3-million chopstick factory in Meadow Lake.[37] It was never explained how the privatization of the sawmill was related to these two projects. Little more has been heard of the chopstick factory since the initial announcement. The pulp mill proposal is proceeding with different owners than initially announced. However, the privatization of the Meadow Lake sawmill has remained relatively immune from political challenge since the sale was made to local groups with a broad membership in the community.

The three privatization schemes outlined above were significant because they were the first initiatives following the creation of the Department of Public Participation. They involved three different models, namely a sale to single buyers (Sask Minerals), a share offering (Westbridge), and an employee/interest group buy out (Meadow Lake Sawmills). However, in dollar terms, they were all relatively small. There were two further privatization initiatives in 1988 that involved hundreds of millions in assets.

The federal and provincial governments undertook the privatization of the uranium industry in a cooperative fashion. The federal government's stake in the uranium and mining industry was represented by Eldorado Nuclear. This company, which had originally been nationalized during World War II to facilitate the production of uranium for the Manhattan Project,[38] owned refineries in Blind River and Port Hope, Ontario, the Rabbit Lake mine in northern Saskatchewan, and a 16⅔% interest in the world's largest and richest producing uranium mine at Key Lake. It also had a mountain of debt, and a history of operating losses through most of the 1970s and 1980s.[39] Saskatchewan's share of the industry was held by the Saskatchewan Mining Development Corporation (SMDC), which had a 50% stake in the Key Lake Mine and a 20% share in the province's third operating mine at Cluff Lake. In addition to its shares in these producing mines, SMDC also held a 50% interest in the world's richest known uranium deposit at Cigar Lake and shares in a host of other uranium properties in northern Saskatchewan. It also was a major player in the province's gold exploration boom. Total assets were valued at $914 million at the end of 1987. Unlike Eldorado, SMDC had a healthy debt:equity ratio, a history of profitable operation, and a promising future. Its net earnings in 1987 amounted to slightly more than $60 million or 20.2% of the province's equity.[40]

While both levels of government were in a privatizing mood, their ability to sell off their uranium companies differed. The profitable SMDC would be snapped up by investors, while it was unlikely that anyone would be too interested in purchasing the troubled Eldorado Nuclear. The solution was for the Devine Conservatives to lend a helping hand to their federal counterparts by agreeing to an amalgamation of the two companies. The new corporation, called the Canadian Mining and Energy Corp (CAMECO), would be the largest uranium mining and refining company in the world.

The amalgamation was announced on 22 February 1988. The federal government would own 38.5% of the new corporation and Saskatchewan 61.5% The amalgamation agreement promised that there would be a series of share offerings which would result in CAMECO being 30% privatized within 2 years, 60% within 4 years, and 100% within 7 years.[41] The amalgamation required legislative changes by both levels of government, which were completed in 1988. However, CAMECO soon ran into difficulties. The company was plagued by operational difficulties, the most visible being a series of spills of contaminated water at the Rabbit Lake Mine. Falling prices and low demand for uranium threatened to lead to losses. In March 1989, CAMECO laid off 200 workers. These difficulties led to delays in the promised share offering. [42]

The most publicized privatization deal in 1988 was also the most complex. In April, the government announced that it was selling Sask-Power's natural gas reserves to Sask Oil for a stated price of $325 million. Payment consisted of $125 million in cash, 13 million shares of Sask Oil stock, cash flow instruments, share purchase warrants, notes, and royalty flow-throughs. [43] Making a precise valuation is almost impossible. Sask-Power then announced the flotation of a $210-million bond issue to Saskatchewan residents. Bonds worth $130 million would be convertible into Sask Oil stock at a predetermined, fixed price. SaskPower would provide the stock out of the 13 million shares it had received for its natural gas reserves. In discussing his company's acquisition of the natural gas reserves, Sask Oil President Ted Renner said "We had to be innovative in how we financed it. The Toronto guys are still trying to figure it out." [44]

For investors, the deal was characterized as "the best of both worlds." They could buy guaranteed bonds offering a lucrative interest rate, and if the price of Sask Oil stock rose, they could convert the bonds to stock at the predetermined price and cash in their profits. A year and a half after the bond issue, with Sask Oil stock trading in the $14 range, the investors could convert their bonds for stock fixed at a price of $10.53 per share. An instant, risk-free, 40% profit was possible. If Sask Oil stock fell, they could simply hang onto the bonds and collect their interest. To make sure that investors got the point, SaskPower launched a massive promotional campaign featuring television, radio, and newspaper ads; 27 public meetings; and several direct mailings to every household in the province. The cost of the two week promotional blitz was estimated at $2 million. [45] The government hailed the result as a resounding vote in favour of "public participation" because the issue was over-subscribed, with 41,000 applicants wanting to buy the bonds.

The complicated deal was a classic privatization scheme, and clearly bore the intellectual signature of Oliver Letwin and the other British advisors imported by the Saskatchewan government. It accomplished a major privatization in a way that offered tens of thousands of Saskatchewan voters a substantial, risk-free profit. The advertising campaign accompanying the bond issue not only ensured that this bond issue would be sold out, but it also celebrated the advantages of privatization in general. As the profits were distributed and the investment dealers beamed in satisfaction, it seemed as if a political climate was being created in which the only question that would be asked about privatization was "when is the next one going to happen?"

ALAMO AND WATERLOO

The government could look back on its first year of an integrated privatization policy with a great deal of satisfaction. It had seized the political initiative and set the terms of the debate. The opposition appeared disorganized and unsure of its strategy. In short, it seemed as if the advocates of privatization could deliver their promise of electoral success through the promotion of free enterprise.

The dream turned into a nightmare in 1989. Despite its successes, the government had not yet attempted the privatization of a corporation that was central to the economic or political fabric of Saskatchewan. The public utilities such as SaskPower and SaskTel had pieces of their operations split off and sold, but the services with which the public had day-to-day direct contact had not yet been touched. Despite repeated promises, the sale of the general insurance side of SGI had not been attempted and PCS, the most visible and largest of the resource crowns, was still in public hands. The government was determined to change this in 1989.

The year began with Devine making a 30-day tour through Asia on a trade mission. Privatization was high on his agenda. Reports and press releases began to trickle back to Saskatchewan stating that the premier had offered a 25% share in PCS to the Chinese government, a 25% share to India's state-owned Minerals and Metal Trading Corporation, a share to the Namhae Chemical Corporation of South Korea, an unspecified share of the company to unspecified European investors, and the sale of PCS's Cory mine to Japanese interests. The Washington-based fertilizer-trade newsletter, *Greenmarkets*, reported that the offer to India was accompanied by a promise of a 10-year payment holiday on its investment, "although it is not clear what payments would be forgone during this time." [46] While Devine was jetting about the Orient offering a stake in PCS to whoever might be interested, back in Saskatchewan his senior cabinet ministers were attempting to limit the resulting political damage by insisting that control of the PCS would remain in Canadian and Saskatchewan hands after privatization. Upon his return to the province, Devine himself quickly attempted to allay fears of majority foreign ownership by stating that "we'll probably be offering something like 15 or 20 percent [to foreign investors]. Nothing has been decided." [47] The Year of Privatization was off to a shaky start with Devine's tour. Even the Regina *Leader Post's* business editor, normally an enthusiastic backer of privatization, was compelled to observe that:

> The whole notion of seeking foreign investors, who are also potash customers, strikes some industry observers as strange.
> After all, potash consumers have a vested interest in large inventories, increased production and competition and low prices – the exact opposite of what potash producers want.
> Needless to say, the trial ballooning of the PCS privatization has hardly raised the confidence level of the investment community in the provincial government. [48]

Although Devine's junket had found no buyers for PCS abroad and no praise at home, the premier and his government were undeterred. When the legislature opened the following month, the government promised that it would pass legislation to privatize PCS, SaskEnergy, and the general insurance side of SGI. The omnibus privatization bill which had died on the order paper the previous year was the first bill introduced by the government in the new session. After the Speech from the Throne, Devine told reporters that he expected a major legislative battle over privatization. "I expect as much noise and bell-ringing and hollering as you've ever seen," he predicted accurately. The premier was confident of victory. Waving a copy of *Newsweek* with the cover story "The Decline of the Left," Devine stated that the NDP, a "radical, left-wing organization" would be destroyed in the privatization debate. "This is their Alamo, this is their Waterloo, this is the end of the line for them." [49]

By the end of the year, many in Saskatchewan were wondering who had been cast in the roles of Davy Crockett, Santa Anna, Napoleon, and Wellington. Of the three major privatizations on the government's agenda for 1989, the only one to be implemented was the sale of PCS. The government was in disarray. In a desperate attempt to salvage some hope of reelection, Devine was promising to listen to the people rather than to actively mould public opinion.

PCS has occupied the centre stage of the ideological and political debate in Saskatchewan since it was created by the Blakeney government in 1975.

The NDP's first term in office after 1971 featured a series of disputes with the potash companies over the government's right to regulate and tax the industry. The companies refused to pay taxes and royalties imposed by the province on the grounds that they could not afford them. They also refused to release production and financial information to the government to enable an evaluation of these claims. A series of court cases were launched challenging, on constitutional grounds, the province's right to collect these taxes and royalties.[50] In response, the Blakeney government passed legislation enabling the province to nationalize all or part of the province's potash industry. By 1982, PCS had purchased the Cory, Lanigan, and Rocanville mines, a major share of the Allan mine, and potash reserves adjacent to the International Mineral Corporation's mine at Esterhazy. In all, PCS controlled 40% of Saskatchewan's potash production capacity.

Although the Blakeney government had initially attempted to present the potash nationalization in nonideological terms as simply a good business deal, the Liberal and Conservative parties, the potash companies, the Saskatchewan Mining Association, and the Saskatoon Board of Trade launched a major opposition campaign to the nationalization. A filibuster in the legislature and massive advertising campaigns were conducted against the creation of the new crown corporation. In the end, the government was forced to scale down its nationalization program, and to avoid outright expropriation of mines by paying relatively generous purchase prices. However, despite the high cost of acquiring its mines, PCS was immediately profitable under NDP administration, with profits of $24 million in 1978, $78 million in 1979, $167 million in 1980, and $141 million in 1981. After tax return on equity ranged from 21% to 34% per year.[51]

Upon its election, the Devine government set about discrediting PCS. In order to lay the groundwork for privatization of what had become an increasingly popular corporation, it was first necessary to prove that public ownership did not work. Once the electorate had been convinced that the NDP, in their socialist zeal, had stuck the province with a money-losing white elephant, it would be much easier to get rid of the most visible symbol of the Blakeney era. Among its first decisions in 1982, the Devine government reversed a decision to withdraw from CANPOTEX, the common offshore marketing arm of the Saskatchewan potash industry. PCS's share of offshore sales declined from 59% in 1981 to 42% in 1985. By 1988, PCS was operating at 67% of capacity, while the private companies in the province were humming along at 88% capacity.[52] The government's efforts to weaken PCS were assisted by a downturn in the cyclical potash industry.

PCS operated at about the break-even point between 1982 and 1984. Despite this, the government took out $162 million in dividends, which burdened the company with debt. The resulting interest charges contributed to large losses in subsequent years.

The Devine government accomplished three things with its first-term policies regarding PCS. First, it quietly managed to effectively privatize a portion of Saskatchewan potash production by transferring market share from the public to private corporations. Second, it created the conditions whereby the electorate could be convinced that the company was a bad investment, and that the government should get rid of its money-losing mining company. However, the third result of its management policies for PCS had the unintended effect of making PCS more difficult to sell. Having been converted from a healthy, profitable corporation into a money-losing venture, PCS had become less attractive to potential investors. While the government needed a money-losing PCS to sell privatization at the ballot box, it needed a profitable corporation to sell on the stock exchange. In Devine's second term, as the government moved closer to actually selling the corporation, the imperatives of the stock market took precedence. Chuck Childers, a former executive from the International Minerals Corporation, PCS's largest private competitor, was brought in with the mandate to prepare the company for sale. By 1988, PCS had declared a $106-million profit, with the minister responsible, Gary Lane, proclaiming that "certainly the time to sell is when the company is strong." [53]

It was in this context that the government introduced its potash privatization legislation in mid-April while suggesting that it wanted to be ready to issue a share offering in June. The terms of the legislation contained a number of provisions designed to allay fears of foreign ownership that had surfaced during the premier's tour of the Pacific Rim. No investor would be allowed to buy more than 5% of the outstanding shares in PCS, and total foreign ownership would be restricted to 45%. Foreign investors would be limited to 25% of votes cast at any meeting of the company. Other "safeguard" provisions in the legislation specified that the head office of the company would have to remain in Saskatchewan, that a majority of directors would have to be Canadian citizens, and that three directors would have to be residents of Saskatchewan. [54] However, the legislation did not give any details as to the timing, form, or pricing of future share offerings.

The debate on the PCS privatization was the longest on any piece of legislation in the history of the Saskatchewan legislature. The NDP members proved to have more endurance than the government had patience. After extended sitting hours failed to do the trick, the opposition filibuster was stopped with the introduction of closure for the first time in the history of the province. The debate was also very one-sided. After Gary Lane, the minister responsible for PCS, introduced the bill in April, there was not another government speaker on the bill until August. A single NDP member, Bob Lyons, spoke longer on the bill than did the entire government caucus.

The PCS debate followed predictable themes. The government members speaking in favour of privatization argued that private, not public, enterprise should be in charge of the province's economy. This basic ideological position was reinforced with descriptions of the future prosperity and economic diversification that privatization would bring. The NDP argued that by privatizing PCS, Saskatchewan would be losing both revenue that could fund social programs and control over the province's economic destiny.

Six weeks after the enabling legislation was passed, the sale of PCS began. The sale consisted of a convertible bond issue, the flotation of a stock issue, and a small scale, but lucrative, stock option plan for employees of PCS.

The convertible bond scheme was a device to win local political support for the privatization. Imitating the SaskPower/Sask Oil scheme of a year earlier, residents of Saskatchewan were given the opportunity to purchase government bonds (called PCS ownership bonds by the government) bearing an interest rate of 10.75%. The bonds were convertible into PCS shares at fixed prices, thereby giving the purchaser the opportunity to place money in a secure investment, watch the stock market, and if share prices rose, to make the conversion for shares and reap windfall profits. As the *Leader Post's* financial editor stated in a column, "everyone . . . agrees that the so-called (ownership bonds) are a good deal for investors." [55] Not surprisingly, sale of the bonds was "brisk." Investment dealers came up with financing arrangements to make purchase easier for those with little money. [56] As the likelihood of an oversubscription and a resulting limitation on the amount available to single buyers loomed, rumours began to surface of promoters stalking the bingo halls looking for people to apply to purchase the bonds. The promoter would put up the money in exchange for a contract to turn over the bonds after they were received. [57] The bond issue was accompanied by a multi-million dollar advertising campaign designed to ensure that everybody in the province would hear of the bright future for the privatized PCS, and about the opportunity to make a sure buck.

The share offering on the stock exchanges met with less enthusiasm. Thirteen million of the 35 million shares in the company were offered to investors at a price of $18 per share on the Toronto, Montreal, and New York stock exchanges. Thirty-seven percent of the equity in the corporation was being sold for $230 million. The share offering coincided with a slump in fertilizer sales, leading to slow sales of the stock and an initial drop in share prices.[58]

The PCS share issue sparked debate over the price of the corporation. Industry analysts stated the replacement cost of PCS' mines would be $2 billion. The depreciated book value of its assets was fixed by the company's auditors at $1.114 billion. The sale of the 37% equity share for $230 million would mean that if all shares were sold at that price, the government would take in $630 million.

The initial drop in share prices lent some credence to the government's claim that it had received a good price for its equity in PCS. However, industry analysts suggested that the share offering occurred in the midst of a short-term slump in the fertilizer market, and that a delay would have increased the price of the share offering.[59] However, Devine had compelling reasons for haste. After entering 1989 proclaiming that his privatization program would mean the end of socialism in Saskatchewan, it appeared as though his program might mean the end of his own political future. While it had been tough going pushing through the privatization of PCS, it was nothing compared with the second of the three major initiatives promised for the year. The attempted SaskEnergy privatization was a political disaster for Devine. What remained of his credibility within his own party depended upon being able to show evidence of at least one victory.

The Devine government's privatization program was derailed by the Saskatchewan voters' attachment to the utility crown corporations. There had been some public ownership in electrical power in the province in the form of a government department since 1908. In 1929 these holdings became an independent commission, and in 1949 formed the basis of a new crown corporation, SaskPower. In 1950, responsibility for the distribution of natural gas was added to the mandate of SaskPower. The new crown corporation quickly embarked upon a rural electrification program that extended the distribution system to all parts of the province. Rural electrification was an accomplishment that both contributed to the Douglas CCF government's longevity and created a mystique around the utility corporation that is unmatched in any other jurisdiction in Canada.[60]

In its first term, the Devine government laid claim to this heritage by extending natural gas service to the rural areas. Just as Douglas had brought one energy source to the farmers, so too would Devine. The program was extremely popular in rural Saskatchewan, and contributed to his government's reelection in almost every rural constituency.

However, in its privatization zeal, the Devine government squandered this reservoir of political good will. Devine appeared to have been aware of the dangers of utility privatization at the start of his privatization program. In the fall of 1987 and throughout 1988, he repeatedly stated that the utilities were not privatization candidates.

The first sign of a possible threat to an operating wing of the utilities came in May 1988. SaskPower was reorganized, with the natural gas distribution system becoming a subsidiary named SaskEnergy. When Eric Bernston, the minister responsible for SaskPower, was asked in the legislature whether this was a prelude to privatizing SaskEnergy, he replied unequivocally "to that rather lengthy straightforward question, the answer is no." [61] Outside the legislature, Bernston insisted to reporters that the reorganization had "absolutely nothing to do with the sell off of anything." [62]

The new SaskEnergy Corporation was an attractive company. While the electrical division of SaskPower was burdened with a debt of close to $2 billion and operating losses in seven of the previous 10 years, the natural gas division had a healthy debt/equity ratio and had been consistently profitable. [63] This had been achieved despite the expense of rural gasification.

In January 1989, George Hill, the president of SaskPower and a former president of the Saskatchewan Conservative Party, began to drop hints that SaskEnergy might, in fact, be privatized. In March's Speech from the Throne, these hints were confirmed as the government announced that SaskEnergy was a privatization priority.

The government introduced legislation to allow the sale of SaskEnergy on Friday, 21 April 1989. This touched off the most intensive political mobilization in Saskatchewan history since the 1885 Riel rebellion.

The NDP opposition called for a standing vote on first reading, or introduction, of the legislation. They then left the legislature and headed home, leaving the division bells ringing. NDP Leader Roy Romanow said that the time had come to "draw the line" on the government's privatization program. "This is the day that the Devine government broke its solemn promise never to privatize one of Saskatchewan's utility corporations." [64] The division bells rang until 8 May, the longest legislative impasse in Canadian parliamentary history. When the NDP reentered the legislative building, the government's program was a shambles and its political future bleak.

The NDP caucus's tactic of delaying the introduction of the legislation was accompanied by unprecedented grassroots political activity. Radio call-in shows and letters-to-the-editor sections of newspapers were deluged with protests against the sale of the utility. The NDP organized a series of rallies across the province. With only a week's preparation, the meetings filled halls to overflow capacity, and appeals for funds to keep up the fight raised thousands of dollars. An army of volunteers took to the streets, going door to door with a petition protesting the sale. In two weeks, 100,000 signatures were collected.

The efforts of the NDP were matched by those of other organizations. The Saskatchewan Federation of Labour and the Social Justice Coalition quickly mobilized opposition to the government's privatization program. Informal groups sprang up in communities across the province to organize educational events, collect petition signatures, and conduct demonstrations.

The opposition campaign hammered away at four themes. First, it pointed out that the government had broken a promise not to privatize the province's utilities. Because the government was reversing an explicit promise, the opposition argued it should seek a mandate for its action through an election. Second, the opposition paid homage to the past accomplishments of SaskPower. The corporation's success in rural electrification and in keeping utility rates low were raised at every turn. This heritage was said to be threatened by privatization. Third, the opposition predicted that the privatization of SaskEnergy would lead to higher utility prices since the private investors would insist upon the payment of dividends. Finally, the opposition argued that SaskPower had been a mechanism whereby Saskatchewan people had asserted some control over their economy. Privatization would lead to a loss of this control to the financiers in Toronto and New York.

While the opposition was hitting the streets, air waves, and meeting halls with this message, the Conservatives sat in the legislative building waiting for the NDP to return to vote. They hoped to portray the NDP as irresponsible radicals "highjacking" the due process of government. "We will not be held up to ransom by people who do not respect the democratic process. We are here to govern . . . We have a mandate by virtue of being the duly constituted government of Saskatchewan," Bernston told reporters. [65] In addition to portraying the opposition as antidemocratic, the government argued that the privatization would foster economic diversification in the province. SaskEnergy would become, it was claimed, another Nova Corporation. This Alberta energy company had diversified into areas such as petrochemicals in recent years. Bernston also attempted to deal with the broken-promise charge by arguing that SaskEnergy was not a utility but merely a gas distribution company. This piece of sophistry earned more ridicule than support.

Two weeks into the legislative standoff, Saskatchewan's news media declared a winner in the battle for public opinion. A poll conducted for the *Leader Post*, the Saskatoon *Star Phoenix*, and CKCK radio made it clear that the privatization issue was propelling the government toward electoral disaster. Opposed to the sale of SaskEnergy were 67% of respondents, while only 22% supported the move. A majority of Saskatchewan residents wanted an election over the issue, and, were such an election to occur, 54% said they would vote for the NDP while only 33% said they would support the Conservatives. Even in the government's rural stronghold, the Conservatives were 15 points behind in the polls. A quarter of all voters said the privatization issue would determine how they cast their ballots, while another 40% said that it would influence their decision.[66] Having staked its political future on privatization, the government was looking at the prospect of overwhelming defeat.

The publication of the media poll marked the turning point in the government's approach to privatization. It began to look for a way out of the quagmire.

Devine, who had been strangely silent throughout the confrontation, reappeared on the scene. The government began vacillating between two approaches. On the one hand, it offered some conciliatory gestures such as the promise of a commission of inquiry prior to proceeding with the privatization of SaskEnergy. On the other, it claimed that its only fault was it had not been effective in getting its message out, but that this was being rectified. Regardless of the approach, Devine had lost control of his legislative agenda.

The legislative standoff ended on 8 May. On the strength of the promise of a commission of inquiry, the NDP members trooped back into the legislature, allowed the SaskEnergy legislation to be introduced, and resumed their filibuster of the PCS legislation.

If the government's strategy during the bell ringing had been a disaster for them, its initial recovery strategy fared no better. Days after the NDP reentered the legislature, Justice Minister Bob Andrew introduced legislation to limit the time that the bells would be allowed to ring. The NDP stated that this rule change was an attempt to make the privatization of SaskEnergy possible prior to the report of the commission of inquiry, and promptly launched a filibuster on the rule change. It died on the order paper. In the meantime, the government made its own attempt to take its case directly to the people of the province. SaskEnergy began a major advertising campaign promoting its own privatization. Four hundred thousand letters were mailed out explaining the financial benefits of privatization, and SaskEnergy executives were dispatched to a series of 80 public meetings across the province. They undoubtedly wished that they had been allowed to stay home. The meetings were very poorly attended, and those who turned up were almost all strongly and vocally opposed to the privatization. [67]

Meanwhile, the Saskatchewan Securities Commission was expressing concerns about advertising financial details of a share offering in advance of a prospectus being filed. The commission chairperson, Marcel de la Gorgendiere, said that if a private company engaged in that type of behaviour, "we'd be proceeding with it as a situation of incomplete disclosure . . . There shouldn't be any advertising or anything under our policies until a prospectus has been filed." [68] The threat of charges from the Securities Commission forced the government to stop its advertising campaign. [69] It subsequently passed an Order in Council exempting itself from the securities regulations.

While the government's aggressive strategy was stumbling badly, it was also encountering difficulty with its conciliatory strategy. The centrepiece was the promised commission of inquiry.

The commission was attacked for both its composition and its terms of reference. The commission was chaired by Lloyd Barber, a commerce professor and the president of the University of Regina. Barber was also a founding board member of the Institute for Saskatchewan Enterprise. The commission's terms of reference were restricted to examining the impact of privatization on SaskEnergy itself. Its mandate did not include the key question of whether Saskatchewan people wanted the corporation privatized, or what the economic and social impact of privatization would be on the province as a whole. [70]

The Barber Commission held a series of public hearings throughout the summer. At the hearings, SaskEnergy and SaskPower officials were charged with the task of presenting the government's arguments in favour of the sale. [71]

The privatization proposal called for the sale of shares in SaskEnergy. SaskEnergy would issue $300 million worth of shares and borrow $487 million. SaskPower would keep half of the shares, with the remaining $150 million sold in a share offering. SaskPower would thus retain $150 million in SaskEnergy shares, and receive a cash injection of $637 million. This represents the proceeds from both the proposed share issue and the debt taken out by SaskEnergy. In addition to privatizing SaskEnergy, the scheme would allow SaskPower to cash in the $227-million difference between the book value and the appraised value of SaskEnergy.

With this $637 million in cash, SaskPower was to pay off a portion of its debt, reduce electricity rates, create an economic diversification fund with contributions of $10 million per year for four years, reduce the electrical rates for skating and curling rinks by 50%, and give electrical consumers a $100 credit on their electrical bills.[72] The scheme followed the privatization experts' advice to distribute a share of the proceeds from privatization as widely as possible in order to buy political support.

To nobody's surprise, the Barber Commission concluded that the privatization of SaskEnergy made economic sense. However, it recommended dropping the political gimmicks such as the credit on electrical bills, the rate reduction for skating rinks, and the economic diversification fund. Instead, Barber recommended that proceeds from the deal go exclusively toward reducing the debt of SaskPower.[73]

The Barber Commission used two devices in order to reach the conclusion that the privatization of SaskEnergy made economic sense. First, much of the report was devoted to discussing the impact of the cash injection on SaskPower. Not surprisingly, it found that this would strengthen the electrical utility. However, it ignored the effect that amortizing the $227-million difference between its book and appraised value would have on SaskEnergy. The proposal would lower the debt of SaskPower while increasing it for SaskEnergy. The commission, however, only discussed the impact that the lower debt would have on SaskPower. Second, the Barber Commission joined the government in treating equity investment as free money to the corporation. Converting debt into equity, it was stressed, would save money because interest charges would be eliminated. However, this ignored the fact that investors would be expecting, or insisting upon, a rate of return at least equivalent to current interest rates.

The Barber Commission was politically irrelevant by the time it reported. Two weeks earlier, Devine had officially buried the government's aggressive privatization campaign, promising that "we're not moving on SaskEnergy until we're convinced people believe its a good idea, period."[74] The government's reaction to the report was consistent with the new mood of caution and the sounding of public opinion. "The government is not looking upon it as a green light to privatize. As the premier has indicated, the government will not privatize until such time as the public is comfortable with the idea," said the new minister responsible for SaskEnergy, Gary Lane.[75]

While the government succeeded in privatizing PCS and faced political ruin in its abortive attempt to privatize SaskEnergy, the third major privatization promised for 1989 simply disappeared from the agenda for a year. The 1989 scheme to privatize the general insurance side of SGI had called for the division of SGI into two corporations, the Auto Fund and Saskatchewan General Insurance. The Auto Fund would provide basic, compulsory auto insurance and would remain publicly owned. Saskatchewan

General Insurance would be comprised of the remainder of SGI. A share issue was to have been floated for 60% of the equity in the corporation, with the Auto Fund holding the remaining 40%. In turn, the Auto Fund would contract out its own administration to the new Saskatchewan General Insurance. Proceeds from the sale of shares were to have been retained by Saskatchewan General Insurance in order to establish reserves which are required by statute for privately owned, but not publicly owned, insurance companies. The scheme would have meant that the province would have sold 60% of its general insurance business, and allowed the purchasers to keep the money that they had paid to buy the company. The SGI privatization plan was swallowed up by the debate over PCS and SaskEnergy. Its enabling legislation was never even introduced in the legislature.

Shortly after the 1990 spring legislative session ended, the government announced that it was preparing to privatize SGI. This time, Devine intended to avoid legislative debate. A new company known as SGI Canada was created to take over the general insurance business. Since this new company was not created through legislation, no legislative approval would be required for a share offering. SGI President Alex Wilde said he would have the company ready for privatization by the end of 1990. [76]

The attempt to avoid legislative debate quickly ran into problems. The union representing workers at SGI launched a court action to prevent the sale. It argued that the enabling legislation for SGI prohibited the reorganization and sale. Court of Queen's Bench Justice Ken McLeod ruled that the proposed sale was, in fact, illegal under existing legislation. This ruling was upheld by the Saskatchewan Court of Appeal, which stated that "it is evident that SGI, under its constituent statute, had no power to reorganize itself, in part, into a securities issuing company, partly owned by someone other than the Crown." Grant Schmidt described the court ruling as a "mere nuisance." Saying that "we'll respect the law as it's currently stated," Schmidt promised to introduce legislation in 1991 to enable the government to privatize SGI. [77]

The government entered 1989 with an agenda to privatize three major crown corporations and to shape public opinion in the process of doing so. It left the year in disarray. Its omnibus privatization bill failed to pass for the second year in a row, and two of the three high-profile proposals were shelved. Privatization Minister Graham Taylor announced late in the year that he was leaving politics. Early in 1990 he was sent off to Hong Kong as the Saskatchewan government's trade officer. The new minister, Lorne Hepworth, promised that "we're rethinking that whole agenda" [78] and that the government would follow and not attempt to lead public opinion.

CONCLUSION

The attempt to use privatization as an active policy to shape political opinion in Saskatchewan was the defining feature of the Devine government's second term in office. After attempting to build a free-enterprise-oriented province through public exhortation and the use of tax breaks in its first term, the government imported the Thatcher model from Britain and launched a comprehensive, politically sensitive privatiz-ation program in its second. The goal was nothing less than a fundamental transformation of the political culture of the province. Devine was seeking to purge the Saskatchewan electorate of all traces of its collectivist and social democratic heritage, and to replace this with an idolatry of the marketplace. If this strategy succeeded even electoral defeat would not undo his government's work since ownership would be so widely diffused within the province that renationalization would be either politically impossible or prohibitively expensive. Further, the structure of decision making in the province would have been changed, with a reduction of political scope and a corresponding increase in domination by the marketplace. In one of his more candid moments, Bernston told the NDP members of the Crown Corporations Committee of the legislature that "we're going to make it very difficult for you people to take it over again, when you get back into power, if that ever happens." [79]

Ironically, what this privatization campaign revealed was the lack of public support for the Conservatives' free market agenda. The citizens of Saskatchewan showed that they were not willing to abandon their attachment to public ownership and public provision of services, and Devine was forced to abandon his program or face the certainty of electoral defeat. Once the issue of ownership and control of the economy was raised, a large majority of Saskatchewan people explicitly rejected the workings of an unrestricted free market and private control of public services.

But it is likely that the government always knew that these policies would not be accepted by the electorate. To succeed, the privatization program depended upon the public's acceptance of an unrestricted market, and was thus accompanied by a chorus of praise for the miracle of free enterprise. Market-determined choices, it was claimed, would inevitably result in a provincial economy that was prosperous, profitable, and equitable. However, in the midst of this song of praise to an unrestricted and unregulated market, the government was busy imposing restrictions on the workings of the market in most of its major privatization initiatives.

Restrictions on the number of shares a single individual or corporation could own, restrictions on foreign ownership, legislation guiding future investment decisions by the privatized corporations, and schemes to eliminate risk for Saskatchewan investors were built into every major privatization deal. These provisions were all in violation of the conservative logic of the market. While the government was claiming that unfettered private ownership would cure the ills of Saskatchewan, it was enacting "safeguards" to persuade people that there would be no harmful effects. Therefore, even at the height of its privatizing and free enterprise zeal, the government was making a tacit admission that Saskatchewan people would insist upon some protection from the marketplace before they would buy into it. These safeguards and complicated formulas to ensure that the privatized corporations would continue to offer traditional benefits were designed to build political support, but instead they contributed, by the government's acknowledgment of their necessity, to suspicion and distrust of the entire agenda.

By the end of 1989, Devine was forced to admit that instead of being the device to build a permanent conservative majority, the privatization program was leading to inevitable defeat. The program was dropped. The premier and his ministers promised to be guided by public opinion rather than attempt to shape it.

The Devine government's grudging promise to abandon its program did not, however, lead to a recovery in popularity. By the summer of 1990, the Progressive Conservatives' support among decided voters had fallen to 18%. The Conservatives were in third place in the polls behind the second-place Liberals,[80] and reports began to surface of long-time Conservative supporters switching to the Reform Party.[81] The government lost the support of swing voters with its 1989 privatization initiatives, and then lost many of the solid supporters of free enterprise when it abandoned the program.

With its attempt to create public opinion favouring privatization, the Devine government placed itself in a difficult predicament. It discovered that privatization was unacceptable to the majority of Saskatchewan voters. Persisting with the policy made electoral defeat appear inevitable. However, it had succeeded in selling the program to its core supporters. Abandoning privatization succeeded only in disillusioning the Conservatives' most fervent supporters.

Devine likely regrets having bought the Thatcher recipe for political success. It now appears that he has created a situation wherein if he proceeds with his privatization program, he will be defeated in the next election. Should he not proceed with the program, he will likely be defeated even more soundly.

PROTECTING GOD'S COUNTRY

by Peter Prebble

C oncern about the environment has become one of the major issues of the 1990s. The decisions that we make today about the destruction of our forests and wildlife habitats, the erosion of productive farming land, and the pollution of our water, land, and air will have consequences that will be felt well into the next century. Efforts to improve our environment demand the cooperation of the public, corporations, and government, but so far there has been little national leadership.

In Saskatchewan, environmental policy has not kept pace with growing national and international awareness about the environment. During the NDP's 1971 to 1982 tenure of office, important pieces of legislation were passed which facilitated the protection of the environment, and major strides were taken in the promotion of energy conservation. At the same time, the NDP supported the expansion of uranium mining. Although improved standards to regulate the industry were implemented, uranium mining not only poses a significant threat to the environment in Saskatchewan but is directly connected to the production of the ultimate environmental hazard, nuclear weapons.

Since the Progressive Conservatives assumed power in 1982, there has been a major shift in policy: the record indicates that the Tories have shown a disturbing disregard for the environment. The government has actively supported the development of megaprojects at the expense of the environment, but the most significant change has been the undermining of the environmental review process. Since the Tories came to power, no major project has been subjected to a full-scale public inquiry assessing the project's environmental impact. The consequences of ignoring environmental issues are visibly exemplified by the spills of radioactive water at Key Lake and Wollaston Lake, and the construction of the Rafferty-Alameda dam project. An examination of these issues reveals government and corporate ineptitude, and disregard for the environment and the well-being of neighbouring communities. It is only in the areas of wildlife habitat and soil conservation that the Tory government has taken some significant steps to protect the prairie environment.

THE NDP RECORD ON THE ENVIRONMENT

The Environment Department was established by the Blakeney government shortly after the election of the NDP in June 1971. The Environment Department's budget was approximately $12 million per year, a relatively small amount when compared to the total provincial budget of $2.25 billion. The department was successful in attracting some excellent professional public servants, most notably Grant Mitchell (deputy minister) and David Penman, a widely respected expert in the area of chemicals and health care. In addition, cabinet appointed an Environmental Advisory Council, a knowledgeable group of citizens concerned about environmental issues, who freely criticized the government and issued annual reports on future directions for environmental policy.

In the course of its first decade of operation, there were several areas where the Environment Department gained genuine credibility with the public and environmental organizations. One of the most important events was the appointment of the Churchill River Board of Inquiry by the NDP cabinet to review the development of the proposed Wintego Falls hydroelectric dam.[1] The board recommended that the hydroelectric project be abandoned—a recommendation which cabinet accepted. In the early 1980s, a number of important pieces of environmental legislation were passed, including: the Ecological Reserves Act, which allowed the government to set aside environmentally sensitive areas; the Department of Environment Act, which governed the reporting and cleanup of hazardous spills; and the Environmental Impact Assessment Act, which specified the type of projects subject to environmental assessment and guaranteed immediate public notification when an assessment was undertaken.

The mid-1970s also marked a period of success in the area of public participation in land-use planning. The Department of Urban Affairs designated funds for the establishment of the Meewasin Valley Authority (MVA), a joint endeavour by the province, the City of Saskatoon, and the University of Saskatchewan.[2] The goals of the MVA were to protect and enhance the Saskatoon riverbank and surrounding areas, and to improve public accessibility to the riverbank. The resounding success of the MVA led to the development of a similar project between the government of Saskatchewan and the City of Moose Jaw.

During its 11-year term in office, the NDP also provided a high level of funding to expand urban transit in larger Saskatchewan cities.

Finally, the NDP government, working in cooperation with the private sector and the research community, made Saskatchewan a world leader in the energy conservation field. By 1982, Saskatchewan was considered to be the North American counterpart to Denmark, Europe's energy conservation leader. Visitors from around the world came to see a model energy-efficient solar house in Regina and a model street of energy-efficient homes in Saskatoon.

The provincial government set up a well-staffed Office of Energy Conservation which offered a range of services including: an interest-free loan program for residential energy conservation[3] which was widely used; advice to other provinces about creating financial incentives for families to conserve energy; an energy audit service to farms and private businesses which identified opportunities for conservation that could yield effective returns for the dollars invested.

Despite these accomplishments, inadequacies in the NDP's environmental policies surfaced in other areas. In 1978, the public learned about a PCB spill at Federal Pioneer in Regina.[4] The spill was not reported by the company at the time it occurred and when officials of the department learned about it, they failed to notify the public or arrange immediately for cleanup. The mishandling of this incident was a source of embarrassment to the government in subsequent years. The government was also criticized because it approved the Poplar River coal-fired generating station at Coronach, a project built without scrubber technology adequate to remove sulphur dioxide emissions.

In 1976, the Saskatchewan Economic Development Corporation, working in conjunction with Eldorado Nuclear (a uranium mining and refining company), purchased land options to construct a uranium refinery along the South Saskatchewan River near Warman, Saskatchewan. But the project was strongly opposed by the Mennonite community in Warman and in Saskatoon because the refinery was closely connected to the production of nuclear weapons and therefore conflicted with the pacifist beliefs of the Mennonite community.[5] As a result of public pressure, the federal government held public hearings on the refinery proposal in 1980.[6]

Opposition remained vociferous and ultimately, Eldorado Nuclear was forced to abandon the project.

The uranium refinery controversy marked the beginning of the most difficult environmental issue facing the NDP government, namely the question of whether the Saskatchewan uranium industry should be permitted to expand. The debate led to the establishment of the Bayda inquiry in 1977.[7] In its 1978 report, the Bayda inquiry supported the construction of new uranium mines, despite their acknowledged connection to the proliferation of nuclear weapons.

Two large mines, Cluff Lake and Key Lake, were constructed during the 1978–82 term of the NDP government. Both projects were subject to a comprehensive public inquiry. As a result of the hearings, the NDP government chose to supersede the federal environmental and occupational health regulations governing uranium, and to implement a stiffer set of provincial standards which were enforced through a formal lease agreement between each of the mining companies and the government.[8]

However, the government continued to be criticized for its uranium development policies, particularly because there was no safe disposal method for nuclear wastes and because uranium products were being sold to nuclear weapons states, such as France and the United States, and to military dictatorships such as South Korea.[9]

What was the role of the Progressive Conservative opposition party re the environment during this period? It is fair to say that the Tories did not portray themselves as anti-environment. They argued that the role of government should be restricted to regulating an industry rather than developing major projects. The environment would be better protected by the Department of Environment, they argued, if a crown agency was not involved in the development of the project being assessed for its environmental impact. On the uranium mining issue, the Tories sat on the fence. The Conservatives abstained on a 1979 motion in the legislature advocating the expansion of the uranium industry in Saskatchewan.[10] Ralph Katzman, the local Conservative MLA for the constituency of Rosthern, opposed the construction of the uranium refinery.[11]

The Conservative's most thoughtful move was the introduction of a private member's bill proposing the adoption of an Environmental Magna Carta in Saskatchewan.[12] The bill embraced several progressive environmental principles including: the right of residents to protection of the environment from pollution and degradation; freedom of information and public participation in environmental regulation; the provision of monies to groups in order to ensure that all significant bodies of opinion are adequately represented during environmental proceedings; and the passage of legislation allowing actions to be brought in Saskatchewan courts to recover the costs for damages, for degradation and contamination of the environment.[13]

Overall, the NDP made significant progress in the areas of environmental protection and energy conservation. The expansion of the uranium industry, however, was one of the most controversial issues facing the party. Although the NDP implemented stricter standards for the regulation of the uranium industry, the NDP's decision to support the expansion of the industry was vehemently opposed by many environmental groups in the province.

THE EARLY YEARS OF PROGRESSIVE CONSERVATIVE GOVERNMENT

If the Tories appeared neutral on environmental issues before the election, they proved to be increasingly anti-environment after the election. The election of the Devine government in 1982 led to a series of rapid changes in environmental policy. The most notable change was the demise of the Office of Energy Conservation in the provincial Department of Energy, Mines, and Resources. Within 18 months of being elected, the Progressive Conservative cabinet closed the Office of Energy Conservation in Regina and eliminated funding to the storefront energy conservation information centres based in Saskatoon and Regina. In addition, the interest-free loan program to improve residential energy efficiency was abolished. Finally, research in energy conservation was scaled down significantly in government-controlled institutions such as the Saskatchewan Research Council.[14]

These cuts brought a rapid end to the leadership role which Saskatchewan had played in the energy conservation field. Many people with expertise left Saskatchewan and some contractors who had begun to specialize in energy efficiency moved into other fields.

Apart from cutbacks to the energy conservation programs, immediate cuts were made to the budget of the Department of Environment. In the fiscal year 1981–82, the NDP's last year in office, the department's budget was $9,273,197. For the fiscal year 1983–84, one year after coming to power, the Progressive Conservatives allocated only $8,172,877 to the Department of Environment.[15] Given that inflation in the intervening period exceeded

10%, the real dollar cutback was in excess of $2 million.

One of the most significant changes in policy was the manner in which the new cabinet and the Department of Environment consulted the public on environmental issues. The NDP had attempted to solicit public input on environmental issues through a variety of mechanisms ranging from the appointment of an advisory council to public hearings on the environmental impact of new projects. When the Tories came to power, public consultation on environmental issues was severely curtailed. Soon after assuming office, the Conservatives cancelled the budget for the Environmental Advisory Council and ceased to appoint members to it. The council's annual reports and its critique of Saskatchewan government environmental policy were no longer published. In addition, plans for public consultation on potential site locations for the disposal of hazardous wastes were dropped and planning for a disposal site was postponed. There were also immediate reductions in grants to Saskatchewan organizations working on environmental issues.

Finally, the tradition of holding public hearings on major development projects which could have a significant impact on the environment was abandoned. This had a two-fold effect: it reduced the opportunity for public input into environmental decision-making, and it reduced media coverage of the environmental implications of several major Saskatchewan mega-projects.

THE UNDERMINING OF THE ENVIRONMENTAL REVIEW PROCESS IN SASKATCHEWAN

Since the Devine government was elected, no full-scale public inquiry has been conducted into a new development project in Saskatchewan. The government has used the discretionary powers of the minister of the environment under the Environmental Impact Assessment Act to circumvent the need for an inquiry. Under the act, the minister of the environment is responsible for determining whether there is "sufficient" public concern about a project to justify a public inquiry.

Examples of projects which should have been the subject of a public inquiry with full-scale public hearings include the test uranium mine at Cigar Lake, a series of uranium mine approvals around Wollaston Lake, the Millar Western Pulp Mill at Meadow Lake, and the Saferco Fertilizer project at Belle Plaine.

The Test Uranium Mine at Cigar Lake

The test mine at Cigar Lake is intended to pave the way for the largest uranium mine operation in the world. The huge Cigar Lake uranium deposit is located 700 kilometres north of Saskatoon and contains over 380 million pounds of uranium.[16] To date, 5,000 tonnes of uranium ore have been removed from this mine to assess three different mining methods.

Substantial capital investment has been made in the Cigar Lake mine. The principal partner is CAMECO (a crown corporation owned by both the government of Saskatchewan and the government of Canada), and CAMECO's major partner is COGEMA Ltd, which is 100% owned by the French Atomic Energy Commission.[17] This agency is responsible for testing atomic weapons in the South Pacific and has developed the French neutron bomb. (France is *not* a signatory to the Nuclear Non-Proliferation Treaty.) The Saskatchewan government has thus placed itself in partnership with a company that is directly connected to the nuclear weapons industry.

In addition to CAMECO'S links to the production of nuclear weapons, the mine poses serious health risks. Radiation levels at Cigar Lake are the highest of any underground uranium mine in the world. Uranium ore levels at Cigar Lake reach 60% in places and average 14% throughout the deposit.[18] In comparison, ore grades in most other uranium mines in the world range from 1–3%. The high radiation levels resulting from high concentration of ore compounded with poor ventilation pose serious health risks to workers. In addition to these risks, the uranium deposit has very poor ground stability (making it subject to cave-ins).[19]

Despite all of the questions raised by this project, the Cigar Lake test mine was subjected only to a written Environmental Impact Assessment. Copies of the assessment were made available at public libraries in Saskatchewan for 30 days during which time written comments from concerned citizens were received by the minister of the environment. The details of these written comments have not been made public. No public hearing of any type was ever held prior to the approval of the project.

The Collins Bay A Zone and Collins Bay D Zone
Uranium Mines and the Eagle Point Uranium Mine

Collins Bay A Zone and Collins Bay D Zone and Eagle Point are uranium deposits located in and underneath Wollaston Lake, a magnificent water body in northeastern Saskatchewan and a valuable recreational and commercial fishery source. Approximately 22 million pounds of uranium will be mined at Collins Bay A and D Zone and 133 million pounds of uranium will be mined at Eagle Point.

As in the Cigar Lake project, the Saskatchewan and Canadian governments have substantial investments in these mining projects. The Saskatchewan and Canadian governments have sole ownership of the two Collins Bay projects through CAMECO and own a large share of the Eagle Point project, although the German firm Uranerz Exploration and Mining owns 33.33% of the Eagle Point North deposit. [20]

Because these mining operations are located on or underneath Wollaston Lake, they pose a serious environmental risk. If a spill occurs, it is likely to pollute the lake. The Collins Bay A Zone mine will be an open-pit operation. The current uranium deposit extends about 700 feet offshore into Wollaston Lake and is currently submerged in waters that are over 45 feet deep. A little over a mile away, the Saskatchewan government has approved the Collins Bay D Zone uranium mine. This deposit extends 300 feet offshore into Wollaston Lake in water depths up to 25 feet. [21] Approval has been given to build a large dike from the shore of Wollaston Lake around each deposit. Water within the dikes will be removed to Collins Bay but continual pumping will be necessary to maintain a dry mine operation.

The Eagle Point mine is to be an underground uranium mine straddling the shoreline of Collins Bay. If it opens, the mine is expected to be in operation for approximately 19 years. Consequently, it will extend uranium mining in Saskatchewan well into the 21st century.

Approval for all three uranium mine projects was given simultaneously on 6 January 1988 following the completion of an environmental impact assessment study and a 51-day period for public review and written comments. [22] Despite numerous requests for public hearings, Environment Minister Herb Swan rejected the need for public hearings and refused to make public the written comments he had received on the projects.

The Millar Western Pulp Mill at Meadow Lake

In early 1990, Millar Western Pulp Ltd. and the provincial government announced plans for a chemical thermo-mechanical pulp mill near Meadow Lake. The proposed pulp mill is to produce 240,000 air-dried metric tonnes of pulp per year, using aspen as the wood source. [23]

It was clear from the outset that the Millar Western project would have a significant environmental impact on the Beaver River. In the first two years of its operation, the Millar Western pulp mill would be discharging liquid wastes into the river. The project developer also intended to use 13,800 cubic metres of water per day from the Hatfield Valley aquifer, resulting in a drawdown of the aquifer in the Meadow Lake area. [24]

Despite full knowledge of these facts, the minister of the environment announced on 2 February 1990 that the mill project would not be the subject of a public hearing or an inquiry.[25] Public concerns about the project, however, forced the minister to change his position. Four public meetings were held in Prince Albert, Saskatoon, Meadow Lake, and northwestern Saskatchewan to explain the project, invite comments, and answer questions.

These public information meetings were very different from the type of public inquiry held during the period of the NDP government. They were evening meetings that lasted approximately four hours; the first half consisted of a formal presentation by the proponent of the proposed project, which was followed by a question-and-answer session and an opportunity for members of the audience to make comments and suggestions about the project.

In contrast, a full-scale public inquiry would generally span several weeks and would involve both formal and informal hearings. At the formal hearings, each section of the environmental impact assessment would be reviewed in depth and company spokespersons would be subjected to cross-examination to establish whether their approach to safeguarding the environment was the best available. In addition to formal questioning of company officials under oath, independent expert witnesses knowledgeable in environmental protection would be called to testify and to critique the company's proposals in a given area. Verbatim transcripts would be published and informal hearings would then follow. This provided an opportunity for members of the public to comment, ask questions, and express their concerns. Finally, a formal report with recommendations would be issued by members of the board of inquiry.

None of this took place in the case of the Millar Western project, which was subjected to a much lower level of public scrutiny.

In late March 1990, the government announced that it was approving the pulp mill project on the condition that it be a zero liquid-effluent mill from the beginning of its operation. This amended the original proposal by Millar Western to discharge liquid wastes into the Beaver River for the first two years of the project, after which time it would shift to a zero liquid-effluent operation.[26] Although this condition was an improvement, the inadequacy of the environmental review process which the government had adopted quickly became evident. In early June, only two months after the government had given approval for the Millar Western project, the mill owner sought permission to take water from Meadow Lake (the water source for the town of Meadow Lake) rather than from the Hatfield aquifer.

In the legislature, opposition environment critic Ed Tchorzewski drew attention to the shortcomings of the environmental review process:

> One must seriously question the process, when scarcely two months after the Minister has approved the project, the company is back asking for approval of a completely new source of water . . . Was the company's initial work so poor that it overlooked a water source it now says is the environmentally preferred source? Or the other question: Was the government's environmental review process so poor that it approved a water source which it now concludes is environmentally objectionable and should be changed?

Tchorzewski went on to raise a second major problem:

> This pulp mill will require 10,000 acres or almost 16 sections of forest a year, yet no environmental assessment has been made by the department [of Environment] to determine the effect that such clear cut areas will have on wildlife or fish or birds . . . air quality, oxygen production or the ecology generally. [27]

Thus, one of the most important, if not the most important environmental impact of the pulp mill project, was outside the terms of reference of the environmental review process which the government had established.

The Saferco Fertilizer Plant

This is a $435-million project to be located at Belle Plaine, Saskatchewan. The provincial government is providing $64 million in capital equity while CARGILL is providing $65 million. An undisclosed third party is investing $1 million. In addition, the government is guaranteeing a $305 million loan to CARGILL, [28] the wealthiest private corporation in the United States.

The fertilizer plant will use large quantities of natural gas and will draw water from Buffalo Pound, the water supply for the cities of Moose Jaw and Regina. Unanswered questions remain about the impact of uncontrolled emissions of anhydrous ammonia from the plant and the fate of waste products.

In early 1990, the provincial government gave approval to the project despite the fact that it had not been subjected to a proper Environmental Impact Assessment study. Nor was any form of environmental hearing conducted. Environment Minister Grant Hodgins based his decision on a 70-page report on the environmental impact of the nitrogen fertilizer plant which he and Premier Devine refused to make public.[29] But under public pressure, CARGILL and the provincial government announced in June 1990, "after the fact," that an environmental impact study would be conducted and would be made public.[30] However, the whole process lacked credibility because approval for the project was given and its development could proceed despite the fact that the environmental impact study had not yet been completed.

The Rafferty-Alameda Dam Controversy

The need for an independent evaluation of the environmental impact of a project is most clearly illustrated by the Rafferty-Alameda dam controversy. In 1985, the provincial government gave approval for the construction of the Rafferty dam without an adequate Environmental Impact Assessment and before the completion of federal public review processes.

The purpose of the dam, now in an advanced stage of construction on the Souris River, six miles upstream from Estevan (the premier's home riding), is to create a cooling reservoir for the Shand coal-fired generating plant, also currently under construction. In addition, the Rafferty dam is seen as a way of eliminating downstream spring flooding in both Saskatchewan and North Dakota, and creating a water body which can be used for recreation and irrigation. The United States is contributing $40 million toward the $154-million project because it will receive flood-control benefits.

Closely tied to the construction of the Rafferty dam is the plan to build the Alameda dam downstream from Estevan. This dam will primarily serve as a "water bank" by ensuring that the legally required streamflow at the Canada-U.S. border will be maintained. The dam, then, has national and international implications because it affects downstream water quality in Manitoba and North Dakota.

Since the Souris River streamflow will be dramatically curtailed by the construction of the Rafferty-Alameda dams, there have been a number of environmental objections to the project.[31] The dam will flood productive farmland in the valleys of the Souris River and destroy several local parks including the Dr. Mainprize Park. The dam will flood wildlife-habitat areas and, at the same time, 40,000 acres of wetlands in the upper reaches of the Souris River basin may be drained to help fill the Rafferty dam reservoir. Finally, and most important, it is feared that the Rafferty project will lead eventually to a water shortage. Given the already existing water demands on the Souris River and the natural evaporation from the Rafferty reservoir, combined with the demands on water resources from the Shand power plant and the proposed irrigation schemes, the projected water use is expected to exceed the total amount of water in the Souris River currently flowing from Saskatchewan into North Dakota. In a recent issue of *NeWest Review*, Bert Weichel, president of the Saskatchewan Environmental Society, neatly summarizes this problem: "The plan is to lose and use water at such rate that in 42 out of 100 years there wouldn't be any (water) left for the river at all." [32]

Given the serious implications for the quality and level of downstream water supplies, the Environmental Impact Assessment of the Rafferty-Alameda project conducted by the Department of Environment was woefully inadequate. It did not include an adequate consideration of the impact of the Rafferty dam upstream or the impact of the Rafferty and Alameda dams downstream. The study also ignored contingency plans (such as pumping groundwater supplies upstream of the dam) necessary to ensure an adequate water supply.

Despite extensive criticisms of the environmental impact study, provincial approval was granted to the Rafferty-Alameda project. However, while Premier Devine controlled the provincial decision-making process, approval by the federal government was not guaranteed. Under the 1984 environmental assessment review procedures approved by the federal cabinet, an environmental assessment review process must be conducted before irrevocable decisions are taken. In the event that a project has significant environmental implications, the minister of the environment must appoint a public review panel consisting of members who are without bias or political influence and have special knowledge relevant to the matter under investigation. [33]

In order to gain federal approval, the Saskatchewan government's main strategy was to limit the involvement of all groups concerned about the Rafferty-Alameda dam project because some federal officials were opposed to the project. This strategy was outlined in a letter written by George Hood, director of planning for the Souris Basin Development Authority:

> The principals involved in this project have deliberately attempted to keep the initial number of agencies involved on both sides of the border to as few as possible . . . It will come as no surprise to you, I am sure, that a number of federal officials have in the past expressed

their aversion to this particular project. Given that a number of these individuals are still working in related areas, the distinct possibility exists that if given the opportunity, they would deliberately attempt to scuttle the project. Our strategy has been, and will continue to be, to take the project as far as we possibly can on our own and build as much momentum behind it before we open the process up to other governments.[34]

In keeping with this strategy, work on the dam began in spring of 1988 *before* initial federal approval was given. The federal license was granted in June 1988 by then federal environment minister Tom McMillan, but it was followed by the resignation of Elizabeth May, his executive assistant.[35] She opposed McMillan's decision to grant a federal license to the Rafferty project because federal environmental review procedures had not been followed adequately.

Despite the government's attempts to exclude public participation in the decision-making process, a number of groups challenged the government's actions. In March 1989, SCRAP (Stop Construction on Rafferty-Alameda Dam), a coalition of individuals and groups attempting to stop the Rafferty project, won a court order forcing the government's proponent of Rafferty, the Souris Basin Development Authority, to release the files related to the project. This was quickly followed by the Canadian Wildlife Federation's successful legal challenge to the federal license.[36]

The response of the federal government was to conduct a hurried initial environmental evaluation. However, despite the fact that the project had significant environmental consequences, no independent review panel was appointed. On 31 August 1989, federal Environment Minister Lucien Bouchard issued a second federal license to the Rafferty dam project and construction proceeded.[37]

Since the federal government had not complied with its own legislation, the Canadian Wildlife Federation returned to the courts. On 28 December 1989, the federal court ordered Bouchard to establish a review panel by the end of January 1990 or else the license would be suspended.[38] In turn, on 26 January 1990, Bouchard announced a five-member assessment panel chaired by Donald Gray, chair of the hydrology division at the University of Saskatchewan. The Saskatchewan government also announced that it had agreed to suspend all construction on the Rafferty and Alameda dams while the panel was conducting its review.[39] However, the project license remained intact.

Under a federal-provincial agreement, Saskatchewan was compensated $1 million for every month of work stoppage. Only work necessary to ensure public safety was to be continued. However, the provincial government has proceeded with work that appears to go well beyond this stipulation.

By late March 1990, opposition critic Bob Lyons was pressing the government to explain how "building golf courses, digging river channels and building causeways in the Souris River Basin" could be justified under the spirit of the federal provincial agreement.[40] (The causeway construction alone was estimated to require the bulldozing of 2,000 acres of forest.[41]) In late April 1990, the government confirmed that it would be doing the above-mentioned work and that by the end of the summer of 1990, work on the dam would be 80% complete.[42] This, in effect, meant that the work of the independent review committee was being rendered meaningless.

The Saskatchewan government's flaunting of a federal court order while receiving $1 million a month of federal compensation drew criticism from environmentalists. Lorne Scott, a Canadian Wildlife Federation board member, summarized the provincial government's strategy: "Their attitude is the sooner they can get rid of the trees and destroy the valley, the sooner the environmentalists will go home."[43]

The provincial government's actions also drew an angry response from Ottawa. In early May 1990, Environment Minister Bouchard wrote to Hon. Harold Martens, minister responsible for the Souris Basin Authority, stating that:

> The announced construction would appear to extend beyond what is necessary to meet the requirements of the independent dam safety review board and will definitely be viewed as contravening the spirit of the Canada-Saskatchewan agreement . . . Activities such as the construction of causeways and bridges in the reservoir area and the continuation of work on the new Dr. Mainprize Park, as well as channelization of the Souris River downstream of the Rafferty dam, have already resulted in misgivings being expressed by environmental groups and could compromise the work of the panel.[44]

Despite Bouchard's warning, the Devine government announced that construction on the Rafferty dam would continue as scheduled. Shortly afterwards, on 22 May, Lucien Bouchard resigned (over Prime Minister Mulroney's Meech Lake policies) and Robert de Cotret became the new federal environment minister. De Cotret took no steps to stop construction of Rafferty or to revoke the Rafferty licence through the critical construction months of June, July, August, and September.[45] By the end of September 1990 the Rafferty dam was only weeks away from being complete.

On 11 October Premier Devine announced his intention to start work on the Alameda dam project, arguing that his order to begin work was based on an agreement that he and de Cotret reached during a 5 September meeting in Saskatchewan.[46] De Cotret publicly denied any such agreement had ever existed and insisted that the 26 January agreement between Saskatchewan and Ottawa had never been altered.[47]

In response to Devine's announcement, the Environmental Review Panel resigned on 12 October 1990, and de Cotret requested an injunction to stop work on the Rafferty-Alameda project.[48] Significantly, however, de Cotret's request was not filed in Federal Court but rather before a provincial judge in Regina's Court of Queen's Bench.[49] Under Saskatchewan law (the Proceedings against the Crown Act), an injunction cannot be granted against a crown corporation. The federal case against the Souris Basin Development Authority and the Saskatchewan Water Corporation thus was doomed to fail.

The Devine government launched its own legal proceedings designed to block Ottawa's injunction request and simultaneously launched an expensive public relations campaign to sell Rafferty to Saskatchewan voters.[50] The campaign included a half-hour television production entitled "Dreams in the Dust" that was aired on Saskatchewan CTV and STV stations and offered a one-sided view of the benefits of the Rafferty project to Saskatchewan, all paid for with Saskatchewan taxpayers' money.[51]

On 15 November 1990, Saskatchewan Court of Queen's Bench Chief Justice Donald MacPherson rejected Ottawa's request for an injunction on the grounds that Saskatchewan law prohibits injunctions against the crown and on the grounds that Ottawa had not shown it had a *prima facie* case against Saskatchewan.[52]

The decision came as no surprise. Rod MacDonald, a Radville lawyer and director of SCRAP (Stop Construction of the Rafferty-Alameda Project) summed up the view of many environmentalists intimately involved in the struggle against Rafferty: "What a stupid application for [de Cotret] to make. He didn't want to win this. He just wanted to create a three-ring circus to divert attention from the main issues."[53] MacDonald went on to say "What's interesting is that if they [Ottawa] went to the Federal Court, that [provincial law] wouldn't be there."[54]

While it is impossible to reach any certain conclusions about federal motives in this affair, several factors support SCRAP's contention that Ottawa's interventions were largely window-dressing. First, de Cotret and Bouchard neglected to get authorization for the 26 January agreement by the federal cabinet.[55] Second, while proceeding on the Rafferty court case, de Cotret brought before the House of Commons environmental legislation (Bill C–78) which weakens the existing Environment Assessment Review process and if passed would make the citizens' court challenge to Rafferty impossible to launch in the future.[56] Third, Ottawa's failure to enforce federal court orders to protect the environment in the spring and summer of 1990 was not limited to Rafferty. Despite a March 1990 federal court ruling ordering a full environmental assessment on the Oldman River dam in Alberta, the Alberta government continued construction for "safety reasons" and the federal government again declined to intervene.[57]

The full implications of the federal-provincial dispute over Rafferty are still unravelling. For example, the possibility has been raised that the Rafferty dam is a pivotal part of long-standing water-diversion plans to export water from Canada to the United States. The group Citizens Concerned About Free Trade maintains that the most obvious place to obtain water in the long term to fill the Rafferty Dam is the Qu'Appelle River, approximately 160 km away, which in turn is linked to the South Saskatchewan River system. A pipeline or channel from the Qu'Appelle to the Souris would, in effect, give both the Rafferty dam and the Americans access to a secure mountain-fed river system. David Orchard and Marjaleena Repo point out that maps of long-standing water diversion plans show a crucial dam at the precise location Rafferty is being built.[58]

At the time of writing, the future of the Rafferty-Alameda project is largely dependent on one final court case. Two Alameda farmers whose land will be flooded if the Alameda dam is built are appealing the December 1989 Federal Court ruling that left the project license in place. Ed and Harold Tetzlaff are asking the Appeal Court to quash the license so that an environmental review panel can do its work before the dams are completed.[59] The outcome of that case could have an important bearing on Rafferty's future.

Whatever the end result, it is clear that at both the provincial and federal levels, the current environmental review process lacks credibility, is not properly enforced, and fails to protect the environment.[60]

The Great Sand Hills Threatened

One of the important environmental issues emerging in Saskatchewan is the Conservative government's decision to sell mineral rights to gas and oil companies in the Great Sand Hills, located west of Swift Current. Three natural gas firms – Lone Pine Resources, North Canadian Oil Ltd, and Ocelot Industries – are seeking the right to develop over 300 gas wells which will affect 20,000 hectares in the most highly sensitive area of the Sand Hills.

This unique ecosystem has been designated by the World Wildlife Fund as one of Canada's wilderness areas most in need of protection. [61] Farmers in the area are concerned that clearing land for gas pipelines and well sites will cause erosion and destroy sensitive vegetation. Local residents are also concerned that road construction leading to the gas wells will harm wildlife and make the area more accessible to hunters.

Despite these concerns, the Conservative government is ignoring a 1980 study by the Saskatchewan Department of the Environment which concluded that the Sand Hills' ecosystem of rolling hills, sand dunes, and unique vegetation "is intolerant of greater than natural physical disturbance." [62] In addition, the government is also ignoring requests from the Saskatchewan Natural History Society to designate the area as a parkland or an ecological reserve.

In July, Saskatchewan Environment ordered a temporary development moratorium on approximately 40% of the Great Sand Hills area, while a planning committee does a land-use study of the region. But, as the leading Saskatoon *Star Phoenix* editorial noted on 25 July 1990, "the underlying premise of both the study and the moratorium seems to be that development should continue in the Great Sand Hills." [63]

At the time of writing, Lone Pine Resources Ltd. is the only firm to file an environmental review of its project. North Canadian Oil Ltd. and Ocelot Industries are in the preliminary stages of environmental assessment. The World Wildlife Fund has proposed that all development be suspended until a comprehensive study of the Sand Hills ecosystem has been conducted; so far, the government has failed to act on this request.

The Key Lake and Wollaston Lake Spill

Since its election in 1982, it was clear that the Conservative government intended to give low priority to the monitoring of northern uranium mines. The northern monitoring committees were disbanded. Existing lease agreements between the mining companies and the government were not

127

enforced. New lease agreements governing environmental safety, occupational health, and northern hiring were significantly weakened.

On 5 January 1984, a break occurred in a large reservoir at the Key Lake uranium mine, releasing 100 million litres of radioactive water into Gerald Lake.[64] At that time, it was the most vivid demonstration of the environmental hazards of uranium mining in northern Saskatchewan. It also revealed the inability of the uranium industry and the Saskatchewan Department of Environment to respond quickly to such accidents when they occur.

This was not the first spill. The 5 January spill was preceded by six earlier radioactive spills at the Key Lake site,[65] but no remedial action was taken by Department of Environment officials. When the 100-million-litre spill occurred, no one could find it. For the first week, the Key Lake Mining Corporation and federal and provincial officials believed that none of the radioactive water had contaminated any of the lakes in the area. Officials believed that the spill had ended up between two lakes when, in fact, it had spilled into Gerald Lake. Concern about the ability of company and Department of Environment officials to respond to a radioactive accident was intensified by the revelation that only two days later, on 7 January, another radioactive spill occurred at the Key Lake uranium mine.[66] It was not reported for two days by the Key Lake Mining Corporation, despite the fact that Saskatchewan Environmental officials were at the mine site at the time of the spill.

Not only was the reporting of the spill poorly handled but responsibility for the cleanup was marked by intergovernmental infighting. The federal Atomic Energy Control Board argued that there was no need for a cleanup, but the provincial Department of Environment argued that water from Gerald Lake would have to be removed, treated, and then returned to its natural environment. Eventually, the provincial government won because it had a lease agreement with the Key Lake Mining Corporation which served as an enforcement tool.[67]

The cleanup was carried out but no public inquiry was ever conducted into the events surrounding the Key Lake spill and the Key Lake Mining Corporation was not prosecuted for failing to report radioactive spills in a timely manner or for polluting commercial fishery waters. In addition, the incident reflected the low priority given to environmental monitoring at uranium mines by the provincial government. In the 21 months following the 1982 election, the staff in Mines Pollution Control Branch was reduced from 13 to 7 persons.[68] The northern monitoring committee, which functioned as a condition of the Key Lake lease agreement, was disbanded.

In the end, the consequences of the 100-million-litre spill of radioactive water could have been far worse; good luck rather than good management prevented a major environmental disaster. If the accident had occurred in the summer, contaminated water would have moved quickly into the environment rather than freezing in the cold January temperatures, and cleanup would have been more difficult.[69]

The Devine government might have concluded that spills like the one at Key Lake were an inherent feature of uranium mining, and stopped any further investment of public and private monies into the expansion of the industry. It might have concluded that: at least uranium mines should not be constructed in environmentally sensitive locations such as Wollaston Lake; the surface lease agreements between the provincial government and each uranium mine company needed to be strengthened and vigorously enforced; and that provincial inspection of uranium mines needed to be improved, with weekly inspections or a full-time provincial inspector at the site on a year-round basis.

Regrettably, it reached none of these conclusions, thus paving the way for a second major spill of radioactive water, this time in the rich commercial fishery waters of Collins Bay on Wollaston Lake.[70] The events surrounding the spill have some remarkable parallels to the Key Lake spill and the uranium industry performed no better in the prevention of or the response to the Wollaston Lake spill than it did six years earlier with the Key Lake spill.

The Wollaston Lake spill occurred on 6 November 1989, when a valve broke on a pipeline carrying radioactive water. One million litres of radioactive water spilled into a stream leading to Wollaston Lake.[71] Like the Key Lake mine, the mine/mill operation at Wollaston Lake had been the scene of constant smaller spills before the 6 November 1989 spill. In the period 1981 to 1989, 48 spills occurred. Twenty-eight were radioactive.[72]

The Wollaston Lake spill was undetected for almost 17 hours. A pipeline patrolman passed by the broken pipe eight times in 16 hours without noticing that the catchment pond was overflowing. A computerized alarm system in the mill should have sounded when the spill occurred but it had not been functioning for years—a problem which had gone unnoticed in numerous federal and provincial inspections. Monitors in the uranium mill actually recorded a 35% reduction in the flow of the leaking pipeline. This was noted by the staff yet nothing was done.[73]

When the spill was finally discovered, CAMECO prepared initial reports which underestimated the level of radioactivity by a factor of 20. Radium levels in the spilled water proved to be 10 times the allowable provincial limit.[74] CAMECO also failed to notify the nearby Hatchet Lake Indian Band.[75]

The uranium industry must have experienced a case of deja vu when a second spill occurred two months later in the same pipeline that failed in November.[76] The leak of 90,000 litres of radioactive water was adequately contained this time.[77] Both accidents led to demands for a public inquiry by Cumberland NDP MLA Keith Goulet and Prince Albert NDP MP Ray Funk, northern leaders, and environmental groups. As in the Key Lake spill, the request was denied by the Conservative government.

Unlike the Key Lake spill, however, charges were laid against CAMECO by both the federal and provincial governments. In April 1990, CAMECO was fined $10,000 for two violations of the Atomic Energy Control Act, and in November 1990, the company was fined $50,00 for violating Saskatchewan environmental law.[78]

Studies prepared by the Saskatchewan Research Council and Saskatchewan Environment were presented in the November 1990 court proceedings and indicated that no serious harm has occurred to water quality or to aquatic life in the area.[79] The long-term effects of the spill are still unknown. Of particular concern is the effect of the spill on the local commercial fishery, which is an important source of livelihood for the Hatchet Lake Indian Band. The contaminated water emptied into whitefish spawning grounds and the spill occurred during whitefish spawning season. Hatchet Lake Band Chief Ed Benoanie continues to push for a public inquiry into the spill, noting that the money from the fines simply goes into government coffers and never reaches his people, who must live with any environmental consequences that may ultimately result from the accident.[80]

The provincial government held the controlling interest in both the Key Lake and Collins Bay B Zone uranium mines at the time of the spills. It also had a major responsibility for monitoring the safety of the mines, in conjunction with the federal Atomic Energy Control Board. The incompetence of the crown-controlled mining companies and the provincial government monitoring agencies, combined with the provincial cabinet's refusal to initiate a public inquiry into the spills, is a serious condemnation of the Conservative government.

Soil Conservation and the Preservation of Critical Wildlife Habitat
Saskatchewan's soil and wildlife habitat resources have been seriously
eroded during this century. Already more than half of certain key nutrient
elements have been lost from Saskatchewan soils. Soil salinity is spreading
and wind and water erosion cause serious problems for Saskatchewan
farmers. With respect to wildlife habitat, 75% of the natural habitat in
southern Saskatchewan was destroyed during the period 1960–1985.
Clearly, these are issues which the NDP and Liberal governments of the
1960s and 1970s failed to address and they remain critical problems in
the 1980s and 1990s.

To its credit, the Conservative government has shown some willingness
to address these problems. In its 1989–90 budget, the government
announced a three-year, $54-million soil conservation agreement with
the federal government.[81] The agreement has three major elements. First,
the government is implementing a field shelterbelt planting program. The
goal of the program is to plant approximately 2,100 miles of field
shelterbelts in Saskatchewan each year until 1992. Second, the government
is providing financial and technical assistance to help groups establish
permanent cover on lands that have been under irrigation, but are no
longer suitable for irrigation farming. Third, and perhaps most significant,
the government has started a "Permanent Cover Program." This program
provides financial incentives to Saskatchewan farmers to seed marginal
lands with trees, shrubs, or perennial forages for wildlife, recreation, or
forestry purposes.[82] The program is intended to take environmentally
marginal and fragile lands out of production, eliminate the soil damage,
and restore these lands to a more suitable land use. Since this program
has only been operating in Saskatchewan for a few months, it cannot be
fully evaluated. But it is a welcome initiative and Saskatchewan is the first
province to take such a step.

The major stain on the government's record on wildlife and water
conservation is the destruction of wildlife habitat resulting from the
construction of the Rafferty-Alameda dam project. However, the government
has made some attempt to address other problems in the area of water
and wildlife conservation. The most significant initiative was the passage
of the Critical Wildlife Habitat Protection Act which is designed to protect
rare and endangered species in the province. The Department of Parks
and Renewable Resources identified 3.4 million acres of crown land that
warranted protection under the act, and Hon. Colin Maxwell introduced

a schedule for the initial protection of 1.2 million of these acres. In the summer of 1988, an additional 714,000 acres of critical wildlife habitat, mostly grasslands in southeastern Saskatchewan, were added to the schedule.[83]

The government, under Maxwell's leadership, has also played an important role in the North American Waterfowl Management Plan. As a result of his efforts to manage wildlife in an environmentally sensitive area, Colin Maxwell received the Ernest Thompson Seton Award from the International Association of Fish and Wildlife Agencies.

ISSUES OF SURVIVAL:
THE DEVINE GOVERNMENT'S RECORD

In the 1960s and 1970s there was growing concern about the threat posed by nuclear weapons testing and nuclear weapons proliferation. In those years nuclear reactors also came under increasing attack for their accident record. In 1986 the reactor controversy was reignited by the Chernobyl nuclear accident in the Ukraine. Above all, the 1980s were marked by increasing concern over the threat to life on earth posed by the greenhouse effect and ozone depletion. No assessment of the Devine government's environmental record would be complete without a brief examination of the contribution, or lack thereof, that the government made to the resolution of these important concerns.

Nuclear Weapons Testing

It is widely agreed by antinuclear activists that the key to suffocating the nuclear arms race is to end the testing of nuclear weapons systems. Cruise missile testing was authorized by the Trudeau Liberals in the early 1980s, and testing of the Stealth Cruise was approved by the Mulroney Conservatives in 1988. The missiles are released by a B–52 bomber over the Beaufort Sea and pursue a flight path along the Mackenzie River Valley and over Alberta before landing on the Primrose Air Weapons Range located on the Saskatchewan-Alberta border, north of Meadow Lake.[84] The Saskatchewan government has given its approval to the testing of these missiles.

The Saskatchewan portion of the weapons range is provincial crown land that is leased to the government of Canada. Saskatchewan is compensated $391,000 a year for the loss of resource revenues from the land.[85] The Saskatchewan government could have attempted to amend or cancel the lease agreement in order to prohibit nuclear weapons testing on the Saskatchewan portion of the range, but it has declined to do so.[86]

Uranium Mining and Nuclear Weapons Proliferation

As noted earlier in this chapter, the Devine government significantly expanded the uranium industry in Saskatchewan, especially in the area of Wollaston Lake. It also exported most of its uranium production to nuclear weapons states, despite mounting evidence that only a small portion of the uranium being purchased was being used as fuel in nuclear power stations.

In September 1985, the national television program W–5 alleged that uranium from Saskatchewan's Key Lake mine was making its way into the US nuclear weapons industry. W–5 found that the bulk of the uranium from Key Lake never reaches civilian US nuclear power plants, but instead remains at the US enrichment facilities where it can be drawn on for the manufacture of hydrogen bombs and other nuclear weapons.[87]

In May 1988, Deputy Premier Eric Bernston acknowledged that of 3.389 million pounds of uranium sold to the US by the Government of Saskatchewan in 1987 approximately 2.9 million pounds never reached the American utilities.[88] The Atoms for Peace Treaty between Canada and the United States clearly says that Canadian uranium is not to be used for military purposes.[89] Despite considerable evidence that this treaty had been violated, the Devine Conservatives continued to export Saskatchewan uranium to the US and to other nuclear weapons states, most notably France.

Ignoring the Consequences of Global Warming

Global warming is a warming trend in the temperature of the earth that is caused by the introduction of carbon dioxide, chlorofluorocarbons, and methane into the atmosphere. Scientists indicate that the temperature of the earth could rise between two and four degrees Celsius by the year 2050 unless the amount of carbon emitted into the atmosphere is reduced by burning less fossil fuels (particularly coal and oil), stopping the manufacture of products containing chlorofluorocarbons, and stopping the massive deforestation taking place on our globe.[90]

As agricultural producers, the Prairie provinces have a great deal at stake in this issue. A two to four degree increase in average temperature may lead to serious droughts in parts of Saskatchewan.[91] Yet Premier Devine's government has pursued policies throughout the 1980s that have worsened rather than improved the impact of the greenhouse effect. Energy conservation programs were eliminated. Widespread clearcutting has been permitted in northern Saskatchewan. And the government is building yet another coal-fired generating station, the Shand Power Plant in Estevan,

Saskatchewan. Simply put, the Devine government has refused to take global warming seriously, despite the huge stake Saskatchewan people have in its resolution.

Slow Action on Cutting CFC Use

The earth's ozone layer, which protects us from harmful, cancer-causing ultraviolet light, is deteriorating. Skin cancer rates are increasing and scientists worry that the depletion of the ozone layer will cause serious crop damage.

The main cause of this problem is chlorofluorocarbons. They are used in automobile air conditioners, as solvents in refrigerators, and in the production of bubbles in plastic foams. Whenever CFCs are used they are eventually released into the air and their chlorine atoms break up the ozone layer.

This spring the Devine government passed legislation giving cabinet the authority to start phasing out the sale of products containing CFCs. This was a positive step, but the proposed phase-out schedule is far too slow. During debate on the legislation the minister of the environment proposed a 50% reduction in the sale of ozone-depleting substances in Saskatchewan by the year 1998.[92] Yet it will require at least an 85% reduction in the use of CFCs to prevent ozone depletion from becoming worse. Under the government's proposed schedule Saskatchewan will continue to contribute to ozone depletion into the 21st century.[93]

CONCLUSION

In assessing the record of the Progressive Conservative government on environmental issues from April 1982 to June 1990, the most significant policy change is the erosion of the environmental review process. Opportunity for the public to have meaningful input into environmental decision making has declined dramatically. Ironically, this comes at a time when public interest in environmental matters is at an all-time high. By shutting the public out of the decision-making process, the Conservative government has succeeded in pushing ahead with several projects without a full environmental review.

The provincial government's failure to establish public hearings on the environmental impact of these projects underscores the need to revise Saskatchewan's environmental impact legislation. Clearly, the decision to hold public hearings should no longer be left to the discretion of the minister of environment. This task should be left to an independent environment protection commission, which would be responsible to all parties in the Saskatchewan legislature. The commission would operate at arm's length from the government; environmental studies would be contracted out on an independent basis rather than by contractors hired by the proponents of the project, which is the current practice. The commission would hold public hearings whenever a project was deemed to have significant environmental impact. On the basis of the hearings, the commission would recommend to the legislature whether a project should be permitted to proceed. Such a commission would provide a mechanism for objectively evaluating the environmental impact of a new project and would increase public participation in the decision-making process.

The Conservative government has undermined the environmental review process, and its actions and policies have undone many of the progressive steps which the NDP was making in the area of environmental protection. The elimination of energy conservation programs and municipal assistance grants for public transit, the real dollar cuts in monies for urban parks, and the lengthy delay in the establishment of a hazardous waste disposal site for Saskatchewan are all examples. The only area in which the Conservative government has taken significant steps is the urgent issue of soil conservation.

Finally, the Saskatchewan government has not adequately addressed the big environmental risks that threaten our health, our quality of life and, in some cases, our very existence on the planet. By expanding uranium mining, the Conservative government has exacerbated Saskatchewan's contribution to the nuclear waste problem. By supporting Cruise missile testing in Saskatchewan's north, the Conservative government has failed to promote an end to worldwide nuclear weapons testing and, de facto, an end to the nuclear arms race. By cutting energy conservation programs and building the Shand coal-fired generating station in Estevan, the Conservative government has increased Saskatchewan's contribution to the build up of greenhouse gases in the atmosphere. While the government has tried to take some legislative action on the question of phasing out ozone depleting substances, the targets for CFC reductions are woefully inadequate.

In the end, our young people and future generations will pay the greatest price for the Devine government's environmental record.

CHAPTER 7

NATIVE LAND CLAIMS: OUTSTANDING TREATY LAND ENTITLEMENT IN SASKATCHEWAN, 1982-89

by Richard H. Bartlett

Although the settlement of treaty land entitlement is a federal responsibility, the lands owed to Indian bands are no longer under federal administration, and historically, provincial administrations have not favoured the establishment of Indian reserves. Little action was taken to settle outstanding treaty land entitlement in Saskatchewan until 1968. Under the NDP administration, a formula to determine entitlement was agreed upon by the provincial and federal governments, but it was not incorporated into a formal agreement. When the Progressive Conservatives were elected in 1982, the absence of a formal agreement allowed for substantial differences in the interpretation of the formula. One of the major issues was the criterion for validation of entitlement claims. The federal government insisted on a restrictive definition using population at the date of first survey as the criterion for validation of entitlement claims; the province adopted a much broader definition based on a band's population as of December 1976. At the same time, the provincial government attempted to change the Saskatchewan formula, requiring that special value be given to lands rich in mineral and forest resources. Negotiations have been complicated by the presence of third party interests and the federal government's refusal to contribute to the purchase of private lands.

From 1982 to 1989, the Conservative government in Saskatchewan has shown little initiative in settling outstanding land claims; no lands have been transferred in northern Saskatchewan with the exception of the Fond du Lac claim, and the only claim to be settled in the southern part of the province was the "unique" Lucky Man claim. The adoption of a "band-by-band" approach indicates a general unwillingness on the part of the Conservative government to resolve this issue.

THE LEGAL AND HISTORIC BACKGROUND

All of Saskatchewan was originally subject to the aboriginal title of Indian tribes. The terms of the "numbered" treaties[1] (1873–1921) provided that in return for the surrender of aboriginal title, the federal government would set apart lands for reserves, guarantee hunting and fishing rights, pay annuities, and offer certain social and economic programs. The area to be set aside was usually specified as "one square mile for each family of five," that is, 128 acres per capita. Some land for Indian reserves was set apart, but not enough to fulfil the treaty entitlement. At the same time, the federal government granted much of the remaining arable land to settlers. By 1930, only 3 million acres of unoccupied crown land remained in the southern part of Saskatchewan.

The federal government retained administration of lands in Saskatchewan until 1930, when the provincial government was granted the administration of crown lands by an amendment to the Constitution. The outstanding treaty land entitlements were protected under the amendment.[2] It was then believed by the federal government that little treaty land entitlement was outstanding in the southern part of the province, although substantial entitlement was readily acknowledged in northern Saskatchewan. However, little action was taken to meet outstanding treaty land entitlement in Saskatchewan until 1968.

THE NDP ADMINISTRATION 1971–1982

Between 1968 and 1973, approximately 185,000 acres in northern Saskatchewan were set apart, purportedly in full satisfaction of the treaty land entitlement of the Lac La Ronge, Lac La Hache, and La Loche bands, and in partial satisfaction of the entitlement of the Stoney Rapids and Fond du Lac bands. The arrangement for these transfers had largely been made in the early and mid-1960s under the administrations of NDP Premier Lloyd and Liberal Premier Thatcher. In the later years of the Thatcher administration, the premier became more reluctant to complete the transfer of land. The NDP administration completed the outstanding transfers in 1972 and 1973.

In 1973, following the decision of the Supreme Court of Canada in Calder,[3] the federal government announced its determination to ensure that the "lawful obligations" to the Indians would be met, and it sought a new initiative with respect to treaty land entitlement. However, since

1930 a number of changes had taken place in Saskatchewan. The population of the Indian bands had begun to increase dramatically with improved health and social services. At the same time, more of the province, including the north, had become settled and developed. As a result, any attempt to fulfil outstanding treaty land entitlement faced a number of major problems including: ascertaining the amount of land owed; identifying funds to purchase land in the south; dealing with the occupants of claimed crown land; and determining whether all lands were to be equally valued whether rich in minerals and forest or not.

In 1975, at the federal government's urging, the Department of Indian Affairs, the Federation of Saskatchewan Indians (which later became the Federation of Saskatchewan Indian Nations, FSIN[4]), and the government began discussions regarding a settlement of the outstanding obligation. The first federal figures provided suggested that the outstanding entitlement in southern Saskatchewan was small.[5] However, by December 1975 the FSIN had identified 23 bands with outstanding entitlement, and the claims were based on current population statistics. Ted Bowerman, the minister of northern Saskatchewan, admitted that "these outstanding entitlements are much larger than the Province had been given to understand."[6] Legal advice to the government stressed "considerable legal doubt" over the appropriate population figure to be used in the calculation of a base formula. The possibilities included: population at the date of treaty or date of first survey, the current population, or a formula incorporating one or more of these elements.

In August 1976, Bowerman wrote to the FSIN stating that the Saskatchewan government was prepared to negotiate the outstanding land entitlement using the population as of 31 December 1976.[7] The area owed would be calculated by multiplying the band's population by 128 acres and then subtracting land already set apart. The offer was made on the assumption that federal and provincial, unoccupied and occupied crown land, would be made available. Bowerman emphasized that if private land was claimed, the funds would have to be provided by the federal government. The FSIN accepted the offer.

The federal government took much longer to reply. The federal government believed that the provincial government had interpreted its obligations "very broadly."[8] In particular, it was concerned about federal contributions for the purchase of private land in southern Saskatchewan. In April 1977, Warren Allmand, the minister of Indian affairs, wrote to

Bowerman confirming that "Cabinet has considered and generally agrees with the settlement proposal," [9] and specifically identified the 1976 population figures as usable in the base formula. But Allmand added that the federal government was hopeful that the provincial government would provide all land and resources required, although "Canada would be prepared to consider making available federal lands where possible." No reference was made to the purchase of private lands.

Although the provincial and federal governments tried to reach a formal agreement, the efforts failed. The federal government offered to make federal crown land available on the same basis as provincial crown land and to contribute funds to purchase lands for bands in southern Saskatchewan, but only on a cost-sharing basis to be established in a federal-provincial agreement. The provincial government, however, was not prepared to enter into a cost-sharing agreement. As a result, federal-provincial negotiations were abandoned. The federal minister announced that action would be "taken on a band by band basis" and the 23 August 1976 arrangement would be implemented "to the extent possible." [10]

Acting on a band-by-band basis, approximately 92,000 acres were set aside in northern Saskatchewan for the Canoe Lake, English River, Fond du Lac, and Stony Rapids bands. The lands set aside for the Stony Rapids Band were purported to be in full satisfaction of treaty land entitlement. The remaining lands were set aside in partial satisfaction. All of the transfers relied on the Saskatchewan formula to determine entitlement, despite some misgivings expressed by the federal minister. None of the settlements involved the purchase of private lands.

Negotiations of the northern claims were complicated by the provincial government's newly announced policy on mineral lands. Land rich in mineral resources would "not be available on an acre per acre entitlement exchange. There will have to be consideration for the improved value of the land." [11] This announcement indicated a major departure from, and discounting of, the original Saskatchewan formula.

The provincial government began negotiations for the transfer of lands in southern Saskatchewan, and in 1981 it committed 211,976 acres of crown land. One of the main conditions of land commitments was that existing interests must be protected. But negotiations with third parties did not go well and local opposition, especially from community-pasture patrons, was considerable. At the same time, the provincial government expressed concern about the ever-increasing number of claims announced by the

FSIN. By year end, the negotiation process had deteriorated, with recriminations being made by all parties, and with threats of litigation by pasture patrons. By the time of the provincial election in April 1982, the patrons of only one community pasture had consented to the terms of transfer. This opposition by community-pasture patrons was a significant factor in the loss of rural support for the NDP in the election.

At the time of the NDP government's defeat, progress in the settlement of treaty land entitlement had been uneven. A formula to determine entitlement had been agreed on but it had not been formally incorporated. Ninety-two thousand acres had been transferred, but they were all in northern Saskatchewan, not in the south where the problems lay. Negotiations with third-party interests on occupied crown land had not been successful. The provincial government never obtained the federal government's agreement to contribute to the purchase of private lands in southern Saskatchewan. Implementation of the Saskatchewan formula was difficult without such an agreement.

The provincial government was committed to the Saskatchewan formula, but the federal government was not. The federal government explicitly stated in 1980 that population at the date of first survey was the basis for the validation of treaty land entitlement claims. The Saskatchewan formula was, in the federal government's view, a generous offer by the provincial government to provide land which was in excess of treaty obligations. These difficulties were compounded by the provincial government's attempt to change the Saskatchewan formula, requiring special value to be given to lands rich in mineral resources. The differences between the federal and provincial governments were unresolved at the time of the election in 1982.

THE DEVINE ADMINISTRATION, 1982-1989

Differences in the interpretation of the Saskatchewan formula were exacerbated after the election of the Tories. On 7 July 1982 John Munro, federal minister of Indian affairs and northern development, wrote to Gary Lane, the new provincial minister responsible for treaty land entitlement, indicating that the federal government considered population at the date of first survey as the criterion for validation of entitlement claims.[12] He stated that "Canada had interpreted its lawful obligation to be the shortfall between what the band should have received at its first survey and the lands it has actually received over the years." But Munro added that the federal government still agreed with the Saskatchewan formula. The federal position was, to say the least, confusing, and it appeared that the federal government was trying to back out of the Saskatchewan formula agreement.

Discussions between the provincial and the federal governments were rescheduled. But in the week before the meeting, the provincial Conservative government met to review provincial policy on treaty land claims.[13] Like the NDP, the government decided that Indian bands must give up more acreage than on an acre-for-acre basis for lands with proven mineral value. But, while the NDP had refused to consider a cost-sharing scheme, the Conservative government concluded that a cost-sharing scheme between the federal and provincial governments must be developed for the purchase of private lands in order to extinguish treaty land entitlement. Finally, the government decided to conduct a review of all treaty land claims and, as a result, a "freeze" on all transfers was imposed while the review was taking place.[14]

As part of the review on land entitlement claims, the provincial government attempted to clarify the federal government's position. In addition, the provincial government attempted to determine the legal status of the Saskatchewan formula. The Department of Justice concluded that the Saskatchewan formula was not legally binding on the provincial government. The department also expressed doubt about the appropriate date for determining quantum of entitlement, but it leaned toward the date of treaty or date of first survey.

In November 1983, Sid Dutchak, minister responsible for Indian and Native affairs, wrote to Munro seeking clarification of the federal position on its "lawful obligations" with respect to the quantum of entitlement and on the "legal status" of the Saskatchewan formula. Based on the federal government's interpretation of the Saskatchewan formula, Munro estimated there were 30 valid claims. He also suggested that the Saskatchewan formula was legally binding[15] but he stressed the limited nature of federal responsibility. He asserted that the sole responsibility for the purchase of private lands lay with the provincial government. He gave only the faint assurance that the federal government would make available "whatever federal lands it can release"–but the examples which he cited represented less than 100 acres.

In his rejection of federal responsibility, Munro emphasized the "substantial resource subsidy" paid by the federal government to the province of Saskatchewan under the terms of the Saskatchewan Act of

1905.[16] He argued that compensation was provided under the act since the provincial government would "not have the public land as a source of revenue." Munro did not respond to Dutchak's question about the federal government's "lawful obligations."

Munro, however, sought to proceed with the "unique" Lucky Man claim. (The population of the band at the time of first survey and at 31 December 1976 was the same, and, therefore, whatever method of land entitlement was adopted the result was the same.) He proposed to transfer part of a community pasture to the band. Most of this land was provincial crown land leased by the federal government; the remaining land was federally owned. He also proposed that the federal and provincial governments cost-share a $1.1-million upgrading program of the lands in the parts not transferred to the band to meet "the concerns of current users of this portion of the Meeting Lake Pasture." However, since the provincial government had yet to adopt a land entitlement policy, Dutchak argued that such steps would be "premature."

In June 1984, the Conservative government developed a policy of land entitlement based on the assumption that any departure from the Saskatchewan formula might result in litigation which the government ran "a serious risk of losing." In fact, the provincial government feared that it might be required "to transfer more land than the 1976 formula would require."[17] The proposal consisted of four main ideas:

1. Negotiations would be carried out on a band-by-band basis, resulting in different settlement packages for different bands.
2. The 1976 population base would be used as a guide for quantifying a band entitlement (whether in land or land and add-on elements).
3. Financial compensation for third-party interests would be made by the federal government.
4. Tax exemptions, mineral rights, resource revenue sharing, and cash settlement were considered legitimate substitutes for land.

In October 1984, cabinet approved the proposal but it also insisted that existing interests on lands selected by bands must be satisfied before provincial and federal approval for setting apart and the transfer of land was given. Cabinet agreed that the claims of the Lucky Man, Fond du Lac, and Nikaneet bands were to be negotiated first. As a result, the provincial government sought federal funds to meet the costs of improving the balance of the pasture not transferred to the Lucky Man Band; and it reaffirmed its position that federal funds were required to meet the costs of any purchase of land that was necessary to meet the Nikaneet's claims.

In March 1985, David Crombie, then federal Conservative minister of Indian affairs, approved the provincial policy: "I believe that the suggested provincial settlement components of land, cash compensation and other rights and benefits reflect a fair negotiating approach worthy of consideration by all parties." [18] But he made no reference to occupied federal lands and he rejected "the purchase of land as a condition of a band's settlement." The federal government showed great reluctance to make federal lands or funds available.

The FSIN expressed concerns about the band-by-band approach. In particular, it stressed the need for equity between bands, the right of bands to take land in accordance with their entitlement acreage rather than trade any part for other components, and the place of a land purchase formula in satisfying entitlement. But the federal government did not alter its position or provide increased funding, and in 1985 the FSIN declared that the "1976 Land Entitlement Formula is in danger of being terminated" and that the provincial government's band-by-band policy "is seriously jeopardizing the federal government's legal and trust obligations under the Constitution and the Treaties."

In the intervening time, negotiations with respect to the Fond du Lac, Lucky Man, and Nikaneet proceeded. Although the lands had originally been committed in 1978, settlement of the land entitlement of the Fond du Lac was not reached until August 1985. The agreement was signed in March 1986. [19] In June 1985, the provincial cabinet agreed in principle to transfer the Lucky Man selection. The federal government agreed to bear the entire cost of improving the balance of the pasture not transferred to the band. Progress, however, on the Nikaneet selection was thwarted by the absence of a purchase policy respecting private lands.

In April 1986, the federal and provincial governments agreed on "Draft Treaty Land Entitlement Criteria" (Draft Criteria). The Draft Criteria confined the selections of northern bands to the north, and inevitably, to crown lands. More significantly, the Draft Criteria operated on the assumption that band entitlement was to be measured as if it was an entitlement to unimproved land in a 25-mile radius around the existing reserve. Improved land would count for more acreage; bands would be required to trade or "offset" some of their acreage when receiving improved land or other settlement components. If land purchase was required, the federal and provincial governments would attempt to reach agreement on a purchase policy. As a result of this new policy, the bands rejected the Draft Criteria but the federal government attempted to negotiate on that basis; consequently, negotiations on the Nikaneet entitlement remained stalled.

In October 1986, Bill McKnight replaced David Crombie as minister of Indian affairs. He indicated that "the federal government continues to support the 'Saskatchewan Formula' as the basis for the settlement of treaty land entitlement claims," but he also stressed that an agreement needed to be reached with the bands on land entitlement criteria "in order to place the subject of treaty land entitlement on a sound footing." [20]

Clearly, the federal government wanted changes in the Saskatchewan formula and it was not surprising that a year later McKnight announced a position which conflicted with the Saskatchewan formula. McKnight indicated that settlement would only be considered by the federal government where quantum of entitlement was based on population at the date of first survey. In November 1987, on the advice of the Department of Justice, the director of Specific Claims Branch confirmed that the federal government's only "lawful obligation" was the extent of the shortfall in acreage provided measured by the population at the date of first survey.

The provincial government decided to test the federal government's resolve by approving the transfer of lands to the Canoe Lake and English River bands. The transfer of land to both bands would exceed their entitlement based on population at the date of first survey. Indeed, on the basis of shortfall, neither band had any treaty land entitlement.

The federal government rejected the proposed transfers. The Specific Claims Branch pointed out that there was nothing to prevent the provincial government from transferring the land to the band, but it would be transferred with the understanding that such land "may not necessarily be given reserve status." [21] The federal government's refusal to accept the provincial government's proposal made it untenable for the province to offer a settlement to the bands or for the bands to accept any transfers that exceed the entitlement based on population at the date of first survey. Grant Hodgins, the provincial minister of Indian and Native affairs, described the federal position as "new" and stated that "it necessitates a change in the provincial government's position on treaty land entitlement." He argued that "we are not willing to supply more land than the federal government requests to fulfil its treaty entitlement obligations." [22] Hodgins later confirmed in the legislature that cabinet had rejected the 1976 formula. [23] In particular, he referred to its lack of flexibility and inequity. Hodgins affirmed the provincial government's intentions to meet its obligations under the Natural Resources Agreement of 1930, but he also observed that "the federal government has now taken the position of date of first survey and legally we are bound . . . to follow that obligation." [24]

Adopting the population at the date of first survey as the basis of entitlement would, of course, lead to a substantial reduction in acreage entitlement to the bands, and it brought the federal government into immediate conflict with the FSIN. In response to the federal government's refusal to accept the transfer at Kyle Lake, the FSIN declared that the "new Federal position" was "extremely detrimental to Saskatchewan Entitlement Bands and is evidence of a clear breach of trust," and urged the "immediate confirmation" of "the '76 agreement and formula." [25]

Having received legal advice that the 1976 Saskatchewan formula was contained in a binding agreement and that an action based on the agreement would stand a reasonable prospect of succeeding in a court of law, the FSIN and the chiefs of Piapot, Ochapowace, Muskowekwan, and Star Blanket bands met with McKnight and threatened to take legal action unless the 1976 Saskatchewan agreement was affirmed by the federal government. At that meeting, an agreement in principle was reached establishing a "third party commissioner approach" to facilitate the settlement of treaty land entitlement.

Frustrated by the lack of progress on negotiations, the FSIN and the Star Blanket and Canoe Lake bands filed a statement of claim in Federal Court in 1989 seeking a declaration that the 1976 Saskatchewan formula constituted a binding agreement. In April and May 1989, a formal memorandum of agreement was reached between the FSIN and the federal government to establish an independent "Office of the Treaty Commissioner" to make "recommendations concerning rules for application in interpreting the terms" of the treaties, in particular with respect to treaty land entitlement. In September the federal government filed a statement of defence which denied that the Saskatchewan formula was a legally binding agreement. In the same month, Clifford Wright, the former mayor of Saskatoon, was appointed treaty commissioner.

Meanwhile, little progress had been made on the vast majority of treaty land entitlement claims. The Canoe Lake and English River bands remained blocked by the date of first survey policy. The Nikaneet and the southern bands were blocked by the absence of a policy for the purchase of private lands. The only movement was in the "unique" entitlement claim of the Lucky Man Band and in the transfer of federal crown lands. The Department of Indian Affairs was expecting a federal Order in Council to set apart 7,860 acres for Lucky Man in October 1989. And, in 1988, 35.33 acres of federal land in the city of Saskatoon were transferred to the Muskeg Lake Band in satisfaction of 421.2 acres of entitlement. The Muskeg Lake transfer recognized the principles of trading or "offsetting" entitlement acreage for the "improved" value of land, and also the need to reach an agreement with the municipality which surrounded the land.

CONCLUSION

Outstanding treaty land entitlement in Saskatchewan dates from the late 19th century. Provincial governments have never been sympathetic to the transfer of crown lands to meet the entitlement. The NDP administration did more than most to endeavour to settle entitlement by the establishment of a formula to determine the quantum of entitlement. But it did not secure a formal agreement about the meaning and implementation of the formula with the federal government. Moreover, the provincial government never obtained the federal government's agreement to contribute to the purchase of private lands in the south. In the end, little land was transferred in pursuance of the formula. The formula and the NDP's approach were far from entrenched.

The absence of a formal agreement led to the collapse of any understanding about treaty land entitlement after the election of the Devine administration. The federal government never liked the Saskatchewan formula and became even more reluctant to apply it. The provincial government sought to clarify the federal responsibility, whereupon the federal government explicitly stated that transfers based on population other than at the date of first survey would not be accepted. The provincial government chose to test the federal government's resolve by approving the transfer of a quantum of land based on later population figures to the Canoe Lake and English River bands, but the federal government rejected the proposed transfers.

The Devine administration waited over two years before deciding on a policy for land entitlement claims. The band-by-band policy adopted in 1984 rejected a comprehensive approach to the question in favour of ad hoc negotiations with each band, leading to considerable delays in the settlement of outstanding land claims. The Conservative government's policy relied on a broader view of the NDP's notion of the "improved" or enhanced value of land and sought to require bands to trade entitlement acreage for that value.

Unlike the NDP government, the Devine administration indicated a willingness to cost-share with the federal government on the purchase of private lands to meet the entitlement of bands in southern Saskatchewan. In 1986 both provincial and federal representatives restated their willingness to reach a cost-sharing arrangement as part of the package of "Draft Treaty Land Entitlement Selection Criteria," but the criteria were rejected by the Indian bands. As a result, no arrangements were made for the purchase of private land, resulting in further delays in a settlement with the Nikaneet Band.

No assessment of the Devine administration's treatment of the treaty land entitlement to 1989 can be very sympathetic. During that time no land has been transferred in northern Saskatchewan with the exception of 30,576 acres to the Fond du Lac Band in 1986, representing the completion of initiatives taken by the NDP administration. The only transfer made in southern Saskatchewan was in the "unique" case of the Lucky Man Band. The Devine administration initiated a "freeze" in order to review its land entitlement policy, and it has barely been lifted.

The reluctance of the provincial government to settle treaty land entitlement has been compounded by the need to work with the federal government. The federal government's rejection of the Saskatchewan formula and the adoption of population at the date of first survey as the determinant of the quantum of entitlement has made progress toward settlement difficult. The settlement of treaty land entitlement will continue to be delayed until a formal agreement between the federal and provincial governments and the bands has been reached.

LABOUR PAINS: THE BIRTH OF A NEW INDUSTRIAL RELATIONS ORDER IN SASKATCHEWAN, 1982–1990

by Ian McCuaig, Bob Sass, and Mark Stobbe

The Devine years have been difficult ones for workers and their unions. A new order in labour relations has featured the virtual destruction of unions in the construction industry, legislative restrictions on the ability of unions to organize and bargain collectively, and the refusal to actively enforce labour standards and occupational health and safety legislation. Regressive policy initiatives have been accompanied by a continuous barrage of "union bashing" by prominent members of the government. The results have been a deterioration in the physical and job security of workers, cuts to their incomes, and a deterioration of their working conditions. With the possible exception of the Bennett/Vander Zalm governments in British Columbia, the attack on working people in Saskatchewan from 1982 to 1990 has been unmatched by any jurisdiction in Canada since the Second World War.

Since 1944, the pattern in Canada has been for both federal and provincial departments of labour to be the workers' (particularly organized workers) representative within the government. This representation was limited and had a dual nature. As Rianne Mahon puts it, officials in departments responsible for "interest groups" such as labour were supposed to provide "representation of the specific interests of their respective groups in the negotiation process, and regulation – the attempt to 'persuade' and/or coerce their group into accepting the compromise" that had been reached within the government.[1] The Department of Labour would thus attempt both to maintain discipline within the workplace by deciding, for example, which unions would be "recognized" or under what time periods and conditions strikes were permissible, and to advance the interests of workers during policy debates. Thus the Labour Department was the body within government that would advance the case for increases in the minimum wage or for changes to labour legislation that would make organizing and collective bargaining easier. While the balance between representing the interests of workers within government and convincing these same workers to act in a manner judged to be appropriate by the government would vary from time to time and administration to administration, ministers of labour would consistently adopt the mantle of "friend of the worker."

In Saskatchewan prior to 1982, the representational role of the Department of Labour was more pronounced than in most other jurisdictions. Organized labour was an intrinsic part of the ruling NDP, and there was close contact between the officials in the Labour Department and the leaders of the trade union movement. Those in this department clearly believed that their mandate was to promote measures that would benefit working people, and labour leaders were always confident that their concerns would be seriously considered. To be sure, there were differences at times, and labour never got all it wanted. In part, this was because the Labour Department was still one of the more "junior" branches of government. Nonetheless, labour leaders were accustomed to working with a set of officials who shared their views and usually worked within government to advance their positions.

This all changed abruptly in 1982 with the election of the Devine government. While nobody expected that the close relationship of the NDP era would be maintained, few expected the complete transformation of the Labour Department. In very short order, this branch of government was changed from one which sought to represent labour within government to one which took the lead in imposing the business agenda on working people.

Devine never made a pretence of having this branch of government represent workers. His first appointment as minister of labour was Lorne McLaren, a Yorkton businessman who had earned notoriety as one of the most aggressive anti-union employers in the province. When McLaren was replaced in 1985 in a preelection cabinet shuffle, his successor was Grant Schmidt, who was universally acknowledged as the most ideologically right-wing member of the government.

In commenting on the American labour relations scene, Jack Barbash notes that under Ronald Reagan there was a dramatic shift in labour policy. The political shift to the right "brings *de facto* amendment of labour laws by administrative rule, staff retrenchment, weak enforcement, and administrators unsympathetic to the laws they administer." [2] The same process applied in Saskatchewan, with the added addition of actual, as well as *de facto*, legal amendment.

The new goal of the Saskatchewan Department of Labour was not to mitigate the harshness of the economic system for workers, but to force workers to adapt to the free market. Saskatchewan was to be "open for business," and this meant that the province's workers would have to be flexible, competitive, and cheap. A symbol of the change was the 1986 renaming of the Department of Labour to the Department of Human Resources, Labour, and Employment. The term human "resources" categorizes labour as a factor of production no different from electricity, natural gas, or potash ore. And if there is one thing that business knows, it is that resources were placed on this earth to be exploited for the greatest possible profit.

THE ASSAULT ON ORGANIZED WORKERS

Labour departments and labour policies tend to be preoccupied with organized workers, who are able to demand some attention. The union movement certainly received attention from the Devine Government. Changes to the Saskatchewan Trade Union Act, a series of rulings by the Conservative-appointed Labour Relations Board (LRB), and the government's treatment of its own employees all resulted in severe restrictions on the union movement's ability to organize or to secure benefits for their members.

The changes to the Trade Union Act were introduced in June 1983, in the dying days of the legislative session. Bill 104 contained 17 amendments to the existing legislation. These amendments had the effect of weakening institutional union security, making organizing more difficult, and weakening the power of the strike.[3]

One amendment gave the LRB wider discretion to exclude people from the bargaining unit, thereby making it easier for management to increase the number of out-of-scope workers. For example, for years the Saskatchewan Liquor Board had attempted, without success, to have store managers removed from the union. Following the passage of Bill 104, a successful application was made to the LRB to have 97 store managers excluded.

Another provision introduced the "duty of fair representation" which made unions liable to lawsuits from members who believed that the union had not been vigorous enough in protecting their interests. This was combined with an amendment that cut down the already restricted ability of unions to discipline their members. The 1983 amendments went so far as to remove the ability of the union to discipline members for crossing a picket line during a strike, so long as the member paid dues. The allowable maximum term of a collective agreement was extended from two to three years.

The core of Bill 104 was a series of provisions making union organizing more difficult. The clause with the most obvious origins was one that specified that where an application for certification has been dismissed, another application cannot be made for six months. The union movement referred to this as the "McLaren amendment" in reference to a prior certification incident in which Minister of Labour Lorne McLaren had been involved. Before entering politics, McLaren had been the general manager of Morris Rod-Weeder Ltd., a farm implement manufacturing company in Yorkton. The Retail, Wholesale, and Department Store Union initially failed in its bid for certification on 1 February 1973. Upon the defeat of the union, the company rubbed it in by changing wages and working conditions. The result was that the union quickly signed up a majority of employees, and reapplied for certification. The board ruled in favour of certification, and said that a second vote was not necessary. McLaren, as minister of labour, ensured that this event would not be repeated.[4] (During McLaren's association with Morris Rod-Weeder between 1972 and 1977, six unfair labour practice decisions were issued against the company by the LRB. McLaren had been personally cited.)

Before Bill 104, if 25% or more of the employees at a company had signed cards and the union requested a vote, the LRB was compelled to direct one. The amendment now left the question of a vote to the discretion of the board. Bill 104 also included a "build-up principle" which permitted an employer who was faced with an organizing campaign to argue before the board that the staff complement had not yet been filled. If accepted, this would result in the application being dismissed for six months.

Bill 104 also permitted employers to "communicate" with their employees during all stages of the industrial relations process, from organizing drives to collective bargaining. The encouragement of employer "free speech" legitimized greater employer resistance to union-organizing drives.

The legislation also made the use of the strike more difficult for unions. A provision was enacted requiring that unions give at least 48 hours written strike notice to the employer and the minister of labour. Thirty days after the commencement of a strike, a new strike vote was mandatory upon application from the union, a group of employees, or the employer. This enabled the employer to force a vote on its final offer after a 30-day strike. The legislation removed the protection of recall, seniority, and other employee rights during a strike. Pension rights and other benefits (with the exception of health rights or benefits and medical rights or benefits) also lost their legal protection should the workers engage in strike action. These amendments dramatically increased the risks for workers of going on strike, since they now faced the prospect of losing their seniority, their jobs, and their pensions.

During the debate on the legislation, the minister of labour stated that no union in Saskatchewan had requested any of the changes to the Trade Union Act that he was proposing. Indeed, the amendments were condemned by the Saskatchewan Federation of Labour and by unaffiliated unions. On the other hand, Bob Findlay, the executive director of the Saskatchewan Chamber of Commerce, said the bill "is a step in the right direction." [5] The president of the Construction Labour Relations Council, Jim Chase, was more enthusiastic. He was quoted by the Regina *Leader Post* as saying that "most of the things they have done we've advocated, so we're generally pleased." [6]

The changes to the Trade Union Act were accompanied by a reorientation of the Saskatchewan Labour Relations Board. Shortly after the 1982 election, the government appointed Estevan lawyer Dennis Ball to chair the LRB. Ball, who had little previous experience in labour law, became the highest-paid board chairperson in the history of the province. [7] Under Ball, the LRB made a series of innovative rulings that undermined long-standing union protection in three areas. These decisions facilitated employers' objectives in "concession bargaining" by: allowing them to unilaterally change the terms and conditions of employment following service of notice of expiration of a collective agreement by the employer; changing long-standing policies regarding decertification applications; and facilitating the destruction of the building trades unions by allowing "spin-off" nonunion operations.

A clause in the Trade Union Act specifies that where no collective agreement is in effect, it is illegal for an employer to unilaterally change rates of pay, hours of work, or other conditions of employment "without bargaining collectively respecting the changes with the trade union representing the majority of employees in the appropriate unit." [8] This provision had been instituted by the Liberal government of Ross Thatcher in 1966, and historically had been interpreted as meaning that these conditions could not be unilaterally changed by the employer unless the union agreed. With Ball as LRB chair, this interpretation of 20 years standing was dropped.

The Retail, Wholesale, and Department Store Union had been meeting with Canada Safeway to negotiate a new agreement for the employees in the company's grocery stores. After 17 bargaining meetings in which the union failed to agree to Safeway's demands for concessions, the company unilaterally implemented new hours of work and rates of pay. Confident of success, the union took Safeway before the LRB on a charge of having committed an unfair labour practice. On 10 January 1986, the union was stunned when the board ruled that Safeway could unilaterally change the conditions of employment and rates of pay so long as they had bargained collectively in good faith. Thus, Safeway, having "attempted" to reach an agreement, was enabled, unilaterally, to implement the change it wanted.[9] As a result of this decision, any employer was free to terminate a collective bargaining agreement by giving notice to the union in the time periods provided for. Having done so, the employer need only go through a period of collective bargaining in which it tries in "good faith" to persuade the union to go along with changes to the agreement. Should the employer fail to obtain the union's consent, it is free to unilaterally change the terms of the contract. The union is then put in a position of either accepting the change or launching a strike. For unions in a poor bargaining position, the change in interpretation meant that they could no longer at least hold onto what they already had in negotiations. For companies in Saskatchewan wishing to bring their wages into line with competition from other parts of Canada or other parts of the world, the Safeway decision made achieving the "adjustment" much easier.

Another example of the surprises awaiting unions before Ball's LRB came in a case involving the Communications Workers Union and Northern Telecommunications. The collective agreement in this case contained a provision allowing it to be reopened for negotiations during a 30 to 90 day period prior to the expiration of the agreement. While the Trade Union Act stipulates that notification of a desire to reopen the agreement must be given within a 30 to 60 day period before the expiry date,[10] it had long been understood that if the parties had agreed to a longer re-opening period in their collective agreement, the longer period would apply. The logic was that if the bargaining could begin earlier, there would be a greater chance of an early settlement. More harmonious industrial relations would be the result. However, in the new industrial relations climate, company objectives had become more important than harmonious relations. After the Communications Workers Union had given the company notice of their intent to bargain within the period stipulated in their agreement with Northern Telecom, the company refused to enter into negotiations on the grounds that the union had missed the time period specified in the Trade Union Act. The LRB upheld the company's position.[11] The effect was that the company was not required to bargain for a new contract for another year, and the union was prohibited from striking during this period.

In another case, the LRB was considering an application for decertification of employees at Revelstoke Lumber. The LRB had ordered a vote on the decertification. The result was a tie. Forty years of LRB practice dictated that in the event of a tie vote on a decertification application, the application was dismissed. In this case, the LRB ruled that the union would be decertified as a result of the tie vote.[12] In effect, the board now required unions to "re-prove" their majority support whenever challenged by a decertification application. In this case, the point that Ball ruled upon had not been argued by either party, and the language that he was reinterpreting had existed unchanged since 1946.

In these and other rulings, the LRB under Ball changed the way many clauses in the Trade Union Act were interpreted. In each of the cases in which new ground was broken, the board used an innovative interpretation of the legislation to rule against the union. Not surprisingly, those involved in the union movement concluded that Ball was biased in favour of management. In 1989, Ball resigned as chair of the LRB and joined the Regina law firm of MacPherson, Leslie, and Tyerman. This is the largest law firm in the province that has a significant practice in the management side of labour law. Ball was replaced on the LRB by Richard Hornung. The union movement's suggestions for appropriate people for the positions were ignored. Hornung's Conservative credentials were impeccable, since he had headed the party's fund-raising effort among the province's lawyers leading into the 1986 election.

The changes in the Trade Union Act and the decisions by the Conservative-appointed LRB have had a substantive impact upon union organizing efforts, the number of union members, and strike activity. Since 1981, the last full year of the NDP government, the percentage of the nonagricultural labour force who belong to unions dropped from 32.9 to 29.2.[13] The number of applications for certification dropped from 183 in 1982–83 to 78 in 1987–88.[14] Unions in most sectors of the economy have suffered drops in membership during the Devine years. Table 8.1 outlines, by sector, the year in which union membership reached its peak, membership during the peak year, and membership in 1989. Construction unionization reached a peak in 1983, and has dropped by 39.3% since then. Unionization in manufacturing and mining peaked in 1982, while unionization in public administration and trade did not begin to decline until 1987. The only sectors in which membership was continuing to grow right up until 1989 were the service sector and finance, insurance, and real estate.

For five decades, the union movement in Saskatchewan had undergone almost uninterrupted growth. Since records began to be kept in 1937, union membership increased for 42 out of 46 years. In the seven years between 1983 and 1989, membership declined in four years. While difficult economic conditions no doubt had some effect on union membership, the role of the regulatory regime should not be understated. During the 1982–1989 period, while union membership in Saskatchewan declined in sectors under provincial jurisdiction, it increased slightly in industries under federal jurisdiction.[15]

While unions were finding organizing more difficult, their members were also far less willing to strike. Table 8.2 outlines the history of strike activity in Saskatchewan in the years before and after Devine's election. In the five full years prior to the Conservative victory, there was an average of 44.2 strikes involving 11,321 workers. In the five full years afterwards there was an average of 13.6 strikes involving 4,107 workers. The average number of work days lost due to strikes per worker dropped from 0.45 to 0.15.

If the proof of the pudding is in the eating, the proof of the labour relations policy is in the paycheque. Figure 8.1 outlines the real weekly income of workers in different sectors of Saskatchewan's economy, and Figure 8.2 provides a comparison of real earnings in Saskatchewan and other jurisdictions. With the exception of the construction industry where the decline in wages was almost immediate, the effects of the new regime began to show up in most sectors by 1986. During the second half of the decade, most workers in Saskatchewan began to suffer substantial drops in their purchasing power. The only industrial sector to experience an increase in real wages during Devine's term in office was the transportation sector in which most unionized workers fall under federal jurisdiction.

While all workers in Saskatchewan felt the effects of the Devine government's new labour policies, two groups of workers were singled out for special treatment: construction workers and the government's own employees.

156

SPECIAL TREATMENT FOR SPECIAL CASES

Of all groups of workers in Saskatchewan, the construction workers and their unions were hit first, and hit hardest. The building trades unions have been virtually destroyed as effective organizations during Devine's tenure in office, resulting in unemployment, blacklisting, and a dramatic drop in income for construction workers. Many have been forced to leave the province.

After the election of the Conservatives, the provincial unemployment rate doubled. It was worse in the construction industry. By 1984, two thirds of the unionized plumbers, pipefitters, and labourers were unemployed. [16] In this environment, the Conservative government repealed Bill 88, the Construction Labour Relations Act (CLRA), which had allowed for industry-wide collective bargaining in the province by a process of "accreditation." Section 17 of the CLRA prevented unionized contractors and firms from setting up nonunion subsidiaries. According to Jim Chase, president of the Saskatchewan Construction Association and the Saskatchewan Construction Labour Relations Council, the employers "went for that change" (repeal) because "it was the only way that we could get rid of Section 17." [17] Since the repeal, almost all contractors have established "spin-off" nonunion companies.

Following the repeal of the CLRA, the construction industry moved to take advantage of the situation. On 12 December 1983, the Saskatchewan Construction Labour Relations Council sent a letter to its member firms stating that the council recognized that "a large number of you are already operating a non-union firm . . . Consideration is being given to develop programs to unify, assist, and perpetuate this trend." [18] In a follow-up letter to all member firms dated 22 February 1984, the council advised:

> that if unionized contractors were to give the building trades unions notice of termination of collective agreement effective May 1, 1984, and if they were also to terminate the employment of unionized employees, they could operate as if they had never been unionized. They could, for instance, hire new employees at whatever wages and conditions the market would bear. [19]

On 1 March 1984, a letter was sent by the council to local trade unions. The letter terminated every collective agreement then in effect. The result devastated construction workers and their unions. For example, the Operative Plasterers and Cement Masons Union saw the number of active unionized employers drop from 40 to one in the space of two years. The Saskatchewan local saw unemployment rates among its members rise from 20% to a staggering 95%. As UIC benefits ran out, many of these workers were forced onto welfare.[20]

Within months of the repeal of the CLRA, the Saskatoon *Star Phoenix* reported that "virtually every major construction project is going non-union. At least 60% of the industrial and commercial construction in Saskatchewan is being done by non-union workers." Chase was reported as saying that:

> the swing is a direct result of the Progressive Conservative sweep to power two years ago. The sympathetic labour legislation enacted by the New Democratic Party has been replaced by pro-business legislation enacted by the Conservatives. And it has left the labour unions floundering, not knowing which way to turn.[21]

Trade unions attempted to prevent "double breasting" or non-union spin-off operations by charging these companies with unfair labour practices under Section 37 of the Saskatchewan Trade Union Act. Section 37 had formerly been interpreted as protecting a certification order and collective agreement where an employer disposes of all or part of his business "unless the Board otherwise orders" in respect to the new employer.[22]

The Carpenters Union, therefore, accused a contractor engaged in a spin-off operation of committing an unfair labour practice. The Saskatch-ewan Labour Relations Board heard the application on the 2nd and 3rd of May 1984. On 4 December 1984, the board chairperson, Dennis Ball, found that the company was guilty of an unfair labour practice so that the certification of the union remained intact, but he ruled that the col-lective agreement was no longer in effect, and that the parties had to renegotiate a new collective agreement. The decision stated:

> The application in effect asks the Board to confirm that the same collective bargaining agreement should apply to Pan-Western. In our opinion, a decision of that kind would fail to recognize and balance the interests of all of the parties in a market economy. It would no doubt extinguish Pan-Western's ability to remain competitive, which in turn would mean less work to be allocated among union members, which in turn could only dilute the strength of the union. It would fail to recognize that the interests of contractors, trade unions, and tradesmen are interdependent in the construction industry, and that

the most prominent relationship of a construction worker is with the union representing his trade and not with the contractors for whom he has worked.[23]

This decision is most unusual since the LRB took into consideration the substantive issues of collective bargaining (i.e., wages) rather than concerning itself exclusively with the process of collective bargaining. Chairperson Ball supported the economic arguments of the employer that the existing wage levels in the collective agreement were too high and would make the company noncompetitive in regard to its bids. Thus, Ball reinterpreted Section 37 of the Trade Union Act as though it had been amended to implement the objectives underlying the repeal of the Construction Labour Relations Act.

This decision, in effect, increased the number of nonunion operations in commercial and industrial construction, and assisted employers in achieving greater concessions in collective negotiations with trade unions. The Carpenters Union, for example, has been unable to negotiate a collective agreement with Pan-Western since the decision was taken.

It was in this context that construction unions began their bargaining under the new regime. The pivotal year was 1984. The *Star Phoenix* reported that "19% of Saskatchewan's unionized sheet metal workers have agreed to major wage roll backs and other concessions in hopes of making their employers more competitive in a cut-throat market place . . . the contracts set a rate of $1.50 an hour below the former $22.41 hourly wage package, including benefits, for a journeyman doing commercial construction work."[24] The construction council demanded 25% wage cuts as a negotiating stance. "In one recent test case, a union attempted to test the waters by agreeing to wage roll backs of $3–$5 an hour. The contractors represented by the Saskatchewan Construction Labour Relations Council (SCLRC) told them to go to hell. Even $5–25%–wasn't enough." Widespread "blacklisting" of union members in the industry began. It was made possible by the SCLRC, "which has the names of all union members in the 17 construction trades in Saskatchewan on a computer because of the joint administration of their pension plans."[25] In a report to a 1984 NDP task force, the business manager for Local 442 of the Operative Plasterers and Cement Masons Union, Kerry Westcott, wrote:

The other night at our regular monthly union meeting, a member stated that "I am 46 years old. I've got three kids. I'm number 93 on the hiring board. I've been a job steward for the last ten years. I smell of the union so bad I couldn't buy a job. Cement finishing is the only thing I know. I'm flat broke, just what the hell am I supposed to do?" [26]

Since 1984, the situation has deteriorated further: wages have dropped substantially and subcontracting and "spinoffs" now characterize this sector of the economy. The building trades unions have had their power broken by the employers' offensive. Even where construction workers have organized, the trade unions have been reluctant to go to the Labour Relations Board for certification, since they know that it will be almost impossible to negotiate a collective agreement. There have been no strikes in the industry since 1983 and, with the exception of the heavy oil upgrader in Regina, every major construction project in the province has gone to nonunion companies. In the case of the Weyerhaeuser paper mill in Prince Albert, the unionized Commonwealth Construction presented the lowest bid. The contract, however, went to B.E.K. Construction from Alabama. This company, notorious for its anti-union practices south of the border, introduced innovations such as mandatory drug testing for employees.

The unions are running out of working members. The Cement Masons Union has seen its membership decline 50% since 1982. The remaining members still talk about their 1982 collective bargaining agreement, since it was the last one to be signed. The Carpenters Union has seen its membership in the province shrink from about 1,800 members to 600. Of these, only 150 are working. The bricklayers have only 100 members remaining in the province, and have only one unionized contractor to work for. Many long-time trade unionists in the construction trades have now lost interest in their organizations, and are simply worn out and dispirited.

Not content with destroying the trade union organizations, the government and the employers in the construction industry have also set about undermining the very basis of these unions: the specialized expertise of craft and trade workers, and the exclusion of those who did not have these skills certified. At many of the job sites in the province, construction companies have replaced job designation on the basis of trade with the designation of "utility worker," meaning someone who knows a little about each trade and works without regard to the traditional boundaries in the industry. As specialized workers are replaced with a "generic" construction worker, the underpinning for union organization disappears, and along with it goes the workers' skills.

The undermining of traditional trade boundaries and specialized skills was actively abetted by the provincial government. An extremely low priority was placed upon apprenticeship training; the Trades Advisory Board and the varied committees representing the different trades atrophied; and the jurisdiction for apprenticeship training was transferred from the Department of Labour to the Department of Education. As apprenticeship programs are dismantled and the journeyman status in a trade becomes irrelevant, the government and employers are succeeding in ensuring that the building trades unions will never be reconstructed in their previous form.

The pattern of spin-off operations, the widespread blacklisting of union members, the deterioration of union conditions, and the complete disregard for minimum standards was imported into Saskatchewan from Alberta. Union contractors from Alberta entered Saskatchewan following the repeal of the CLRA. Nonunion shops were set up, and nonunion employees in Alberta were invited to work on Saskatchewan construction sites at lower than union rates. The carpenter's union estimated that 68% of all workers at the Nipawin dam site, the first major construction project in Saskatchewan following the 1982 election, were from out of province.[27] At the same time, unionized construction workers in Saskatchewan were forced by the resulting unemployment to go to Alberta to work on non-unionized projects at reduced wages there. The contractors' strategy supported the nonunionized firms, and a competitive, interprovincial market led to workers competing against other workers for scarce jobs.

Employment in the construction industry dropped from 27,000 in 1981 to 22,000 three years later,[28] with little improvement since then. Those construction workers lucky enough to find a job were still not doing well. Figure 8.3 traces the path of real construction wages in the three Prairie provinces. Real (and nominal) wages dropped dramatically in Alberta and Saskatchewan, while in Manitoba, the only Prairie province where the unions survived the employers' offensive, real wages were relatively stable.

The employers' offensive in the construction industry was extremely successful in Saskatchewan. With the legislative changes and the Labour Relations Board rulings, the government created a situation in which the construction companies could operate without unions. The companies were quick to take advantage of the new opportunities. Indeed, some are now concerned that they may have been too successful. As skilled construction workers led the migration out of Saskatchewan, some employers and industry spokespeople began to bemoan the resulting shortage of skilled labour. Should the economy improve, they cried, it might even be impossible to take advantage of the boom.

In addition to changing the rules governing relations between employers and employees in the private sector through the changes in the Trade Union Act and the rulings of the LRB, the government also set the tone for provincial labour relations through its treatment of its own employees. Over the period of the Devine administration, people working for public institutions were subjected to unilateral declarations of wage freezes, back-to-work legislation, having union bargaining rights stripped away by legislative fiat, privatization, mass layoffs, and a dramatic move toward part-time, temporary, or casual employment in the public sector.

Before the 1982 election, relations between the Blakeney governments and the public sector unions had been strained. In 1979, members of the Saskatchewan Government Employees Union (SGEU) had engaged in a month-long strike. In a classic example of alienating its own constituency, the NDP government legislated an end to a strike by hospital workers immediately before calling the 1982 election. As a result, many unionists did not take an active part in the election campaign, and the Saskatchewan division of the Canadian Union of Public Employees went as far as running a candidate against the minister of health. When Devine took office, therefore, he enjoyed a honeymoon of sorts with the public sector unions since his victory had at least "taught the NDP a lesson." Further, during the election campaign the Conservatives promised to end patronage in the public service. In election advertising they promised that "under a Progressive Conservative government, promotions and positions will be based on ability and seniority." [29]

This honeymoon has long since ended in divorce. The Devine government has engaged in behaviour toward its employees that most governments in Canada have not even contemplated. It began with a series of purges of public employees, collectively described as "NDP Rats," at the first convention of the Conservative Party following the election. The waves of firings broke a tradition in Saskatchewan dating back to the first CCF victory in 1944, of avoiding large-scale firings upon a change of government. According to political scientists Hans Michelmann and Jeffrey Steeves, the firings were often based on "unsystematic and sometimes suspect information . . . there appeared to be a number of dismissals based on rumours and guilt by association." [30] The purges of real or imagined

NDP supporters in the public service quickly created a climate of fear and uncertainty. The purges were accompanied by gag orders placed on civil servants to prevent the workers from speaking out about working conditions or government policies, and a campaign to portray civil servants as lazy, stupid, and unproductive.

It was in this atmosphere that SGEU began to collectively bargain with the Devine government for the first time. When negotiations began in August 1984, the government presented a package that severely undermined job security, hours of work, and the scope of the union bargaining unit.[31] SGEU members had good reason to be concerned about their job security. Table 8.3 outlines changes in the employment status of public servants. As previously noted, there has been a dramatic shift toward the use of temporary, part-time, and casual employees by the government. The increased use of temporary and part-time employees also allowed the government to bypass the Public Service Commission for the hirings. Patronage appointments were thereby extended into the lowest reaches of the public service.

SGEU was unable to make any progress with negotiations, and the union began conducting rotating strikes at the end of 1985. The government responded first with threats and ultimatums, and early in 1986 passed legislation imposing a contract and ordering an end to the strikes. This legislation gave the Saskatchewan government the dubious distinction of being the first government in Canada to use the "notwithstanding" clause to override the Canadian Charter of Rights and Freedoms.

The use of the constitutional override was not the only unique use of its legislative powers in dealing with its employees. The government also legislatively decertified workers being transferred to the Saskatchewan Water Corporation in 1984, and to the amalgamated technical institute in 1988. In the latter case, the government also set out within the legislation the nature of the bargaining units, should the workers reorganize. This task had traditionally been performed by the LRB, but the government wanted to ensure that any new bargaining unit within the technical institute would be fragmented. The SGEU was forced to spend approximately $250,000 reorganizing workers it had represented for years.

In March 1987, Finance Minister Gary Lane announced that the government was unilaterally declaring that "wage increases for government employees will be held at a maximum of zero percent for at least the next two years."[32] The freeze was to extend not only to direct employees of the government, but also to bargaining groups that had some nominal autonomy from the government, such as hospitals, nursing homes, and school boards. This arbitrary fiat made bargaining in the public sector extremely slow and difficult. Eventually, settlements were reached that broke the second year of the two-year freeze. These settlements were far from generous, and contained a number of special bonuses and cash payouts designed to allow the government to claim that it had, in fact, maintained the two-year freeze.

Nonetheless, public sector employees in Saskatchewan have seen their real incomes deteriorate during Devine's tenure in office, particularly during the second term. Even physicians have not been exempted from the restraint policies. Between the 1982 election and the end of 1988, for example, general practitioners in urban group practice saw their average weekly earnings expressed in 1981 dollars fall from $1,834 to $1,617. [33] Those public sector employees who have seen their incomes decrease in this fashion, are, however, in a real sense the fortunate ones. The contraction in employment, the reduction in job security, the move toward temporary and casual employment, and privatization campaigns resulting in the mass layoffs of whole groups of employees ranging from highway workers to dental therapists, have resulted in thousands of civil servants losing their jobs completely.

For organized workers, therefore, the Devine years have been hard ones. Legislative changes and LRB rulings have made union organizing and collective bargaining much more difficult. Public sector workers have been treated in an arbitrary and capricious fashion, and have on several occasions been publicly vilified by senior members of the Devine government. The attitude of this government toward workers has been demonstrated in other areas as well. In particular, the protection of the unorganized by the Labour Standards Branch of the Department of Labour and the protection of all workers' health and safety deserve some attention.

THE ASSAULT ON THE UNORGANIZED

Workers in relatively powerless positions are often characterized by academics as "the unskilled, the unlucky, and the unorganized." The basic assumption which underlies all minimum employment standards legislation is that ordinary workers subject to the "individual contract of employment at common law" are simply unable to strike an equal or fair bargain with the employer, who can exercise considerable coercion over employees who may fear loss of their jobs. Social legislation, such as labour standards, establishes the lowest permissable standards for wages and working conditions. These are enforced by the state rather than by labour-market competition.

When the Conservatives took office in 1982, they inherited a minimum wage that at $4.25 per hour was the highest in Canada. A series of 25-cent-per-hour increases was scheduled for six month intervals. The new government cancelled the scheduled increases, and the minimum wage has remained frozen except for preelection increases of 25 cents per hour every four years. Between Devine's assumption of office and January 1990, the purchasing power of a worker on minimum wage has declined by 28%.[34] As it geared up for an election expected in 1990, the government announced two further 25-cent-per-hour increases.

While the real income of the poorest workers in the province was dropping, those unfortunate enough to be working for unscrupulous employers were obtaining less support from the Labour Standards Branch, which was now far less aggressive in pursuing complaints. In the five-year period from 1983–84 to 1987–88, the number of complaints to the Labour Standards Branch rose from 2,300 to 3,120. At the same time, the number of prosecutions commenced dropped from 55 to 7. A 37% increase in the number of complaints was accompanied by an 87% decrease in the number of prosecutions.[35] In 1986, the branch stopped the practice of making routine inspections, and acted only on the basis of complaints. This change made it impossible for the enforcement officers to investigate a complaint without alerting an employer to the fact that an employee had in fact filed a complaint. The potential for reprisals was thereby increased.

It was not until 1988 that the Devine government turned its attention to actually changing Saskatchewan's labour standards legislation. In the 1988 legislative session, Labour Minister Grant Schmidt introduced Bill 73, or the Employment Benefits Act, to replace the Labour Standards Act. The legislation was allowed to die on the order paper, with the promise that it would be reintroduced and passed in the next (1989) session.

When he introduced the legislation, Schmidt claimed that "it is a fair and reasonable Bill . . . it improves and tidies up the benefits for workers in Saskatchewan, primarily the non-union workers of Saskatchewan."[36] And indeed, the new legislation did offer a few improvements to workers: maternity, paternity, and adoption leaves were extended; employees were given the right to seek damages should an employer cancel a scheduled vacation; the method of calculating pay for statutory holidays was simplified; provision for unpaid sick leave was established; and protection against unjust dismissal was provided. The legislation also called for the establishment of an Employment Benefits Board which would adjudicate on disputes without the necessity for expensive court action, and gave part-time workers pro-rated fringe benefits once they had reached two years of uninterrupted service with the same employer.

However, despite these improvements, the Employment Benefits Act represented a major attack on the protection offered to workers in Saskatchewan. Most important, the benefits and protection under the new legislation would not be mandatory. Each individual employee would have to request the benefit, and the act allowed for private agreements between employers and employees to opt out of the benefit. The mandatory floor for benefits and working conditions in the old labour standards legislation thus became subject to voluntary agreement. Employers would be allowed to insist, as a condition of employment, that workers waive their rights under the legislation. Those workers who were most vulnerable to exploitation without labour standards legislation would be precisely the ones forced to waive their legislated rights in order to keep working. The waiving of benefits could be done both individually in the case of unorganized workers and collectively in the case of organized ones. The existing labour standards legislation stipulated that less-favourable provisions in employment agreements are superseded by statute. The new legislation removed this provision, and thus would effectively destroy a collective bargaining strategy of building on statutory provisions which might not otherwise be capable of being bargained.

The voluntary nature of benefits was the most serious flaw in the Employment Benefits Act. There were also a number of specific measures that weakened protection under the Labour Standards Act. Employees in the retail trade could be compelled to work two shifts in a day once a week without the payment of overtime. The requirement for two consecutive days off would be weakened. Both of these changes were designed to accommodate the needs of retail stores in an era of unrestricted shopping hours. Employers would be granted the right to deduct any alleged cash shortages or property losses from an employee's wages. Employees would be compelled to give seven days notice before quitting a job. It would become possible for an employer to reduce wages or hours of work without regard to the length of service of the employee. The provision for notice, or pay in lieu thereof, would be eliminated for temporary layoffs. The basis for comparison for pay equity would be narrowed. The requirement that employers provide transportation home for female workers whose shift ended between 12:30–7:00 A.M. would disappear.[37]

The Employment Benefits Act provoked an outburst of outrage from a wide sector of Saskatchewan society. The Saskatchewan Federation of Labour led a campaign against the bill, joined by church and community groups and the NDP. Numerous leaflets explaining the impact of the legislation were printed and distributed, public meetings were held, and letter-writing campaigns to the government were mounted. In Regina, high school students organized a group to explain the impact of the proposals to their fellow students, and to conduct demonstrations against the legislation.

The 1989 legislative session came and went without the legislation being reintroduced. Already buffeted by the opposition to its privatization program, the government chose to avoid the fight over labour standards. With Grant Schmidt muttering that if people did not want what was good for them then he would not give it to them, the Employment Benefits Act was allowed to die a quiet death. Even if the benefits under the labour standards legislation that Devine inherited were not being vigorously enforced, the legislation itself survived on the books. It was one victory against the government's labour policies.

THE ASSAULT ON WORKERS' HEALTH AND SAFETY

When Grant Devine took office in 1982, Saskatchewan's system for enforcing Occupational Health and Safety (OHS) was widely acknowledged to be among the best in any jurisdiction in North America. The program, evolved during the previous decade, centred on the involvement of workers in the monitoring and enforcement of health and safety conditions in the workplace. The centrepiece of the program was the joint labour-management OHS committee. It was mandatory for every workplace with more than 10 employees, and was charged with the responsibility of ensuring that the workplace was as safe and healthy as possible. Workers had also been given the right to refuse any job that presented an unusual hazard to their health or safety, and had the right to information about potential hazards in the workplace. The program thus rested on the trinity of the workers' right to participate, refuse, and know. The role of the Occupational Health and Safety Branch of the Department of Labour was to provide educational and technical services to the OHS committees. In addition, its officials conducted inspections, investigated and adjudicated cases where a worker had refused a job thought to be unsafe, and prosecuted employers who violated either the OHS legislation or regulations.[38]

A year before Devine's election victory, a study prepared for the Economic Council of Canada confirmed the success of the approach that had developed during the Blakeney years. However, its authors noted that:

> A new government could destroy the effectiveness of the program without altering its basic structure. The committees gained legitimacy in large measure because program administrators want them to be the instrument through which decisions are made. Management and labour know that labour department administrators want problems solved in committees. They also gain stature as a result of their role in arbitrating work refusals. A change in attitude by administrators towards the problem resolution role of committees, or an alteration of the arbitration role, might significantly undermine the stature of the committees.[39]

This prediction was extremely accurate. There has been no legislative change for Saskatchewan's OHS program. However, the administration of the program has undergone a dramatic change since Devine's election.

After the 1982 election, the new minister of labour, Lorne McLaren, quickly clarified the new policy by stating that "Management is saying to us: 'Get off our backs, let us do the job'. So my response to them is, 'Okay, we'll get off your backs . . .'" He added that the new approach would be a "management responsibility system" since "after all, it's still the employers' plant." His deputy minister was even more explicit: "We're open for business and that means that we're not going to put employers out of business by pursuing academic occupational health and safety rules."[40]

The director of the OHS Branch was quickly fired and replaced by John Alderman, the former chief mines inspector. McLaren reported that he had received accolades from employers and condemnation from unions for this action.[41] Alderman had his own ideas about what caused accidents and how to prevent them. The new director said that the key to effective accident prevention is "the influence that management can exert in the workplace . . . over workers." The new task of the OHS Branch was to assist management in their efforts to "develop that attitudinal environment which is conducive to doing the job properly."[42]

The impact of the new regime was immediate and dramatic. Two years after Devine had taken office, spending by the OHS Branch on research and education had disappeared as a line item in the provincial budget. The number of inspections by the Health and Safety Standards Unit of the OHS Branch dropped in this period from 2,629 to 1,864. The number of contacts with workplace committees dropped from 1,519 to 847. The number of notices of contravention dropped from 947 to 681. The record of the Mines Inspection Branch was even more dramatic. There, the number of notices of contravention dropped from 2,474 to 180 in two years.[43] Instead of issuing notices demanding compliance with mining regulations, the inspectors began issuing informal "notices of hazards." These had no legal standing, and effectively constituted friendly suggestions for improvements. The government also instituted a temporary moratorium on prosecutions which lasted for close to two years. Alderman said the moratorium was necessary "to evaluate what we wanted to accomplish with them."[44] Even after the moratorium ended, most observers agreed that the OHS Branch was now extremely reluctant to prosecute an employer for violating OHS regulations.

Because the Saskatchewan OHS program was reliant upon active, functioning committees that management was forced to take seriously and upon the protection of the worker's right to refuse unsafe work, it is difficult to capture the changes in the program with an outline of the number of inspections and prosecutions. The crucial issue is the dynamic within the workplace and whether workers, their committee members, and employers expect complaints about OHS conditions to be supported by the Department of Labour. If the threat of "calling in an inspector" is a real and effective one, then most employers will attempt to resolve complaints internally. If the threat is perceived to be an empty one, then employers are more likely to ignore complaints and requests from workers.

A clear illustration of the change in the philosophy of the OHS Branch is the change in treatment of workers who exercised their right to refuse work they believed was unsafe. The director of the OHS Branch from 1972–1982 took the position that this right was a fundamental cornerstone of the program, to be upheld whenever it was utilized. His successor had a different view of work refusals. According to Alderman:

> Really the only ones which come to us are those where the employer thinks he's in the right *which are usually fairly marginal cases* and usually arise because someone's had an argument with a supervisor and got sent home and they turn around and say they got sent home

because it was unsafe. At that stage, they suddenly try to make it into a section 26 and we get dragged into it. (emphasis added)[45]

This change in attitude toward work refusals makes it less likely that a worker would refuse to perform a job that he thought was unsafe since the chances of employer retaliation are increased.

A dramatic example of the effects of the new policy came in 1985 at the Prince Albert Pulp Company (PAPCO). A long-term effort by the worker members of the OHS committee to force a cleanup of asbestos insulation culminated in a worker refusing to work with asbestos-contaminated material. He was suspended. When the OHS Branch refused to get involved in the case, the other 385 workers at the mill launched a wildcat strike. The strike lasted a month, and was only ended with a court injunction which ordered the workers back to work and the asbestos contamination cleaned up. PAPCO then launched a $1-million damage suit against the union, which was subsequently settled out of court.[46]

In this case, the refusal of the OHS Branch to get involved either by ordering a cleanup or supporting the work refusal led to a month-long strike and a major lawsuit against the union. It is worth stressing that the court injunction that ended the dispute imposed a mechanism for dealing with the asbestos that was essentially the same as what already existed in provincial legislation and regulations. However, the OHS Branch's refusal to enforce these regulations made the cost of demanding a cleanup extremely high for the workers at PAPCO. In this climate, it is probable that in many workplaces workers simply put up with conditions that they would not have accepted before the 1982 election. Alderman himself provides a succinct summation of how the government policy change has played itself out in individual workplaces:

> Now we have a situation where the committees are still theoretically just as good and just as well staffed and everything, but where the people in the union or the work people represented on the committees are being very careful about what they do. They have a certain amount of bargaining power still, but they're not wasting it.[47]

Two further examples serve to illustrate the approach to OHS under the Devine government. In 1981, the NDP government enacted a regulation that specified that where a job could be performed while sitting, a chair would be provided.[48] The regulation was aimed at the retail sector, and was intended to relieve the strain of standing in front of a cash register all day. Although the regulation is still on the books it has never been enforced, and many workers are still standing.

In another case, the government did change a regulation. Without any public notice, Section 249 of the Occupational Health and Safety Crane Regulations was changed to allow workers to be hoisted in swing-type "man baskets" that are not fixed to the boom of the crane. These baskets are cheaper than those that are fixed to the boom of the crane. Four months later, 19-year-old Jason Greenwood was killed when the newly legalized basket that he was working on fell to the ground. Initially, the OHS Branch did not intend to prosecute the employer, but letters and a petition campaign organized by Jason's mother eventually resulted in charges on six counts.[49]

Perhaps the best summary of the changes in the OHS Branch comes from an internal memorandum. After a survey of Saskatchewan unions, the director of the OHS Branch was told by one of his senior officials that:

> There is a general feeling of mistrust by organized labour in Saskatchewan supported by the feeling our Branch of Government is not acting in the best interests of the workers of Saskatchewan. The open door policy and Branch support of workers that was so prevalent up to 1982 no longer exists. By our actions we have lost long term continuity of programs so crucial to expanding the overall Health and Safety programs in Saskatchewan.[50]

In 1989, Alderman was replaced as director of the OHS Branch. The appointment of his successor was greeted with cynicism by the union movement. Myles Morin had been in the process of applying for a job as an occupational health officer when he suddenly withdrew his application. A short time later, he was appointed as director. This led to the suspicion that his experience as a defeated Conservative cabinet minister was given greater weight than his lack of experience in the field of OHS.

The general attitude of the Workers' Compensation Board has also changed. Workers unfortunate enough to be injured on the job stand a greater chance of running into trouble with their Workers' Compensation Board (WCB) claim than they would have before 1982.

Workers' compensation was implemented in Saskatchewan in 1929. In its legal underpinnings, it is similar to the system in all Canadian provinces. Workers are legislatively stripped of the right to sue their employer for

171

any injury suffered on the job. In exchange, they are supposed to receive medical treatment and wage-loss protection from a fund which is administered by a board appointed by the government and paid with premiums levied against employers. Workers' compensation is therefore a compulsory, no-fault liability insurance scheme for employers. It is a legislated exchange: employers are protected from negligence suits while workers are assured protection from financial loss as a result of a workplace injury.

With the trade-off inherent in a workers' compensation system, the key for workers is how claims are adjudicated. If the claim of an injured worker is denied, then the worker has lost the right to sue for negligence without receiving any compensation for the injury. The attitude of the claims adjudicators is in large part determined by the composition of the board itself. While all three board members are appointed by the government, in theory it should be composed of an independent chair, one member to represent the interests of the employers who pay the premiums, and one member to represent the interests of employees. Since 1929, the worker representative on the board has been chosen in consultation with Saskatchewan's labour movement. This practice changed in 1987, when the term of the worker representative appointed by the NDP government expired. Labour Minister Grant Schmidt ignored the names put forth by unions.

The chair of the board is the crucial position in determining policy regarding claims adjudication. The Devine government allowed the NDP-appointed board chair to finish out his term in 1984. Since then, three people have served in that position. The first person appointed by the Conservatives resigned in less than a year. Since 1985, the position has been held by Garnet Garvin.

During Garvin's tenure, there have been some dramatic shifts in the operating statistics of the Saskatchewan WCB (see Table 8.4). The number of permanent impairment claims has dropped from 583 in 1984 to 91 in 1989. The average duration of claim dropped in this same time period from 37.4 days to 25.4.[51] While this theoretically could be due to a reduction in the number and severity of workplace injuries, two things suggest that the real reason is a tougher claims adjudication procedure. First, the total number of claims has remained relatively constant. If the remarkable decline in the number of permanent impairment awards and the average duration of claims was the result of safer workplaces, it would be reasonable to expect that there would also be a reduction in the volume of claims. Second, there has been an equally dramatic increase in the

172

number of appeals of WCB decisions. Table 8.5 outlines these statistics. In 1981, there were a total of 191 appeals launched. By 1985, the numbers had grown to the point where it had become necessary to establish a separate appeals committee to reduce the number of appeals reaching the board. By 1988, a total of 839 appeals of WCB decisions were launched. In 1981, one in 100 decisions involving injuries severe enough to necessitate a loss of time from work were appealed. By 1988, better than one in 20 of these decisions were appealed. A comparison of the permanent impairment awards and the appeals figures suggests that the reconstituted board was toughest on those workers who were most seriously injured. Their claims, often for injuries causing chronic back problems, had been the most expensive for the WCB since they involved long-term income replacement. The cheaper solution was to terminate the benefits, usually on the grounds that the back difficulties were caused by a hitherto unnoticed and undiagnosed noncompensable degenerative condition rather than the compensable workplace injury.

The policy that reveals the most about the attitudes of the reconstituted Workers' Compensation Board centres around the word "deeming." Prior to 1979, the Saskatchewan Workers' Compensation Act treated long-term disability arising from a workplace injury in the same manner as in all other jurisdictions in Canada. Once a permanent injury had stabilized, a "meat chart" was used to determine the percentage of disability, and a pension was paid out according to this physical impairment rating. The problem with this approach was that a percentage physical impairment rating often had no correlation with the effect on the worker's ability to earn a living. For example, a 45-year-old construction worker with a grade eight education and a bad back might receive a 10% physical impairment rating and a pension based on 10% of his pre-injury earnings. However, without extensive rehabilitation, this worker would be 100% vocationally disabled.

In 1979, the Saskatchewan Workers' Compensation Act was changed so that a calculation of the income lost due to the effects of the injury, rather than the severity of the injury itself, became the determining factor in the level of long-term benefits. This was widely hailed as a major improvement in the system. However, when Garvin became chair of the WCB, this provision quickly became a device to terminate or reduce benefits. For example, an injured worker would receive a letter stating that "in view of your age, work limitations, prior work experience, etc., we deem that you are capable of performing suitable work as a service station attendant, parking lot attendant, or parts person earning the equivalent of $10.00 per hour or $400.00 per week." Compensation benefits would be reduced accordingly. The determination of what an injured worker was entitled to was therefore not based on the actual income loss from the injury, but on the income loss after the WCB had "deemed" what the worker's income should be. If he or she was not earning this income, the WCB argued that the cause was due to such things as high unemployment rates or low wage rates which are not the WCB's responsibility.

The WCB's practice of "deeming" quickly met with widespread condemnation. A 1986 committee of review into the operations of the board chaired by Judge Muir and composed of equal representation from workers and employers unanimously concluded that "it is not the responsibility of the Board to guess what the worker's earnings would be if only that worker could get a job. It is the Board's responsibility to rehabilitate that worker and aid the worker to return to productive employment." [52] The committee of review argued that deeming what a worker "should be" earning should be applied only in exceptional circumstances, and that as a widespread and general practice, it should be stopped immediately. It was a year and a half before the WCB responded to this "urgent" recommendation. In a policy directive, the members of the board relaxed some of the criteria for deeming, but insisted that "the workers' compensation system is responsible to return injured workers to a position where they can seek gainful employment. The system cannot insulate injured workers from the economic realities which all workers face. The Workers' Compensation Board cannot guarantee employment opportunities, but it can guarantee 'job readiness.' " [53] The WCB was saying that it did not care what a worker would be making "but for" his or her injury. All that mattered was what it was theoretically possible for the worker to earn after the injury, whether or not this was, in fact, possible.

In the area of workplace health and safety, the Devine years are therefore characterized by both a reduction in the enforcement of OHS conditions within the workplace, and more restrictive policies for claims adjudication for workers who were in fact injured on the job.

CONCLUSION

During eight years of the Devine government, the province has had ministers of labour who were vocally and actively anti-union. Senior administrators were at best ignorant of legislation and programs they were responsible for, and at worst, actively opposed to the philosophical under-pinnings of those programs. Administrative changes were accompanied by legislative ones as the new Department of Human Resources, Labour, and Employment became the instrument whereby the government sought to force workers to adapt to its vision of the free market. By 1990, the circle was complete. Grant Schmidt, the minister of labour, also became minister of economic development.

During Devine's two terms in office, union membership dropped, organizing stagnated, real incomes of workers dropped, and OHS and labour standards legislation went almost unenforced. From the govern-ment's perspective, its labour policies have been very successful.

For a time, these policies met with little opposition. Long accustomed to enjoying a close working relationship with the government in general and the Department of Labour in particular, labour leaders were bewildered by the sudden and dramatic changes. For several years, Devine even refused to receive the Saskatchewan Federation of Labour's annual brief to the government! The government's hostility toward organized labour was matched only by its contempt for its leaders.

While the union movement's early responses to the Devine agenda for labour were ineffective, during the government's second term there has been more effective resistance. The SFL has played the major role in organizing the two largest demonstrations in the history of the province. It has also played a leading role in organizing broader-based coalitions of individuals and groups who have been hurt by the government's policies. The anger over the lack of enforcement in the OHS program has long been simmering, and appears to be boiling over. An informal support group organized around the death of Jason Greenwood has attracted support from around the province as it worked to compel the government to prosecute. Most significant, the government was made to back down from its legislative agenda when the union-led opposition campaign forced the withdrawal of the Employment Benefits Act.

The Devine years have been harsh ones for organized labour. However, it is by no means assured that the government will be able to fully implement its agenda. Its very severity has begun to arouse more militant resistance.

BUILDING BINGES AND BUDGET CUTS: HEALTH CARE IN SASKATCHEWAN, 1982-1990

by Lesley Biggs

T he concept of health care as a just and due right has a lengthy history in Saskatchewan. The province has been a leader in the provision of health care services both in Canada and internationally. Saskatchewan was the birthplace of medicare in Canada and many other innovative health care programs were pioneered here. Although the implementation of these programs was controversial, the people of Saskatchewan have come to accept medicare as part of the fabric of Saskatchewan society.

However, the right to accessible and affordable health care has been severely threatened by the policies of the Devine government. The Conservatives have embarked on a massive building program in the hospital sector while squeezing operating expenditures. This approach has resulted in understaffing, lengthy waiting lists, and equipment shortages. At the same time, the government has cut programs which primarily serve disadvantaged groups in Saskatchewan society–the poor, the elderly, women, Natives, children, the mentally handicapped, the disabled, and victims of abuse. This has led to increasing inequities not only in the provision of services but in the health status of Saskatchewan residents. The burden of cutbacks has been shouldered by individuals, families, and health care workers.

BACKGROUND

Residents of Saskatchewan have attempted to provide accessible health services even under the most adverse conditions. In the 1920s, several rural municipalities developed municipal doctor plans in order to attract physicians to sparsely populated areas.[1] By 1930, 32 plans were in operation. In 1947 the CCF introduced the Saskatchewan Hospital Services Plan which removed all financial barriers to hospital services by providing universal hospital insurance. In 1948, the Swift Current Health Region began providing compulsory universal medical insurance to residents in the area.

The most significant event in the provision of health services in Saskatchewan and Canada was the introduction of universal medical insurance in 1962. The introduction of the Medical Care Insurance Act led to a bitter confrontation between the medical profession and the CCF government, culminating in a 23-day strike by 625 of the 700 doctors practising in the province. A climate of fear and hysteria was created as the merits of socialism and state interventionism were hotly debated. The province was deeply divided. Community clinics sprang up to provide services by doctors who supported the plan while the "Keep Our Doctors" committees organized rallies and collected petitions to oppose the government's actions.

The dispute was eventually resolved with the assistance of Lord Taylor, a member of Britain's House of Lords who had been asked to mediate the dispute. Under the Saskatoon Agreement which ended the strike, the Medical Care Insurance Commission (MCIC) was created to administer the plan. Physicians were able to bill MCIC on a fee-for-service basis but retained the option to bill private insurance companies which, in turn, would be reimbursed by MCIC.

Since the introduction of universal medical insurance, other programs have been implemented including the Saskatchewan Hearing Aid Plan (1973), Saskatchewan Dental Plan (1974), the Saskatchewan Aids to Independent Living Plan (1975), and the Saskatchewan Prescription Drug Plan (1975). These programs were designed to meet the needs of Saskatchewan residents by reducing the costs of direct services.

Health is a political issue. Elections have been won and lost over the provision of health services. (This was a hard lesson learned by the Thatcher government which introduced unpopular hospital utilization fees and was subsequently defeated in the 1971 election.) Since there was widespread satisfaction with the delivery of health care services in Saskatchewan when the election was called in 1982, the Progressive Conservatives did not make health care the centre of their political platform. In the past, the Conservatives had opposed a universal medicare scheme and were, therefore, particularly vulnerable on health issues. Aside from occasional references to improving health care and wanting to be "number one in Canada," the Tories treated health care as a nonissue.

While the Tories were silent on health issues, the NDP was embroiled in a bitter dispute with non-nursing staff in hospitals. The NDP made the fatal error of introducing back-to-work legislation for non-nursing staff just before calling the 1982 election. The labour movement was disenchanted with the NDP's actions and withdrew active support for the party.[2]

HEALTH CARE UNDER THE TORIES: THE FIRST TERM OF OFFICE, 1982–86

In 1983 the Conservative government proudly paraded a health budget of close to $1 billion, apparently up by $250 million from the previous year.[3] The expenditures were cited as proof that the Tories were concerned about health care which, it was argued, had been neglected by the NDP. However, much of the increase was due to "creative accounting." Programs were transferred from the Northern Saskatchewan Branch and Social Services Department, amounting to over $176 million dollars or 70% of the health budget increase. The largest single transfer was from the Department of Social Services to the Department of Health for grants to special care facilities ($147,467,650) and grants and allowances for home care ($18,380,040). The other main transfer was from the Department of Northern Saskatchewan, amounting to $3,482,110. While a case could be made for including these services under the Department of Health, the presentation of these statistics as if they were a real increase was grossly misleading.

The most significant real increase in spending was in the area of hospital construction and upgrading. This accounted for 25% of the Health Department increase. This increase was not a one-time event but signalled a major shift in the direction of expenditures on health care. Throughout the Tories' first term of office, the government vigorously pursued capital projects at the expense of operating budgets. Millions of dollars were allocated toward hospital construction and upgrading while little money was available for staffing and equipment. At the same time, more vulnerable programs, primarily serving the poor, children, the elderly, and the mentally ill, were cut.

The construction of health care facilities became the centrepiece of the Tory program in health care.[4] The government embarked on a massive building program including construction on hospitals in Lloydminster, Nipawin, and Cut Knife, the construction of a new cancer clinic in Saskatoon, funds for the Kinsmen's Childrens' Rehabilitation Centre in

179

Saskatoon, 97 new nursing home beds, a new four-bed pediatric intensive care unit at Royal University Hospital, and the upgrading of cardiac services at the Plains Health Centre.

The trend toward capital-intensive projects continued in 1984.[5] Substantial funds were allocated to Pasqua and Regina General and Royal University hospitals ($14 million for construction from the Special Projects Fund). In addition, the government announced a five-year, $25-million nursing home construction program, giving the province 1,000 new long-term beds and replacing another 500 beds. In 1985, the government announced the Partnership in Progress Plan, a five-year $290-million hospital construction program for Saskatoon and Regina hospitals.[6] In 1985–86 almost half of all hospital construction grants went to Regina and Saskatoon.

While the Tory government pursued capital projects, other (less-visible) programs were cut. In 1983, the Psychiatric Services Branch suffered the most staff cutbacks.[7] The branch itself lost 13 positions and the psychiatric centres at Yorkton, Weyburn, and North Battleford lost 23 positions, for a total loss of 36 jobs in psychiatric services. In addition, 23 staff positions were cut in the Saskatchewan Dental Plan. In 1984, grants for home care, the Saskatchewan Dental Plan, and the Saskatchewan Health Research Board were all cut.[8] Overall funds for psychiatric services increased, particularly to nongovernment agencies, but staff positions in the psychiatric centres at Weyburn, North Battleford, Yorkton, and Prince Albert were once again cut. Similarly, the overall budget for Northern Services was increased but the food subsidy program (costing $250,000) was cut.

The government provided little rationale for these cuts. The elimination of the northern food subsidy was justified on the basis that it was being abused. Sid Dutchak, minister responsible for northern affairs, stated that northern outfitters were taking advantage of the subsidized food and selling it at a profit to tourists from the south. The claim was vigorously denied by the Tourist Industry Association of Saskatchewan.[9] The consequences of removing the food subsidy were dramatic. The price of bread in Stony Rapids rose from $1.25 to $1.52, two litres of milk rose from $1.41 to $1.94, a five-kilogram bag of potatoes rose from $4.50 to $8.50, and a package of six porkchops rose from $4.00 to a whopping $7.00.[10] Given the undisputed relationship between health and nutritional status, this funding cut inevitably led to a worsening of health status in the north.

These cutbacks were particularly difficult to swallow after it was revealed that the government spent $321,000 promoting its spring budget[11] and that it spent $41,000 in 1985 to hire a public relations firm to prepare copies of the finance minister's speeches.[12] These speeches, in turn, were mailed to 2800 people and formed the basis for the minister's "consultation" process.

By 1985, the financial squeeze on the provincial government was apparent to all. With the accumulated deficit approaching $2 billion, the government sought measures to reduce costs and there was no doubt that "spiralling" health care costs were seen as a major source of the problem. The government quietly began to renege on its commitments to health care expenditures.[13] In 1983–84 the government spent $16 million less than budgeted on health care including: $2.5 million less than projected for grants to hospitals and health centres, $1.4 million less than budgeted for home care programs, and $3.8 million less than budgeted on nursing homes.

The most visible sign of financial constraint was the alarming rise in surgical waiting lists, particularly for Saskatoon hospitals. For example, the surgical waiting list at St. Paul's Hospital had almost doubled, from 1,200 in 1982, to 2,000 in 1986. In order to cope with its operating deficit, the hospital was forced to periodically reduce the number of operations. Out of sheer frustration, seven anesthetists at St. Paul's Hospital withdrew all but emergency services for one day in June 1986, an action which coincided with a visit to the hospital by Health Minister Graham Taylor.[14]

In addition, more and more reports were appearing in the media concerning the introduction of other cost-saving measures by hospitals so that they could balance their budgets. For example, Regina General Hospital raised its crutch-rental fees and was discharging patients at 11 A.M. to save the cost of a noon meal.[15] There were also reports of shortages of equipment such as CT scanners, leading to waiting lists of six to eight weeks.[16] Finally, there were reports of staffing shortages. The Saskatchewan Union of Nurses initiated a campaign to draw attention to the inadequate care in hospitals due to staff shortages.[17]

The lengthy waiting lists, the understaffing of hospitals, and equipment shortages were all a result of the government's policy to expand capital expenditures by squeezing the operating side. Although there is no doubt that some existing facilities required upgrading and there was a need for new facilities, the Tories' program led to a gross discrepancy between capital and operating expenditures.

By the 1986 election year, the government was politically vulnerable on health care. It responded with some band-aid measures by providing supplemental funding to Saskatoon hospitals to shorten hospital waiting lists. [18] In addition, the government announced on the eve of the election a five-year, $100-million plan to provide improved hospital and nursing home services. The first $40 million was to be spent on reducing waiting lists, providing new equipment and diagnostic services, and creating new nursing positions. The remaining $60 million was to be spent on staffing and other operating expenses at new facilities.

If the hospital administrators were nervous about balancing their budgets, the medical profession became increasingly anxious about its position in the health care system. Under the new Canada Health Act passed in 1984, the federal government attempted to eliminate extra-billing by imposing a penalty on provinces which allowed the practice to continue. (The federal government deducted one dollar from its transfer payment to a province for every dollar that was extra-billed by a physician.) The Tory government assured its traditional conservative ally, the SMA, that it would absorb the penalty. [19] Several months later, however, in response to the heavy penalties imposed under the Canada Health Act, the government reneged on its promise and announced that it would eliminate extra-billing with or without the cooperation of the medical profession.

Despite the tough stance taken by the provincial government toward the medical profession, the SMA was appeased when the government agreed to a statutory bargaining process. The SMA signed the Saskatoon Agreement II on 22 May 1985. Although the SMA was angered by the government's actions, "the [SMA] was satisfied that the bargaining process had served us, the government and the public well. Our anger dissipated." [20]

The truce was short-lived. The medical profession became increasingly frustrated by the government's unwillingness to negotiate new contracts. In June 1985, after a three-day strike, Saskatchewan's 205 interns won the right to submit any and all issues except academic and training issues to binding arbitration. [21] Similarly, when the government refused to discuss all of the economic issues brought to the bargaining table by the medical profession in 1986, the physicians began to hold study sessions. Eight of the 10 anesthetists in Prince Albert withdrew their services to reinforce their demands for a better fee structure. An agreement was reached but only after the premier intervened. [22] With his eye on the upcoming election, Premier Devine wanted to avoid a public confrontation with the SMA.

During the Conservatives' first term of office, overall health care expenditures were not subject to the same restraints as other areas of government spending. Dale Eisler, political columnist for the Regina *Leader Post*, maintains that this strategy prevented the NDP from reclaiming health, the centrepiece of NDP policy, as a political issue.[23] Moreover, when concern began to be expressed about the imposition of hospital user fees, which may have given the NDP an opportunity to reclaim health care debate, the Tory government reassured voters that hospital user fees would not be implemented despite a resolution calling for the introduction of user fees at the annual P.C. convention.[24]

On the eve of the election Graham Taylor declared that "health care is no longer a political football and that's because the province's system is generally regarded as one of the best in Canada . . . Saskatchewan people are generally satisfied with the province's health-care program which explain[ed] why it was not a major election issue." Taylor added that "there were no significant announcements about health care during the past election campaign because the government has embarked on long-range planning."[25]

THE TORIES SECOND TERM OF OFFICE, 1986 TO THE PRESENT

Although the government was exploring measures to reduce health expenditures prior to the 1986 election,[26] there was no overt indication in the 1986 election campaign that the government was going to make major changes in the delivery of health services. There were, however, warning signals. In 1986, George McLeod replaced Graham Taylor as minister of health and announced that he was looking for "innovative solutions." "We need to come up with innovative ways to provide the service that people rightfully expect with the resources that are available." While rejecting user fees, McLeod clearly believed that the private sector should assume more of the burden. In particular, he strongly supported the Regina hospital lottery through which Regina hospitals hoped to raise money by selling $100 tickets for prizes that included a house and vacations. However, McLeod reassured the public that "Health is one of the four pillars of this government . . . You will not see a change in priority that is placed on health or in the direction (we are taking)."[27]

Early in 1987, rumours about cutbacks in health care began to circulate before the introduction of the budget. Anticipating the worst, agencies began to trim budgets and to streamline services. They also kept a low profile. "Most were reluctant to speak against cuts to health care in case this criticism affected their own funding. This resulted in minimized public outcry or advocacy. The suspense alone was demoralizing." When the cutbacks finally came, "they occurred in a piecemeal fashion. Government did not produce a comprehensive summary of their planned reductions but rather notified agencies independently without public announcement." [28] Overall, the government's strategy has excluded public participation in the policy-making process and stifled criticism by presenting a fragmented program to individual agencies.

The cutbacks were extensive. [29] The school dental program for adolescents was cut and dental services for children from kindergarten to grade eight were contracted out to private dentists. The government estimated that it would save $5.5 million. Two hundred and ninety-four workers lost their jobs including: 111 therapists, 148 assistants, seven equipment technicians and 16 in clerical and administrative positions. Most of these were women working in rural areas where there was little chance of employment.

Cuts were made to the drug plan. Families and individuals were required to pay a $125 annual deductible for prescription drugs, senior families pay $75, and single seniors pay $50. The government reimbursed 80% of the costs after the deductible was reached. The government estimated that it would save $60 million by having people pay part of the costs for prescription drugs.

Although the changes to the drug and dental plans received the most publicity, the government also cut a number of other programs including: $1 million from the mental health services budget and over $550,000 from the Saskatchewan Hearing Aid Plan. The budget for community services was cut by close to $200,000. Responsibility for a special equipment and repair program under the Saskatchewan Aids to Independent Living was transferred to the Saskatchewan Abilities Council, resulting in a loss of 12 jobs. [30]

Other programs under the Department of Health were more fortunate. The budget for the Saskatchewan Alcohol and Drug Abuse Commission (SADAC) was more than doubled from $5.4 million to $13.2 million, including $3.2 million for substance abuse programs and $1.5 million for the Whitespruce Drug and Alcohol Treatment Centre. The government announced a 15-cent increase on everyone's monthly phone bill in order to pay for equipment and services for the hearing impaired. In addition, the government promised funds to "respond to the growing problem of

AIDS" but the amount was unspecified. The sum of $7,000 was eventually given to AIDS Saskatoon and AIDS Regina. No cuts were made to the five-year construction programs.[31]

The Effect of the Cutbacks

The presentation of cutbacks in dollar figures does not adequately capture the hardships endured by both staff and the clients who they serve. In a report commissioned by the Saskatchewan Public Health Association, *Profiles of Reductions in Health Care in Saskatchewan*, Carol Brown documented the economic, sociological, and psychological effects of the cutbacks in health care.[32] However, the Saskatchewan Public Health Association chose not to publish the report, ostensibly because the information was considered outdated by the time it was collected.[33] It was not until the report was leaked to the press that the extensive damage and hardship created by the cuts became public knowledge.

Brown identifies five general trends in the process of cutbacks and their future implications: limitation of services, transfer of costs, privatization, increasing inequities, and erosion of health professions.

Limitation of Services

One of the main effects of the cutbacks was manpower shortages across the province. Some staff were fired, as in the case of the dental assistants, but most staff cuts were imposed through an early retirement scheme. The determining factor in how much a program was affected was the number of older workers rather than the demand for services. As a result, agencies have been forced to cut back on services, shorten hours of operation, expand summer bed closures, centralize operations, and create or increase user fees.

Transfer of Costs

Brown points out that the government's cost-reduction strategies have not meant a decrease in the real costs but rather costs have now been shifted from the government to other agencies, municipalities, community groups, families and the individual. The cutbacks to the drug plan are the best example of transferring costs from the government to the individual. The introduction of the deductibles created unnecessary hardship for the people who could not afford to pay the upfront costs of medication. As a result, many patients simply did without the prescription or were forced to make sacrifices in other areas of their budgets in order to pay for the prescription.

Privatization

Privatization of services has emerged in direct and indirect ways. The contracting out of dental services is the most vivid example of privatization. Under the new plan, children's dental care is only available through private dentists. This imposes an undue hardship on those parents who must transport their children to a dentist who is not located in their community. Clearly, the rural areas bear a disproportionate burden since many people must travel hundreds of miles to the nearest dentist. The cutbacks to the children's dental plan left many communities with no dental services and they had little opportunity to attract new dentists because in an earlier budget, the government cut back funds subsidizing newly graduated dentists.

According to Brown, privatization occurs in more insidious ways. Clients who are unable to get their needs met through traditional nonprofit agencies may seek help elsewhere – if they can afford to pay. This opens the door for private agencies to expand their market by offering direct services or offering insurance coverage for health care. Brown points out that "in privatizing services government sacrifices quality control, consistency and universality." [34] Quality of care is sacrificed when profit is the driving force.

The most significant example of indirect form of privatization is the 66% increase in user fees for home care services announced in the 1987 budget. Although seniors are eligible for a subsidy, they must submit first to a form of "means test," which for many elderly conjures images of the hated means test of the premedicare days. This dramatic increase in the user fee may force individuals on a fixed income to seek care in an acute care hospital rather than depend on home care. Acute hospital care, however, is the most expensive and least effective way to deal with many of the needs of the elderly. At the same time, the home care program may be forced to limit services even further due to declining revenues. Those who can afford to pay will seek the services of a private homemaker or a private nursing home.

Increasing Inequities

The burden of the cutbacks which took place in the Tories' first term of office was shouldered by disadvantaged groups. In the Tories' second term of office, this trend was intensified. Brown concludes that:

> There is evidence that suggests cutbacks were specifically targeted . . . Over and over again the prime client groups hurt by service reductions have been the most disadvantaged groups within society.

The ones with limited public voice. At an agency level, many high profile, traditional health care agencies were minimally effected by health care cuts. It was at the expense of agencies offering service targeted to disadvantaged groups. In answering the question of who loses one concludes that natives, youth, children, the elderly, the disabled, psychiatric patients, the mentally handicapped and victims of abuse are the losers.[35]

Since the government has actively undermined services which have provided a minimal safety net for disadvantaged groups, Brown argues that the government's policies perpetuate systemic social inequality.

Erosion of Health Professions

One of the main strategies of the government's policy was to "downsize" the public service. This was achieved by firing health care professionals as in the case of the dental therapists and assistants or by forcing numerous individuals to accept early retirement or by not filling vacant positions. The effect on health care professionals has been catastrophic. Brown reports widespread demoralization among front-line health care workers since they have been forced to cope with staff shortages and increased workloads. "They have been demoralized by the lack of consultation, the loss of valued peers and leaders, and by various austerity measures."[36] Overall, Brown presents a bleak picture of the impact of the cutbacks on health services.

Were the 1987 cuts justified? In his budget address, Gary Lane argued that "the health care sector was beset with structural and systemic problems . . . Structural problems include a disjointed, layered system, built up over the years through a simplistic add-on mentality." The government identified two major problems: the distribution of health services and the lack of accountability in the health care system. Lane argued that services were underutilized in the rural areas and excessive pressure was placed on urban hospitals, resulting in long waiting lists. He noted that "the present system can also cause the excessive utilization of physician services and medical procedures." Finally, Lane noted that administrative costs were escalating and he pointed to an administrative structure consisting of 500 boards to manage the health system.[37]

However, the cutbacks did not address the problem of maldistribution of services and a lack of accountability in the health care sector. With the exception of the drug plan, the cuts represented only 4.4% of the total health budget. Moreover, the cutbacks do not make sense in terms of the health care philosophy which emphasizes prevention rather than cure.

187

Most of the cuts, again with the exception of those to the drug plan, involved programs which in the long term are designed to reduce overall health costs by reducing the need for expensive curative services.

The government justified many of these cuts by claiming that people were abusing the system. The drug plan was singled out as a particular source of abuse. While there is no doubt that double-doctoring occurs (a practice where individuals obtain prescriptions from different doctors in order to support a drug habit), attention should also be directed at physician prescribing practices. For example, a report appearing in the Saskatoon *Star Phoenix* in December 1987 revealed that while 812 charges were laid against people suspected of attempting to satisfy their drug habits by "double doctoring," almost one half of the 5,400 prescriptions were issued by just nine doctors.[38] Mechanisms can be introduced to monitor these abuses without punishing the entire population.

If the cutbacks do not make sense in terms of the economic and health benefits derived by Saskatchewan residents, they make even less sense when viewed in a broader context. In a stinging critique of the government's policies, Dale Eisler of the *Leader Post* argues that "McLeod's fiscal argument rings hollow when considered in the light of other events." More specifically, he points out that the government heavily subsidized the Newgrade heavy oil upgrader by providing 15% or $105 million in equity and lending Consumers Co-operative Refineries $35 million for its portion of the project's equity and guaranteeing the majority of the remaining borrowed loan. Eisler points out that the government spent more than $100 million to help create 100 jobs and eliminated 294 jobs to save $5.5 million.[39]

Response to the Cutbacks

Public response to the cutbacks was swift and furious. Editorials appearing in the province's daily papers, the *Leader Post*, and the *Star Phoenix*, either condemned the government's cutbacks to the children's dental plan and the drug plan or questioned the political wisdom of the government's actions. In addition, the press sympathetically reported on numerous cases in which individuals or families were faced with high drug prescription bills, some amounting to hundreds of dollars per month.

The NDP continually attacked the Tories in the legislature and Pat Atkinson, NDP health critic, repeatedly drew the legislature's attention to the hardships endured by individuals and families who could not afford the costs of services and prescriptions as a result of the cutbacks. The

NDP was able to mobilize public protest against the cutbacks and presented a petition with over 100,000 names to the legislature in September 1987. The petition was dismissed by Premier Devine as "childish antics by the NDP." [40] Finally, the Saskatchewan Union of Nurses installed a health care hotline so that people could register their complaints about the provision of health services in the province. In the first week of operation, SUN received over 150 calls.

The negative reaction to the cutbacks, particularly to the financial hardship created by the cutbacks to the drug plan, forced the government to do some damage control. Under public pressure, the government established a drug review panel to deal with hardship cases. [41] In addition, the drug plan was extensively criticized because the sole responsibility for recovering prescription costs rested with individual residents. Under the new plan, Saskatchewan residents submitted receipts to the government and were reimbursed later. This process was inconvenient, cumbersome, and led to long delays in repayment. In order to streamline the accounting process, the government introduced the Saskatchewan health card which is presented each time an individual uses health care services, including the purchase of prescription drugs.

While these changes have no doubt improved the efficiency of the current drug plan and health services, they do not amount to major changes in the delivery of care. Rather they were implemented in response to shortcomings in the government's hastily introduced and poorly conceived policies. The government remained firmly committed to reducing health expenditures, arguing that cutbacks were necessary if a universal health care program was to survive. The government plowed ahead despite opinion polls indicating that "providing enough, good medical care" was "the number one priority in all of Canada" at that time. [42]

THE CRISIS IN HEALTH CARE IN SASKATCHEWAN?

The government's position on health care is a confusing one. Prior to the 1986 election, Graham Taylor, the minister of health, assured voters that Saskatchewan's health care system was one of the best in Canada and no major changes were required. Just four months after the election, the government announced major spending cuts. The Tories also argue both that health care costs are out of control and that new private money is needed to offset the problems of long waiting lists, understaffing, and equipment shortages. What is the nature of the health care crisis?

Expenditures on health care have increased over the past 10 years. Since the Tories came to power, expenditures on health care have doubled from approximately $500 million in 1980–81 to over $1 billion at present. Health care expenditures have increased 12.7% annually[43] and now represent one-third of the total provincial budget. The four major sources of expenditures are physician services, drugs expenditures, hospital services, and grants to special care facilities, representing 18.3%, 5.0%, 44.5%, and 15.1% respectively of the total health budget.[44]

A study of the utilization of health services in Saskatchewan found that between 1977–78 and 1985–86, expenditures on physician services increased from $65.3 to $153 million, representing an increase of 152.9%.[45] A significant proportion of this increase can be attributed to fee adjustments. The Medical Care Insurance Fee Schedule increased by 94.7%. The average annual income for physicians has risen from $126,000 in 1982–83 to $148,600 in 1985–86.[46]

In addition to an increase in physician expenditures, there was also a 29.9% increase in the volume of services provided.[47] While this figure includes changes in population growth and an aging population, the most significant factor leading to an increase in physician expenditures is the number of services per person. In particular, the largest single increase in the volume of services can be attributed to an increase in diagnostic services which has more than doubled in the past 10 years. Much of this increase can be attributed to the introduction of new technology.

Expenditures on prescription drugs increased from $15.2 per person in 1977–78 to $58.69 per person in 1985–6, representing a 273.3% increase.[48] While part of this increase can be attributed to the availability of brand new products and an increase in price, the number of prescriptions per person has increased by 43.4%. Only a small proportion of the increase in the utilization of drugs can be attributed to the aging population. One of the most significant factors contributing to the escalating costs of prescription drugs was the tendency toward "no-sub" policy by physicians. Doctors were less willing to substitute lower-priced generic drugs for more expensive brand-name drugs. This added about $8 million to expenditures on prescription drugs.

Finally, hospital expenditures have increased from $412 million in 1982–3 to $527 million in 1987–8, representing an increase of 28%.[49] The increase in hospital expenditures can be attributed primarily to a shift in utilization of hospital services from rural to urban areas. Rural residents go to base or regional hospitals for most diagnostic and therapeutic procedures and all surgical procedures.[50]

One of the major causes of the current crisis in hospital care can be attributed to the Tories' policy of funding capital projects at the expense of operating costs. Table 9.1 presents the annual increase/decrease of hospital operating and capital costs. The annual increase for operating costs has been approximately 5% whereas the annual increase for capital costs has been approximately 37%. Overall, capital costs as a percentage of total payments to hospitals have increased from 6.2% in 1981–2 to 14.4% in 1987–8.[51]

A similar trend of favouring capital projects over direct services can be found in the provision of long-term beds in special care homes. In 1984, the government announced a five-year, $25 million special care home construction program under which 1,000 new special care beds would be built.[52] In 1984 there were 8,634 beds and by 1988, there were 9,437 beds, representing 803 new beds. On average, $5.5 million was spent annually in construction and renovation costs for special care facilities.

The Tories maintained that new extended-care beds were needed because when the NDP was in power, a moratorium had been placed on the construction of special care beds. The rationale behind the NDP strategy was not to ignore the needs of seniors as the Tories claimed. The NDP government was implementing a home care program which would keep seniors (and other groups with special needs) in their homes and out of institutions. Despite the fact that home care is a cost-effective preventative program, the Tories have not actively promoted it. In the first term of office, the Tories provided increases to the budget of the home care program but the level of funding was not commensurate with the demand. As a result, the government was forced to give $700,000 in emergency funds to the home care program in 1986. With the introduction of the cutbacks in the 1986–7 budget, the budget of home care was reduced by 0.14%.

The major sources of health care expenditures are physician services and hospital costs. Despite this, it was the low-cost community services that were cut back. Much of the increase in health care expenditures can be attributed to physician-induced demand. Physicians are the gatekeepers to the health care system – they order the tests, admit patients to hospital, perform surgery, and prescribe medication. Yet it is evident that the

191

government is unwilling to make substantive changes in the payment mechanism for physicians.

Although hospital expenditures have not risen at the same rate as physician services, funds within the health care sector have been reallocated toward capital projects. This strategy has led to a gross discrepancy between capital and operating expenditures. The result is gleaming white hospitals but no nurses to take care of patients.

THE EFFECTS OF THE TORY SPENDING PRIORITIES

The Tories' health care policy was riddled with contradictions. On the one hand, the Tories had engaged in a massive building program. On the other hand, hospitals were forced to cut programs and close beds in the summer, in order to contain their operating costs. The effect of these policies reverberated throughout the health care system. Every interest group in the health care system has been affected by the Tories' mismanagement of the health care sector.

The Problem of Surgical Waiting Lists

Although the government introduced supplemental funding to reduce surgical waiting lists in Saskatoon just before the 1986 election, this did not solve the problem. In part, the lengthy surgical waiting lists can be attributed to the centralization of medical services, technology, and staff in Saskatoon and Regina. As a result, rural residents are forced to come to Saskatoon and Regina for medical services, taxing already limited resources in the cities.

But the problem of long waiting lists was exacerbated when hospital operating budgets were frozen for two years in July 1987. As a result, hospitals were forced to streamline their budgets. Since the hospitals were reluctant to cut staff, they sought to reduce costs by not replacing staff who went on holidays, imposing a hiring freeze, reducing educational and travel funds, and encouraging staff to take unpaid leave. The most effective method to reduce costs was to shut down beds in the summer.[53] The total number of beds shut down in the summer of 1987 was 309 beds for the three acute care hospitals in Saskatoon and 102 beds for the three Regina hospitals. The Victoria Union and the Holy Family hospitals in Prince Albert closed their operating rooms for six weeks.[54] The consequences of the bed closures were dramatic. By September there were 11,403 people on waiting lists in Saskatoon and 2,649 in Regina.

The government's response to the problem of growing waiting lists was to downplay their significance. Health Minister George McLeod suggested that the long waits were only affecting nonemergency patients who were waiting to see specialists.[55] He further claimed that the waiting lists in Regina "were not a serious problem." However, some physicians challenged McLeod's claims and indicated that in fact, many of the cases did require urgent treatment. For example, one woman was diagnosed with a cancerous growth on her kidney but was forced to wait five weeks for surgery.[56] In response to the negative publicity generated by the waiting lists, Premier Devine announced in October 1987 that additional funds for overtime would be provided to Saskatoon hospitals so that 2,000 additional operations could be performed.[57] The additional funding has led to a significant reduction in surgical waiting lists. For example, City Hospital reported in November 1989 that its surgical waiting list had been cut by 27% in the preceding 18 months.[58]

The Impact on Hospital Workers
The combination of cutbacks, misallocation of funds and centralization of services has had a major impact on hospital workers. One of the greatest concerns of health care workers is chronic understaffing leading to increased workloads for individual workers. The care of patients is labour-intensive and has become increasingly complex with the introduction of new, sophisticated technologies.

The most revealing and perhaps most disturbing trend in patterns of hospital employment is the increasing reliance on part-time work. Although the total number of positions in Saskatchewan general hospitals has increased from 10,682 in 1976–77 to 13,138 in 1987–8 representing a 23% increase,[59] these figures obscure the dramatic shift to part-time work. Table 9.2 indicates that part-time workers have increased from 20.4% of all hospital workers in general public hospitals in 1976–77 to 38.7% in 1984–5. This trend is evident for all major groups working within the hospital.

In part, this reliance on casual labour represents the hospital's attempts to balance its budget since it does not have to pay the same benefits to a part-time worker as to a full-time employee. This shift to part-time work also represents workers' response to stressful working conditions–a conclusion which is reinforced by the high turnover rates in the hospital sector, particularly in the nursing profession.

The shift toward part-time work has led to widespread concern about the quality of care in hospitals because part-time workers are unable to provide continuity of care. The fear is that patients will receive fragmented care from a variety of people even within one shift. Under these conditions, it is difficult to monitor the progress of a patient and more important, assess early warning signs.

The increasing workload and the accompanying high levels of stress have not been offset by improved wages. In the negotiation of contracts, there has not been a year since the Tories came to power in which the wage increase has approached the cost of living. [60] The real purchasing power of hospital workers has declined. The only new benefit negotiated by the Canadian Union of Public Employees, Saskatchewan Union of Nurses, and the Service Employees International Union since 1982 was a provincial dental plan available to all public service employees. It provides minimum assistance for dental services.

The situation in the hospital sector was critical and it was only a matter of time before it reached a crisis point. In October 1988, the Saskatchewan Union of Nurses staged a province-wide strike. The three major issues were wages, job security, and the nurses' right to speak out about patient care. The Saskatchewan Union of Nurses (SUN) wanted nursing review committees to be established which would make recommendations on patient care. Most important, nurses wanted the right to make hospital issues public. After a seven-day strike and overwhelming public support, SUN and the SHA reached a settlement which included a quality review committee. In response to the nurses' concerns about understaffing, the Tory government created 370 new nursing positions in its 1989 budget. [61]

Although this strike was resolved, there have been other signs of discontent in the health care sector. Immediately following the nurses' strike, the hospitals faced the possibility of another strike by 4,500 non-nursing hospital employees. [62] In November, 31 employees of Integ Management and Supply Services Ltd. went on strike. [63] The central issue was contracting out of services. Also in 1988, nursing supervisors in regional health offices questioned the advisability of an administrative reorganization leading to the reduction of nursing supervisors. [64] As a result of the cutbacks, there will be six regional nursing supervisors to administer 10 regions. The nursing supervisors argued that the reduction of their numbers combined with other cutbacks could threaten the quality of care since nursing standards would not be properly monitored.

The prognosis for the future of Saskatchewan hospitals is bleak.

Although the government has provided additional funding to hospitals, the practice of funding capital projects at the expense of operating costs led to a major crisis in the hospital sector most graphically illustrated by long surgical waiting lists, bed closures, and unrest among hospital workers. These tensions culminated in a province-wide strike by the majority of nurses working in Saskatchewan. The burden of these decisions has been shouldered mostly by patients and workers within the hospital but other groups, most notably physicians, have not escaped the attention of the Tory government.

The Relationship between Physicians and the Government

Although physicians occupy a privileged position within the health care system, there are signs that the Devine government is willing to challenge the ideological dominance of physicians within the health care system and where it hurts most–in the pocketbook.

The first challenge was the abolition of the Medical Care Insurance Commission (MCIC) in 1987. As part of its attempt to streamline health care by saving on administrative costs, MCIC, a public commission, was absorbed into the Department of Health.[65] There was little reaction to the elimination of MCIC by the SMA despite the fact that the commission was created after the 1962 doctors' strike to quell doctors' fears that "state medicine" would not infringe upon physicians' independence. As Dale Eisler perceptively commented, "the years have managed to soothe those concerns" particularly since medicare has provided physicians with unprecedented economic security. "The demise of MCIC represents a major step in a process that has slowly, but steadily drawn doctors into the system of universal, publicly funded health care."[66] The abolition of MCIC represented a symbolic challenge to physician control because the government did not consult with the doctors on a major policy matter.

If the elimination of MCIC was a symbolic challenge to physician control of the health care system, the unilateral introduction of a fee cap was a direct assault on physicians' pocketbooks. In November 1987 the government imposed a $189-million cap on payments to doctors.[67] Doctors would have to pay back the government anything above the fee cap or work for free. The government's decision was upheld by the Medical Compensation Review Board but was subsequently overturned by the Saskatoon Court of Queen's Bench. The government appealed this ruling but it was upheld by the Saskatchewan Court of Appeal.

Although the doctors won that round, the lack of consultation on health policy indicates that the relationship between doctors and the government is changing. Physicians no longer determine what happens in the health care system but are forced to negotiate not only the fee structure but all other policy areas with the government.

The Inequities in Health Status

Throughout this chapter, little has been said about the relationship between health status and the provision of health care. This is not an oversight. The dominant philosophy of the health care system, held by most physicians, health care administrators, and government bureaucrats, is that more health care leads to better health. Thus the majority of health care funding is directed toward hospitals, drugs, physician fees, and new technologies. But this approach is contraindicated by mounting evidence linking health and socioeconomic status. Studies conducted in Canada and elsewhere have consistently shown that those with the lowest income have the poorest health. [68]

Perhaps the most vivid demonstration of the relationship between poverty and ill-health is the health status of Natives in Saskatchewan. Registered Indians experience high rates of unemployment ranging up to 90% on some reserves and 70% in the urban areas. On average, the life expectancy of registered Indians [69] (both male and female) is 10 years below the life expectancy of the Canadian population. [70] (The life expectancy of registered Indian females was 69 years compared to 79 years for all Canadian females in 1981. The life expectancy of registered Indian males was 62 years compared to 71.8 years for all Canadian males in 1981.) The infant mortality rate was 1.5 times greater than for the general Canadian population. Fifteen of every 1,000 Indian babies die in their first year compared to 10 per 1,000 live births for the total Canadian population. Registered Indians have higher rates of accidents, suicides, and death from infectious, parasitic, and respiratory diseases. All of these causes of death are strongly associated with poverty; most of them are preventable.

The continuing disparity in health status between registered Indians and the general Canadian population leads to serious questions concerning the allocation of resources in the health care sector. More hospitals and physician services will not solve the problems of poor housing, lack of sanitation, poor nutrition, and unemployment.

The Devine government has failed to address these issues, and its policies have led to "the pauperization of the already poor" (Riches and

Manning, in this volume). In the past eight years, Saskatchewan has experienced rising unemployment and the mass exodus of young people from Saskatchewan to other provinces in search of jobs. At the same time, the real basic allowance for individuals and families on social assistance has dramatically declined. This has led to a growing reliance on food banks to supplement the food budget of the needy—of whom the largest single beneficiary group is children.

WHAT HAS THE GOVERNMENT'S RESPONSE BEEN TO THESE PROBLEMS?

The Tory government cannot afford to ignore health care, especially since elections have been won and lost over health care issues. The Tories are painfully aware of this fact as their second term of office rapidly comes to an end.

But in an attempt to improve its popularity, the government introduced a fat budget for health care in 1989.[71] The Tory government injected a 10.8% increase or $130 million into the health care system, raising total health care expenditures to a record $1.37 billion. (It should also be noted that $22 million more than budgeted was spent in 1988.)[72] The money was targeted for 370 new nursing positions, hospital renovations, increased surgical capacities, a breast cancer screening project, and a program to fight drug and alcohol abuse. In addition to these attempts to provide adequate funding, Minister of Health Grant McLeod rejected Consensus Saskatchewan's recommendation to reintroduce user fees for hospital services. This recommendation would not only be a violation of the Canada Health Act but it would also be politically unpalatable.

But despite these positive steps, the Conservatives have been unsuccessful in distancing themselves from health issues since the cutbacks in 1987. In 1987, a public furore was created when the Schwartz report on rural hospitals was released.[73] In his report, Schwartz recommended the establishment of a "Certification of Need" program to determine the need, location, and scope of service for hospitals, special care homes, ambulance services, and home care services throughout the province.[74] Many critics interpreted this recommendation as the end of many rural hospitals. As a result of the public controversy, the report's recommendations were not implemented.

In June 1988, Premier Grant Devine and Health Minister George McLeod kicked off a $2-million "Everyone Wins" health promotion and advertising campaign.[75] Although it was released with much fanfare, the campaign quickly became embroiled in a controversy when it was revealed that between $500,000 and $600,000 was being spent on advertising in the first year. Critics maintained that the funds could be effectively used in the provision of direct services.

In addition to the physicians and nurses, the government also managed to antagonize other professional groups in the province. In 1987, the government considered imposing a limit on the number of visits to a chiropractor.[76] In response, the chiropractors launched "a fight back" campaign; the government was forced to back down from its decision. In 1988, the Professional Association of Interns and Residents of Saskatchewan, which had gone on strike three years earlier, wrote letters to prospective interns across the country warning them about the heavy work loads and low wages. The association advised students to "consider the decision carefully" before accepting positions at Saskatchewan hospitals.[77]

The dental cutbacks made in 1986 returned to haunt the government. In June 1988, 45 dental therapists sat in the public gallery of the legislature and openly criticized Premier Devine while he gave reasons for the end of the program. At the time, the dental plan's annual reports indicated that the government saved only $500,000 through the privatization of the dental plan compared to the predicted $5.5 million;[78] enrolment of eligible children receiving the service had declined by 6%; and, only 50 of 111 dental therapists had found jobs.[79] In 1989, Willard Lutz, the auditor-general, found no record of the revenue generated from the sale of the dental equipment in the consolidated fund.[80] A month later, the *Leader Post* reported that the government had sold only one-third of the dental equipment, amounting to $700,000, and the leftover dental equipment had been scrapped.[81]

Finally, in March 1990 a civil jury found that the College of Dental Surgeons interfered in the employment contract between the government and the dental workers. On the same day that the government fired 294 dental therapists, it signed a memorandum of agreement with the College of Dentistry allowing dentists to provide dental services for school children. Two dental workers were awarded $10,000 each and a third was awarded $3,500. The government which fired the dental therapists "escaped unscathed"; the government's lawyer successfully argued that this issue was a labour grievance.[82]

When a government has a credibility problem, the usual Canadian strategy is to appoint a royal commission in order to deflect public opinion. The government opted for a task force which does not have the subpoena powers of a royal commission. The Task Force on the Future Directions in Health Care was announced in the March 1988 throne speech, and Robert Murray was appointed chairperson of the seven-member committee. The committee conducted public hearings around the province.

The report, which was released on 1 May 1990,[83] recommended the replacement of approximately 434 health care boards and agencies with 15 health services divisions. Each division would be run by elected officials from the local area and would be responsible for all aspects of health care. In addition, the report recommended the expansion of community services, particularly in the areas of mental health and home care. It also suggested new methods of payment for physicians and expansion of nurses' responsibilities.

At the time of writing, none of the report's major recommendations have been implemented, with the exception of the consolidation of hospital services in Saskatoon. This issue has been the subject of numerous studies over the years and all three hospitals have supported, in principle, the concept of rationalization, but no changes have taken place. In February 1989, George McLeod, minister of health, proposed the concept of "Centres of Excellence" resulting in the concentration of specialities at specific hospitals. However, one-third of the general practitioners and specialists at City Hospital publicly opposed the plan, and negotiations between the government, the hospitals, and the College of Medicine broke down.[84] The problem was referred to the Saskatchewan Commission of Directions in Health Care which commissioned consultants from out-of-province to study the issue further.

In July 1990, the study panel consisting of Dr. John Atkinson, Ralph Coombs, and John MacKay presented to the commission its final report (hereafter known as the Atkinson Report). Its main recommendations were: that City Hospital should be a centre for maternal and child care; St. Paul's should specialize in geriatrics and rehabilitation; Royal University Hospital should become a trauma team specializing in neurosurgery and oncology.[85]

The report indicated that there was no agreement among the hospitals about the implementation of this model. St. Paul's Hospital had rejected the plan because it was not willing to relinquish obstetrical care. St. Paul's had just completed a $53-million expansion including eight new birthing rooms and operating rooms for high-risk delivery.[86] Almer Schwartz, the president of City Hospital, did not completely agree with the panel's recommendations or the tone of the report. He was not convinced about the centre of excellence concept.[87] The only hospital that whole-heartedly supported the report was the Royal University Hospital.[88]

In addition to these objections, many of the city's general practitioners were opposed to the plan. They believed that family practitioners would be excluded from providing in-hospital, family-centred care. Louise Gagne, a spokesperson for the family practitioners, also pointed out that there was little information about the problems of amalgamation nor was there any discussion about the costs of the plan or the cost-effectiveness of amalgamation.[89] (These issues were not addressed in the Atkinson report.)

The panel believed that rationalization of hospital services was a pressing issue and demanded immediate actions or the quality of services would decline. Therefore, in order to resolve the differences among the Saskatoon hospitals, the panel recommended the establishment of a Saskatoon Hospital Services Authority "with full responsibility for determining priorities, defining services and allocating funding."[90]

The minister of health, George McLeod, promised quick action and indicated that the Atkinson report would form the basis of his proposals.[91] On 26 October 1990, McLeod announced the creation of the Saskatoon Health Services Authority, and Bill Bergen, former chief executive officer of the Federated Co-operative, was appointed the chair of the new board. But McLeod did not follow the recommendations of the Atkinson report regarding the rationalization of hospital services: St. Paul's retained its maternity wing and will specialize in kidney care and adult psychiatric services; City Hospital will specialize in geriatric medicine, rehabilitation, orthopedics, and opthalmalogy, and will provide acute-care services in general medicine and surgery; the Royal University Hospital will remain the city's emergency centre, will continue to provide services to northern and central Saskatchewan, and will expand its pediatric and maternity services. Doctors with privileges at one hospital will retain the same privileges at other hospitals.[92]

All of the hospitals have accepted McLeod's proposal, but its final configuration is the result of a complex process of negotiation and compromise. The most contentious issue was the location of the maternal-child care centre. St. Paul's was adamant that it would retain its obstetrical unit, but responsibility for maternal/reproductive care could not lie solely with St. Paul's since the board was opposed to abortions, tubal ligations, and birth control. Hence, these services have expanded in the Royal University Hospital.

Many of the issues facing Saskatoon hospitals have been attributed to the "turf wars." The problems of coordination and allocation of funds are assumed to be the result of petty rivalries and jealousies among the stakeholders. Yet this assumption remains largely unexamined. The delivery of hospital services needs to be placed in a much broader context. The most important question concerns responsibility for the allocation of health care dollars. As pointed out earlier in this chapter, the Conservative government has granted over $150 million in hospital construction costs to St. Paul's and City hospitals over the past five years. At the same time, operating expenditures have not kept pace with need, resulting in surgical waiting lists and staffing and equipment shortages. Thus, problems in the delivery of hospitals services are not simply due to interhospital rivalry but to inadequate planning and management of public funds by all stakeholders, including the government, which controls the purse-strings.

A further, more in-depth examination of "interhospital rivalry" reveals that intraprofessional rivalries also have played a significant role in shaping negotiations. The "town versus gown" debate centres on competing interests between teachers-researchers and practitioners. The trend toward specialization and centres of excellence is strongly supported by the Royal University Hospital, which has close ties with the University of Saskatchewan College of Medicine. It is also supported by the College of Medicine, particularly since some believe that the college is in danger of losing its accreditation.[93] In contrast, City and St. Paul's hospitals and the family practitioners support the provision of general services, which emphasizes family-centred, community-based care. This tension is inevitable but rarely acknowledged publicly.[94]

CONCLUSION

In the first term of office, the Tories engaged in a massive building campaign leading to a gross distortion between capital and operating costs. The most visible effects of this policy were the alarming rise in surgical waiting lists, the understaffing of hospitals, and equipment shortages.

After reelection in 1986, the Conservative government unveiled major changes in the delivery of health services to an unsuspecting public. The school dental program was cut, a deductible for prescription drugs was introduced, and substantial cuts were made to mental health and community services programs.

The effects of the cutbacks have been devastating: services have been reduced, the workloads of health care workers have increased, morale has plummeted. Most significantly, the economic and social costs have been shouldered disproportionately by the poor, women, children, Native people, the elderly, the sick, and the mentally ill. Devine's Conservatives have not only failed to address inequities in health status but the cutbacks have perpetuated systematic inequality among disadvantaged groups.

POST-SECONDARY TRAUMA: HIGHER EDUCATION IN SASKATCHEWAN, 1982–89

by Brett Fairbairn

The 1980s were a decade of turmoil for post-secondary education in Saskatchewan. Under the Conservative governments elected in 1982 and 1986, the province's technical institutes were built up, cut down, and finally amalgamated to form a new Saskatchewan Institute of Applied Science and Technology (SIAST). The province's community colleges ceased to exist: they were amalgamated into other institutions or reorganized into new kinds of entities. Private vocational schools flourished as public institutions choked on swollen enrolments and restricted admissions. Only the universities were spared from these sweeping rearrangements, perhaps because their arm's-length governance structure prevented direct government intervention. Instead, they saw their funding go from bad to worse as successive ministers exhorted them to change. The University of Regina, awash in red ink, tried to sell its library. The University of Saskatchewan balanced its books for a while, but its administrative style in doing so helped rouse professors to the first faculty strike in the province's history. There was labour unrest in both the technical institutes and universities, and anxiety among students as they faced rising tuition fees, declining grants, fewer jobs, and tighter and tighter quota restrictions.

It was not a peaceful or prosperous eight years.

And yet those in the post-secondary sector did not fare as badly as did single employable people on welfare or minimum-wage workers. This was because there was a certain positive commitment to education in the ideology of the Conservative government that set out in 1982 to transform Saskatchewan society. Some developments that emerged almost unnoticed by the public may be with us for a long time, such as the growth of distance education, the development of satellite and fibre-optic communications, and the delivery of university and technical courses by regional colleges. Other lasting legacies may be the built-up resentment of teaching staff who see themselves as underpaid and their institutions as overburdened, and of students and aspiring students who see themselves denied access to meaningful careers and rewarding lives.

There are two actors hidden behind the scenes in this story. One is Saskatchewan's pre-1982 NDP administration, which began exercising fiscal restraint with respect to higher education in the mid-1970s. Because of this, the post-secondary system entered the era of recession and Conservative rule under-financed and thinly stretched. As late as 1985 one Conservative supporter could still blast "the previous administration's low priority of post-secondary educational financing . . . The records show clearly that the universities' operating portion of provincial expenditure fell from 7.28 per cent in 1969 to 4.6 per cent in 1982. The falling trend stopped." [1] This is no longer true.

The second and much more important hidden actor is the federal government. With education being a provincial responsibility, Canadians frequently forget that Ottawa plays a $7-billion role in financing education. Federal cuts to Established Programs Financing (EPF), which funds health care and post-secondary education, helped trigger provincial restraint in the 1970s. In 1983, the Liberal government in Ottawa applied its "six and five" restraint program to the post-secondary education component of EPF. With Brian Mulroney came more of the same. A 1986 law limited the rate of growth on federal transfer payments over five years to save $6 billion. In Finance Minister Michael Wilson's 1989 budget, Ottawa shaved a further 1% off EPF payments. This restraint came in part because successive federal governments have felt that they do not get credit for their role in education, and that provinces are not shouldering their share of the load.

As a political issue, post-secondary education is part sacred cow and part sacrificial lamb. No party will campaign *against* higher education; and yet it is also rare for any party to feature it as an issue of high priority. Not since 1971 has higher education surfaced as a significant province-wide issue in an election campaign. As a result, post-secondary education is not highly politicized (unlike health care, for example). Once in power, parties elected with vague post-secondary policies have to figure out what to do with a complex and expensive system. Pragmatism generally prevails, but ideology tends to seep in to fill the policy vacuum. The Devine governments follow this pattern, but with more ideology seeping in than had been the case before.

A CONSERVATIVE PHILOSOPHY OF EDUCATION

When Conservatives got excited about higher education in the 1980s, they were usually talking about one of two themes: technology or trade. Both are part of the stated Conservative goals of making Saskatchewan more flexible and responsive to world markets, more aggressive in its trading, and more high-tech and modern in its adaptation to the emerging global economy. In setting these goals, the Conservatives followed business leaders and think tanks. A 1989 study by the consulting firm Clarkson Gordon pointed to "educational inadequacy" in North America, citing statistics showing that the Japanese are ahead in the "literacy race." The report called for "increased corporate participation" to shore up and improve the educational system since "education and training are key issues in North America's ability to compete globally." [2]

Market-oriented Conservatives attach importance to education, but couple this with a suspicious and critical attitude toward established educational institutions.

One of the early actions of Devine's Conservatives in January 1983 was to endorse all the recommendations of a government task force on high technology. According to press reports, Education Minister Colin Maxwell said the government would "shape post-secondary education so it supports high-technology industry." [3] Prior to the 1983 budget, the government reorganized the old Department of Continuing Education into a Department of Advanced Education and Manpower. The purpose of the change was to tie educational expenditures more closely to the short-term needs of the economy. Maxwell boasted in 1983 that his was "the only growth department within government." [4]

On the international playing field, the score is sometimes measured by literacy rates. Literacy became one of the priorities of the government. In 1983, the new department received a report on adult basic education (ABE) which argued for a comprehensive adult education system. It touted distance education, computer-assisted learning, and other applications of technology as means to deliver basic education to all citizens. ABE became a major thrust of the community colleges as the Department of Social Services selected welfare recipients to take courses. In 1987, a literacy council was appointed to run ads and sponsor programs promoting literacy. Its chairperson explained, "if we expect our economy to be responsive, we have to have a labour force that can be responsive." [5] The Conservatives managed to involve both high technology and corporate participation in their literacy drive. In 1988, Grant Devine and IBM Canada announced that they would jointly fund a three-year, $2.5-million, computer-based literacy-teaching system. This was spurred by millions of dollars in *federal* government funding.

In similar high-tech vein, Maxwell hinted in 1983 that mathematics and science would be made compulsory for high school students, saying 15 year olds are too young to decide for themselves what subjects they should take. The government did its best to promote science in the school curriculum, and opened a science museum in Regina. In doing so, Maxwell denied disrespect for the arts. "There's nothing wrong with getting a B.A. or a B.Ed. Students just have to realize there won't necessarily be a job waiting for them at the end of it." [6]

For adults, the mechanism to provide job-oriented, high-tech education was to be the technical institutes.

Technical Institutes: The Great Expansion

In the summer of 1983, the government announced a $120-million program for the following four years. Its goal was to expand student positions in technical training by 60% from 5,500 places to 8,600. "There can be no permanent long-term economic recovery unless we do something to increase the number of technically skilled people," said Minister Gordon Currie. [7] At the fall P.C. convention, Colin Maxwell noted that Saskatchewan was ninth among the provinces in vocational spending, but that the government hoped to yank it up to third place in Canada in just four years.

The government quickly began to implement its expansion plan. A major expansion was announced at Wascana Institute in Regina in 1983. In 1984 an advanced technical training centre was announced for Kelsey Institute in Saskatoon. It was funded by $1.6 million in provincial funds plus $2 million from the federal government. The centre, chaired by SED Systems president Alex Curran, was intended to service 55 high-technology companies in Saskatoon. A new technical institute was announced for Prince Albert, making that city the fourth in the province to be home to a major educational establishment. The $35-million construction project started in 1984.

This should not be taken to mean that the techs suffered no cutbacks in those years. There was a redistribution of resources to suit the high-tech philosophy of the government. In 1984, for example, although the budget of Kelsey Institute in Saskatoon increased because of the addition of a new program in computers, 13 teaching positions spread across several different programs were cut. [8]

The Prince Albert Institute eventually opened in the fall of 1986 as the Northern Institute of Technology (NIT). It was intended as a state-of-the-art, high-tech learning centre using a competency learning system that replaced lectures with self-study and computerized testing. Principal Bob Gervais explained, "the learner starts on the program and contracts with us on the number of competencies he or she wants to achieve per week. Their progress is monitored by a computer-managed learning system . . . Learners must maintain that contract performance or else they will be called back by a training adviser to discover why." [9] The system has advantages such as permitting learners to enter and exit constantly to suit their own home and work schedules rather than being tied to a standard academic year. In political terms, it appeals to the high-tech mentality.

The NIT deal exemplifies another new factor in educational politics: education as economic development. The institute was no sooner opened than local MLA Paul Meagher said it had more significance for the city than the Weyerhaeuser deal. "It's going to change the whole image of Prince Albert . . . we've had forestry, we've had a pulp mill . . . but this is a fundamental change in what Prince Albert is as a city." Meagher's claims were backed by an NIT study which claimed the institute would provide $10.5 million in spin-off benefits to the city, and benefit virtually every resident. Mayor Dick Spencer called the study's conclusions "amazing." [10] The institute was opened, coincidentally, shortly before the 1986 election campaign. "Ultimately, a college for Prince Albert is our commitment," said local MLAs Meagher and Sid Dutchak during the campaign, trying to make education the cornerstone of the P.C. platform in the city. [11]

In presenting an educational institution in the guise of local development, as a prize the city had somehow won, the Conservatives opened a Pandora's box. In Melfort a committee of civic and hospital board officials, school trustees, and businessmen began campaigning for a junior university college in their city. Once any community gets an educational institution as a boost to its economy, why not all the others? By letting local boosterism instead of educational policy serve as the justification for spending, Tory politicians run the risk of making it into a commodity that towns and cities bid for.

In 1985 technical school enrolment in Saskatchewan reached an all-time high. Some 26,467 students enroled as full- or part-time in the province's three established institutions. This represented an increase in student numbers of almost one-third since 1982, and the new NIT was still to come on-stream. In a survey of graduates, students rated the technical institutes highly, with 14% saying they were excellent, and 42% very good. Only 3% called them poor or very poor. Six months after graduation 78% of respondents had jobs with 80% of these training-related.[12] Demand for positions was high, with large waiting lists for many courses. But 1986 was an election year, and within a few months of voting day, the great technical expansion had run its course.

In February 1987, the new minister, Lorne Hepworth, held the first of 17 meetings with business leaders and invited guests to discuss new directions for post-secondary education. The minister's press release stated, "government is coming to the view that some changes are required in the province's adult education system. We face some tremendous challenges as enrolments sky-rocket."[13] In April Deputy Minister Laurie McFarlane stated that the "major educational initiatives to help Saskatchewan meet the technological revolution will be announced within weeks." The government was about to "embark on a vast new enterprise to help Canada and Saskatchewan meet the post-industrial challenge."[14]

THE YEAR OF THE CUTS: 1987

Soon after the 1986 election, the Saskatchewan public learned that Finance Minister Gary Lane had underreported the magnitude of the government's deficit. In the spring 1987 budget, the axe fell on a wide range of programs, including education. To wield the axe in education, Grant Devine's government chose a new minister of advanced education and manpower, Lorne Hepworth. Advanced education and the Department of Education (responsible for Kindergarten to Grade 12) were soon merged into a single department.

In May 1987 Hepworth announced the layoffs of 142 instructors and 74 nonteaching staff in technical institutes. The explanation was that the government was amalgamating and consolidating the institutes.

The cuts fell heavily on the smallest of the three older institutes. Students at the Saskatchewan Technical Institute in Moose Jaw "reeled with shock, confusion, and fear" as 42 instructors lost their jobs. Another 32 elected to take early retirement. Students and staff called the day of the announcement "Black Tuesday." Principal Andy Nicol, who just one month before had said, "it's going to be tight . . . we'll try to maintain service and avoid layoffs," was fired along with his staff.[15]

At Kelsey Institute in Saskatoon, 67 full-time permanent instructors and 7 labour-services workers were given layoff notices. Six programs were cut, including barbering/hairstyling, cabinet making/millwork, cosmetology, dental assistant, nursing assistant, and office education. The programs had an enrolment of 247 students, and had a waiting list of 831. The choice of programs reflected the government's thrust: five of the six primarily trained female students for the service sector, and high technology programs escaped the axe. In addition, 12 other programs had staff and enrolment cuts. In total, 533 student positions at Kelsey were cut, and the 74 layoffs and 39 early retirements represented nearly one-third of Kelsey's staff. The outgoing president of the student association, Todd Benko, estimated that after the cuts four out of every five applicants to Kelsey would be rejected for lack of space. Two days after the cuts were announced, 24 new labour-services positions were created. The new positions had less job security and fewer benefits than the permanent positions that had been abolished. Most had a 185-day contract year compared to 200 days for the axed permanent positions.[16]

Right-wing columnists like Nancy Russell, business editor of the Saskatoon *Star Phoenix*, crowed with delight. "Saskatchewan's small business sector should be privately smiling to itself this week," wrote Russell. She said that cuts were "long overdue . . . The drain on the provincial treasury has been growing in leaps and bounds." Russell's comments may well indicate what kind of advice Hepworth received in his closed meetings with business leaders and invited guests. "The program and staff cuts are bound to translate into a further increase in the number of private vocational schools in the province,"[17] said Russell with satisfaction.

The technical institute cuts did indeed coincide with an increase in the number of private vocational schools. Until early 1987, the number of private schools in the province had been stable at 28. In three months leading up to and including "Black Tuesday," 12 new ones applied for licenses, including two in the three days following the announcement of the technical institute cuts. Within weeks of the cuts at Kelsey, private vocational schools in Saskatoon announced plans to offer the six programs eliminated by the public institution. Robertson Career College expressed an interest in the dental assistant program (and intended to charge students $4,000 compared to $471 for the old Kelsey course); Saskatoon Business College announced it expected more students; and Marvel Beauty School eyed the barbering/hairstyling and cosmetology courses. Marvel president

Dave MacNeil declared that "there is no need for government to get involved because we can do it better and cheaper in the long run, and at no cost to the taxpayer." [18] Cheaper to everyone except unemployed students desperate for jobs who would be paying thousands for their privatized courses.

In March 1989, Hepworth assured Kelsey students and staff that post-secondary education would not be privatized. In the same month he appointed a vocational school advisory committee stacked with school operators and business representatives. By then, there were 5,000 students enroled in 48 private vocational schools, up from 1,755 in 18 schools in 1983.

Private colleges come in many varieties; many are old and respected; many do things that public institutions will not or cannot do. The proliferation of private schools under the Tories, however, opened the doors to "edubusiness," in which the interests of students often seem to be secondary to monetary gain. Students at Bridge City College in Saskatoon found this out the hard way.

Bridge City hit the headlines in 1989 when nine employees met a *Star Phoenix* reporter to described alleged abuses. The chief abuse was the admission of many students who had no hope of passing courses or getting jobs. Three thousand dollars and more in tuition fees were being collected from each student, most of whom borrowed on government-sponsored student loans, while instructors were not being paid on time. Former instructor Carol Kirkland said, "one student couldn't even read or write. She lost all her money. The problem is [the school is] preying on a certain population that is most vulnerable"–transient, unemployed, and poorly-educated people. Other instructors criticized high cost and a poor curriculum, the lack of support staff, and broken-down facilities and poor equipment. One reported that a television and VCR had been repossessed in the middle of a class. A student who dropped his management course in disgust said simply, "the program kinda sucked . . . There was nothing practical." He was left with a $2,200 debt. [19]

Four hours after the story broke, most of those who met the reporter were out of jobs. School director Dorothy Prior stated, "they resigned on their own initiative." She proclaimed that "Our future is solid," and that the school did have some credentials. Lorne Sparling, the government's superintendent of vocational schools, added that "our role is to ensure a quality program is offered, and the consumer is protected," and assured the press that the department had been in constant contact with Bridge City. All requirements, said Sparling, had been satisfied. Just one day later he was admitting that the school was under investigation for its extremely high dropout rate and high student loans. Nearly $1 million in loans had been issued to the 205 students enroled in the college. Only 25 remained in class in June.[20] A report on Saskatoon's CBC Newsday on 27 September quoted anonymous students as saying most of their classmates had registered in order to get student loans, and that many then dropped out as soon as they received their money.

In the legislature, NDP advanced education critic Herman Rolfes noted the province appeared to have no regulations for private colleges except a requirement for a $5,000 bond. Rolfes cited instances in which Bridge City charged $2,160 for a 72-hour acting course, $3,000 for "speech communication for business professional practices," and $3,600 for a "care companion course" that involved learning how to read to people, drive their cars, help them dress, and push their wheelchairs.

The market for the new private schools had been created by a combination of ready student loans to students at the private schools, and cuts to the public institutions that offered higher quality courses at a fraction of the cost—but to only one prospective student in four.

AMALGAMATION AND LOSS OF AUTONOMY

The program cuts were accompanied by the merger of technical institutes and some community colleges to form the Saskatchewan Institution of Applied Science and Technology (SIAST). It was part of being responsive to the new technological economy, said the government. Not everyone agreed. Brendon Ballon, representing the student executive council of technical institutes in Saskatchewan, said, "I'm concerned that our views weren't really given any meaningful consideration."[21]

Opposition to the amalgamation was strongest in Prince Albert. A survey of Prince Albert community college and NIT students and staff, school boards, and the Chamber of Commerce, conducted by NDP MLA Myron Kowalsky, indicated that "over 93%" favoured autonomy and local control for technical institutes.[22] Three hundred people gathered to protest the merger of the Prince Albert Regional Community College into SIAST. The entire board of the community college threatened to resign over the issue, but Deputy Minister Laurie McFarlane assured the press that, "I'm confident, in the end, they will decide to participate." When they did resign en masse, Hepworth called it an "unfortunate glitch," and "a case of sour grapes." [23]

Chairperson Murdine McCreath of the community college said her board simply did not want to "rubber stamp something that's become so ludicrous." She said "there was just too much of a contrast between our conception of adult education and theirs. It's as if people don't have a need for anything other than work." Hepworth defended the amalgamation on the basis of his prior meetings in closed session with businesspeople ("there was consultation . . . I held plenty of meetings") and said the changes were necessary "if we're to position ourselves for the 21st century." [24]

With the exception of Prince Albert, opposition to the technical institute amalgamation was limited, and the enabling legislation was proclaimed on 1 January 1988. The business manager of the Kelsey student association observed, "we are not as vocal in our complaints as the universities" because students come only for short courses, and staff fear reprisals because they are public servants. [25]

The staff had good reason to be nervous. When SIAST was created, the legislation decertified all of the unions at the technical institutes and the affected community colleges. The new management claimed that all previous contracts were void. The response of staff and faculty was not outspoken, but it was firm. In March 1988 the Saskatchewan Government Employees Union (SGEU) re-won the right to represent the 600 nonacademic staff in SIAST. For the 1,100 academic staff, matters were more complicated. The more conservative-sounding "SIAST Faculty Assoc- iation," which SGEU complained was employer-dominated, had emerged and was attempting to organize the academic staff. Finally, in April 1988 the academic staff voted by about 540–522 to join the SGEU. This was a narrow but major victory for SGEU. In August 1988, SIAST board chairperson Merv Houghton promised that SIAST's "new and innovative approach" to education would extend to collective bargaining, and in November 1988 talks finally resumed. [26]

In the spring of 1989 talks broke down over the employer's refusal to recognize the former collective agreement, and over SIAST's insistence on hiring according to "job suitability"–on merit, not seniority, which union negotiator Gary Crawford complained "allows managers to make subjective decisions." [27] Management's approach was innovative but not legal. In the midst of the impasse, the Labour Relations Board handed down a ruling on two claims of unfair labour practices filed by SGEU in June 1988. The

Labour Relations Board found SIAST guilty of laying off senior instructors in Regina and hiring less qualified ones in their places, and that the agreements in place before the amalgamations were in effect until a new contract was signed. Second, SIAST was found guilty of failure to act on grievances of harassment, unjust termination, and improper application of seniority.[28]

Bargaining for the SIAST collective agreement was long and bitter. Rumours began to circulate that SIAST had already run up a $6 million deficit, and that special teams were preparing plans for cutbacks and layoffs. The SGEU members began rotating strikes in the fall of 1989. The government eventually responded by requesting that both sides enter mediation, and by hinting that if this did not solve the dispute, legislation would follow. When mediator Vince Ready began his work, a new education minister, Ray Meiklejohn, threw cold water on the process by stating that even if a wage increase was recommended, SIAST would not get any more money. However, in February 1990, over two years after SIAST was created, the first collective agreement was signed.

The pattern of labour unrest may be a more general one, for an even more dramatic example occurred when professors went on a full-scale strike at the University of Saskatchewan in the spring of 1988. That event was also conditioned by an educational policy that veered between "facing the 21st century" in idealistic moments, and promoting deficit-justified cutbacks at budget time.

A TALE OF TWO UNIVERSITIES

The Devine government's treatment of universities was much more straight-forward than that of technical institutes. The Conservatives simply restrained growth in grants and let inflation and mounting student numbers put greater and greater pressure on students, staff, classrooms, laboratories, and libraries. They did this not out of malice – they were frustrated by universities and suspicious of them, but never explicitly hostile. The reasons for the budget restraint were several. First, universities seemed less directly linked to the short-term performance of the economy and the productivity of business than were the technical institutes. Second, the size of the budget deficit required that cuts be made somewhere, and universities do not have the broadest and deepest support in society. Finally, Conservatives believed that education needed to be reformed, to be flexible, to be responsive, while the universities jealously guarded their independence and were so complex as to be not only difficult to change, but absolutely impenetrable and incomprehensible to the eye of the outsider. To a cabinet minister (perhaps of any party), money put into a university disappears into a complex and unseen mechanism whose products are often intangible.

The real story is not the monotonous tale of government cuts, but the ultimate effects of those cuts and the different responses of the two universities. The U of S is older, dating back virtually to the founding of the province. It is replete with an expensive array of prestigious professional colleges and is more conservative, more willing in its smugness to assume its reputation and its superiority. The U of R has been an independent university only since 1974. It is smaller, and struggles with some adverse economies of scale. It has less political and academic clout, and angles for advantageous programs and unfilled niches. It is more influenced by the social sciences and by the politics of the capital.

The two universities do not dislike each other, but are simply jealous of each other's existence. At the U of S one can still find those who do not think Regina should be a university, that instead it should be closed down with the money diverted to Saskatoon. In Regina one senses a feeling that the U of S gets too much, and that maybe it should spare one of those professional colleges or fine buildings to give to its grown-up offspring. In a 1986 interview, for example, U of R president Lloyd Barber asked for "some of the generosity the provincial government has recently shown the U of R's Saskatoon counterpart" with respect to capital grants. The city of Regina went so far as to form a committee (with Barber as a member) to examine "what appears on the surface to be an inequity" between the two universities in capital funding. The committee estimated that over 12 years, 1974–86, the U of S had received $139 million for buildings and the U of R only $14.5 million.[29]

In the 1980s, the administrations of the two universities offered contrasts in style. The U of S administration, led by Leo Kristjanson from 1980 to 1989, fought a war of quiet resistance to government cuts. The president would warn publicly that government budget decisions would cause problems. He would argue the value of education to society and the need for the government to invest in it. The administration would then balance the budget. The university had the advantage of a large institution that could spread cuts more evenly across a broad base. The battle for funding was fought not in the newspapers, but in confidential meetings where U of S administrators worked on successive ministers (and on their own government-appointed board members) to turn them into allies and thereby come out better in next year's budget. The university had the advantage of its size, history, and tradition. It could take the time to play the backroom game with the long term in mind.

U of R president Lloyd Barber did not mince words quite so often. He regularly denounced funding shortages. Unlike Kristjanson, he was willing to run a deficit when the law and the government frowned upon it.

The contrast between the two styles was striking. For example, in August 1984 the government announced an extra $900,000 in enrolment-related funding to supplement the 5% grant increase that spring. Barber said the U of R "will still be plagued with broken laboratory equipment, over-crowded classes and a shortage of full-time instructors." He demanded "a lot more money" and an end to the government practice of asking universities to "do more with less." Kristjanson refused to comment. Until meeting with his senior administration, he would not say whether there would be cuts. "There could be. We really won't know the magnitude of this until we've studied it." [30] In declining to say that his university was suffering from shortages and broken equipment, Kristjanson was following a long-standing U of S tendency to protect its reputation rather than publicize its problems. Similarly, in 1987, facing continuing restraint and inevitable cuts or shortfalls, he did protest, "it's going to very difficult," but he also commented, "I think all of us realize the government has some major financial problems. We may not be happy with (less money), but we can appreciate that we're all going to have to work on it." [31]

It is likely that of the two universities, Regina ended up the worse off. Of the two administrators, Kristjanson got the rougher ride.

REGINA'S DEFICIT: SELLING THE LIBRARY?

Already in July 1982, a Canadian Press story cited university cutbacks across Canada, resulting both from fiscal restraint and growing enrolments. At the U of R, vice-president Don Shaw explained the dilemma of universities, whose program commitments are largely inflexible: "there are courses where the demand exceeds what we can accommodate," and other courses which must be maintained, even where enrolment has declined, because "otherwise this just wouldn't be a university." [32] Both Saskatchewan universities found things to eliminate (the U of S cut its Institute of Northern Studies that year) but neither could find any rationale for eliminating major programs.

There was one cut that went mostly unlamented in the universities. The Tories abolished the Saskatchewan Universities Commission, which had done statistical analyses of the universities and acted as a go-between for the government. University leaders had complained the commission was a buffer that prevented them from influencing cabinet directly. Of course, if that interpretation was correct, universities should have been able to win better support after the commission's abolition in 1983.

In fact, in 1983 and 1984 there was some success. The universities received special supplemental grants in recognition of their record enrolments. "We're playing it year by year until the bulge [in enrolment] works itself out," said a department spokesperson who emphasized that these special grants would not become part of the base budgets.[33] The "bulge" theory was one of the most unfortunate misconceptions to which the government ever gave credence. As it became more and more clear that high enrolments would continue, the government became tighter and tighter with funds. In the fall of 1984, the government required universities to submit operating forecasts based on grant increases of only 2%, less than the rate of inflation, let alone the rate of enrolment increase.

In response to such warnings, the U of R presented the government with dramatic cost-cutting proposals including closing the Conservatory of Music (1,300 students, 45 teachers) and the Norman Mackenzie Art Gallery; cancelling the noncredit extension program (16,000 students, 500 instructors); ending intervarsity sports; and increasing tuition by 15%. This proposed list of cuts hit every public and community user of the university, and served to demonstrate to the government the political undesirability of further cuts. The government was to make the university pay for his political hardball.

By 1985 the U of R's accumulated deficit was growing at an increasing rate (according to the Universities Act, Saskatchewan universities are not supposed to run deficits). In 1984–85 the university's debt increased by $600,000 to $2.6 million, with a forecast of $700,000 in additional debt to be incurred in the following year. In a bid to slash the deficit and take dramatic action, the U of R cancelled one-half of its off-campus extension program in fall 1984, cutting 63 classes and $150,000. The community colleges, which advertised and delivered many of the courses, were not told until after the cuts were made.

Extension classes have strong support in the community and appeal to governments who want to have education available and visible to the wider off-campus population. About one-third of the cancelled classes were restored when the government came up with an extra $50,000. However, nothing significant was done for the university's ever-mounting financial crisis, or for the serious deterioration in the quality of education as enrolments surged further and further ahead of capacity.

By 1986, academic vice-president Reid Robinson cited a 50% increase in enrolment over the five years from 1979 to 1984. Only 15 full-time teaching positions were created during the same period. After so much increase, there was some expectation that a peak had been reached. University officials were startled, therefore, when fall 1986 brought a dramatic 12.5% increase. "The courses needed in order to graduate are pretty well packed," admitted Robinson. Students found they could not take required classes. "I tried to take English 100," said one student, Denise Ramsay, "but there wasn't room for me this semester." The English class is required for all degrees and for prejournalism, which she wanted to enter. Full parking spaces were a less serious problem than full classes, but became more than annoying for anyone trying to visit (or attend, or work at) either university. "If you don't get to school by 8:30 A.M.," said a student, "you can forget about finding a legal parking place."[34]

As with technical institutes, restraint got worse after the 1986 election. In response to a student demonstration early in 1987, new minister Lorne Hepworth said, "as a politician I would like nothing better than to say you can count on our government to keep on giving as in the past. But I would be less than honest if I said that. Our province faces severe economic challenges and controlling and reducing the deficit calls us to set priorities, cut waste and eliminate unnecessary spending at the top."[35] Hepworth told the protestors that the economic conditions created by a changed world economy required all sectors of society to work together.

There was worse to come. Among the things the government was willing to spend money on was management consultants' reports. The U of R, its deficit now $4.7 million, was given $100,000 by the government to hire the firm of Woods Gordon to report on nonacademic operations. At the same time, a task force was appointed to review academic programs. The Woods Gordon report contained a mix of comment both favourable and unfavourable to the university. Hepworth leaked the report to the press and heavily emphasized the negative aspects. He quoted the report as saying "the size of the administration is too large" and that "the credibility of the senior administrative organization of the university is questioned

217

by both internal and external parties." Hepworth claimed that a minister of education had to be "somewhat troubled" by this. [36]

Administration and students were outraged. The student president, Lyndon Surjik, told the press the government was "twisting statements made in the Woods Gordon report to its own advantage." The Regina *Leader Post* noted "the department seems to have gone to pains to emphasize the passages of the report reflecting poorly on the university administration." And Barber admitted that he had sought legal advice on whether Hepworth's statements were libelous. "There is a point," he is quoted as saying, "where half-truths become lies." [37] Hepworth's comments clearly portrayed the university deficit as the result of bad management. This was a softening up for what came next. In March 1987, rumours of a freeze in university grants began to circulate. Barber asked college deans to come up with "hypothetical exercises" of budget cuts ranging from 3% to 9%. The dean of Arts developed a scenario for the elimination of the sample survey and data unit, history, philosophy of science, and classics, and cuts in sociology and social studies. [38]

Whether the release of these projected cuts to essential core programs was a political ploy or not, intended to up the stakes and forestall any cutbacks at all, is hard to say. But if the public release of this information was intended to influence the government, it did not do so in any positive way.

Hepworth proceeded to meet with the U of R board. In his brief, he delivered an ultimatum that the university's accumulated deficit, now projected at $5.5 million, must be completely eliminated within four years. Hepworth dictated an annual schedule of the surpluses the university would be required to run from 1987 to 1991 in order to accomplish this feat. He announced, simultaneously, that university operating grants were indeed frozen for the next two years, and that universities should not plan on increases greater than the rate of inflation in 1989–90 or 1990–91. The minister conceded that the university had a right to academic freedom, but proceeded to offer his opinion that the "primary focus of the U of R should be . . . high-quality undergraduate programs in the high demand areas of administration, arts, science and education." It should do this "if need be at the expense of withdrawing from other program areas." He also forestalled any attempt by the university to make up revenue through tuition fees. The university, he said, should not ask students to "shoulder a disproportionate share of the burden." (Previous restraint had already made U of R tuition fees the highest of any western university.) He left no doubt that the university was to cut programs. Implicitly, he suggested that the targets were graduate studies, social work, the School of Human Justice, physical activity studies, and possibly engineering and journalism.

Playing off one university against the other, Hepworth noted that "a plan to erase the debt over four years isn't unrealistic," since the U of S remained in the black.[39]

Barber soon announced, in effect, that the university had capitulated to the government's ultimatum. The School of Human Justice would be eliminated; the faculty of social work would be sharply cut back by eliminating its Saskatoon and Prince Albert offices. These cuts were greeted by protests, rallies in all three of the affected cities, and by efforts to sway public opinion and rally networks of community groups. Mayor Dick Spencer of Prince Albert saw the cuts as a setback to the city's hopes of becoming a university centre. He had hoped, he told the press, that the two services spared from restraint would be health and education.[40] One social work student related the university cuts to the wider cuts in social services. Blair Wotherspoon said, "it's obvious human justice has been given to the government as a sacrificial lamb to appease the Tory agenda."[41] Tuition fees were increased a further 9.4%, on top of cumulative increases of 32.5% in the four years from 1982 to 1986.

The administration of the university also took criticism. "They're messengers of the Progressive Conservative government," said Wotherspoon. Barber protested, perhaps a little too loudly, "it's purely and simply a financial decision, that has nothing to do with any philosophical proposition. It is purely financially driven." After years of angling for advantage, of trying to force or bribe or extort more money from the government, the U of R ended up in the position of being blamed by the government for the university deficit, and blamed by public critics for its cutbacks. The truth of the matter was that the university, dependent on government funding, bankrupt and perhaps in violation of the law, was no longer capable of resistance. Barber was prostrate before government demands.

Meeting the government's schedule of surpluses proved difficult. An early retirement offer to convince professors to retire at 60, permitting the university to hire young professors at about half the cost, was taken by only six of 30 eligible professors in 1987. In April 1988 the head librarian announced that the library was taking donations of grain from Saskatchewan farmers to buy more books and periodicals. "In effect, we're knocking door-to-door in the rural community and asking for grain." The librarian said he got the idea from Brazil.[42] In September 1988 the university, its accumulated deficit growing further to nearly $6 million instead of shrinking, hired a private fund-raising consultant to design a campaign. Most spectacular, however, was Lloyd Barber's attempt in June 1988 to sell his university's library holdings and computer equipment to a private company in return for cold, hard cash.

The practice of selling libraries had been pioneered by a number of Ontario universities a few years earlier. The benefits to the university are obvious: cash, and the ability to continue making use of the assets. The purchasing corporation, because of the bizarre effects of the depreciation provisions in the income tax system, could actually save enough in taxes, by buying an asset like a university library that it did not actually need, to more than pay for buying the library in the first place. If this seems like a win-win situation – perhaps of somewhat dubious ethics, since it involves selling assets purchased by the public in order to avoid taxes being paid to the public – the federal government did not agree. Barber was just "two or three days away" from clinching the deal when Ottawa announced a moratorium on such sales.[43]

There were new initiatives at the U of R in the 1980s. Barber's administration looked for money in the opportunities of the moment. It announced expansion in trendy fields like computers, robotics, co-operative work-study programs, second languages and languages for trade, and even made a foray into committing the university to testing cold fusion. But then the $200,000 to finance work-study programs in 1985 was federal money. So was the $17 million out of which the language training centre, the campus's first new building since 1973, was developed in 1988.

QUOTA, TENSION, AND RESTRAINT

At the University of Saskatchewan, the effects of budget restraint developed differently. There the administration chose to live within its fiscal means, and to attempt to protest the funding levels without damaging the academic reputation of the university.

U of S president Leo Kristjanson avoided making public threats of large and visible program cuts. Instead he chose to cut clerical staff and to squeeze all programs instead of cutting some. "The university," he told the 1983 spring convocation, "chooses to give priority to retention of instructional staff" on the grounds that "basic goals of a university . . . the values of a liberal education as distinguished from a technical education" dictated that academic faculty be protected while secretarial and clerical workers, part-time and student assistants, were cut.[44]

Professors have tenure and academic freedom which make it difficult and expensive to lay them off. Since 80% of a university budget is for salaries and it is very difficult to cut staff, a university has few options to reduce its budget. It can leave vacancies unfilled, make sessional appointments instead of permanent ones, offer early retirement to professors to hire cheaper, younger replacements, and just squeeze and cut everything else.

The budget-paring process at the U of S was an exercise of "probe and add back." Every college and department was asked to respond to a specified cut in its budget. The total of the requested cuts was greater than what was needed to balance the university's budget. The goal was to free up about a million dollars that could then be reallocated, and allow for flexibility and innovation. This process had two effects. First, the decisions redistributed money from the professional colleges and the Extension Division to the College of Arts and Science, which was sagging under the weight of record enrolments. However, it did not do this quickly enough to match the growth in enrolments. The second effect was that no one was satisfied. All units were squeezed and all units faced cutbacks every year. Those that gained relative to the rest, like Arts and Science, did not do so quickly enough.

The largest program cut was the elimination of the College of Home Economics in 1987, but this was not directly due to budget considerations. The decision was made on academic grounds by the university council and senate. In the background, though, was the conclusion of university leaders that the college was too small, its program too little developed, its staff too few for quality programs in all its areas. It had to grow or die, and in the climate of restraint it had to die. Eva Lee, the dean of the college, commented philosophically that "change is sometimes difficult."[45] She went on to become the first president of the amalgamated SIAST where she surely discovered once again the truth of her words.

Other cuts included the dismemberment of the Department of Far Eastern Studies and the dispersal of its staff among other departments. The medical program in Regina was eliminated, and funding for the Diefenbaker Centre was discontinued, leaving the centre to seek federal money. Besides cuts, there were some significant failures to grow. The most important was the inability of the university and the refusal of the government to establish a School of Occupational Therapy. The Saskatchewan Society of Occupational Therapists lobbied unsuccessfully for most of the 1980s to get their profession, in which there is a shortage of graduates, established on campus.

Meanwhile, there was some growth on the U of S campus. Kristjanson spearheaded a new research park which grew throughout the 1980s. The biggest project on the old campus was the new agriculture building. The $90-million construction project was funded by a $78 million government grant with the remainder raised by the university. Opposition leader Allan Blakeney had promised a new agriculture building in the fall of 1985. Grant Devine, with better timing, announced the government's decision to build shortly before the 1986 election. There were also other new projects: a toxicology centre, expansion of the linear accelerator laboratory with $900,000 in provincial funds so that it could capture $5.8 million in federal research grants, and a $6-million federally funded biotechnology project.

However, the most important development at the university was the combination of soaring enrolments and fiscal restraint. The resulting strain on resources, and simple overcrowding, led to perceptions of a deteriorating quality of education, labour unrest, and enrolment quotas.

The decision to restrict enrolment was a slow one. In the spring of 1983 (the time of the first Conservative budget) Kristjanson, using the university senate as his platform to address the public of the province, warned that "we may have reached the limits of our ability to accept further student numbers" given the level of operating grants and the restrictions of physical facilities. He cited an overall enrolment increase of 18% in the three previous years, concentrated in Arts and Science (41%) and Education (12%). During the same period, full-time teaching positions increased by only one-half of 1%. Kristjanson insisted that the university "must try to its utmost to accept all qualified students, in light of the high youth unemployment rate and the potential it has to develop innovative thinkers who can contribute to economic recovery and long-term productivity." Because of such considerations, Kristjanson declined to impose quotas in 1983.[46]

However, the pressure on the university's resources continued to grow. In 1985, quotas took effect in Agriculture, Physical Education, and Commerce. The university resisted quotas in Arts and Science, the largest of its undergraduate colleges and the last without enrolment quotas. However, as Dean Art Knight observed, the enrolment growth was continuing and the college was stretched past acceptable limits. "We are operating with temporary solutions to what is now a permanent problem. We are in a situation where we can't handle any more students." [47] Finally in 1986, quotas were approved for Arts and Science. They took effect in the fall of 1987. A limit of 6,000 was set on total enrolment in the college, with admission dependent primarily on high school grades. The grade required to enter the college increased from 65% in required classes to 73%. Over 400 students were turned away from the university, bringing criticism from high school students and their families, from teachers and rural leaders, that the university was elitist.

In 1987–88, when the government announced its two-year funding freeze for universities, Kristjanson sounded the warning that "difficult, controversial, and unpleasant decisions" lay ahead. [48]

The budgetary pressures on the university also brought to a head difficulties in governing the university. The governance structures of the campus have never worked well. The unwieldy 1,100-member academic council has had trouble getting a quorum for essential business. Its structure is expressly designed to deflect important decisions to committees who never report on much of what they do. A key recommendation of a 1987 report on governance was to create a new representative council to give faculty a more effective voice. [49] This recommendation has now become a priority of the new president, George Ivany.

Throughout the 1980s, faculty have lacked an effective role in university governance. Given this vacuum and the prominence of budgetary and managerial questions, the faculty turned to their certified union, the Faculty Association, to represent their interests. One effect of underfunding was to heighten the tension between the union and administration. Furthermore, a private consultant's report similar to the U of R's resulted in an administrative reorganization which intended to increase the effectiveness of management. A side-effect, however, was an increase in the number of vice-presidents who buffered and isolated the president from the campus as a whole.

One university veteran noted that in the face of enrolment growth, budget restraint, and government demands for accountability, the university "responded by increasing the number of administrators, introducing elaborate administrative procedures and imposing across-the-board budget cuts." This "separated students and faculty from the president by an ever-increasing hierarchy" of vice-presidents, associate and assistant vice-presidents, deans, and associate and assistant deans.[50] "We moved to a more hierarchical model," admitted an administrator. "That was a disaster."[51] As the governance report had noted, "our institution suffers because of a perception that the most important decisions are made in remote and secretive councils." It also warned, "in recent years . . . we have seen the difference between employer and employee accented rather more than is healthy."[52]

PROFESSORS ON STRIKE: UNDERFUNDING AND HOW NOT TO FIX IT

In 1988, the fiscal pressures on the U of S culminated in a professors' strike. The faculty of the most conservative educational institution in the province traded their lecterns and libraries for the picket line.

Bargaining between the faculty association and the university had become more and more difficult throughout the 1980s. The 1986 contract was only settled following a one-day study session held to protest the lagging talks. Binding arbitration eventually settled the dispute, with the arbitrator awarding the faculty a 4.1% increase for that year.

The negotiations for the 1987 contract became even more bitter. In February 1988, 64% of association members voted in a mail ballot in favour of some kind of job action. The main issues were salary and working conditions. The chair of the Faculty Association, Peter Millard, charged that the university had enough in reserves to give faculty salary increases equal to the rate of inflation. In March, when faculty voted to hold a strike ballot, Millard added, "people are fed up with the refusal of administration to listen to faculty. There is a strong lack of confidence in the priorities set by administration."[53] The demands expressed at the time of the strike vote were a salary increase equal to the rate of inflation plus one-half of 1%, and a say in the appointment of senior administrators through the academic council. The addition of the latter demand suggests that the association may have been looking for ways to focus professors' resentment of and anger at the university administration. The ballot was held and, in an extremely close vote, faculty voted 424–412 to authorize strike action.

With that slim mandate, the association executive called the professors out on strike. The strike was far from total, but it was enough. Professors continued to do their research and stopped performing their teaching duties only. In many of the professional colleges, classes continued. But Dean Knight of Arts and Science estimated that in his college, the largest on campus, only 10% of classes were being taught.[54]

During the strike the faculty association directed its criticism at the university administration. Millard insisted that the provincial budget was irrelevant to contract talks. "It's not a question of how much money is given to the University in the budget, it's a question of priorities that the administration sets. This is what the strike is about—we disagree with their priorities."[55] One of the picket-line slogans from the strike captured the faculty association's assessment of the blame for the problems at the university: "Create Teaching Positions Not a Budget Surplus." A key part of the argument by striking faculty was that the university was sitting on $10.6 million in reserve funds.

The president of the student union, Kevin Doherty, attacked this argument. (Doherty disowned the strike early and said faculty should be satisfied with their lot when students were suffering 10% tuition increases as well as quotas.) In a speech to the senate in April, Doherty noted that the funds identified by faculty were of a variety of types. Part of the alleged $10-million was one-time-only money, accumulated surpluses from previous years which were not part of the base operating budget. Such funds could not finance annual salary increases. Another part of the sum consisted of "fall-in" accounts in departments and colleges, an innovation under the budget-cutting system which permitted those units to retain and reallocate some money and encouraged them to make savings. Though these were indeed "surpluses" in a sense, they were a necessary part of the budget system and few faculty wanted their departments stripped of them. What remained was about $2.8 million in actual annual reserves, which the administration insisted was essential for flexibility in the budget, and which would not have covered the full salary increases demanded. It was misleading, said Doherty, for faculty to claim that the president "had a pot of gold in his closet."

For this reason among others, one history professor said he was breaking with the majority of his department and "putting myself into exile by refusing to support a strike that is based on false information and that punishes only students."[56]

Despite the faculty association's blaming of the university administration, specific complaints related directly to the provincial government's funding

225

decisions. Early in March, before the strike, demonstrating professors said they were concerned about larger classes, less time for individual students, and the imposition of enrolment quotas. Placards at the Memorial Gates read "re-open the gates of the U of S to qualified students," and "restore quality university education." "Less cuts!" chanted some students who supported the strike on 29 March ("Fewer Cuts!" corrected a faculty member next to them). [57] A professor of education said he was on strike because the university had "deteriorated . . . classrooms . . . are over-crowded, far too many part-time lecturers rather than full-time professors teach our students, qualified students are not admitted because of quotas, retiring faculty members are rarely replaced." [58]

It is possible that hostile professors were so angry at the administration that they simply did not believe or did not care about its budget statements. It may be that they thought the university should run a large deficit in order to maintain its programs. Whatever the reason, they saved their antagonism and, in some cases, outright hatred for those they knew best.

At a brief meeting of the academic council on 8 April, one professor gave notice of motion demanding the resignations of senior administrators. At a subsequent meeting a month and a half later, the motion passed 274–166. Once again, those criticizing the administration offered budget cuts, large classes, and quotas as evidence of the "incompetence" of their administrators. Nursing professor Joan Sawatsky said facilities and equipment were "inadequate and an embarrassment." [59] By and large, the government escaped blame, and Kristjanson was blamed instead as its "messenger."

As English professor Paul Denham later told the *Star Phoenix*, he believed Kristjanson "was very careful to please the government. He's not as independent as he ought to be." Denham added, "I don't think Kristjanson knows what a university is about. He thinks of it as a kind of upscale technical institution." [60] Geology professor Fred Langford wrote, "These problems are not unique here. Why then was there a strike here? At other universities, the faculty, the presidents and the boards were united trying to keep university standards and in fighting for the required resources. At the U of S, the president and the board acquiesced to the government's readiness to sacrifice standards." [61]

The government did directly intervene in the strike – it legislated the professors back to work. As late as 3 April 1988, Deputy Minister Laurie McFarlane assured the press that back-to-work legislation was something "we should leave for only if there is an ultimate breakdown." But Hepworth had already staked his ground on 31 March: "whatever happens, the exams must proceed on schedule and . . . means must be found in the next few days to ensure this." The university's failure to guarantee all students their exams was "unacceptable." Meanwhile, academic vice-president Bruce Schnell noted that about half of the required exams had been submitted to the registrar already—about normal for the time of year. There was every possibility that most students would write their exams in spite of the strike. But on 4 April Millard issued a dubious clarification: "we're not directing them (our members) one way or the other" about submitting exams. "But we're simply pointing out that a strike is a withdrawal of services, full stop. Of course, in a strike, you don't do any work, it's obvious." [62] The next day, even though conciliation talks were still in progress, Hepworth introduced legislation to force professors back to work.

In the legislature, the NDP tried to pin the blame for the educational crises on the government. MLA Ed Tchorzewski stated that "clearly this bill is a result of under-funding of our universities." The argument received little support from the disputants on campus. [63]

After the legislation ordering the faculty members back to work for the examination period was passed, bargaining continued. The dispute was eventually settled in 1989 on the basis of a recommendation from mediator Howard Tennant of the University of Lethbridge. The terms of the agreement were only marginally more favourable to the faculty than was an offer that was narrowly rejected in the spring of 1988. [64] The issue of who appoints senior administrators was the subject of a report issued in July 1990, which offered more faculty positions on the hiring committees which advise the board of governors. Since the board is legally accountable for the university's finances, it will presumably always have the final say.

In addition to the terms of the contract, a series of grievances arising from the strike lingered on for a year. The faculty association argued that professors should not be docked pay for the time they were on the picket line, since most had continued to carry out research. Since only a part of the professors' duties (teaching) had not been carried out, the faculty association demanded full pay for the strike period. The university administration took the position that a strike was a strike, and that meant no pay. An arbitrator ruled in the administration's favour on the first of the association's 300 grievances. The administration, to clear away the remainder, said it would pay anyone who worked provided they filed a letter saying they had worked.

Public reaction to the faculty strike appeared to be against the professors. Hepworth seemed very sure of himself when he intervened in the name of the students. The *Leader Post* said what many outside of Saskatoon were thinking when it saw "self-serving" motives in the strike, "meanness" in its timing to take advantage of the students' predicament, and hypocrisy. "The faculty association seems disposed to wrap what is essentially a salary dispute in the trimmings of high-sounding academic principles." The newspaper took pains to note the "privileged position" of "members of the robed ranks." The newspaper pointed to the professors' average $50,000 salaries, the fact they rejected a contract very similar to what Saskatchewan teachers had just received, and reported demands of a 20% raise and free tuition for their children. "There is not a huge pool of public sympathy for the position taken by the U of S faculty association." [65] Nor was there a great deal of criticism of the government's role in setting the stage for the strike through its funding policies.

In his fall 1988 address to the senate Kristjanson stated, "we have now reached a crisis point in our funding." The university, said Kristjanson, had now depleted its carefully built-up reserves, and would be facing a shortfall of $5 million in 1989–90. The measures to deal with such a deficit would "make the last three or four years appear to have been a 'Utopian era' in the University financial history." [66] The university cited figures showing that funding, corrected for inflation, had fallen from $9,000 per student in 1979–80 to $7,000 in 1987–88.

During the 1980s, Saskatchewan universities maintained most of their programs, and did not lay off faculty. Quality and accessibility were both squeezed heavily. The U of R ran a deficit, and eventually suffered cuts virtually dictated by the government. The U of S balanced its budget, and suffered a strike in which a key issue was President Kristjanson's alleged failure to stand up to the government. One might be forgiven a certain sympathy for administrators required to chart a course between the Scylla of financial catastrophe and the Charybdis of faculty rebellion.

Neither university administration was popular, certainly not among its own staff nor among groups in the communities affected by the cuts. Both universities cut, among other things, their off-campus classes, their extension divisions. It is a paradox of university decision making that the programs most entrenched in the community, being the least entrenched in the university, are cut first. The legacy is social workers in Prince Albert and elsewhere furious at the U of R, regional college officials angry at both universities for cutting extension classes, and middle-range high school students everywhere turned away by the U of S quotas.

The government knew in the 1980s that it was giving universities less than they needed to deal with enrolments. Ministers expressed displeasure with university enrolment quotas and with tuition fee increases. Clearly, they expected universities to cut whole programs and reallocate if they couldn't cope. The universities refused to do so, often citing the fact that no quick savings could be made from cancelling programs because of commitments to pay off any faculty who were cut, and commitments to students already in the programs who expected to be able to finish. The universities ignored government hints that things would only get worse, and acted as though there were only a few tough years to be weathered.

The government largely escaped blame for the difficulties in the universities. The question of overall funding levels was for the most part ignored, and criticism was directed toward university administrations whenever a specific action was taken to deal with the fiscal crises. Whether it was the U of R attempting to sell its library, closing colleges, or cutting extension courses, or whether it was the U of S imposing admission quotas or having its professors hit the picket line, the political repercussions were internalized within the university. The government tightened the screws and joined in the chorus of "it's not just money that is going to build a great university." [67]

REGIONAL COLLEGES AND THE HIGH-TECH QUICK FIX

The reorganization of the technical institutes and the inadequacy of both technical and university funding to maintain accessibility came together in the changing role of Saskatchewan's community colleges (more recently, regional colleges).

The government likes these colleges because they are cheap and flexible, but its support has limitations. Prior to 1987, the colleges were ignored by the government and eked out a marginal existence. In 1986, the college trustees association presented a study to Minister Hepworth with 105 recommendations, and concluded that "colleges are stretching their human and financial resources." Shrinking budgets and "the suspense of waiting for the annual provincial budget plays havoc with staff and forward planning," especially given simultaneous cutbacks in federal employment grants. [68] These problems have by no means been eliminated, but at least in rhetoric the colleges have come to assume a larger role in government plans.

In 1987, Deputy Minister Lawrie McFarlane promised a community college conference, saying that "the community colleges are in the very frontline of the future and I think you will soon see that both provincial and federal governments are prepared to give you the responsibility of fulfilling the future." Soon after, Hepworth commented that the strongest message he received from people was that they wanted greater access to adult education in or near their own communities. He announced a new "outreach" policy for education, including a standardized first and second year arts and science course by extension, available at colleges throughout the province, and more technical institute certificate courses by extension. To accomplish this, the eight rural community colleges in southern Saskatchewan were converted into regional colleges, with the additional mandate of offering university and technical institute courses on a brokerage basis. Hepworth also announced a $3-million "educational outreach fund" to pay for library materials, equipment, and satellite and cable delivery for courses, and appointed a distance education council to advise him. As the technical institutes were cut and university funds frozen, the government's new darling was the regional college system and distance education.[69]

At the same time the regional colleges were created, the urban community colleges were amalgamated with the four SIAST campuses, and several northern community colleges were amalgamated into a single Northlands Career College.

The result is a network of regional colleges in rural Saskatchewan. Each covers a defined territory and concentrates on three basic functions: adult basic education (continued from the mandate of the old community colleges), technical classes from SIAST (purchased by the colleges from SIAST with money from the Saskatchewan Skills Extension Fund), and university extension classes. The original, general adult education function of the colleges declined. In 1987 the college system was a $30 million operation. The province provided $20 million in operating grants and adult education funding, and the federal government $8 million. Tuition fees provided the remainder.

The political significance of regional colleges is substantial, particularly to a government justifying itself in terms of rural areas, technology, and reform to suit the changing marketplace. Colleges are spread through the province and are highly visible in the community. The trustees on their local advisory committees, plus their instructors and staff, constitute a

230

new element and a new lobby in the post-secondary constellation. The existence of such colleges, and their expanded mandates, also creates expectations that the post-secondary system is not funded to meet. As Lloyd Barber commented, there is a concern that "too many expectations might be built up about community colleges eventually becoming junior colleges." [70] In at least some areas, thinking runs in that direction. A committee of Melfort civic and community officials presented a brief to cabinet in January 1989, and organized a conference in October to promote the idea of a junior college system for Saskatchewan. They justified their arguments on the basis of the economic impact of such colleges on their host communities. The spokesperson for the Melfort group, Dub Henderson, referred to the centralized universities as "taking much needed money out of the community." In contrast, a junior college would enhance the quality of life and keep younger people in the community. [71] Such priorities, however, raise the spectre of educational policy being driven by boosterism or even political pork-barrelling.

Meanwhile, because demand by regional colleges for university classes grows, so do expectations of what the universities should provide. While the universities argue that budget restrictions prevent them from offering more extension classes, the colleges criticize them for not offering more. [72] Once again, the result of institutions being short of money is that they are at each other's throats.

The government may, in fact, be lukewarm about the college idea, since to do it right costs a lot of money. It appears that the government thinks it can get more bang for its buck by investing in technology for distance delivery of centralized education.

In the 1980s, Saskatchewan universities were pioneers of a sort in this area through the Saskatchewan Tele-Learning Association (STELLA), which rented time on the Anik-3 communications satellite to broadcast U of R and U of S courses to 30-odd sites around the province. The classes (in subjects like History, English, Psychology, French, Sociology) had lectures delivered on television screens in the remote sites, with on-site and phone-in discussion afterwards. They were well-received in rural areas that had not previously had any university classes, but less so in cities like Prince Albert that were used to face-to-face extension instructors. Reasons for resistance to the satellite courses included concerns about the quality of instruction and that they divert students from the regional colleges and SIAST campuses, which otherwise can generate revenue from holding regular face-to-face university classes.

Still, the limitations of the technology were handled well by STELLA, perhaps because as a cooperative consortium it remained flexible and responsive both to students' comments and to the universities' concerns. A lot of effort was put into doing a few classes well.

The government established a new Saskatchewan Communications Advanced Network (SCAN) as a centralized crown corporation intended among many other things to replace STELLA. SCAN will set up fibre optic communications to dozens of sites around the province where video, computer, and telephone equipment will permit educational communication, and will operate an educational channel on regular cable television. "It will therefore be possible," says a SCAN brochure, "for universities, correspondence schools, technical institutes, government departments, non-governmental agencies and non-profit organizations to deliver programs to the general public as well as to specific interest groups in smaller or rural locations." That, at least, is the theory. The public-access SCAN channel was due to come on-stream early in 1990, though the shape of the corporation, particularly the other services and who will control them, is still unclear and contested by the groups involved.

SCAN is a perfect symbol of the government's technological and electronic populism. It merges high technology with centralized control and appeal to the rural areas in Saskatchewan. Whether a centralized medium with an educational bureaucracy will serve the needs of the province's formal learners is an open question. SCAN seems likely to develop in this way at the expense of the control of educational institutions, as under the STELLA model. If so, then in effect the Conservative government will have created another post-secondary agency in the province, a major educational player, to add to the other organizations and amalgamations—and all this, without funding any of those agencies to the level they consider adequate.

CONCLUSION

Perhaps if Saskatchewan post-secondary institutions could rise above their competitive instincts and their unique but similar grievances, their response for the 1990s might be: no more changes, until there's proper funding. They could also add that education is a task in its own right, and not a subsidiary to trade or technology, or to privatization.

There is of course no indication that post-secondary institutions will pull together in any such way. Given the relatively low political profile of post-secondary issues and the lack of large, organized lobby groups, the government mostly has control.

The Conservative government in the 1980s has had two opposite approaches to post-secondary education. On the one hand it has been pro-education, seeing it as supportive of business, international competitiveness, globalization, and social change. On the other hand it has pushed for privatization, and tended to be suspicious of public institutions. One approach has dominated the speeches; the other has wielded the cost-cutting axe. New initiatives worth hundreds of thousands of dollars have been announced, while cuts to save the government millions were carried out.

Who benefited? Clearly not instructors (numbers down, student load up, salaries behind inflation). Clearly not students (tuition fees up, opportunities reduced, facilities and services declining). Clearly not the administrators who had to cope with all this. Private vocational school operators benefited. Business people and corporations got more say in how the educational system was run. But the list of those who benefited is really rather short. The experience of the 1980s can only be justified on the basis of deficit cutting, and to some that is justification enough. Except that even by the Conservatives' own philosophy, education must not be cut in the bad times, in the times of rearrangement and change. It is precisely in the bad times that education is most needed.

FROM BAD TO WORSE: DAY CARE IN SASKATCHEWAN, 1982–1989

by Judith Martin

During the 1980s, the problem of accessible, quality child care became a major public policy issue. Governments could no longer ignore the demands of parents, day care advocates, and child care workers to replace the old selectively subsidized user-fee approach with a universally funded, nonprofit child care system. Some provinces have made substantial progress toward the implementation of this goal. In Saskatchewan, however, the provision of adequate day care services has not kept pace with developments in the rest of the country. Tory times have been sorry times for child care in Saskatchewan.

Unfortunately, the issue of child care has been neglected by all governments in Saskatchewan. In 1969, the Liberal government under the leadership of Ross Thatcher introduced the province's first child care legislation using Section 66 of the Child Welfare Act. This legislation established child care in Saskatchewan as a selectively subsidized, user-fee service. In practical terms, the Liberals established a small monthly subsidy for low-income parents who used licensed spaces, a universal operating grant of $5.00 per licensed space per month, start-up grants for nonprofit centres, and minimum criteria for licensing profit and nonprofit child care. The legislation established minimum standards of care including: staff-child ratios of 1:10 for preschoolers, indoor space requirements of 35 square feet per child, and outdoor space requirements of 60 square feet per child. These standards of care remain in effect today or, in the case of outdoor space requirements, have been downgraded.[1] Like the Canada Assistance Plan Act (CAP) which was passed in 1966 enabling Federal-Provincial cost-sharing of subsidies for low-income child care users, the Thatcher initiatives operated under the assumption that the care of preschool children was a private family responsibility that should be resolved through existing market mechanisms except in the case of low-income parents.

When the 1971 election was called, Saskatchewan had 636 licensed child care spaces and a day care budget of $18,854. In March of that year, in preparation for the upcoming election, Thatcher signed an Order in Council to remove the requirement that only nonprofit centres should get the start-up grant. This same Order in Council permitted day care operators to pocket operating grants instead of deducting them from user fees as had been previous practice. At that time, the requirement that all centres provide hot meals was eliminated; it has not been reinstituted under either NDP or Tory governments. The overall effect was to reduce the quality of children's care for politically expedient reasons.

Following the election of the NDP, after significant and consistent pressure from child care advocates and grassroots members of the NDP,[2] Allan Blakeney's government fulfilled its 1971 election promise to "provide child care centres and after school programs for working parents."[3] The government increased its 1974–75 day care budget from $100,000 to $1.7 million.

The 1974 Child Care Policy,[4] which represents the only policy initiative the NDP undertook with respect to child care during their 1971–82 tenure, was based on assumptions similar to those that informed the policy of Ross Thatcher's government. Child care was seen primarily as a private family responsibility which ought to be resolved via market mechanisms. The 1974 policy entrenched the selectively subsidized, user-fee model of child care in Saskatchewan.

The NDP, however, saw the state taking a more generous role in assisting low-income families. As a result of the NDP's 1974 initiatives, start-up grants and parent subsidies were increased, and more staff were hired to assist with the development of new spaces. A new Family Day Care Home Program was added which enabled the government to licence individuals to care for a maximum of eight children in their homes. But centres and family day care homes were expected to operate like small businesses; parents' user fees (including the government subsidy) had to cover operating costs.

The criteria for licensing remained minimal: hot lunches were not required; child-staff ratio of 1:10 for preschoolers remained in effect; windowless basements without yards were licensed; no criterion for group size was established; and the government required only a 40-hour training program for staff. These policies provided minimum standards of care and reflected the extent to which the government was out of touch with child development research; at that time, group size and staff training were identified as key determinants of quality. Since no capital funding was provided, day care centres remained the tenants of church basements and other low-cost spaces.

In policy terms, many child care advocates argued that Allan Blakeney had simply become a more generous Ross Thatcher. While this was true to a large extent, one critical aspect of the NDP's 1974 policy distinguished it from previous policies and from child care policy in other provinces, namely that all newly established child care centres in Saskatchewan were to be controlled by nonprofit boards of which at least 51% were to be parent users. Although the Blakeney cabinet never developed an adequate number of spaces and never gave the support that parents needed to provide high quality care, the institutionalization of parent-controlled, nonprofit child care was a bold and significant step in 1974. At that time, 50% of the then licensed centres in Saskatchewan and 42% of all spaces in the country were located in the commercial sector.

After the 1980 day care review and a show of unprecedented child care advocacy in the province, the NDP started to spend more money on child care. The 1981–82 budget was increased from $3.4 million to $6.9 million and the 1982–83 budget estimates,[5] which the NDP was not able to implement, indicate that a 23% increase had been assigned for child care. However, the NDP cabinet remained opposed to universal funding for child care, which prevented the spending of these new dollars in a way that would have improved and protected the nonprofit, parent-controlled model.

During the 1979–82 period, the position of child care advocates crystallized. They argued that the problem was not simply a matter of more money; rather, it was a matter of establishing significant universal funding for centres in the form of a direct operating grant which would have allowed the quality of care and the salaries of caregivers to improve. This did not happen and the NDP's failure to properly fund the nonprofit system unwittingly eased the way for Grant Devine's Tories to reintroduce commercial child care into the province.

CHILD CARE "COMES OF AGE" IN CANADA: THE TORY RECORD IN CONTEXT

Before examining the Tory record on child care, it is important to examine the development of day care policy in Canada more generally. Throughout the 1980s, child care "came of age." Canadians came face to face with the fact that we, as a nation, were putting the next generation at risk because of the lack of decent child care. While over 51% of mothers with children under the age of three were in the labour force, only 15% of their children had access to quality-controlled care. The media called it a national crisis.

The Canadian Day Care Advocacy Association (CDCAA), which formed out of the militant 2nd National Child Care Conference held in Winnipeg in September 1982, finally succeeded in convincing the federal government to take action on this issue, even though it fell under provincial jurisdiction. The CDCAA argued that the federal government had already put in place a child care policy, albeit ineffectual, through the 1966 Canada Assistance Plan Act and through changes to Section 62 of the Income Tax Act, allowing tax deductions for child care. In addition, the CDCAA pointed out that the federal government had already taken a leadership role in the funding of health and university education, programs which were also under provincial jurisdiction.

The argument for federal leadership (and, of course, the need for women's votes in 1984) captured the imagination of both the federal Liberal and Conservative parties. The Liberals set up a Ministerial Task Force on Child Care just before the 1984 federal election, and only a few days into the federal campaign, Brian Mulroney took up the child care issue and promised a parliamentary task force if elected, a promise which he fulfilled.

As a result of these two national task forces on child care and numerous conferences and symposia, day care received wide public attention. The central question was: who should get public dollars to help pay for care of children? Under the original legislation passed in 1966, federal dollars for day care were limited to low-income parents. Like Saskatchewan, most provinces had followed this lead. But, in the 1980s, middle-class parents were demanding financial assistance for child care and also insisting on better quality care.

The relationship between the quality of care and the type of funding (selective individual subsidy or universal direct grants to centres) began to make sense to federal officials and some provincial leaders. In their 1986 report, the Liberal-appointed ministerial task force recommended a long-term plan to replace Canada's user-fee child care system with a universally funded program.[6] Brian Mulroney's task force also had harsh words for the operation of Canada's child care system and, while the Tory task force did not recommend the replacement of Canada's user-fee day care system, it did recommend significant universal federal funding to all licensed spaces, which if it had been implemented and matched by the provinces, would have established a pattern of significant partial universal funding for child care.[7]

Other jurisdictions finally recognized the need to go beyond (at least partially) the old selectively subsidized user-fee approach to child care: Manitoba moved to increase the amount of universal funding for day care which it had begun in the 1970s; Quebec enhanced the universal funding which it had started in 1979; Alberta provided major universal dollars for each licensed space; and in 1987, Ontario implemented partial universal funding.[8]

In summary, the 1980s were a period of promise for child care. Even promises, however, were not put forward in Saskatchewan. Shortly after their election in 1982, the Tory government moved not only to limit funding but also began the process of dismantling the current system and returning Saskatchewan's child care system to its pre-1974 days when commercial care was acceptable.

THE NEED FOR CHILD CARE IN SASKATCHEWAN

In order for parents of young children to participate in the labour force, access to high-quality day care is a necessary precondition. But the number of spaces available is woefully inadequate to meet the needs of working parents. Table 11.1 describes the position of Saskatchewan children in 1981 with respect to the employment status of their parents and the percent of these children who had access to licensed child care in 1987. The data indicate that in 1987 only 13.1% of children of full-time working parents had access to licensed day care in Saskatchewan; this number declines to 9.4% if parents working part-time and students are included.

The fact that a child's parents are working in the paid labour force does not, of course, mean that a licensed child care space is needed. But determining the number of child care spaces needed at any given time is a complex question which is not easily answered. The only attempt to address this question systematically took place in 1978 when the Sample Survey and Data Bank Unit of the University of Regina surveyed the need for child care in Saskatchewan. The study indicated that the province needed about 28,000 full time spaces[9] but, as of April 1989, there were only 6,060 spaces.[10]

In the 1970s, most of the demand for child care spaces came from the urban centres in Saskatchewan. But, in the 1980s, with the large number of farm wives pressed into the labour market and the maturation of the child care debate, strong demands for child care came from the rural areas. For example, in September 1984, representatives of parent groups from Tisdale, Candle Lake, Christopher Lake, and North Battleford held a news conference in Saskatoon to draw attention to the fact that their plans to set up centres were being stalled by the government's refusal to approve both start-up funds and the selective subsidy which assists low-income parents in paying user fees.[11] Rural spokespeople pointed out that less than 4% of all licensed spaces were located in rural areas of Saskatchewan despite increasing on-farm and off-farm employment of mothers. In addition, they pointed to the dangers of inadequate care by noting that from 1979 to 1984, 93 children age four and under were hospitalized in this province due to farm accidents. Despite their claim to be supporting rural Saskatchewan and the rural family in particular, the government of Grant Devine has not felt obliged to meet the child care needs of rural families.

THE TORY RECORD

Child care policy in Saskatchewan is provided through three specific programs: the Parent Income Subsidy Program, the Neighbourhood Day Care Centre Program, and the Family Day Care Home Program.[12] These programs were regulated under the Family Services Act until August 1989 when the government passed the Child Care Act. The programs are administered by the Day Care Branch within the Department of Social Services.

The Parent Income Subsidy Program provides a subsidy for specific users of licensed day care. The subsidy is tied to gross family income and assumes that all parents, no matter how poor (except those on social assistance), should pay at least 10% of the user fee. The government arbitrarily determines the maximum subsidy and the family income levels of eligibility for the subsidy program.[13]

The Neighbourhood Day Care Centre Program provides financial start-up assistance, licensing, annual monitoring, and support to groups who want to establish day care centres which can serve a maximum of 60, 18-month to 12-year-old children. Until August 1989, these centres were nonprofit organizations and parent-users represented at least 51% of the board of directors. With the exception of a limited start-up grant of $600 per space (which has been frozen since 1981), this program assumes that the centres will run essentially as small businesses. All operating costs must be recovered through user fees.

The Family Day Care Home Program allows a maximum of eight

children (aged six weeks to school age) to be cared for in private dwellings by an individual who has been approved by day care officials. Like the Neighbourhood Day Care Centre Program, the Family Day Care Home Program assumes that individual providers will operate as a small business. Although they are given a small start-up grant, they are then expected to recover their costs including salaries through user fees.

These three programs are the basis of Saskatchewan's child care policy and only minor modifications have been made to these programs since the Devine government was elected in 1982. In April 1986, a $20 per month per space "maintenance" or direct grant was introduced for all licensed group day care spaces in Saskatchewan. This grant replaced the annual equipment grant of $100 per year per space. In addition, an equipment grant of $50 per year per space (to a maximum of $400 per year) is available to approved family day care homes.

In examining the Tory record, it is clear that two issues – accessibility and quality of care, which are considered central issues by day care advocates and researchers – have been systematically ignored or undermined by the government. In the following sections, these issues will be examined in more detail.

Accessibility

In March 1982, there were 3,914 licensed child care spaces in Saskatchewan, representing 31 spaces per 1,000 children under the age of six. (In comparison, B.C. had 69 spaces per 1,000 children under the age of six, Manitoba had 84, and Alberta had 73.) By 1989, the number of spaces had increased to 6,060, indicating that the Tories opened on average the same number of spaces annually as the NDP did during its 11 years in power. Compared to other Canadian provinces except Newfoundland, Saskatchewan had a much lower number of children with access to licensed care in 1987 (see Table 11.2).[14]

While the total number of spaces provides one criterion for examining the Tory record on day care, it is also necessary to examine the growth of spaces in licensed centres and family day care homes. In 1982, 20% of the licensed spaces in Saskatchewan were in the Family Day Care Home Program. By 1987, 35% of all day care spaces were in the Family Day Care Home Program. In comparison, family day care spaces represent approximately 12% of all spaces across Canada.[15] This shift toward privately operated day care homes reflects the Tories' support for the traditional concept of the family.[16]

The lack of licensed spaces is only one of the child care accessibility problems facing working parents in Saskatchewan. Even when parents can find a licensed space, many families cannot use the space because the user fees are prohibitive. In March 1982, the average user fee in the province was $230 per month (in some city day care centres, the user fee was $300–$325 per month) and parents who qualified for the user-fee subsidy received up to 90% of the user fee to a maximum of $235 per month. The Tories considered this subsidy too generous and although seven years have passed and the average user fee in 1988 was $310 ($395 in some cities), the maximum subsidy remains at $235 per month. As a result, the poorest of working parents are now paying from $65 to $160 per month per child for care in Saskatchewan.

In addition to underfunding the Parent Income Subsidy Program, the Devine government has refused to raise the income level at which parents are eligible for user-fee assistance. The "subsidy turning point" (the gross family income below which maximum subsidy is available) was set at $18,000 by the NDP in 1982, where it remains today. If the Progressive Conservative government had adjusted the subsidy program for inflation and maintained the modest levels set by the NDP in 1982, the monthly subsidy maximum would be $300 (compared to $235) and the subsidy turning point would be $22,500 (compared to $18,000).

The Tory decision to underfund the child care program has hit hardest those who are struggling against the greatest odds to raise their children. As the National Welfare Council pointed out in 1984, a single parent with a minimum-wage income received less public support for child care in Saskatchewan than a single parent working in Alberta, Manitoba, Ontario, New Brunswick, Nova Scotia, Prince Edward Island, the Yukon and the Northwest Territories.[17]

The Tories were only in office a few months when they first moved to make child care less accessible for low-income families. On 15 November 1982, without any prior notice, the government reduced the period for which unemployed parents could receive the child care subsidy from 6 months to 2 months. This policy change created unnecessary hardship for unemployed parents and their children. Under the regulations, parents are required to give one month's notice to their centre. An unemployed parent, therefore, must give notice after only four weeks of unemployment, only perhaps to need the space again a month or so later. In addition, the reduction in the child care subsidy for unemployed parents greatly hinders an unemployed parent's opportunity to look for a job when no child care is available.

QUALITY OF CARE

The decidedly inadequate standards that were in place in 1982 are still in effect today.[18] The overall child care situation in 1990 is not the same as it was in 1982, however: levels and quality of care have steadily deteriorated. The government's decision to restrict the subsidy program not only reduced access to child care, but also lowered the quality of care available in the province. Since the maximum monthly user-fee subsidy has been fixed at $235, child care centres and providers have been forced to keep user fees as low as possible in order not to create undue hardship for poorer families and to keep spaces fully occupied. As a result, fewer resources are available for quality programming. Marlene Bokshowan, president of the Saskatchewan Child Care Association, argues that:

> quality is more and more precarious – rent, cost of food has gone up a good deal since 1982 – costs of field trips, supplies, crafts have also risen and of course most centres have given staff wage increases – so centres are operating closer and closer to the minimum regulations and consideration of quality of what is best for the child is more and more like a luxury every day.[19]

With respect to quality of care, one key item is the wages of care givers, representing 78–85% of a child care centre's operating budget. The average starting salary for a child care worker in Saskatoon is approximately $1,000 and after three years' experience, it increases to $1,300 per month.[20] As a result of the Devine government's decision to freeze parent subsidies, day care workers in Saskatchewan have spent the last decade living on wage levels close to those set in the early 1980s. In comparison, the governments of Manitoba, Alberta, and Ontario have taken some steps to reduce the extent to which workers subsidize the user-fee child care system.

The pressure on staff has not been limited to those working directly in the provision of care. As part of its cost-cutting measures, the government has refused to fill vacant program development positions within the Day Care Branch and, in the 1988 budget, the government cut two full-time positions reducing the 16-person complement of staff to 14. These cutbacks have had a profound impact on the activities of the government's day care staff. Their job is to assist in the establishment of new centres and family day care homes and to monitor the quality of care being provided. With the cutbacks, however, the government has reduced the staff's monitoring role to visiting each centre or home once a year as part of the licensing renewal process.

THE TORY SPENDING RECORD

Although child care has never been a major priority for any government in Saskatchewan, nonetheless, there is considerable variability in government expenditures on child care. Table 11.3 indicates that from 1971 to 1982, the average annual increase in public expenditures on child care was 82%. The most significant increase (441%) took place in 1974 when the NDP fulfilled its election promise by providing substantial funds to child care. Since the Tory government came to power in 1982 and until 1988, the average annual increase in public expenditures on child care was 13.9%.

If the Tory record is compared to the records of Alberta, Manitoba, and Ontario, the three provinces which did take steps in the 1980s to begin to resolve the child care crisis, the picture is even more dismal. Table 11.4 provides interprovincial comparisons for total budget and per-capita expenditures on child care. The data indicate that in 1986 (the end of the first term of the Devine government), Saskatchewan severely lagged behind expenditures on child care when compared to Alberta, Manitoba, and Ontario. Saskatchewan spent $59.50 per child (aged 12 and under) while Alberta spent $123, Manitoba $116.60, and Ontario $114.50. (The remaining provinces have similar or considerably worse records on expenditures for child care than the Tory government in Saskatchewan.)

The decision to turn away from the NDP pattern of substantially increasing Saskatchewan's child care budget each year was not an arbitrary decision on the part of the Devine government. It reflected the commitment to reducing the role of government involvement in the market.

Although centres and family day care homes in Saskatchewan can charge any level of user fee, the amount of the subsidy directly affects the user fee. When the government holds down the subsidy, centres are reluctant to increase the user fee too much because a large discrepancy between the price of the user fee and the subsidy may force some parents to remove their children from day care. But attempts to keep the user fee somewhat in line with the subsidy threatens the quality of care; centres and homes are forced to economize on wages, meals, and resources. The problem of a large discrepancy between the user fee and the subsidy cannot be offset by the introduction of variable rates for low-and high-income parents whose children attend the same day care because the regulations specify (and rightly so) that only one fee can be charged to parents of each individual centre.

Gordon Dirks, the minister of social services, was aware that parent-controlled centres would be forced to limit increases in the user fees and thus reduce the quality of care. The minister ignored the advice of people working in the system and the inevitable happened. From 1978–1982, user fees in the province increased by 64%; from 1982 to 1986, user fees increased by 30.5%.

How one interprets this trend toward smaller increases in the user fee is a matter of perspective. Some members of the public who are unaware of the relationship between the amount of the user fee and the quality of child care tend to see this price restraint simply as a money-saver. Defenders of the Devine government point out that the public portion paid toward the average child care space increased from 57% in 1982 to 60% in 1986. How, then, can it be claimed that the Tories have cut public support for child care?

If the 1982 to 1986 user fees had increased at the same rate as they did in the period 1978 to 1982, the portion that the public paid toward the average child care space would have fallen from 57% when the NDP left office to 44% by 1986. In brief, after only one term, Grant Devine managed to shift 13% of the cost of each child care space onto the backs of parents, children, and staff.

The underfunding of the subsidy program has exacerbated an inherent problem in the user-fee approach, namely a two-tiered system of day care. Although most child care centres in Saskatchewan are struggling for survival these days, centres serving high-income users continue to raise their user fees and are able to offer a wide range of services, while centres serving a majority of low-income users struggle to keep their fees as close to the maximum subsidy as possible, and struggle to make ends meet.

As the Tories move into the last year of their second term in office, all in Saskatchewan who love the next generation should be troubled by the systematic undermining of day care services. Their NDP predecessors left a vulnerable program which fell far behind child care services in many other Canadian provinces. Instead of strengthening this program, the

Devine Tories have underfunded it in every possible way, whether it was freezing user-fee subsidy and start-up grants, or refusing to raise the income levels eligible for a subsidy, or eliminating government staff who assisted parents in establishing and running centres. Today, Saskatchewan's child care crisis is considerably worse than it was in 1982. But the insensitivity of Grant Devine's government to the care of our youngest citizens is best understood in relation to the Tories' approach to commercial care.

THE TORY LEGACY: THE MOVE TOWARDS A PRIVATE CHILD CARE SYSTEM

The government did not delay in developing a Progressive Conservative approach to child care. In September 1983, Gordon Dirks, minister of social services, appointed Joanne Zazelenchuk, the young Saskatoon woman who had defeated Deputy Premier Roy Romanow in the 1982 Tory victory, to review the day care system in Saskatchewan. This review attracted a great deal of attention, and over 1,400 people requested a copy of the terms of reference. Action Child Care, the Saskatoon-based advocacy group, which successfully convinced the NDP government to incorporate public meetings into the 1979 day care evaluation, also convinced Zazelenchuk to include public meetings in the 1983 review. Zazelenchuk received 150 submissions and attended meetings throughout the province.

Given the ideology of the Progressive Conservative government as well as the major role of commercial child care in Canada (38% of all spaces), it was obvious that the NDP's nonprofit and parent-controlled program was at risk. The problem for the government, however, was that the profit or nonprofit debate was not really an issue in Saskatchewan. Speaker after speaker at the public meetings outlined the benefits of the nonprofit approach to child care. They pressed the Tories, as they did the NDP government under Allan Blakeney, for more licensed spaces and partial universal funding.

As the review proceeded, Dirks found it increasingly difficult to dispute the evidence that commercial care threatened the quality of care.[21] In addition, Dirks was forced to acknowledge that the province would lose federal dollars because provincial support for commercial care would not be cost-shared. The lack of support for private day care and the practical problems of allowing commercial care in the province appeared to have an impact on the minister. On 19 December 1983 he said in a letter to his Day Care Advisory Board:

You may be interested to know that among the individuals and groups who have made submissions to Ms. Zazelenchuk, there has been no support for the introduction of private day care. This sentiment coupled with Ms. Zazelenchuk's personal research has led her to inform me she will not be recommending that private day care for profit be permitted to operate in Saskatchewan.[22]

At a public meeting in Saskatoon on 18 January 1984, Dirks said he did not favour commercial day care. But in a meeting with his Day Care Advisory Board only 12 days later in Regina, Dirks indicated that small commercial day care centres were an option for Saskatchewan.[23] Similar views were held by advisory board members Peter Matthews (later to become president of the Saskatchewan Progressive Conservative Party) and Marilyn Collicult (the owner of Mother Goose Day Care in Saskatoon, which closed its doors in June 1981 after workers attempted to unionize and day care advocates insisted that standards be enforced). As a result, the advisory board voted 5 to 3 in favour of reintroducing commercial child care in Saskatchewan.[24]

In her June 1984 report,[25] Zazelenchuk offered no new programs or innovative policies in child care. Zazelenchuk believed that the selectively subsidized user-fee system was effective, but said it should be more selective! She argued that the income subsidy level should be lowered so that only those who were "really poor" received assistance and that this more selective subsidy should not be frozen as was the case since 1982. She had strong objections to partial universal funding (or the direct-grant concept), and her review did not address the question of minimum standards for care in the province. In short, the report was rather bland except, as was feared, it recommended "owner-operated child care minicentres as one option and alternative for Saskatchewan through the 1980s and 1990s."[26]

By September 1984, Action Child Care had organized paid staff and a broad coalition of labour, women's, and church groups to sponsor major forums in Regina and Saskatoon to protest against commercial day care. The forums were very successful and hundreds gathered in each city to demonstrate their opposition to commercial day care becoming part of the Saskatchewan child care system. After these forums, the government lost interest in promoting commercial child care. No moves were made to implement Zazelenchuk's report.

While Dirks was forced to back down on commercial day care, the

247

federal Minister of Health and Welfare, Jake Epp, was considering changes to the regulations of the Canada Assistance Plan Act which would have provided an additional $51 million for cost-sharing of commercial day care across Canada. While several provinces were lobbying for this change, Saskatchewan was opposed. In September 1985, Dirks wrote to Saskatoon Member of Parliament Ray Hnatyshyn, indicating that:

> While the sharing of commercial centres is not of financial importance to Saskatchewan, other provinces, in particular Alberta and British Columbia, stand to significantly gain from such a change. Other provinces favour the inclusion of commercial agencies under the cost sharing parameters of CAP (Canada Assistance Plan) in order to expand the array of day care services which might be funded by the province and shared by the Federal government. Should a change in Federal legislation (that is the CAP) actually occur for this province, I do not foresee any significant shifts away from the predominantly non-profit, parent controlled centres which presently exist. As you are aware, the level of volunteer participation is very high in Saskatchewan, making parent controlled operations a desirable form of child care from both a parent-child and volunteer perspective. In addition, little pressure exists from within the private sector at present to expand into the day care field. In conclusion, I think it would be fair to say that because we are relatively happy with the Canada Assistance Plan as it currently exists we are not actively promoting any changes to this agreement. Nor do we foresee any significant shifts in the mode of delivering day care service in Saskatchewan should a reinterpretation or regulatory change be made to the Canada Assistance Plan which would eventually result in the cost sharing of commercial operation.[27]

This letter strongly suggests that Dirks was impressed by the strength of opposition throughout the province to commercial day care.

The first term of the Tories came and went (and so did Dirks who was defeated in the 1986 election), leaving Saskatchewan the only province in Canada where the establishment of any new commercial child care was illegal. But the idea of commercial child care was not dead within Tory ranks. In December 1987, Epp unveiled the federal Tories' response to Canada's child care crisis.[28] This program, which did not adequately address the shortage of licensed child care spaces in Canada nor the problems inherent in the user-fee approach, sounded an immediate alarm in Saskatchewan. It appeared that the new program would provide cost-sharing subsidies to commercial care in all provinces.

The Devine government followed Epp's lead and announced, in the 1988 Speech from the Throne, that it intended to introduce Saskatchewan's first piece of separate legislation regulating child care.[29] The government's decision to introduce a bill licensing commercial care appears to have been influenced by pressure from small business people who were interested in establishing commercial care.[30] In addition, the government's decision may have been influenced by the free trade agreement.[31]

The bill, which was introduced in the legislature in June 1988, provided for the licensing of commercial child care centres. Once again, the province was drawn into a battle to preserve the nonprofit approach to child care. From June 1988 to the bill's final reading in August 1989, the Saskatchewan Child Care Association, many labour and women's groups, and the NDP opposition mounted a strong attack on the move toward for-profit child care.

But round two of the struggle against the licensing of commercial child care in Saskatchewan was, unfortunately, quite unlike round one in 1984. In 1988–89, it was almost impossible to arouse public interest in the issue of commercial child care because other issues (i.e., the privatization of the publicly owned natural gas system) dominated public debate. Child care was lost in the larger privatization issue.

In addition, by 1988 the small but fiery Saskatoon-based child care advocacy group, Action Child Care, which had succeeded in uniting many community interests and groups to fight both the former NDP government and the Progressive Conservative government on the child care issue, had disbanded after giving birth to the larger and more broadly based, but less militant, Saskatchewan Child Care Association. Although the final outcome probably would have been the same, the Saskatchewan Child Care Association never focused on the issue of commercial child care to the same extent as Action Child Care. The organization of major rallies with prominent speakers was not part of the 1988–89 struggle against commercial child care. Staff and elected officers of the Saskatchewan Child Care Association did not work full time on this issue.

Finally, it is clear that by 1988 parent users, staff, and providers within the child care system were seriously demoralized. Six years of financially bleeding the program had taken their toll. Parents and staff were exhausted. The enthusiasm for the 1988–89 fight against commercial care never approached the 1983–84 struggle.

249

While the new Child Care Act provides for the licensing of commercial care, the full implications of the act remain unknown. The details of the new Tory plan for child care will be contained within the regulations which have not been passed.[32] Government officials claim that commercial spaces will not be eligible for subsidy. But if the Saskatchewan government had any intentions to cost-share subsidies for commercial spaces when they first introduced the Child Care Act in June 1988, these hopes were dashed when federal Minister of Finance Michael Wilson eliminated Epp's child care initiatives from the 1989 budget.[33] Provision for federal cost-sharing of subsidy to child care is still operating under the Canada Assistance Plan Act, which does not provide for subsidization of commercial spaces in Saskatchewan.

The refusal to provide subsidies and start-up grants to commercial spaces may curtail some criticism about the use of public dollars for private ventures but it also ignores the perpetuation of a two-tiered system of child care. Those with more resources will be able to afford private care (with no subsidy), while those with less money will be restricted to specific centres and spaces that are eligible for subsidy. At the same time, the introduction of commercial care threatens the overall quality of day care. Research indicates that commercial centres operate at levels closer to regulated standards–which in Saskatchewan's case are so minimal that they afford little protection to children.[34] Most important, the experience of Ontario, Alberta, and the United States strongly suggests that once commercial care is allowed, those who have a vested interest become a persistent lobby group which presses for lower standards and public support for commercial care.[35]

CONCLUSION

In Saskatchewan, the child care crisis has intensified under the Tory government. The province has not kept abreast of current research and development in child care policies and services. It lags far behind other provinces in terms of the number of per capita licensed day care spaces, and this problem is particularly acute in rural areas. In addition, the quality of care has eroded under the Tories since publicly financed day care spaces have been continually underfunded.

The introduction of legislation supporting commercial care represents a new era in the provision of child care services. Until 1989, Saskatchewan was the only province which prohibited the development of new commercial child care; since 1974 all new child care centres had to be operated by nonprofit, parent-controlled boards. The passage of the Child Care Act in 1989 is consistent with the Tories' business approach to all aspects of social and economic life. Saskatchewan is open for business even in the area of child care.

Tory times really have been sorry times for children in Saskatchewan. Whether these sorry times will come to an end, however, is not simply dependent on a change in government. The Tories are not entirely to blame for the current child care crisis situation; the sad truth is that working parents and their children have not received adequate support from all three of Saskatchewan's main political parties. The Liberals, under Ross Thatcher, can be credited for implementing a woefully inadequate day care system, and the NDP left a vulnerable and underfunded nonprofit system.

As we move toward an election, it is imperative for supporters of a universal, nonprofit day care system to galvanize their efforts and demand specific commitments from everyone seeking support at the ballot box. Specific proposals are essential: first, the growth of commercial care must be ruled out; second, standards must be improved; third, partial funding through a direct grant to all licensed spaces must be introduced; fourth, a long-term plan should be developed for the establishment of new licensed day care spaces.

However, these proposals are the minimum requirements. Many employed parents wish to integrate their family responsibliities with the need to earn a living, but under the present system these two functions are regarded as mutually exclusive. The child care movement, therefore, needs to expand its political agenda beyond these immediate child care demands. Political parties must commit themselves to initiatives in the area of family/work policy. Such initiatives should include: fully paid parental leaves of at least six months; the right for employed parents of children below six years of age to shorten their work day by one hour; the right for paid days to care for sick children. In order for these changes to take place, politicians must work with organized labour and employers to develop job-sharing and flex-time programs for parents of young children. What is needed is a government that demonstrates a commitment to developing family-work policy of which good child care is an essential component.

THE BREAKDOWN OF PUBLIC WELFARE IN SASKATCHEWAN

by Graham Riches and Loralee Manning

W elfare reform as a policy of the Devine government can be traced to attempts in the 1980s in the United States to transform public welfare. Welfare reform in this context aimed to reduce welfare dependency by moving people off the social assistance rolls and back into the labour force. Achieving self-sufficiency was the prime goal. Other goals included: the reallocation of scarce resources to those most in need, the reduction of welfare expenditures, and the discouragement of fraud and abuse.[1] This was to be achieved by a variety of measures, including increased employment and training opportunities, workfare programs, benefit reductions, and more stringent eligibility requirements. In this way, welfare reform of the 1980s differed from earlier attempts in the 1970s in Canada and the United States which sought to reduce poverty by major expansions of cash welfare.[2]

When the Devine government set out to "reform" Saskatchewan's welfare system, it did so within the framework of the Canada Assistance Plan Act (CAP) of 1966.[3] This federal legislation sets out the terms under which the federal government assumes 50% of the cost of provincial social assistance programs. In order to receive the federal transfer payment, which in 1990–91 was budgeted to total $162 million,[4] the provincial government is obligated to ensure: that financial assistance is adequate to meet basic needs; that there is an appeal process for people who have been denied benefits or have been otherwise unfairly treated; that participation by recipients in any work or training programs is voluntary rather than a condition of assistance; and that eligibility for assistance is based on the fact and not the cause(s) of need.

This Chapter is adapted from: *Welfare Reform and the Canada Assistance Plan: the Breakdown of Public Welfare in Saskatchewan, 1981–1989,* (Working Paper Series No. 4), Regina: Social Administration Research Unit, 1989.

Determining eligibility on the basis of financial need is a central principle of the Canada Assistance Plan.[5] In his review of the origins and development of this program, Carleton University professor Allan Moscovitch writes that "social assistance was to be made available on the basis of a test which would look not only at the income of the person or persons but also at the relation between resources and budgetary requirements in order to arrive at an assessment of need." He goes on to point out that "the use of the term 'need' was meant to signify a change from the older categorical programs in which assistance was based on the particular characteristics of the person applying." The intention was to remove the means test and phase out categorical programs and, in so doing, remove the distinctions between employable and unemployable persons or between the deserving and nondeserving poor. In other words, granting assistance on the basis of need was intended to result in the elimination of the work test or the requirement that persons had "to accept employment as a condition of receipt of assistance."[6] The Devine government's reforms, and the American models to which the government looked for inspiration, challenged this principle. Those who were in need for reasons such as ill health or old age were judged to be deserving of assistance. Those who were at least theoretically capable of employment were judged to be less deserving.

In Saskatchewan, the specific origins of welfare reform lie in a study of the Saskatchewan Assistance Plan (SAP) commissioned in 1982 by the newly elected Progressive Conservative government and published in 1983. Its author was Duane Adams, the former deputy minister of social services in the previous administration. The study included a review of the U.S. experience, and the report's proposals and the welfare reform program instituted in 1984 were almost identical to the U.S. models. The Adams report concluded that SAP was:

> essentially non-productive for clients, helping clients very little except in the payment of minimum financial allowances. The system is dehumanising, adversarial, inequitable, relatively cheap in client benefits but wasteful administratively, inconsistent and unacceptably complex. The program is widely misunderstood by the public.[7]

It is essential to remember that by March 1983 the province was feeling the harsh effects of the economic recession and social assistance rolls were showing the impact of rising unemployment. By 1983, the number of people receiving social assistance from the provincial government had jumped 26.8% above the number two years earlier to 59,724 men, women, and children (see Table 12.1). One year later, when welfare reform was introduced, the number had increased to 63,703, and was still climbing. The figures do not include the approximately 20,000 treaty Indians in Saskatchewan receiving social assistance from the Department of Indian and Northern Development. [8]

The report's major recommendations were to find ways of moving people from social assistance into jobs and training, to streamline what was seen to be an unnecessarily complicated administrative structure, and to make greater use of the private, nongovernment, and voluntary sector.

Welfare reform as a specific government policy was introduced in March 1984, with a second stage being phased in toward the end of 1987. [9] It built on the main principles outlined in the Adam's report but in its intent and implementation adopted a more aggressive, stringent, and punitive approach.

Its stated aims were: (i) to reduce dependency on social assistance by moving single fully employable long-term clients into work and training programs; (ii) to provide equitable benefits for people unable to work; and (iii) to make SAP more efficient and more effective. This latter objective included the goal of reducing fraud and abuse. On the face of it, these seemed like wise and sensible commitments. However, the experience of welfare reform has been very different.

First, single employable people were required to participate in short-term, low-wage jobs through the Saskatchewan Employment Development Program (SEDP) or New Careers Corporation (NCC), and in upgrading and skills courses through the Saskatchewan Skills Development Program (SSDP). This was to be accomplished by cutting their financial assistance benefits by 35% to induce them to accept workfare employment. The $9 million thus saved was spent on short-term job programs and used to provide wage subsidies to business. Essentially it was a case of robbing the poor to pay the poor.

Second, benefit restructuring has not resulted in increased equity because all people on social assistance have seen the value of their benefits decline. Between 1981 and 1988 the real purchasing power of benefits declined by 54% for single employable people and by 28% for families with dependent children (see Table 12.2).

Third, the attempt to increase efficiency has been spearheaded by

255

antifraud activities that have created a stringent and punitive environment for social workers, financial aid staff, and more particularly, for welfare recipients themselves. Not only has the intent been to cut people off assistance, but it has also been to deny them eligibility in the first place.

In other words, as the continuing high numbers on the social assistance rolls attest, welfare dependency has not been reduced. What has occurred is the increased pauperization of the already poor, the development of a climate of fear which makes it difficult for even the most courageous social workers within the system to speak out about current welfare reform practices, and the continuous implementation of welfare policies and practices which violate not only basic tenets of human dignity but also the purposes and conditions of the CAP. It is not possible to provide documented evidence with regard to the fear felt by many workers and clients, although one recent study of the experiences of welfare recipients in Saskatchewan does address this concern. Social assistance recipients reported being accused of lying about their welfare claims, being untrustworthy, not being properly informed of the entitlements and being intimidated by the appeal process.[10]

THE EROSION OF ADEQUACY

In analyzing the impact of welfare reform upon the adequacy of SAP benefits, it is necessary to make a conceptual distinction between an entitlement and the actual benefit which is received by a claimant or recipient. The **benefit entitlement** is the amount of financial assistance to which an eligible person in need is entitled according to the SAP regulations and the CAP cost-sharing conditions, and which the claimant has a legal right to receive. In 1989, the **SAP benefit entitlement** is that amount of financial assistance deemed adequate to meet the basic requirements of food, shelter, clothing, utilities (gas, electricity, telephone, water), household supplies, and personal requirements including travel. In addition, benefits can be provided to meet a range of special needs.

The **real basic allowance** is the amount of dollars or financial assistance actually received by a recipient to meet the costs of food, clothing, household, personal, and travel costs after deductions have been made for rent and for utilities. Families with dependent children receive family allowance payments and child tax credits in addition to the real basic allowance. However, the full value of the family allowance has already been taxed back at a 100% rate from the social assistance entitlement.

Both the benefit entitlement and the real basic allowance can be reduced on account of overpayments, advances, and duplicate assistance, i.e., monies recouped from social assistance cheques. In practice the concept of the real basic allowance is itself somewhat misleading because it fails to take into account these forms of forgone income. One needs to identify what might be termed a forgone basic allowance, that is all the money reclaimed by the government, and finally a net basic allowance, which is the amount people actually receive to meet their basic income requirements.

The welfare reform introduced in 1984 has not led to any overall increases in the levels of benefit entitlements for single, long-term, fully employable persons nor for families on social assistance. Overall, entitlements have been subjected to deep cuts in value and adequacy. In terms of current dollars, the entitlement for a single person declined by 31.5%, from $548 per month in 1981 to $375 in 1989. Savings from these cuts funded the initial employment and training schemes in 1984.

Entitlements for single parent and husband/wife families have remained frozen at current levels for the same eight-year period. While it is true that the amount to meet basic requirements was increased since 1987 for single persons and families, this increase was accompanied by a cut in the allowances for transportation and laundry. Allowances for certain add-ons such as fridge and stove costs have also been eliminated. As a consequence of these changes the overall benefit entitlements remained the same during the 1980s but inflation caused a real decline in their purchasing power.

What this means in cold, hard terms is that in 1989, a single unemployed but employable person in Saskatchewan is entitled to receive $375 a month for all his or her basic requirements including shelter and utilities. A single mother with two children is expected to live on $900 per month and a husband/wife family with four children on $1,384 per month.

When inflation is taken into account for the period 1981–89 (Table 12.2), the extreme seriousness of the situation can be realized. By 1988, the real purchasing power of the entitlement for single fully employable persons had fallen to $207 per month (constant 1981 dollars), or by a staggering 64.4%. For the single mother and her two children, it had dropped by 28.8% to a monthly rate of $652 (constant 1981 dollars) and for the husband/wife family by 27.7% to $1,006 per month (constant 1981 dollars).

When SAP benefit entitlements are measured against poverty lines, minimum wage levels, and average incomes, it is clear that welfare reform has had a devastating impact on the adequacy of the social assistance entitlement. A single person's entitlement in 1988 stands at only 41% of the poverty line. This is less than half of the provincial minimum wage and one quarter of the average Canadian income for an unattached individual. Even on minimum wage the single person, earning twice what he or she would be receiving on social assistance, would be living below the poverty line. The 19th century English poor-law principle of less eligibility, which stated that no one on public relief should receive more than the lowest-paid wage earner,[11] is today being rigorously applied by welfare reform in Saskatchewan.

The single mother with two children is likewise very vulnerable; her SAP entitlement is only 60% of the poverty line and 67% of the average Canadian income for a single-parent family (1986). If a job at minimum wage was her only source of income she would be $2,309 per year worse off and she would also have to start paying for medical drugs and supplies and for eye and dental care. The two-parent family is also better off on welfare than if one of them worked at minimum wage. However, their SAP entitlement is only 62% of the poverty line and less than half of the average Saskatchewan family income (1986).[12]

In the real world of welfare, what one is entitled to receive is one thing, what one actually gets is very different. The fact is that after actual rent and utility costs have been paid, those on long-term social assistance frequently find that the already marginal monthly basic-needs allowance can be reduced by as much as a third to a half depending on family size. One reason for this is that welfare reform has resulted in caps being placed on what the government will allow for rent and utilities. In 1984, the maximum rental allowance for single fully employable persons was reduced from $300 to $200 per month. Actual costs are invariably higher, and the difference has to be made up from the basic allowance. A second reason is that laundry, transportation, and certain add-ons for stoves and fridges have also been cut.

The impact on the real basic allowance is dramatic. Using the CMHC figures for the average cost of a bachelor apartment as an estimate of true housing costs, the benefit entitlement for a single, unemployed, but fully employable person on long-term benefits can be reduced by $75 a month, leaving a real basic allowance of $65 per month or $16 per week. Sixteen dollars a week is all that remains to meet the basic requirements of food, clothing, household, personal, and travel costs.[13]

For families with dependent children the situation is equally depressing. A single mother with two children can be left, after the true cost of housing, with a real basic allowance as low as $26 per person per week;[14] and a husband/wife family with four children with an amount as low as $23 per person per week.[15] Even with the addition of the monthly family allowance cheque and the annual or semiannual child tax credit, it is difficult to understand how families are able to meet their basic requirements on such sub-subsistence levels of income. The short answer, of course, is that they do not.

Another way of appreciating the sheer inadequacy of the real basic allowance is to compare it to Agriculture Canada's weekly nutritious food-basket cost. This is an officially sanctioned and objective measure. Even the SAP food entitlement is below the basic requirement for teenagers (10–18 years) and adult males (19–49 years), although the entitlement for adult females is sufficient.[16] However, the real basic allowance of $16 per week, even if it was just for food, would only be approximately half the amount specified as necessary by Agriculture Canada. Of course, the real amount is much less since the money has to be spent on a range of basic requirements. For families, a similar situation of absolute deprivation applies.

As previously noted, the real basic allowance may not be the same as the actual income received because it does not take into account further deductions for overpayments. It is the net basic allowance which takes into account this additional forgone income.

Overpayments refer to monies received but to which the recipient was not entitled due to administrative error or failure to report income or assets. In Saskatchewan overpayments can be recovered at a rate of up to 10% of maximum entitlement per month or according to a sliding scale.

Advances refer to lump sum payments loaned against future entitlements. They are granted to social assistance recipients (except single, fully employable, and childless couples) to enable them to defray certain unavoidable household costs. Advances are always issued at a rate of $60 per month for up to six months and are reclaimed at the same rate even though for some people the budgetary allowance is $30 per month.

Duplicate assistance refers to the cost of emergency food vouchers received from the Department of Social Services itself and to the price of "free" meals eaten at the Salvation Army. These costs are charged to the government which recovers its expenditures ($3 per meal) from the welfare recipient's cheque.

259

Approximately one-third of those receiving social assistance in the province are having overpayments deducted from their cheques.[17] Repayments can amount to $5 million a year.

A recent decision by the Federal Court of Canada with respect to the Finlay case in Manitoba stated that where the collection of an overpayment results in an assistance recipient's basic needs being left unmet, then the collection is in breach of the terms of the CAP. The rate of overpayments charged against Mr. Finlay's social allowance deprived the recipient of his basic needs; undue hardship was caused. And as Judge Teitelbaum noted, 'it is undue hardship that is caused to a person who may not have sufficient funds to feed himself or at least to look after himself with the basic necessities one requires.'[18] The Federal Court ordered the federal government to suspend CAP payments to Manitoba until its overpayment collection policy conformed with the terms of CAP. The decision has been upheld by the Federal Court of Appeal, and is expected to reach the Supreme Court of Canada. Two points should be noted about the implications of this ruling for Saskatchewan. First, the overpayment collection rate in Saskatchewan at the time of the ruling was higher than that of Manitoba. Second, while most other provinces responded to the ruling by lowering the overpayment collection rate for assistance recipients, the Devine government raised its collection rate a month after the Finlay decision.

The impact of overpayments on the net basic allowances can be devastating. In the case of the single mother with one child, her weekly allowance to meet basic requirements (food, clothing, personal, household, and travel costs) is reduced from $43.16 per person to a real basic allowance of $29.90 per person. If an overpayment is being recovered, she is left with $18.73 each for herself and her child. In other words, her allowance to meet basic requirements has been more than halved.

In the case of the childless couple, after deductions for actual rent and utility costs and for an advance and overpayments, the weekly allowance to meet basic requirements has shrunk from $36.16 per person to a net basic allowance of $8.40 each. It is clear that the combination of rent and utility costs and overpayment deductions can turn subsistence allowances into totally inadequate pittances. In the light of such data, it is not inappropriate to speak of the breakdown of public welfare in Saskatchewan.

Further evidence of the inadequacy of social assistance benefits in Saskatchewan lies in the continued growth of food bank usage. It has been argued elsewhere that the growth of food banks in Canada is concrete evidence of the collapse of the public safety net.[19] In Saskatchewan welfare reform has contributed to this breakdown. The first food bank in the province was established in Regina in 1983 with others being set up in Saskatoon and Prince Albert the following year. They are now springing up in small towns and rural communities. The majority of food bank users are on social assistance and the largest single beneficiary group is children.[20]

What is of interest is that the Regina, Saskatoon, and Prince Albert food banks have seen their usage increase from their first full year of operation to 1988 by 70%, 165%, and 89% respectively. During the same period, social assistance caseloads have declined for each city by 10%, 7.5%, and 9.7% respectively. The sharpest decreases in social assistance caseloads occurred between March 1987 and September 1988 when they dropped by 20% in Regina, 10% in Saskatoon, and 12% in Prince Albert. In the same period, Regina food bank usage increased by 15.9% and between March 1987 and 1989 rose by 42%.[21] It should also be noted that between 1987 and 1988 Saskatchewan was the only province in Canada which saw its labour force and the number of employed people decline and, along with Manitoba, was the only province which saw its rate of unemployment rise.[22]

It could, of course, be argued that the decline in the welfare rolls was due to the impact of welfare reform in returning significant numbers of people to long-term paid employment. However, as noted previously, there is no publicly available data to support this. Given that the steepest declines occurred from early 1987 onwards, the more likely explanations are that increasing numbers of persons have been cut off or denied eligibility or have simply left the province. In this period benefits and earnings exemptions were lowered, shelter and utility caps were imposed, and travel allowances were cut. The effect of these measures is to make eligibility more difficult. At the same time, the Home Verification Unit (formerly the Entitlement Control Unit) and the Special Investigations Branch were introduced and surveillance of welfare clients was increased.

The stark fact is that food bank usage continues to rise because many on social assistance run out of money well before the end of each month. The Department of Social Services advises claimants to go to the food bank instead of issuing vouchers pending approval of applications or granting interim assistance pending the outcome of an appeal. In this way, the food bank is used as a substitute for social assistance. The sad story is that many on social assistance are destitute and are being forced to resort to public begging.

THE FAILURE OF WORKFARE

In 1986 Saskatchewan and Canada signed the first Employability Enhancement Accord between a province and the federal government. The accord, which was one part of the Canadian Jobs Strategy, was designed to ensure cost-shared funding for the province so as to enable a percentage of social assistance clients to gain work and training experience. The stated goals of this endeavour are to be applauded and were consistent with the major recommendations of the Adams Report. Participation in the schemes was to be voluntary.

One problem, however, was that the federal funding which was to be shared with Saskatchewan and other provinces for employability enhancement was to be diverted from the Canada Assistance Plan. No new money was to be expended on the schemes. In one very real sense, the logical outcome would be to reduce welfare benefits. As previously noted, in 1984 the Saskatchewan government had already cut the benefits of single, unemployed, employable persons as an inducement for them to find work. Employability enhancement and workfare were, it would seem, indistinguishable in terms of welfare reform policy.

Another more fundamental issue is that the purpose of Conservative welfare reform is to separate the "employable" from the "unemployable" and force the former into the labour market. Workfare is the device whereby those on social assistance who are unemployed but deemed fully employable are compelled or induced into accepting work or training. Whether the work pays adequate wages or whether long-term employment is available on the completion of the training course are not the issues. The real policy agenda of welfare reform and workfare has been to reduce the social assistance rolls and cut social spending.

It has already been observed that there is little evidence to support the view that the employment and training schemes introduced by welfare reform in Saskatchewan between 1984 and 1989 have resulted in a meaningful decrease in welfare dependency. Indeed, if welfare reform had resulted in the majority or even half of fully employable persons obtaining stable, well-paid, long-term employment, or if they had been trained in areas where new jobs were opening up, one would have to conclude that workfare had been successful. However, there is a different story to tell.

The 1989 Saskatchewan budget papers state that "over 10,000 participants have received skills training and employment from the Saskatchewan Works Program" and that over 1,000 individuals have participated in New Careers Corporation projects with hundreds of individuals being trained for forestry jobs.[23] Given the scarcity of reliable public data in this field, it is difficult to determine the validity of these claims.

What can be ascertained is that between 1985 and 1988 SEDP spent $25 million creating 4,893 job placements for social assistance recipients in 1,516 approved projects.[24] In addition, a number of NCC jobs were provided in provincial parks. Interestingly, 45% of the jobs were in nonprofit agencies, with local government and private business dividing the remainder between them. Ironically, it was the public sector in the shape of municipal government and publicly funded NGOs (nongovernmental organizations) which contributed 72% of the job placements.

These statistics sound attractive until we realize that these placements represent only an average of 16% of the fully employable SAP caseload between 1985 and 1988. The fully employable caseload has shown a decline of 1,678 for the same period, but it should be noted that the fully employable/unemployable categories were changed in 1988, resulting in a significant decrease in the employable classification. Between 1984 and 1987 the fully employable caseload continued to represent 25% of unemployed persons in the province.[25]

The majority of jobs subsidized through welfare reform are short term, lasting 20–23 weeks. This is just long enough for the erstwhile social assistance recipients to be recycled back onto the unemployment insurance rolls. It is not known how many find long-term jobs. There is, therefore, little reason to believe that workfare is significantly reducing welfare dependency in Saskatchewan. This finding is consistent with U.S. studies.[26]

In terms of upgrading and skills training, about one in five of the fully employable caseload participated in SSDP programs between 1985 and 1988. This figure matches that presented in the 1989 budget speech. Clearly for some these are worthwhile programs. Yet the question remains whether the training does translate into long-term employment and adequate wages. This appears unlikely given the fact (as previously noted) that Saskatchewan was the only province in Canada which saw the size of its labour force and the numbers of employed people fall between 1987 and 1988, and was one of only two provinces, the other being Manitoba, which experienced an increase in its rate of unemployment. Perhaps the most

263

significant finding is that five years after the introduction of welfare reform, the provincial social assistance caseloads remain 27% higher than when the current Progressive Conservative administration came to office in 1982.

There is then considerable evidence to suggest that workfare has failed to reduce welfare dependency. The implication from a federal perspective is that the cost-sharing of the Employability Enhancement Accords is a failed strategy. One must therefore look elsewhere to explain the decrease of 1,678 social assistance cases between 1985 and 1988.

Perhaps this decline can best be explained in terms of the increasing application by the Saskatchewan Department of Social Services of a range of mandatory eligibility tests to social assistance recipients. The purpose of the tests has been to restrict or deny eligibility and to cut benefits. The intent is also to deter new applications.

In any needs-based entitlement program, there will a screening process for current and potential recipients. The point is, of course, that if the policy objective is to screen people out rather than ensure that their entitlements are met, then ways have to be found to make eligibility for assistance more exacting. The task of the financial-aid worker then becomes one of denying eligibility or cutting people off benefits.

In theory, according to the Memorandum of Agreement signed between Canada and Saskatchewan on 22 March 1967, all that is required to determine the eligibility of a person in need is for a test to be applied which takes "into account that person's budgetary requirements and the income and resources available to him to meet those requirements." [27] The memorandum further defines a person as being in need "where the aggregate of that person's budgetary requirements exceeds the aggregate of the income and resources available to him to meet his budgetary requirements." [28] The implication is that adjustments are to be made for family size and short or long-term needs.

While such a formula still leaves much room for policy and field-practice discretion in determining what should constitute available resources in relation to a person's income needs, nevertheless, the obligation to meet basic requirements still applies. It is the needs test which remains the prime condition for cost-sharing social programs.

However, the introduction of welfare reform in Saskatchewan reveals a growing gap between the rhetoric of federal and provincial legislation regarding needs testing and the reality of the intensifying eligibility tests. The Devine government, under the guise of welfare reform, has imposed numerous tests which a person must meet in order to receive assistance. In Saskatchewan, it is no longer enough to be in financial need to receive assistance. It is also necessary for the recipient to conduct his financial, personal, and even sexual behaviour in a way that is deemed to be appropriate by the Department of Social Services. Failure to act in the prescribed manner can result in a reduction, termination, or denial of assistance.

The "man-in-the-house" test is a test of domestic interdependence. If it is shown that people of the opposite sex who are sharing the same accommodation are financially and emotionally supportive of each other, then they are deemed to be in a common-law or spousal relationship. If the person who is sharing the dwelling is independent of social assistance, then he (and sometimes she) is assumed to be able to supply the needs of those who are receiving social assistance. If the Department of Social Services makes this assumption, the onus falls on the SAP recipient to prove that she is not involved in a spousal relationship. Its major effect is that a mother and her children will be disentitled to benefits, and any benefits received, usually from the date of application, will be assessed as an overpayment. [29]

In addition to regulating the sexual behaviour, real or imagined, of assistance recipients, the Saskatchewan Department of Social Services also makes a flawless record in the workforce or training programs a condition of assistance. Assistance regulations require, as a condition of eligibility, that a recipient has explored and taken advantage of "every possibility of self support, rehabilitation, and re-establishment." [30]

This rule has been interpreted in such a way that recipients who are categorized as fully employable will be denied benefits if they fail to conduct an "adequate" job search, if they fail to complete an approved training course, and if they quit or are fired from a job. [31] This section has been applied in a particularly punitive manner toward recipients who have some reluctance to participate in government-sponsored programs such as SEDP, SSDP, and the NCC. According to the federal-provincial cost-sharing arrangements for such projects, participation was to be voluntary. [32] This condition reflected the CAP principle that eligibility for financial assistance was to be based on a test of need and by implication ruled out mandatory work requirements. CAP also specifically stated that participation in work activity projects was to be voluntary. [33] With welfare reform, this requirement was ignored.

In addition to making "appropriate" sexual conduct and performance in the employment market conditions of assistance, other mandatory tests for receiving assistance in Saskatchewan include ensuring that any money received by an applicant in the two-year period prior to application was disposed of in a manner approved of by the department, and requiring that a person in need have a permanent and approved residency prior to the granting of assistance. The principle that financial need should be the central test of eligibility for assistance has been abandoned in Saskatchewan.

CONCLUSION

The foregoing analysis of welfare reform in Saskatchewan provides strong evidence of the breakdown of public welfare in the province. On a number of fronts, the evidence is compelling that Saskatchewan's public safety net is no longer capable of responding to the basic income requirements of thousands of men, women, and children who are legitimately entitled to receive adequate benefits. Moreover, it is clear that since the introduction of welfare reform in 1984, many of the federal cost-sharing provisions of the Canada Assistance Plan have not been honoured by the province.

It is not possible to hold any department of social services accountable for the forces which create the general and prevailing conditions which give rise to the need for social assistance in the first place. Yet it is perhaps pertinent to ask: How appropriate it is for those who are publicly charged with the responsibility for advancing public welfare to be presiding over its breakdown?

WELFARE REFORM AS MORAL REFORM IN SASKATCHEWAN

by Diana Ralph and Mark Stobbe

Saskatchewan has been a bad place to be poor during the 1980s. During the tenure of the Devine Conservatives, those unfortunate enough to be forced to rely on the province's income support programs have been subjected to a program of "welfare reform" which has featured cuts in benefits, work for welfare programs, arbitrary treatment, and public insults from political leaders. The preceding chapter by Graham Riches and Loralee Manning has outlined changes to the Saskatchewan Assistance Plan (SAP) which have undermined the adequacy of benefits and imposed criteria other than financial need in the determination of entitlement. This chapter will focus on assistance recipients' day-to-day treatment at the hands of the government.

Under Grant Devine's administration, the Saskatchewan government has sought to reintroduce the concept of the deserving and the undeserving poor. The deserving poor—the old and the infirm—were to receive assistance and support. While this acceptance did not go so far as to entail any increase in benefits, the deserving poor were exempted from the harshest and most punitive aspects of welfare reform.

The undeserving poor comprising all of those judged to be physically capable of working were not so fortunate. For these people, poverty was seen as a sign of moral failing. With this view of the world, people are unemployed not because there are no jobs, but because they are too lazy to find and keep a job. Children are hungry not because their parents do not have enough income to feed them, but because they spend their income on beer and bingo rather than on food. This individualistic and moralistic approach to the problems of poverty is rooted in a fundamentalist theology. Just as the immoral are to be denied a place in heaven and consigned to eternal suffering, so should they be made to pay for their transgressions on earth. The only alternative to this fate of eternal damnation, in this life and the next, is moral redemption. This must be an act of individual initiative. The poor must pull themselves up by their bootstraps, change their ways, and get a job. Even though this is an achievement which can only be accomplished by each individual, there is a role for the government. Instead of being content with ensuring that welfare met recipients' basic financial needs, the Devine Conservatives wanted to reshape the behaviour and personalities of recipients. The social service system has been used to monitor behaviour, to punish wrong doing, and to intensify the consequences of inappropriate action. The Department of Social Services functions as the stern parent attempting to teach wayward children proper attitudes.

The premise that those on assistance are morally flawed led to more than exhortations to the poor to pull up their bootstraps. It inevitably resulted in the belief that "abuse" of welfare programs was widespread. Many, if not most, of people applying for benefits were suspected of being simply out to get something for nothing. Suspicion was institutionalized. For example, a policy of forcing recipients classified as employable to pick up their cheques in person at designated times was implemented. Being late for the appointment, failing to pick up a cheque, having no identification, or having identification with a different address were all taken as indications that the person was not eligible for assistance. After the first month of the cheque pick-up program, Minister of Social Services Grant Schmidt announced that almost 20% of single employable recipients did not receive their assistance that month. These people had their benefits terminated, and the minister threatened to investigate them all for fraud.[1] By August 1989, 2,910 people had been cut off assistance for failing to pick up their cheques at the designated time. Of these, 1,160 were reinstated after they managed to explain why they had missed the appointment. The remaining 1,750 were deemed to be "unaccounted for" and were permanently cut from the assistance rolls. Schmidt presented this as an indication of widespread fraud and abuse.[2] A more plausible explanation is that in the normal course of events, some people do go off assistance. If a recipient found employment or moved from the province, the cheque would not have been picked up because it was not needed any longer. Failure to pick up a cheque that was no longer needed was portrayed as abuse. Meanwhile, over 1,000 people who were in need and were entitled to assistance had their benefits temporarily cut off.

This discrepancy between the claims of widespread fraud and its actual incidence was not unusual. Schmidt regularly claimed that 10% of assistance recipients were receiving benefits fraudulently.[3] These figures were never substantiated. The concrete measures of fraud differed from the estimates in Schmidt's speeches. For example, in 1988–89, 54 assistance recipients were convicted of fraud.[4] This amounted to fewer than one per thousand cases.

However, the government never abandoned its belief that welfare fraud was rampant; the price of fiscal responsibility is eternal vigilance. As a result, a new branch of the Department of Social Services, the Special Investigations Branch (popularly known as the "Fraud Squad"), was created. Composed primarily of former members of the RCMP, its mandate was to root out fraud and punish wrongdoers. The activities of the Special Investigations Branch promptly resulted in allegations of electronic surveillance, opening of mail, and the posting of observers outside of the homes of female recipients. Assistance recipients who were active in welfare rights organizations believed they had an inordinate chance of receiving attention from the branch.[5] The actions of the Special Investigations Branch were defended by Schmidt on the grounds that:

> to use old fashioned terminology, when you look at a barrel of apples, you have a lot of good apples and you have a few bad apples . . . we can't leave them in the barrel so that they ruin the life for the good ones.[6]

The creation of the "Fraud Squad" as a separate unit within the Department of Social Services and the enthusiastic support the squad received from the government is indicative of attitudes towards assistance recipients. However, the day-to-day activity of the department's social workers primarily determines the treatment of recipients. Regardless of the personal inclination of an individual social worker, the attitude of the government towards the poor ultimately has an impact on the way an individual recipient is treated. Decisions on hiring, promotion, demotion, and allocation of cases send powerful clues to employees of the Department of Social Services about what their priorities should be in dealing with recipients. It is difficult to quantify an operating attitude of a government department. In Devine's Saskatchewan, assistance recipients almost invariably report that they feel everything they say is disbelieved. Rudeness, lack of consideration, failure to explain what is happening, and even failure to return telephone calls are pervasive.

One indication of the new regime at the Department of Social Services is the dramatic growth in the number of appeals. Table 13.1 outlines the volume of appeals being launched by assistance recipients. The number of appeals being heard by the first level of the appeal process increased from 200 in 1982–83 to 950 in 1988–89. The number of appeals forwarded to the second level of the appeal process increased from 40 to 164 during the same time period.

This growth in the number of appeals took place while advocacy services to assistance recipients all but disappeared. Before 1988, each major urban centre in Saskatchewan possessed a government-funded agency which provided trusteeship services to recipients, conducted educational activity about welfare entitlements, and provided advocacy services. In June 1988, the government terminated the core funding, and offered fee for service funding to these groups. For advocacy services, the government proposed the fee of $40 per case.[7] With the exception of the Regina Welfare Rights Agency, all of the welfare advocacy agencies were forced to close their doors.[8] Recipients were left to fend for themselves in the appeal process. Few enjoyed any success. In 1988–89, the first year after the abolition of the advocacy services, only 16.3% of appeals before the local appeal panels were decided in favour of the client. This was a decline from 27.1% the preceding year. At the provincial appeal board, the recipient success rate dropped from 16.2% to 10.4%.[9]

In addition to this dramatic growth in the sheer volume of appeals, two new policies are indicative of the new regime.

First, there was an increasing tendency for decisions of the local appeals panels favourable to recipients to be contested by the department. The number of these cases rose from 16 in 1985–86 to 49 in 1988–89.[10] Thus, where the local appeal panel members ruled that the department was violating its regulations, the verdict was not accepted in one third of all cases.

Second, a presumption of the recipient's guilt was instituted. It had been long-standing practice to grant minimal interim assistance pending the completion of the appeal process to any recipient whose application for benefits was denied or whose benefits had been terminated. The rationale was that since SAP is the program of last resort, benefits should not be terminated until the recipient either accepted the termination, or the appeal process had been completed and the action had been found to be justified. This policy placed a high priority on ensuring that all of those entitled to benefits actually received them. Prevention of undue hardship to the innocent was valued more than ensuring that the guilty were punished immediately.

During Schmidt's tenure as minister, the policy on interim benefits changed. To be accused of being ineligible for benefits meant that the recipient would go without benefits until the completion of the appeal process. The denial of interim benefits was continued even in many cases where the local appeal panel had ruled in favour of the recipient, and the department was appealing this decision. The result was that a recipient can be cut off benefits for three to four months prior to the final determination of whether the action was justified.

This new policy of treating all accused as guilty has been applied with a vengeance. In a report of 71 appeals involving the termination or denial of benefits handled by the Regina Welfare Rights Centre over a six-month period, Riches and Manning report that only four were granted interim assistance.[11] It should be noted that this group is not a representative sample because they were among the relatively fortunate few with access to advocates who could press the request for interim assistance.

INDIVIDUAL REFORMATION THROUGH WELFARE REFORM

The punitive approach to dispensing social assistance was not motivated by meanness. The government's policies of welfare reform were aimed at reforming the individual recipient. The social assistance network was transformed into a system wherein action offending the moral code of government members was promptly and severely punished. Singled out for special reforming zeal were the sexual mores and adherence to the work ethic of assistance recipients.

The government was extremely vigilant for inappropriate sexual activity by assistance recipients. The second page of the policy manual for the Saskatchewan Assistance Plan instructs social workers to be on the alert for couples living in common law relationships. The manual outlines "suggested points of enquiry" to determine whether an applicant or recipient is

> living as a family unit having established a common-law relationship . . . an accumulation of these characteristics suggest an interdependence typical of a legally married couple. In situations where a couple appears to be living common law, *it is the client's responsibility to clearly establish otherwise.* [emphasis in the original][12]

Should a social worker rule that a recipient is living common law, assistance is denied or terminated. Any assistance paid since the common law relationship was alleged to have begun is assessed as an overpayment which must be repaid to the department. The person who had been on assistance or had applied for assistance is deemed to be able to receive financial support from their alleged common law spouse. If this person does not have sufficient income, the "family unit," as determined by the Department of Social Services, is able to apply for assistance as a single unit. Admission to the department's allegations becomes the only quick way to continue to receive the income necessary for survival. In cases where an application is made as a newly constituted family unit, the assistance cheque is almost invariably made out to the male. Thus, a female single parent will suddenly have the benefits for herself and her children terminated. In order to retain benefits, she is then forced to have the cheque made out in the name of the man with whom she is allegedly living common law.

In practice, the "man in the house" rule is used any time non-related people of the opposite sex are deemed to be sharing a residence. In order to discover common law relationships, members of the Special Investigations Branch place the homes of single parents on assistance under surveillance, and conduct home visits to count toothbrushes and search for men's clothing.[13] Judgement is often reached quickly and arbitrarily. In some cases, the department could not even name the person who was alleged to be the common law spouse of a recipient. Phone calls from neighbours informing Social Services that "a man" had been seen around the recipient's house were sufficient to result in the termination of benefits. A problem often cited by single parents is that if their ex-spouse visits to see his children, Social Services makes the presumption that the relationship is still intact and terminates benefits to the mother and children. In one case, a single parent offered temporary shelter to her teenage son's friend who was experiencing family trouble in his own home. Her assistance was terminated, and she was told that the newly constituted "family unit" could reapply with her son's friend listed as the head of the household. The cheque upon which she and her five children depended would then be issued to the teenager.[14]

Once it is determined to a social worker's satisfaction that a recipient is living common law, the person is faced with the alternative of admitting guilt and reapplying as a new constituted family unit (if the alleged spouse has little or no income), or with the prospect of a three to four month appeal process. If the department alleges that a recipient is living in a common law relationship with a person who does have an income, the benefits are terminated on the grounds that the recipient can and must receive support from a person who has no legal obligation to provide this financial support. During this time, she and her family will probably have no income, and be forced to justify every aspect of their personal life before a group of strangers. It is worth stressing once again that in this process the onus is not on the Department of Social Services to prove their allegations, but on the recipient to disprove them. The effect of the policy is to impose severe restrictions on a recipient's ability to live anything approaching a normal life, since there is the fear that any inter-action with a member of the opposite sex, no matter how casual, could result in a loss of income.

In addition to ensuring that a recipient is either chaste or in an approved family unit while on assistance, the department also attempts to ensure that fathers of children in households receiving assistance pay for the support of their children. This can be considered a laudable goal. However, the department has pursued this goal in a typically heavy-handed fashion. As a condition of receiving assistance, recipients are required to apply for child support payments and to apply to the Maintenance Enforcement Branch for collection.[15] Any support payments received are then deducted dollar for dollar from the family's assistance cheque. The application of this policy can be criticized on two grounds. First, by making application to the Maintenance Enforcement Branch compulsory, the government has institutionalized the judgement that the ex-spouse of any person on welfare cannot be trusted to make maintenance payments of his own accord. Second, by making an application for child support payments a condition of assistance, the government refuses to allow women to decide whether they should fight for these payments. In some cases, a woman will have good and valid reasons for not wanting to attempt to secure child support payments. These can range from attendant complications in custody pro-ceedings to a fear of physical violence. Once again, however, the threat of denying welfare benefits is used to impose the government's moral agenda.

Just as a recipient's sexual activity, real or imagined and past or present, can become grounds for the denial or termination of assistance, so too can insufficient adherence to the work ethic. According to SAP regulations, as a condition of eligibility every recipient must:

produce evidence that he has explored within the limits of his ability every possibility of self support, rehabilitation and re-establishment including making application for assistance and services provided in Saskatchewan by any department or agency of any government or by any crown corporation.[16]

This regulation has formed the basis for compulsory "work-fare" programs in Saskatchewan. It has also been used to terminate the benefits of hundreds of assistance recipients categorized as employable.

Beginning with the first phase of "welfare reform" instituted under Gordon Dirks in 1984, an alphabet soup of work and training programs was created. The Saskatchewan Employment Development Program (SEDP) was designed to subsidize employers who hired assistance recipients for 20-week periods (i.e., just long enough to qualify for unemployment insurance benefits). The Saskatchewan Skills Development Program (SSDP) was established to provide educational upgrading to recipients who had not previously completed elementary or high school. The New Careers Corporation (NCC) was created as a contracting company employing assistance recipients. The goal was twofold. First, NCC would undertake construction projects designed to enhance the province's tourist appeal. Second, it would teach assistance recipients construction work skills.[17] Later, the Saskatchewan Works Program (SWP) was established to fill the same role as the SEDP. In 1986, the Department of Social Services reached an agreement with the federal government to allow cost-sharing of its work and training programs under the auspices of the Canada Jobs Strategy.[18]

These programs designed to remove people from the welfare rolls suffered from several flaws. For example, only recipients classified as employable could attend classes offered by the SSDP. If a person who was classified as unemployable because of a physical disability wished to attend with the hope of preparing to learn a skill which would be within his physical capacity, he must first be re-classified as employable. For a single person, this results in a cut of $55/month in the basic allowance and a $110/month cut in the maximum allowable shelter allowance. The recipient is thus subjected to a cut of up to $165/month in an already meagre income if he or she attempts to return to school rather than being content to accept assistance indefinitely.[19]

When the NCC contracted with Par Industries of Prince Albert to clear underbrush from forest areas, and with the Meewasin Valley Authority in Saskatoon for development work along the riverbank, workers were hired on a two week on, two week off cycle. At minimum wage, this ensured that their earnings would be the same or less as on assistance.[20] Like the other work programs designed to remove people from the welfare rolls, once a participant accumulated enough weeks to qualify for unemployment insurance, he was released.

But the idiosyncrasies of these programs pale before the fundamental objection to them. Both the Canada Assistance Plan Act and the federal/provincial accord on enhancing the employability of social assistance recipients require that participation in work and training programs be voluntary. However, in practice, failure to participate in an assigned program results in the termination of SAP benefits. In the fiscal year 1988/89, Schmidt notes that 3,800 recipients were cut off benefits for "failing to take a job when it was offered to them or failing to take education or training when it was offered to them." For 902 of these people, the termination of benefits was permanent. Termination for refusing to participate in a work or training program, or for failing to meet the standards of the program, was immediate. It is worth stressing that of the 3,800 people who had been cut off assistance for failure to satisfactorily participate in a work or training program, 2,898 had explanations for their actions that were satisfactory to the Department of Social Services.[21] However, with the "shoot first, ask questions later" policy, these people were forced to undergo the traumatic experience of having their assistance benefits terminated.

The most rigorously applied of the "employment enhancement" programs is the Job Search Training Program (JSTP). This is a three week program in which single employable recipients are taught how to compose a resume and conduct themselves during an interview. There is, in and of itself, nothing particularly objectionable to the training program. However, should a person referred to the program fail to attend the full program or be late for more than one session, assistance benefits are terminated. The recipient's file is then computer coded to prevent access by the local social services office. Thus, even if the social worker accepts the reasons for the failure to complete the program or even if the Appeals Panel rules that the recipient should be re-instated, benefits cannot be processed until senior program administrators in Regina agree to remove the computer coding. Riches and Manning note that this program is the largest single source of appeals by SAP recipients.[22]

When confronted with the provision in the Canada Assistance Plan

Act which states that "no person shall be denied assistance because he refuses or has refused to take part in a work activity program," [23] Schmidt asked, "since when is work illegal?" [24] According to Schmidt, welfare is not a right solely based on financial need. Adherence to the work ethic is a precondition for entitlement. Speaking to the legislature, he explained that:

> I do not apologize to anyone who was cut off welfare for refusing a job. I do not . . . Where people will not go to the trouble of picking up their cheque or will not work when they are offered a job, there is no right to sit on welfare in Saskatchewan or in Canada. The member opposite thinks that is the state of the law. We have a difference of opinion. [25]

Most employable assistance recipients are on welfare not because of a lack of adherence to the work ethic, but because of a lack of jobs. However, the underlying assumption of Saskatchewan Department of Social Services policies is that most people are unemployed simply because they are lazy. Those who have no money because they are lazy have no right to support from tax dollars. A simple screening test gives a recipient one chance for training or employment. Should a recipient fail this test, the presumption of laziness is held to be proven, and benefits are terminated. What happens thereafter does not concern the government, although one can presume that government members assume that hunger will eventually motivate the person to change his attitudes.

In its treatment of those assistance recipients deemed to be lacking in either sexual morals or the work ethic, the Devine government has chosen to ignore the mandate of both federal and provincial assistance legislation. The existence of financial need is legislatively the primary criterion for determining eligibility for assistance. However, standards of morality and behaviour have become additional eligibility criteria for the assistance programs.

THE GOVERNMENT, THE COURTS, AND THE POOR

During the 1980s, two assistance recipients in Canada launched court cases that resulted in new legal interpretations of the rights of recipients of social assistance. In Saskatchewan, Murray Chambers successfully argued that human rights legislation should govern the terms under which assistance is granted. In Manitoba, Robert James Finlay demanded that the legislation authorizing cost-sharing arrangements between the federal and provincial governments be adhered to. Both cases have been hailed as victories for the poor. In Saskatchewan, the victories have been hollow ones.

In the 1984 round of welfare reform sponsored by Dirks, single assistance recipients categorized as employable were singled out for special treatment. Their clothing and household allowances were discontinued, resulting in a cut in their entitlement of $55/month. In addition, their maximum allowable shelter allowance was cut by $100/month.

The cut in benefits to "single employables" was challenged by Murray Chambers, an assistance recipient living in Saskatoon. Chambers filed a complaint with the Saskatchewan Human Rights Commission contending that the new policy was discriminatory on the basis of marital status since childless couples did not face a cut in benefits. The complaint was heard before a one person Board of Inquiry appointed by the minister of justice. The person appointed was Saskatoon lawyer Les Prosser. In April 1987, Prosser ruled that no violation of the Human Rights Code had occurred since assistance was not a service offered to the general public.[26] Had the ruling stood, assistance recipients would have been exempted from coverage under the province's Human Rights Code. However, upon appeal, the Saskatchewan Court of Appeal ruled that Prosser had erred in his rejection of the complaint. The case was returned to the Board of Inquiry, where it was found that discrimination had, in fact, occurred.[27] Three years after filing his complaint, Chambers received the back payment for the assistance he had been illegally denied and a payment for damages. The province was also required to pay back-payments to the estimated 12,000 people who had been discriminated against by the policy. In dollar terms, the ruling was the largest human rights award in Canadian history.

The government's response to the Chambers case is instructive. It not only vigorously contested Chambers' challenge to its policy, it also set out to malign him personally. Schmidt accused Chambers of shirking work and attempting to milk the public purse, stating that "I would think he would be better off using his energy looking for employment than looking for more government money."[28] When faced with the prospect of being forced to repay not just Chambers, but all others who had been discriminated against, Schmidt initially refused. "We've been providing jobs for these people. Since they've got jobs, they don't need back pay."[29] Upon being ordered to make the payments, the government has complied grudgingly. With the exception of including a letter along with the cheques of those still on assistance at the time of the ruling, it has not undertaken active efforts to locate the people who it discriminated against. Instead, it relied upon the victims hearing of the ruling and making an application for compensation. The Department of Social Services took several months to process the applications. Statistics on the number of people who have applied for and received compensation have not been released.

The passive attitude towards compensating those discriminated against contrasts sharply with the Devine government's prompt action to remove the basis of discrimination. Rather than raising benefits for single employable recipients, in December 1987 the government cut benefits to childless couples to levels comparable with those of single people. The reduction in benefits was now in accordance with the provisions of the Human Rights Code.

The second ground-breaking court ruling challenged the right of provincial governments to deduct money from assistance cheques for the recovery of overpayments.

Whenever a SAP recipient receives benefits in excess of what he is entitled to receive, the excess benefits are "posted as an overpayment" and recovered by the Department of Social Services. While the recipient is still on assistance, any outstanding overpayments are recovered at a rate set by the policy manual. Should the recipient no longer require benefits, the outstanding overpayment is sent to a special branch for collection.[30]

Overpayments are caused by a number of reasons, of which fraud is the least common. In general, overpayments occur if the recipient has unexpected income, has fluctuating income, or has changes in the composition of the family unit. They can also occur if the employees of the department make an error. A typical overpayment arises when a recipient is working at a job with fluctuating earnings. Assistance is paid at the beginning of the month on the basis of an estimate of the recipient's monthly earnings. The recipient is required to turn in wage stubs at the end of the month so that the actual earnings can be reconciled with the estimated earnings and the appropriate adjustment made. Because of high case loads, it is not uncommon for a social worker to accumulate the documentation of three or four months earnings prior to performing the reconciliation. If the recipient's earnings have been higher than estimated, suddenly there is a substantial overpayment. The provincial auditor estimates that the error rate in processing assistance benefits was 8.7% in 1987/88. This represented an improvement from 10% the previous year.[31] At any given time, approximately one third of all SAP recipients have an outstanding overpayment. If the recipient is working and has fluctuating earnings, it is almost inevitable that he will eventually have an overpayment assessed against him.[32]

Having an overpayment assessed against them can be a frustrating and bewildering experience for assistance recipients in Saskatchewan. In most cases, they first learn about the overpayment when their cheque arrives and a deduction has been made for recovery. The amount stated as owing on the cheque stub often fluctuates wildly from month to month with no apparent relationship to the amount that has been collected. Efforts to obtain clarification can be extremely frustrating, since the information available to the social worker who calls up the file on the computer is different from that which is printed on the cheque stub. In many cases, the social worker will simply admit that she cannot explain what has transpired, and attribute responsibility to the computer. It usually takes weeks or months, and extreme persistence, to obtain a detailed written explanation. In these cases, even when the department is unable to explain how the overpayment was calculated, the deduction for recovery continues unabated. Just as a recipient who is cut off benefits for allegedly living common law is presumed guilty until proven innocent, so too is a recipient alleged to owe money to the Department of Social Services; the onus is on the recipient to establish that the money is not in fact owed. Assistance cheques are, in effect, garnisheed for the collection of debts that cannot be explained, let alone proven.[33]

In Manitoba, an assistance recipient argued that the collection of overpayments in that province was in violation of the Canada Assistance Plan Act. Robert James Finlay maintained that because the federal government shared the cost of welfare programs under the terms of this legislation, the federal government was obligated to terminate the cost sharing agreement if its conditions were not being met. One of these conditions is that the province must determine the minimum amount of money required to live in that province, and then pay assistance sufficient to enable people to meet their basic needs. Finlay argued that because the Manitoba government had established the level sufficient to meet basic needs, and then paid out a smaller amount because of collection for overpayment recovery, the province was not meeting the obligation to meet basic needs. As a result, the federal government should cease its payments to Manitoba under the Canada Assistance Plan until such time

279

as the provincial program conformed to the conditions of the cost-sharing program.

In a landmark ruling handed down in January 1989, the Federal Court agreed with Finlay.[34] The federal government was ordered to suspend CAP payments to the province of Manitoba. The decision was appealed, with the government of Saskatchewan joining the appeal. In its intervention, the Saskatchewan government argued that:

> There is no obligation on the province to provide a specific dollar amount of social assistance each month. It is clear that the agreement itself does not contemplate that a particular dollar figure can be calculated to represent the cost of purchasing basic requirements.[35]

In short, the Devine government argued that it has no legal obligation to provide assistance to meet minimum basic needs.

On 6 July 1990, the Federal Court of Appeal upheld the decision in a unanimous vote, with Justice Mark MacGuigan writing that "it must not be blithely supposed that it is necessarily in the public interest to bleed those who live at or below the poverty line as a purgative for social health, even if the bleeding is only a little at a time and only once a month."[36] The Court of Appeal delayed enforcing its judgement pending an expected appeal to the Supreme Court of Canada.

The Finlay ruling does not directly affect Saskatchewan or any province except Manitoba. However, if Manitoba is ultimately found to be violating the terms of CAP, Saskatchewan's overpayment collection policies will place its transfer payments in jeopardy. It was for this reason that the government of Saskatchewan intervened in the case during the appeal process. In the wake of the original Finlay ruling, most jurisdictions changed their overpayment collection policy to conform more closely with the guidelines set out for Manitoba. An exception was Saskatchewan, where the overpayment recovery was increased. Saskatchewan's recovery rate is now twice as high as was Manitoba's prior to Finlay's challenge.[37] After the Federal Court of Appeal decision, Neudorf suggested the government would be forced to be even more cautious prior to granting assistance. "I think we're going to be more restrictive, we're going to be less flexible in adapting our programs."[38]

The Finlay and Chambers cases bear remarkable similarities. In each instance, a recipient of assistance has undertaken to challenge the legality of social service policies. In both cases, the challenges were successful.

In both cases, the Devine government has initially claimed not to be bound by the ruling, and contested the ruling in the courts with all of its ability.

CONCLUSION

Social service administration in Saskatchewan during the 1980s has been characterized by three essential features.

First, the government has changed the basis for eligibility for assistance. The legislation for the income support programs and for the federal-provincial cost sharing arrangements both specify that the determining criteria for eligibility is financial need. The Saskatchewan government has added to this requirement a number of tests of attitude and behaviour. In order to qualify for assistance, a recipient must not only be in financial need, but must also demonstrate characteristics such as an adherence to the work ethic.

Second, assistance recipients are treated with suspicion. It is assumed by the Department of Social Services that abuse of the social services system is widespread, and that rigorous screening and monitoring of recipients is needed to protect the taxpayers.

Finally, those who are unfortunate enough to have to be reliant upon social assistance are treated in an extremely arbitrary manner. The escalation in the number of appeals, the reluctance to grant interim assistance pending appeals in the case of denial of benefits, the response to the legal proceedings around the rights of recipients, are indications that the Devine government places a low priority on ensuring that the rights of assistance recipients are protected.

Social assistance is a program of last resort. Those who are forced to rely on assistance payments have no other options to turn to. The consequences for individuals who are denied this assistance can be catastrophic.

CHAPTER 14

PROMOTING THE NEW RIGHT AGENDA

by John W. Warnock

T he previous chapters have outlined the horror story of eight years of Tory government in Saskatchewan. These years parallel the type of Tory government we are getting in Canada on the federal level under Brian Mulroney. The new policies are at variance with the well-established Canadian tradition of the mixed economy and the expansion of the welfare state. Because Canada is such a large country geographically, has a relatively small population, and has to deal with a very harsh climate, it has long been recognized that the state has an important role to play in economic development and in offsetting regional disparities. The state has been an essential tool in our efforts to create a Canadian community, distinct from that of our far more powerful neighbour to the south.

From the St. Lawrence River canal system and the railroads to Air Canada, the CBC, and Teleglobe, the state has played the key role in the development of transportation and communications in Canada. From Ontario Hydro and Hydro Quebec to the Prairie institutions, utilities have been primarily state owned.

In other instances, using the state has been seen as the most practical way of dealing with specific problems. The Canadian Wheat Board confronted the private grain exchanges. A federal medicare program was designed to overcome the inequities and inefficiencies of free market health care. Petro-Canada was created to try to gain Canadian sovereignty over the oil and gas industry, which had been controlled by foreign-owned transnational corporations.

When World War II came along, the Mackenzie King Liberal government decided that it could not wait for the private sector and the "free market" to act, and so the state mobilized capital for investment. Around 75% of this went to 28 newly created crown corporations in the manufacturing area. Another 250 plants were built with state money but were operated under contract by private firms. This industrial expansion formed the foundation for Canada's economic growth after 1946.

Canadian governments have also been involved in "hospitalization" cases, in which bankrupt private firms are subsidized or taken over by the state in order to protect jobs or to maintain an important industry. For example, the British Columbia Resources Investment Corporation (BRIC) originally consisted of three pulp mills and two saw mills abandoned by Celanese Corporation of New York; the NDP government operated them as crown corporations in order to save jobs and preserve isolated northern communities. Another example would be Canada's aircraft industry. The two major corporations, Canadair and de Havilland, were originally developed during World War II as crown corporations; at the end of the war they were privatized. During the Trudeau government they became hospitalization cases, rescued from their foreign owners who wanted to dump them.

State intervention is even more important in hinterland areas such as Saskatchewan. In 1968, the Liberal government of Ross Thatcher financed the $55 million needed to build the Prince Albert pulp mill for Parsons & Whittemore but took only a 30% equity position for the taxpayers. In 1980, when the New York owners wanted to bail out of the project, the NDP government paid them another $162 million for their 70% equity. In 1973, when Intercontinental Packers was in financial difficulty, the NDP government gave them $10 million in return for a 40% equity position in the firm.

As one looks at the top 25 corporations by sales in Saskatchewan, crown corporations or recently privatized crown corporations are the most important: SaskPower, SaskTel, CANPOTEX, SGI, Potash Corporation of Saskatchewan, Saskatchewan Mining Development Corporation, Sask Oil, Prince Albert Pulp Co., and Saskatchewan Housing Corporation. Even more significant is the cooperative sector: Saskatchewan Wheat Pool, Federated Co-operatives, Interprovincial Co-operative, Dairy Producers Co-operative, Credit Union Central, Co-operative Trust Co., Co-operators Life Insurance Co., Saskatoon Co-op Association, and Pioneer Co-op Association. The largest private corporations in the province are Intercontinental Packers and IPSCO Inc., both of which have received substantial government subsidies and investment over the years. Without government involvement, these companies probably would not be in business.

Thus, in Canada, there is a long tradition of state involvement in the economy. In Saskatchewan, it has been crucial. Furthermore, the importance and strength of the cooperative movement bears witness to the weakness of the private sector. It is very clear that there is no tradition of the laissez-faire "free market" in Canada and particularly, in Saskatchewan.

THE IDEOLOGY OF THE NEW RIGHT

The New Right burst on the political scene in the 1970s. It became a dominant force with the election of Margaret Thatcher's Conservative government in Britain in 1979 and Ronald Reagan's administration in the United States in 1980. The New Right has been much less successful in Canada, although it has a very strong presence among the backbenchers of the Tory caucus in Ottawa, and is identified with the Social Credit government in British Columbia and the Tory government in Saskatchewan.

Right-wing economists Milton Friedman and F.A. Hayek originally provided the theoretical underpinnings for the New Right. Once considered cranks, they were suddenly "discovered" in the late 1970s. Friedman and Hayek were economic advisers to the brutal Pinochet dictatorship in Chile. They promoted an ideology of rampant individualism, government deregulation, and a return to private charity. This suited the needs of big business. By promoting the rights of individuals over collective rights, big business could undermine trade unions, costly affirmative action programs, and the general philosophy that a job and social services were basic human rights.

The New Right ideology expounded by Friedman and Hayek would have had little impact if it were not supported by big business and propaganda organizations. In the mid-1970s, the business ideological position was articulated by the Trilateral Commission, an organization composed of transnational corporations and conservative political leaders. The commission attributed the world downturn in the economy after 1974 to excessive demands of the people for increased social services and higher incomes. This was characterized, in one of the commission's major studies, as the "excesses of democracy." [1] The commission argued that trade unions had become much too powerful, government spending on social programs had to be cut, and the expectations of the poor needed to be reduced. Their publications called for a return to a respect for authority, obedience, and the rights of management. The taxation system had to be changed to relieve the burden on corporations and the rich.

Big business has sponsored a cluster of organizations to promote its ideological position. In Canada, there is the Fraser Institute in British Columbia, whose board of directors and financial supporters could comprise a "Who's Who in Canadian Big Business." The Fraser Institute first achieved notoriety when it was acknowledged to have drafted British Columbia Premier Bill Bennett's "restraint" program in 1983.[2] Staff of the institute were early political advisers to the Devine government. Later, our local Tory government became more dependent on Madsen Pirie of the Adam Smith Institute and Oliver Letwin of N. M. Rothschild & Son, both of London. Both have been key advisers to the Thatcher government.

Here on the Prairies, we have the Institute for Saskatchewan Enterprise. As *Briarpatch* magazine documented, almost all of the board members financially support the Tories, and their businesses and professions have a direct interest in privatization of crown corporations and government services.[3] A third element in the New Right is the fundamentalist religious right. This group advocates the preservation of patriarchy and the traditional nuclear family, with the woman at home taking care of the children. The religious right strongly opposes the feminist revolution, sexual freedom and abortion, government-sponsored child care and support services, and extending human rights to homosexuals. REAL Women and various anti-abortion organizations have strong connections to the religious right.

The keystone of the New Right economic policy is support for the "free market." This fundamental principle goes back to Adam Smith and *The Wealth of Nations*, first published in 1776.[4] Like Smith, supporters of the "free market" see all societies as nothing more than a collection of individual consumers. Everyone, in every action, seeks to maximize his or her well being. In this world of competition, we all get what we deserve. Thus, the single-parent woman in Regina has the "freedom" to compete in the marketplace with Conrad Black of Toronto, who inherited extensive business interests from his father.

Business organizations and right-wing "think tanks" argue that decision making should be left to the marketplace. Mainstream economists, hiding away in their ivory towers, produce mathematical formulas, computer models, and curves on a graph to support them. Government decisions are invariably wrong. Competition guarantees that we will all get the best possible goods and services for the lowest prices. Thus, the well-being of all is guaranteed.

But what has the free market produced in reality? Competition among firms has always led to concentration: monopoly and oligopoly power.

The market has a natural tendency towards centralization. Sociologists and political economists have demonstrated that where the market prevails, there are gross inequalities in income, wealth, power, and status. In Canada, the market has produced an alarming degree of foreign ownership and control. Our economy is relatively dependent on the export of natural products and the import of manufactured goods, and as a result has had a level of unemployment usually higher than that in other advanced capitalist states.

But there is an even more fundamental fault in the Adam Smith free market model. People are born into existing societies, where there is a complex division of labour. We are all interdependent and produce goods and services not as isolated individuals but as social beings, in relation to others.

The basic structure of production in Canada and almost everywhere else is one of hierarchy and command. It is an antidemocratic world where power is exerted over us from the top down. We are forced to work under these conditions in order to earn a living; the alternative is unemployment and a struggle to survive physically. The reality of life for the great majority of Canadians is vastly different from Adam Smith's model of a collection of happy consumers.

THE CRISIS FOR CAPITALISM

In the 1980s, people everywhere were being confronted with the New Right and the new business agenda. This was not an accident of history, nor was it due to the arrival on the political scene of a new group of mean-spirited politicians. Transnational capital was trying to cope with a new world economy.

The long postwar economic boom ran out of steam around 1971, the year of the collapse of fixed foreign exchange rates. The rate of inflation rose after 1972 along with the price of primary commodities. This was intensified with the shock of the 1973 jump in oil prices. In 1974, there was the first worldwide recession since the end of the war. Growth rates began to slide, unemployment rates began to rise. The capitalist world experienced "stagflation," high inflation rates during periods of weak economic growth and high unemployment.

But for big capital the main problem was the fall in the rate of profit. In the European Economic Community, the average net rate of return on capital dropped from 13% in 1960 to 4% in 1980.[5] In the United States, the after-tax rate of return on capital investment fell from 10% in 1965 to 4.5% in 1979.[6] There was a growing pool of international capital sitting with no place to invest to obtain a good rate of return, which is why there was such extensive investment in marginal projects in the Third World. By the late 1970s, the new business agenda was taking shape. Its central goals are cutting costs at home and increasing the security of investment abroad.

In September 1979, the World Bank and the International Monetary Fund met in Belgrade, Yugoslavia. The central banks and governments of the major economic powers adopted the tight-money policy of high interest rates. This produced the severe world recession of 1980–82, but it created the climate for a recovery for profits. The new business agenda was born.

High interest rates would bring down the inflation rate and at the same time, discipline the labour force by creating high unemployment. Employers everywhere began demanding wage cuts and concessions from workers. Conservative governments began an open attack on historic trade-union rights. Deregulation would reduce the costs of business operations. Privatization of profitable government operations would open good new investment areas for big capital, and, at the same time, would weaken the bargaining power of public service trade unions.

The rate of profit would also be aided by changes in the taxation system. Corporate taxes were cut further. Taxes on people in the upper income brackets were greatly reduced. Progressive taxes were being replaced by direct consumption taxes. Business interests and their supporters began a massive attack on the Keynesian principle that taxation should be based on the ability to pay. In all countries, spending on social services was being cut and universal programs were being replaced by those which "target the poor." The new business agenda called for the introduction of user fees for all government services.

The free market and free trade emerged as the ideological foundation of the new business agenda. Big capital demanded the right to invest wherever the highest profit could be made. The Keynesian policies of the postwar period had required government intervention in the economy and some controls on the ability of capital and profits to cross national boundaries.

But while big business pushed for cuts in government-sponsored social services, it advocated increased expenditures on the military. In the 1960s and 1970s, expropriations of Western business interests increased in the

Third World. The very significant rise in military spending under Thatcher, Reagan, and Mulroney was designed to provide the power to intimidate radical and nationalist governments bent on controlling their own economies.

In Canada, the Mulroney government quickly became the agent of big business. It fully embraced the new agenda, including the free trade agreement with the United States. For example, while defending her bill to bring reductions in unemployment insurance benefits, Minister of Employment Barbara McDougall noted that:

> Privatization, deregulation, tax reform and free trade are all parts of the same agenda for revitalizing the Canadian economy to meet the requirements of increased globalization of markets and rapid technological change.[7]

In Saskatchewan, the Devine government also embraced the new business agenda. Many of the elected Tory members of the Legislative Assembly openly identified with the New Right. Grant Devine became an ardent supporter of free trade with the United States and free trade within Canada. The Tories proclaimed that Saskatchewan was "Open for Business"– they would create a positive social and economic climate for foreign investors. In their widely distributed 1984 publication, "The Saskatchewan Promise," they declared their new policy:

> Our business climate is being made more attractive: major amend- ments to labour legislation, an overhaul of government structure . . . revised tax structures, and in some cases, reduced or eliminated taxes altogether. The government has divested some commercial interests, allowed greater private sector representation on the boards of crown corporations, and has limited the growth of the crowns . . . Many other positive changes are coming.[8]

REGIONAL DEVELOPMENT—A CANADIAN TRADITION

Regional disparity is a natural part of capitalist development. This should not come as a surprise, for the goal of capitalism is not the promotion of equality but the accumulation of wealth by the owners of capital. Many Marxists have argued that uneven development is quite functional to capitalism. Underdeveloped areas provide a large pool of labour, which migrates to the centre in good times and goes back during depressions. These areas have traditionally been the suppliers of relatively cheap raw materials and food. Capital is also extracted from underdeveloped areas through taxation, merchant profits, and financial institutions. The underdeveloped areas also provide markets for products manufactured in the industrial centres.

Regional disparities increased after Canadian confederation. Under the policy of internal free trade, the Maritime provinces were quickly deindustrialized as business shifted to central Canada. The National Policy and the Tariff of 1879 were designed to industrialize Canada, and this meant central Canada. The Great Depression brought home to Canadians the reality of regional disparity. The hinterland provinces in Canada went bankrupt and had to be bailed out by the federal government. The Rowell-Sirois Royal Commission was established in 1937 to examine Canada's economic and financial structure.[9] The commission's report called for a national system which would permit all Canadians, wherever they lived, to have a similar base level of services. This required federal government grants to the disadvantaged provinces.

The Rowell-Sirois Royal Commission also set forth a general philosophy of economic development which dominated Canadian policy until the adoption of the new business agenda by the Mulroney government. There was an explicit rejection of the free market (or neo-classical) model of development. Canadian governments were obliged to intervene in the economy in an attempt to offset regional disparities.

In the US, on the other hand, capital made the investment decisions, and people were expected to move to where they could get a job. In Canada, it was felt that the American approach would not work. The country was too large. Our population was stretched in a narrow band along the US border. Already there was an imbalance, with population concentrated in the Hamilton-Quebec City corridor. There was also a recognition that regional loyalties were strong in Canada, and large numbers of Canadians did not wish to have to move to central Canada to find a job. Furthermore, there was a general understanding of the economic and emotional hardship that long-distance moving places on individuals and families.

However, the federal government was slow in reacting to the problem. The first program was the Prairie Farm Rehabilitation Act of 1935. The next was the Maritime Marshlands Rehabilitation Act, not in place until 1948. A real commitment to the principles of the Rowell-Sirois Royal Commission did not occur until the election of the Diefenbaker Conservative government (1957–1963). In 1957, the federal government

290

established the first program of equalization payments to the poorer provinces. In 1960, the federal government introduced a series of programs to encourage private investment in high-unemployment areas. In 1961, the Agricultural Rehabilitation and Development Act was passed, and in 1962, the Atlantic Development Board was created. Subsequent federal governments experimented with other regional development programs. This approach culminated in the Constitution Act of 1982, brought in by the Trudeau government. It committed the provinces and the federal government to "further economic development to reduce disparity in opportunities."

The goal of regional balance was also promoted through various income security and social service programs financed by the federal government. Family allowances were introduced in 1945. The Old Age Security Program came into effect in 1951, replacing the Old Age Pension Act of 1927, which was not universal. The federal government used conditional grants to encourage the provinces to expand certain services. The most notable of these have been medicare, post-secondary education, the Canada Assistance Plan to subsidize social assistance, and public housing. In 1964, the guaranteed income supplement was passed to provide financial support to the elderly. In 1965, the Canada and Quebec Pension plans came into effect. Refundable tax credits to support families on low income were introduced in 1978. The Unemployment Insurance Plan even provided preferential treatment for people in high unemployment areas—Canada's hinterlands.

The principles behind these social programs were clear. Under the constitution, the federal government had the major sources of taxation and, therefore, the primary responsibility. Canadians required portability as they moved across the country seeking employment. But most important was the principle that these programs were provided as citizenship rights, and that they were to be roughly the same, wherever Canadians lived.

However, big business in Canada was growing restless. The onset of the economic crisis after 1974 had eventually brought into play the new business agenda—but not in Canada. Canadian business leaders watched with envy the implementation of New Right policies in Great Britain and the United States. Yet, in Canada, the federal government, still under the leadership of Pierre Elliott Trudeau, remained committed to the moderate Keynesian welfare state.

Canada's big business organizations (including the Canadian Chamber

291

of Commerce, the Canadian Manufacturers' Association, the Business Council on National Issues, and the Canadian Bankers' Association) began a major campaign to sell the new policies. First, they concentrated on the Macdonald Royal Commission. In briefs presented to the commission hearings between September and December 1983, they stressed the need for the new business agenda. They won over the commission.

The Macdonald Royal Commission called for the bilateral free trade agreement with the United States and trade liberalization in general. The commission argued that Canada "must be more responsive to international competitive conditions than to internal political pressures to protect the status quo." [10] Canada could do little to promote a policy of economic independence since we are too dependent on international trade. Furthermore, capital now moves freely around the world, and very quickly in the era of microelectronics and telecommunications technologies.

The commission concluded that "a central theme of this Report is that relative to current practice, government should rely more on market forces and less on intervention designed either to frustrate or to anticipate these forces." [11] As several economists from the pro-business C. D. Howe Institute noted, "taken together, the Commission's themes call for a fundamental departure from long-established tradition in Canadian economic policy." [12]

The traditional goals of Canadian economic policy were Keynesian: the objective of economic policy should be full employment and price stability. The thrust of the commission's report was the new business agenda. Government interventions in the economy have distorted incentives and delayed necessary adjustments to international competition. Social policies have often interfered with "economic efficiency." The commission attacked unemployment insurance, and in particular the special provisions for areas of high unemployment; the commission argued that this program destroyed the incentive to work. They advocated a shift away from taxation according to ability to pay and toward a goods and services sales tax. There should be no controls on foreign exchange and no controls on foreign investment.

The Macdonald Royal Commission also attacked the now well-established policies for regional development. These were said to hamper market forces and hinder necessary adjustments. It argued that the federal government "should not involve itself directly in regional job creation." [13] It advocated an end to all interprovincial barriers to the free movement of capital, labour, goods, and services. This was a necessary part of a new policy direction which placed primacy on the free market and free trade.

As we know only too well, the Mulroney government, elected in 1984, quickly adopted free trade and the rest of the new business agenda.

In Saskatchewan, the Devine government threw its support behind the free trade agreement with the United States. But the local Tories have a contradictory attitude toward free market economic development. Devine's government fully accepted the new business agenda's policies, which called for a removal of restrictions on the rights of the owners of capital. Its actions in the area of government subsidy to business to promote regional development have not been as ideologically consistent. At the beginning of its first term, the government apparently believed that once the world financial markets learned that Saskatchewan was "Open for Business" and that the heavy hand of NDP social democracy had been lifted, investment would flow into the province. This expected rush of investment failed to materialize. Left to its own devices, the workings of the capitalist market-place would leave a hinterland area such as Saskatchewan relatively undeveloped. In desperation, Devine was forced to resort to bribing capital to invest in the province.

Thus we have the paradox. The Devine government never ceases to pay homage to private investment and the free market. But in one area it has continued to follow the Saskatchewan tradition: government support for private investment. The Saskatchewan Economic Development Corporation (SEDCO) continues to give private investors a range of subsidies. The government willingly goes into financial markets to guarantee loans for special investors. The Saskatchewan Tax Incentives Program provides personal and corporate income tax credits for investors. The Venture Capital Program provides a 30% provincial income tax credit for investments in businesses. Other government assistance includes cost-shared feasibility projects, the Aid to Trade Program, and the Industrial Incentive Program, which provides businesses with grants for job creation.

At a Tory fund-raising dinner in Moose Jaw on 3 March 1989, Grant Devine reported the results of his Asian tour. "Asian entrepreneurs hoping to cash in on the Canada-US free trade pact can be lured to Saskatchewan with promises of cheap land and labour." [14] The premier argued that Saskatchewan people want investment and don't care where it comes from. We can see how this strategy works by briefly noting the major thrust of the Tory government's chief accomplishments.

First, there is the welcoming of international capital. The Devine government "sold" the Prince Albert Pulp Company (PAPCO) complex to Weyerhaeuser Corporation of Tacoma, Washington, one of the largest pulp and paper corporations in the world. The company received a 30-year, government-backed loan at only 8.5% interest. The price of PAPCO was set at $248 million, but Weyerhaeuser is not required to pay anything on this unless their annual profits exceed 12%. The government guaranteed a loan of an additional $83 million to help build a paper mill. [15]

In September 1988, the governments of Canada, Alberta, and Saskatchewan announced that they would bankroll the construction of a heavy-oil upgrader at Lloydminster for Husky Oil. Husky Oil, owned by Hong Kong billionaire Li Ka-shing, had tried to find private partners for the project, but had failed even with $635 million in government loan guarantees. The three Tory governments pledged $929 million and Husky only $338 million. Grant Devine kicked in $222 million from the Saskatchewan taxpayers. [16]

In May 1989, the Devine government revealed the terms of its joint venture with CARGILL Inc. of Minneapolis, the largest grain company in the world, which is scheduled to build a $435-million fertilizer plant at Belle Plaine. CARGILL will put up $65 million and Saskatchewan $64 million and, in addition, the provincial government will guarantee a loan for $305 million. For providing 85% of the financing, the provincial government will take a 49% equity position. [17]

In August 1989, the Tory government forced through legislation permitting the Potash Corporation of Saskatchewan to sell shares to private investors. For the time being, foreign ownership is limited to 45%. During his tour of the Far East, Grant Devine was trying to find buyers for PCS in China, India, Japan, South Korea, and Hong Kong. The government also announced that shares would be offered in the United States and Europe. While the Tories say PCS is worth $630 million, US experts put the value at around $2.4 billion, the 1987 full replacement cost for the four operating mines. [18]

Second, the government has been generous to Canadian capitalists. Peter Pocklington received substantial subsidies to establish the Gainers meat packing plant in North Battleford. These included a $21-million loan from SEDCO, of which $10 million was forgivable. Gainers also received $7,500 for each job created. In addition, the city provided $825,000 in "incentives." [19]

Intercontinental Packers of Saskatoon has continued to receive government subsidies. In 1973, the NDP government gave the Mendel family $10 million for a 40% interest in the firm. In June 1983, the Tories sold the government's equity back to them for $4.5 million. In turn, Intercontinental opened a plant in Los Angeles.[20] In 1986, they used a federal DRIE grant and provincial job creation grants to expand their Saskatoon plant.

In 1986, Sask Oil, a crown corporation, was privatized; by the end of the year, three-quarters of its common shares were held outside the province. In April 1988, the Devine government announced that it had sold SaskPower's natural gas reserves in Alberta (510 billion cubic feet) to Sask Oil for $325 million. At current market prices, the natural gas was worth $984 million.[21]

Third, some smaller local business operations also receive taxpayers' money. In 1984, the government privatized the government's capacity for road construction and maintenance. Over $40 million worth of equipment was sold for $4.5 million; 30% of this was grabbed by Saskatchewan residents.[22]

Many monopoly operations in our provincial parks have been turned over to local businesspeople to run at a profit. These include facilities in Battlefords, Buffalo Pound, Cypress Hills, Danielson, Greenwater Lake, Moose Mountain, Duck Mountain, Echo Valley, Meadow Lake, Blackstrap parks, and the Moose Jaw Animal Park. Most of these operations have also benefited from government grants and upgrading of facilities.[23]

However, the biggest boondoggle is Grant Devine's megaproject, the Rafferty and Alameda dams on the Souris River and the Shand Power Plant. The Shand plant, which is a very expensive alternative to an energy conservation program or buying power from Manitoba or North Dakota, will cost $942 million. The two dams are a very expensive and inefficient way to control flooding and store water. Their cost is estimated at $126 million.[24]

Thus, the Devine government never hesitates to provide government subsidies to private businesses. But when the Devine government approaches interprovincial trade, it reverts to the ideals of free enterprise and free trade. Traditionally, barriers to interprovincial trade have protected local investment and jobs. But this approach was abandoned when the right-wing premiers of the four western provinces signed the Western Free Trade Agreement in March 1989. The Devine government argued that "the principle behind the Buy Saskatchewan Agency's work is that firms must be competitive in their home market if they are to go on to be competitive in national and international markets."[25]

What we can expect under the new internal free trade policy is illustrated by the experience of the brewing industry. The brewers asked to be exempted from the free trade agreement with the United States in order to adjust their industry for competition with the giant US brewers. Shortly after the agreement was ratified, Molson and Carling merged. They then announced they would consolidate into three plants in Toronto, Montreal, and Vancouver. John Labatt is expected to follow suit. A study by the Conference Board of Canada concludes that the adjustment will cost Saskatchewan 1,400 well-paying union jobs. [26]

These policies of the Devine government are consistent with the new business agenda and the New Right ideology. When Conservatives speak of the "free market" and the benefits of free trade, they really mean the freedom of capital to move wherever it can get the highest rate of return. Governments should not interfere in any way in the pursuit of high profits. But the free market does not mean laissez-faire or free enterprise. Business interests in Canada still expect the government to subsidize them and bail them out when they get into financial difficulties. On the other hand, free trade and the free market mean lack of freedom to employees, communities, and governments, for in the end we have no say over issues which are crucial to our own survival and well-being.

TABLE 1.1
PROVINCE OF SASKATCHEWAN
ANNUAL AND ACCUMULATED DEFICITS
1981–1991

Fiscal Year	Estimated Deficit (000's)	Actual Deficit (000's)	Cumulative Deficit (000's)	Interest Charges (000's)
1990–91 (Est.)	363,145	N/A	4,357,077	493,400
1989–90 (Prel.)	226,060	**377,703	3,993,932	522,937
1988–89	328,213	324,397	3,616,229	312,762
1987–88	577,235	542,477	3,291,832	282,043
1986–87	389,150	1,232,143	2,749,385	192,587
1985–86	291,258	578,877	1,517,242	192,322
1984–85	267,206	379,796	938,365	102,470
1983–84	341,879	331,394	558,569	56,513
1982–83* (PC Budget)	312,134	227,175	227,175	44,701
1982–83 (NDP Budget)	+ 1,442			
1981–82	+ 2,357	+ 7,971		

Notes: + Indicates a surplus rather than a deficit.
  * In March 1982, the NDP government presented a budget. Due to the election, this was never passed. The new government based its spending on the figures in the budget, and in November presented a financial report that revised the figures to account for the changes it had made. The most important of these were the reduction in oil production royalties, the abolition of the pump tax, and the implementation of the mortgage protection plan.
  ** Unaudited figures.

Sources: Compiled from: Government of Saskatchewan *Budget Estimates* 1983–1990; Figures for 1989–90 actual deficit annd interest charges from Saskatchewan Finance, *Saskatchewan Economic and Financial Position,* August, 1990.

TABLE 1.2

OIL PRODUCTION AND REVENUE IN SASKATCHEWAN
1981–1989

Year	Value of Oil Production (000's)	Oil Royalties to Saskatchewan (000's)*	Potential Oil Royalties to Saskatchewan (000's)**	Forgone Revenue to Saskatchewan (000's)***	% of Value of Oil Sales going to Saskatchewan in Royalties
1989	1,170,000	254,251	759,330	505,079	21.7
1988	1,044,200	187,862	677,685	489,832	18.0
1987	1,514,700	347,261	983,040	635,779	22.9
1986	1,173,900	212,926	761,861	548,935	18.1
1985	2,252,100	673,937	1,461,613	787,676	29.9
1984	1,867,800	740,357	1,212,202	471,845	39.6
1983	1,650,800	684,534	1,071,369	386,835	41.5
1982	1,189,400	700,282	771,920	71,638	58.9
1981	821,000	532,712	532,712	–	64.9

Notes:

* Oil Royalties are calculated on the fiscal year while production is calculated on the basis of the calendar year. The royalty figures for each year are those for the closest corresponding fiscal year. (i.e., 1981 royalty figures are for 1 April 1981 to 31 March 1982).

** The potential revenue is based on a calculation of what the revenue for each year would have been had that value of production been subjected to the same percentage royalty rate as was the case in 1981.

*** The forgone revenue represents the difference between actual revenue and the potential revenue.

Sources: Compiled from: Oil production figures from Saskatchewan Bureau of Statistics, *Economic Review* (1986 and 1989). Figures for 1989 from Saskatchewan Finance *Saskatchewan Economic and Financial Position*, August 1990. Figures for royalties are from Saskatchewan Finance, *Budget Estimates*, 1983–1990.

TABLE 1.3

REVENUE TO SASKATCHEWAN GOVERNMENT: SELECTED SOURCES

Source of Revenue	1981–82 Fiscal Year (Actual) (000's)	1986–87 Fiscal Year (Actual) (000's)	1990–91 Fiscal Year (Estimate) (000's)
Corporation Capital Tax	19,522	48,256	107,100
Corporation Income Tax	93,111	118,801	143,100
Fuel Tax	120,686	31,541	206,000
Individual Income Tax	511,684	692,079	896,700
Sales Tax	317,102	356,597	530,300
Tobacco Tax	30,594	78,584	103,000
Transfer from Liquor Board	49,000	140,000	190,000
Fines, Forfeits, and Penalties	6,317	8,846	10,500
Lands, Forests, Fur, Fisheries, and Game	18,950	10,970	11,700
Motor Vehicle Licenses	41,590	61,255	83,800
Sales, Services, and Service Fees	27,139	40,627	45,100
Oil Royalties	532,712	212,926	242,926
Transfer for other Governments	535,493	799,465	1,119,000
Total Revenue	2,663,703	2,800,815	4,278,200

Source: Figures compiled from Saskatchewan Finance, *Budget Estimates,* (1983–84; 1988–89; 1990–91).

TABLE 1.4

SELECTED REVENUE SOURCES AS A SHARE OF TOTAL SASKATCHEWAN GOVERNMENT REVENUE

Revenue Source	1981–82 (%)	1990–91 (%)
Fines, Forfeits, and Penalties	0.2	0.2
Corporate Income Tax	3.5	3.3
Oil Royalties	20.0	5.7
Corporate Capital Tax	0.7	2.5
Fuel Tax	4.5	4.8
Individual Income Tax	19.2	21.0
Sales Tax	11.9	12.4
Tobacco Tax	1.1	2.4
Transfers from the Liquor Board	1.8	4.4
Lands, Forests, Game, Fur, and Fisheries	0.7	0.3
Motor Vehicle Licenses	1.6	2.0
Sales, Services, and Service Fees	1.0	1.1
Transfers for other Governments	20.1	26.2

Source: Calculated from figures presented in Saskatchewan Finance, *Budget Estimates,* (1983–84 and 1990–91).

TABLE 4.1
SASKATCHEWAN FARM INCOME

Year	Net Cash Income (000's)	Realized Net Income (000's)	Value of Inventory Change (000's)	Total Net Income (000's)
1990*	642,241	−9,441	186,608	177,167
1989**	1,565,479	909,617	307,882	1,217,499
1988	1,685,150	1,022,466	−814,754	207,712
1987	1,607,119	924,904	−182,402	742,501
1986	1,345,067	659,138	710,921	1,370,059
1985	1,234,955	548,094	238,560	786,654
1984	1,715,570	1,003,304	−741,135	262,169
1983	1,400,151	702,848	−185,271	517,577
1982	1,607,067	929,112	129,674	1,058,786
1981	1,684,577	1,041,099	465,360	1,506,459
1980	1,494,445	928,541	−314,424	614,117
1979	1,464,226	980,155	−215,967	764,188
1978	1,298,082	790,904	55,461	846,365
1977	1,081,314	719,277	47,342	766,619
1976	1,260,157	939,294	269,188	1,208,482
1975	1,655,070	1,399,510	68,992	1,468,502
1974	1,340,761	1,160,880	−26,135	1,134,745
1973	858,457	728,258	159,944	888,202
1972	720,670	602,305	−220,768	381,537
1971	517,150	403,085	55,807	458,892

Notes: * Outlook
       ** Projection

Source: Statistics Canada, *Agriculture Economic Statistics,* catalogue 21–603E.

TABLE 4.2
SASKATCHEWAN FARM DEBT

Year	Chartered Banks (000's)	Federal Government Agencies (000's)	Provincial Government Agencies (000's)	Total Outstanding Debt (000's)
1988	1,359,079	1,404,864	1,167,599	5,520,936
1987	1,432,152	1,507,802	1,418,863	6,000,783
1986	1,608,000	1,472,636	1,423,158	6,120,433
1985	1,805,000	1,421,372	293,950	5,092,610
1984	1,769,000	1,369,151	149,234	4,714,385
1983	1,725,000	1,316,461	144,838	4,519,796
1982	1,492,000	1,052,600	144,800	3,970,037
1981	1,277,000	985,515	129,523	3,478,802
1980	1,172,000	902,963	100,419	2,988,415
1979	1,057,000	816,205	73,413	2,759,303
1978	903,000	755,852	76,637	2,451,276
1977	748,000	691,862	60,681	2,089,720
1976	683,000	602,554	51,820	1,884,250
1975	545,000	541,044	46,000	1,575,825
1974	445,000	481,797	31,252	1,326,730
1973	397,000	433,331	3,534	1,126,751
1972	314,000	388,009	3,167	957,030
1971	269,000	376,559	2,800	903,816

Source: Statistics Canada, *Agriculture Economic Statistics*, catalogue 21–603E.

TABLE 8.1
UNION MEMBERSHIP IN SASKATCHEWAN
PEAK YEAR AND CURRENT YEAR COMPARISONS

Year	Peak Year	Peak Year Membership	1989 Membership	% Change From Peak Year
Construction	1983	7,292	4,426	− 39.3
Manufacturing	1982	9,962	8,046	− 19.2
Mining	1982	4,740	3,425	− 27.7
Finance, Insurance, and Real Estate	1989	1,781	1,781	−
Transporation, Communications, and Other Utilities	1981	15,710	12,646	− 19.5
Public Administration	1987	29,228	23,972	− 18.0
Trade	1987	7,300	7,256	− 0.6
Service	1989	36,867	36,867	−

Source: Saskatchewan Human Resources, Labour, Employment, *The Saskatchewan Labour Report* Vol. 2 (3) (Winter 1989).

TABLE 8.2
STRIKE ACTIVITY IN SASKATCHEWAN
1976–1987

Year	No. of Work Stopages	No. of Workers Involved	No. of Worker Days Lost	No. of Days Lost per Non-agricultural Worker
1987	7	4,502	26,317	0.08
1986	15	8,307	131,249	0.39
1985	25	5,119	56,659	0.17
1984	11	1,366	12,231	0.04
1983	10	1,239	28,000	0.09
1982	26	11,863	416,245	1.31
1981	33	4,767	61,787	0.19
1980	49	9,731	61,402	0.20
1979	36	25,293	330,987	1.14
1978	50	10,078	164,506	0.60
1977	53	6,738	31,548	0.12
1976	60	17,960	136,265	0.52

Source: Compiled from: Saskatchewan Department of Labour *Annual Reports,* 1975–76 to 1985–86; and Saskatchewan Department of Human Resources, Labour, and Employment, *Annual Reports,* 1986–87 and 1987–88.

TABLE 8.3
CHANGE IN COMPOSITION OF
SASKATCHEWAN PUBLIC SERVICE BY TYPE OF EMPLOYEE
1985–1988

Type of Employee	1985	1988	Actual Change	% Change
Approved Permanent	12,707	10,079	− 2,628	− 20.7
Permanent	11,366	7,511	− 3,855	− 33.9
Temporary	1,000	1,129	129	12.9
Part-time	416	1,413	997	239.7
Casual	495	1,003	508	102.6

Source: Saskatchewan Government Employees Union.

TABLE 8.4
SASKATCHEWAN WCB CLAIMS
1981–1989

Year	Total Claims	No Time Lost Claims	Temporary Impairment Claims	Permanent Impairment Claims	Fatalities	Average Duration of Claim in Days
1989	33,319	19,486	13,706	91	36	25.4
1988	35,915	20,707	15,075	110	23	27.1
1987	36,785	21,272	15,354	132	27	26.3
1986	37,034	20,413	16,402	190	29	28.3
1985	37,437	20,725	16,369	318	25	34.4
1984	38,080	21,488	15,971	581	40	37.6
1983	34,048	18,002	15,492	519	35	37.4
1982	36,942	20,024	16,285	592*	41	38.8
1981	40,280	21,334	17,858	1,012*	76	32.9

Note: * Includes disability pensions awarded under the pre-1979 legislation.

Source: Compiled from: Saskatchewan Workers' Compensation Board, *Annual Report,*
1981–89.

TABLE 8.5
APPEALS OF WORKERS' COMPENSATION BOARD DECISIONS
Saskatchewan 1981–1989

Year	Appeals to Appeals Committee	Appeals to the Members of the Board	Appeals to the Medical Review Panel	Appeals as a % of Total Claims	Appeals as a % of Lost Time Claims
1989	675	218	N/A	2.03	4.89
1988	839	N/A	N/A	2.34	5.53
1987	550	256	28	1.50	3.55
1986	666	157	11	1.80	4.01
1985	606	151	9	1.62	3.63
1984	–	344	12	0.90	2.21
1983	–	254	12	0.75	1.59
1982	–	219	10	0.59	1.30
1981	–	191	2	0.47	1.01

Source: Saskatchewan Workers' Compensation Board *Annual Reports*, 1981–1989.

FIGURE 8.1

CHANGES IN REAL AVERAGE WEEKLY EARNINGS OF SELECTED INDUSTRY GROUPS IN SASKATCHEWAN
(Expressed in 1981 Dollars)

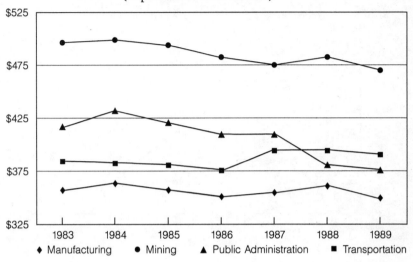

♦ Manufacturing   ● Mining   ▲ Public Administration   ■ Transportation

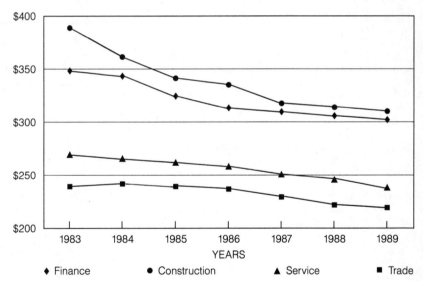

YEARS

♦ Finance   ● Construction   ▲ Service   ■ Trade

Notes:
1. Values for 1983 and 1989 are based on 10 months.
2. All values are calculated using current figures and adjusting for inflation using CPI.

Sources: Compiled from:
1. *Wage Rates*: Saskatchewan Labour Report, Spring 1990 (p.9).
2. *CPI*: Saskatchewan Labour Report, Spring 1990 (p. 8).

FIGURE 8.2

CHANGES IN REAL AVERAGE WEEKLY WAGE, INDUSTRIAL AGGREGATE
CANADA AND PRAIRIE PROVINCES
(1981 Dollars)

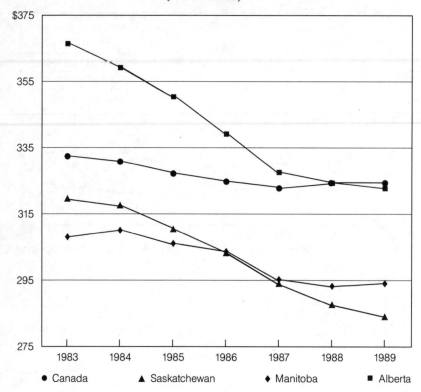

Notes: 1. 1989 figures are based on 11 months.
2. All figures calculated using current figures and adjusting for inflation using CPI.

Sources: Compiled from:
1. Alberta Statistical Review; Fourth Quarter, 1989 (p.29).
2. Saskatchewan Labour Report, Spring 1990 (p. 8).

FIGURE 8.3

AVERAGE WEEKLY WAGE IN THE CONSTRUCTION INDUSTRY
IN SELECTED PROVINCES

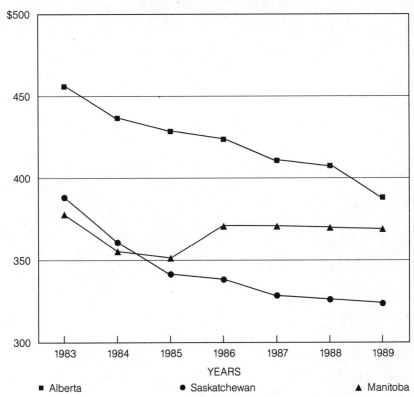

Notes: 1. 1983 and 1989 Saskatchewan figures are based on 10 months.
2. 1989 Alberta figures based on 11 months.
3. All figures calculated using current values and adjusting for inflation with CPI.

Sources: Compiled from:
1. *Alberta:* Alberta Statistical Review; Fourth Quarter, 1989 (p.30).
2. *Saskatchewan:* Saskatchewan Labour Report, Spring 1990 (p. 8).
3. *Manitoba:* Manitoba Statistical Review; Vol. 14, No. 3 (p.22).
4. *CPI Values:* Saskatchewan Labour Report; Spring 1990 (p.9).

TABLE 9.1
OPERATING AND CAPITAL COSTS
SASKATCHEWAN HOSPITALS' BUDGET
1981–82 to 1987–88

Year	Total Hospital Budget	Total Operating Costs	% Change from Prior Year (Operating)	Total Capital Costs	% Change from Prior Year (Capital)	Capital Costs as a % of Total Payments to Hospitals
1987–88	527,085,466	495,201,987	0.14	75,769,344	8.7	14.3
1986–87	524,379,699	494,526,287	7.9	69,700,000	100.3	13.3
1985–86	488,123,220	458,335,387	3.9	34,800,000	41.75	7.1
1984–85	466,184,330	440,262,715	5.2	24,550,276	32.4	5.2
1983–84	443,410,793	418,696,777	7.3	18,546,421	2.5	4.2
1982–83	412,427,578	390,391,274	18.2	18,092,764	– 16.1	4.3
1981–82	348,212,290	330,117,613	N/A	21,572,075	N/A	6.2

Source: Compiled from: Saskatchewan Department of Health, Saskatchewan Health *Annual Reports*, 1981–82 to 1987–88.

TABLE 9.2

PERCENTAGE OF HEALTH CARE WORKERS
IN SASKATCHEWAN WORKING PART-TIME
1976–77 to 1984–85

Year	Nursing Workers	Diagnostic Therapeutic Emergency Workers	Administrative Workers	Total Hospital Workers
1984–85	45.6	30.7	34.8	38.8
1983–84	43.4	29.6	32.9	36.7
1982–83	42.7	25.9	31.8	35.5
1981–82	40.5	22.9	29.1	33.1
1980–81	38.1	21.3	28.0	31.2
1979–80	32.5	19.3	24.8	27.0
1978–79	30.5	15.8	22.8	25.1
1977–78	27.4	14.8	20.9	22.6
1976–77	24.6	12.7	19.2	20.4

Source: Compiled from: Statictics Canada, *Hospital Annual Statistics,* 1976–77 to 1984–85. Cat. 83–232, Ottawa, Ministry of Supply and Services.

TABLE 11.1

CHILDREN IN SASKATCHEWAN BY EMPLOYMENT STATUS
OF PARENT AND ACCESS TO LICENSED DAY CARE

Category of parent	No. of children 12 years of age and under (1981)	Percentage of children with access to licensed day care (1987)
Full-time working parents[1]	43,585	13.12
Full-time working parents plus students[2]	47,515	12.04
Full-time working parents plus students plus parents working 20–29 hours per week[3]	61,055	9.37

Notes: 1. This category includes single parents who are working full-time and two-parent families where both parents are working full-time.
2. This category includes full-time working parents; parents who are full-time students; two-parent families where one parent works full-time and the other is a full-time student; and two-parents families where both parents are full-time students.
3. This category includes full-time working parents; parents in the student category; single parents who work 20–29 hours per week; two-parent families where one parent works full-time and the other works 20–29 hours per week; two-parent families where both parents work 20–29 hours per week.

Source: Statistics Canada, Special tabulations for Health and Welfare Canada, National Day Care Information Centre, Canadian Day Care Advocacy Association, 1984.

TABLE 11.2
PERCENTAGE OF CHILDREN AGED UNDER 13 IN LICENSED DAY CARE
1987

Province	Percentage of children under 13 in licensed day care
Alberta	20
Prince Edward Island	16
Manitoba	14
Ontario	12
Quebec	12
Nova Scotia	11
British Columbia	10
New Brunswick	10
Saskatchewan	7
Newfoundland	4
Canada	13%

Source: Adapted from Table 11.1: Licensed Child Care Spaces and Children of Working or Studying Parents, 1987. National Council of Welfare, *Child Care: A Better Alternative*, Ottawa, December 1988, (p. 4).

TABLE 11.3
SASKATCHEWAN GOVERNMENT EXPENDITURES ON DAY CARE

Fiscal Year Ending	Actual Spending	% Increase Over Previous Year
1988	13,157,065	6.2
1987	12,487,755	12.9
1986	11,058,895	3.5
1985	10,694,481	14.7
1984	9,315,357	11.0
1983	8,392,785	35.6
1982	6,187,098	90.2
1981	3,252,448	19.2
1980	2,727,646	29.2
1979	2,110,982	58.6
1978	1,330,952	68.9
1977	787,818	73.8
1976	453,276	31.4
1975	345,068	441.7
1974	63,700	9.5
1973	58,192	43.6
1972	40,515	123.2
1971	18,154	N/A

Source: Compiled from: Saskatchewan Finance, *Public Accounts*, 1970–71 to 1987–88.

TABLE 11.4
INTERPROVINCIAL COMPARISON OF CHILD DAY CARE SERVICES
TOTAL BUDGET AND PER CAPITA EXPENDITURES
(per children 12 years and under, 1986)

Province	Population 12 years and under	1985/86 Budget (000s)	Per Capita
British Columbia	506,555	26,185.9	51.7
Alberta	470,550	57,856.7	123.0
Saskatchewan	206,525	12,291.9	59.5
Manitoba	204,530	23,841.9	116.6
Ontario	1,615,520	185,000.0	114.5
Quebec	1,195,345	72,412.2	60.6
New Brunswick	148,285	3,093.2	20.9
Nova Scotia	169,270	5,750.6	34.0
Prince Edward Island	26,035	617.4	23.7
Newfoundland	142,305	1,130.9	8.0

Source: J. Martin, *Childcare in Saskatchewan: What We Have, What We Want,* Saskatoon: Action Child Care, 1988.

TABLE 12.1
NUMBERS OF PERSONS RECEIVING
SOCIAL ASSISTANCE BENEFITS IN SASKATCHEWAN
March 1981–88

Year	Cases	Beneficiaries
1988	29,894	60,292
1987	30,544	62,061
1986	30,803	62,707
1985	31,572	64,040
1984	31,446	63,703
1983	29,455	59,724
1982	23,613	48,396
1981	22,605	43,766

Source: Compiled from: Monthly Bulletin of Statistics and Quarterly Statistics, Saskatchewan Social Services, 1981–88.

TABLE 12.2
IMPACT OF WELFARE REFORM ON PURCHASING POWER OF MONTHLY SAP ENTITLEMENTS
Saskatchewan 1981, 1984, 1988

	1981 $	1984 $	1988 $	Loss in Purchasing Power, 1981–88 Constant 1981 $'s	% Loss
Single Employable Person	581	384	375	268	−54
Single Parent, Two Children	916	919	900	643	−30
Two Parents, Two Children	1,391	1,399	1,384	989	−29

Source: Rates calculated from Saskatchewan Assistance Plan Regulations. CPI Index (Regina, 1988) 10-month average of 139.95 applied. Labour Report, *Saskatchewan Human Resources Quarterly,* Vol. 1, No. 2, Table 2, Winter 1988.

TABLE 13.1
NUMBER OF APPEALS OF DECISION BY THE SASKATCHEWAN DEPARTMENT OF SOCIAL SERVICES
1982–83 to 1988–89

Year	Appeals to Local Appeal Panels	Appeals to the Provincial Appeal Board
1988–89	950	164
1987–88	460	102
1986–87	408	103
1985–86	329	55
1984–85	368	82
1983–84	262	51
1982–83	200	40

Source: Letter from The Honourable Bill Neudorf, Minister of Social Services, to Peter Prebble, MLA, 23 March 1990.

NOTES TO CHAPTERS

INTRODUCTION

1. Transcribed from the special television address, 5 March 1990, CFQC TV, Saskatoon.
2. Thomas Nunn, "Conservative steamroller flattens New Democrats," *Leader Post* (Regina), 27 April 1982.
3. Daphne Branham, "Size of victory shocks even Devine," *Leader Post* (Regina), 27 April 1989.

CHAPTER 1

1. Saskatchewan Finance, *Budget Address*, 24 November 1982, p. 5.
2. Saskatchewan Finance, *Budget Address*, 26 March 1986.
3. Saskatchewan Finance, *Saskatchewan Economic and Financial Report*, March 1987, p. 2.
4. Progressive Conservative election ad, *Leader Post* (Regina), 14 April 1982.
5. D. Sprout, "Devine stands by figures on gas tax cut," *Leader Post* (Regina), 15 April 1982.
6. D. Bronhan, "Devine still had some promises left over," *Leader Post* (Regina), 24 April 1982.
7. J. Richards and L. Pratt, *Prairie Capitalism: Power and Influence in the New West* (Toronto: McClelland and Stewart, 1979), pp. 288–291.
8. Saskatchewan Finance, *Budget Estimates*, 29 March 1983.
9. Sproat, "Devine stands by figures."
10. Not included in this total is the fuel rebate to farmers, who were able to purchase tax-free gasoline prior to the 1982 election.
11. C. Thatcher, *Backrooms: A Story of Politics* (Saskatoon: Western Producer Prairie Books, 1985), p. 221.
12. Ibid.
13. Includes all drilling. Saskatchewan Bureau of Statistics, *Economic Review 1989*, vol. 43, December 1989, p. 19.
14. Saskatchewan Finance, *Budget Address*, 21 March 1984, p. 5.
15. Saskatchewan Department of Energy and Mines, *Submission to the National Energy Board – Update of Energy Supply and Demand*, Miscellaneous Report 84–5, January 1984.
16. "Royalty holiday over for oil companies," *Star Phoenix* (Saskatoon), 13 June 1990.
17. "Resource Industry Statistics," *Sask-Trends Monitor*, April 1990, p. 7.
18. Saskatchewan Finance, *Budget Address*, 29 March 1983, p. 17.
19. Saskatchewan Finance, *Budget Estimates*, March 1990, p. 14.
20. Saskatchewan Finance, *Budget Estimates*, March 1990, p. 10.

21. Calculated from figures presented in Saskatchewan Bureau of Statistics, *Economic Review,* 1989, vol. 43, p. 36; and Saskatchewan Finance, *Saskatchewan Economic and Financial Position,* August 1990, p. 7. Figures for personal income are calculated for the calendar year.

22. Calculated from figures presented in Saskatchewan Finance, *Budget Address,* 21 March 1984, p. 21; and Saskatchewan Finance, *Saskatchewan Economic and Financial Position,* August 1990, p. 12. Figures for tax revenues are calculated for the fiscal year.

23. Compiled from Saskatchewan Finance, *Budget Address,* 1984–1990.

24. Saskatchewan Finance, "Saskatchewan's Economic Tax Credits" in *Budget Address,* 30 March 1989, p. 44.

25. Saskatchewan Finance, *Budget Address,* 29 March 1983, p. 19.

26. Saskatchewan Finance, *Budget Estimates,* March 1990, p. 11.

27. Saskatchewan Finance, *Budget Estimates,* June 1987, p. 47.

CHAPTER 2

1. J. Steffenhagen, "Tory reprimanded for racist remarks," *Star Phoenix* (Saskatoon), 11 December 1982.

2. "Devine in Charge," *Star Phoenix* (Saskatoon), 16 December 1982.

3. Dale Eisler column, *Leader Post* (Regina), 5 March 1988.

4. C. Stadnychuk, "Hunger and home economics wizardry," *Briarpatch* 16 (May 1987), p. 2.

5. R. Burton, "Grant Schmidt: Who is this man, and why is he saying those outrageous things?," *Star Phoenix* (Sasktoon), 6 May 1988.

6. E. Fowler, "Devine's statement on AIDS, natives inappropriate," *Star Phoenix* (Saskatoon), 12 June 1987.

7. D. Traynor, "Schmidt rejects call for native inquiry," *Star Phoenix* (Saskatoon), 19 April 1989.

8. "Race Relations require deliberate, timely probe," *Leader Post* (Regina), 21 April 1989.

9. T. Blackwell, "Aide rescues Schmidt after remark about gays," *Leader Post* (Regina), 30 October 1987; T. Blackwell, "Schmidt continues antigay remarks," *Leader Post,* 30 October 1987.

10. Dale Eisler column, *Leader Post,* 3 March 1988.

11. "Devine critical of homosexual lifestyle," *Star Phoenix* (Saskatoon), 2 March 1988.

12. Notice to members of the American Psychological Association, 1984, listing persons removed from the Association. It includes the following: "Paul Cameron (Nebraska) was dropped from the membership for a violation of the Preamble to the *Ethical Principles of Psychologists.*"

    Resolution at membership meeting, Nebraska Psychological Association, 19 October 1984, which reads in part: "The science and profession of psychology in Nebraska, as represented by the Nebraska Psychological Association, formally disassociates itself from the representations and interpretations of scientific literature offered by Dr. Paul Cameron in his writings and public statements on sexuality. Further, the NPA would like it known that Dr. Cameron is not a member of the Association." See also Mike Salinas, "Paul Cameron: Psychological Terrorist," *New York Native,* 27 April 1987, p. 12.

13. *Baker vs. Wade,* case 106 F.R.D. 526 (1985), in *Federal Rules and Decisions,* vol. 6 (St. Paul: West Publishing, 1985), p. 526.

14. D.A. Nicholas Groth, State of Connecticut, Department of Correction, to Dr. Wayne Price, Chair, Nebraska Board of Examiners of Psychologists, 21 August 1984. The letter reads in part: "It has come to my attention that Paul Cameron, Ph.D. is quoting my research in an offensive pamphlet he has authored entitled 'Child Molestation and Homosexuality.' He misrepresents my findings and distorts them to advance his homophobic views . . . I consider this totally unprofessional behavior on the part of Dr. Cameron and want to bring this to your attention. He disgraces his profession."

15. P. Cameron, "What Homosexuals Do (It's more than merely disgusting)," Washington: Family Research Institute, 1987.

16. "Critic of gays accuses customs of censorship," *Star Phoenix* (Saskatoon), 29 March 1988, p. A3.

17. D. Traynor and R. Burton, "Homosexual-crime link claimed," *Star Phoenix* (Saskatoon), 5 March 1988.

18. Ibid.

19. R. Burton, "Gay couples aren't families: Schmidt," *Star Phoenix* (Saskatoon), 15 April 1989.

20. See: Jenni Morton, "Planned Parenthood seeks funds, members," *Star Phoenix* (Saskatoon), 14 February 1984; "Planned Parenthood may close," *Star Phoenix*, 6 December 1986; "Province cuts funding for abortion debate," *Star Phoenix*, 25 April 1987.

21. "High Profile speaker lends moral support to movement," *Melfort Journal*, May 1989.

22. Victorious Women of Canada, Quality Sound Services, 1987.

23. Ibid.

24. Editorial, *Star Phoenix* (Saskatoon), 25 January 1989.

25. D. Herman, "Saskatoon first private agency to handle adoptions," *Star Phoenix* (Saskatoon), 9 October 1987.

26. Dale Eisler column, *Leader Post* (Regina), 5 March 1988.

27. H. MacDonald, "Welfare recipients lash out at Schmidt," *Star Phoenix* (Saskatoon), 20 April 1989.

CHAPTER 3

1. P. Resnick, *Parliament vs. People* (Vancouver: New Star Books, 1984), p. 20.

2. R.J. van Loon and M.S. Whittington, *The Canadian Political System* (Toronto: McGraw-Hill Ryerson Ltd., 1981).

3. *The Saskatchewan Act*, 4–5 Edward VII, chap. 42, sec. 12.

4. Amendment of the Constitution of Canada (Nos. 1, 2, and 3), 1982, 125 D.L.R. (3d), 1 at p. 30 (Supreme Court of Canada). In the same way, the Bill of Rights has a similar significance in other parts of the Commonwealth. Its authority was invoked, for example, in a situation in New Zealand in which a court order was sought to declare illegal a government attempt to suspend the operation of a particular statute rather than to bring in Parliament a bill to repeal it. See W.A. McKean, "The Suspending Power Exhumed," *Public Law* 7 (Spring 1978).

5. In Saskatchewan, this provision is found in s. 33 of The Financial Administration Act (originally enacted as The Department of Finance Act, 1983, S.S. 1983, c.D–15.1, and now located in the looseleaf tables and statutes of Saskatchewan as chapter F–13.3).

6. Those occasions were: 1906, 1908, 1982 and 1985. Special warrants were used only in 1908 and 1982. The 1908 occurrence is not explained in contemporary accounts and thus remains an aberration. In 1982, special warrants were used during a period of dissolution and change of government. This is discussed more fully later in this chapter.

7. In 1864, legislation had been enacted to permit special warrants 'in the event of any accident happening to any public work or building required immediate outlay to repair it" (Province of Canada, *Statutes*, 1964, c.6). When monies became necessary to equip a volunteer force to repel the Fenian raids, it was clear that a special warrant could not be used to authorize the expenditure. In the budget speech of 26 June 1866, Alexander Galt said: "The government are perfectly conscious of the responsibility they incurred during the year now closing, in violating the provisions of the law in regard to the public expenditure and they do not desire to be again put in that position" (cited in H.R. Balls, "Governor General's Warrants," *Canadian Tax Journal*, 1963, p. 186).

The special warrant power was subsequently amended to provide for cases that were not foreseen or provided for or insufficiently provided for.

8. Saskatchewan Legislative Assembly, *Debates and Proceedings*, 30, 24 June 1987, p. 697.

9. Saskatchewan Legislative Assembly, *Debates and Proceedings*, 32, 19–29 May 1989.

10. *Alberta Statutes*, [1938] S.C.R. 101, p.133.

11. In order to avoid prejudicing the trial of an action or interfering with the judicial process, it is the practice of the House not to bring matters awaiting the adjudication of a court of law forward in debate.

12. Saskatchewan Legislative Assembly, *Debates and Proceedings*, 27, 26 April 1984, p. 2095. (Because the bells began to ring on this debate, the parliamentary day is extended; this same issue of Hansard includes the transcript of proceedings for 1 May 1984 at pp. 2102–03.) The other item of business conducted on 1 May 1984 was Royal Assent to the Appropriation Act, 1984 (No. 1), which, in effect, authorizes interim financing of government expenditure pending the approval of the estimates. One can speculate that this pressing financial situation was a factor in the negotiations between government and Opposition in this dispute.

13. It may be the case that funds for activities to be carried on in these "new" departments were previously approved by the legislature in the "old" departments. These old funds may have been frozen so that there is no net increase in the approved level or type of executive expenditure. This cannot be determined on the face of the special warrants that have been issued. Even so, the integrity of Parliament should not be or appear to be compromised for the convenience of the government's bookkeepers.

CHAPTER 4

1. L. Auer, *Prairie Farming, 1960–2000: An Economic Analysis* (Ottawa: Economic Council of Canada, 1989).

2. G. York, "Hard Times: Grant Devine finding family farm no refuge," *The Globe and Mail* (Toronto), 5 March 1990.

3. Saskatchewan Department of Agriculture, *Saskatchewan Agriculture Assistance Programs*, 1987.

4. Saskatchewan Finance, *Budget Address*, 29 March 1990, pp. 9–10.

5. B. Braden, "Provincial seeding program lends $156.9 million to farmers," *Star Phoenix* (Saskatoon), 2 August 1990.

6. Saskatchewan Department of Agriculture, *Saskatchewan Agricultural Assistance Programs*, 1987.

7. G. Dishaw, "Farm Depression Hurts Saskatchewan Economy," *Union Farmer*, April 1989.

8. T. Pugh, "The Invisible Crisis," in *Fighting the Farm Crisis*, T. Pugh, ed. (Saskatoon: Fifth House Publishers, 1987).

9. Auer, *Prairie Farming*.

10. Pugh, "The Invisible Crisis."

11. "New Cargill Plan Packs Wallop," *Star Phoenix* (Saskatoon), 17 November 1989.

12. "Banking's big six make $2 billion," *Star Phoenix* (Saskatoon), 8 December 1989.

13. D. Loehr, "Summary of Effects of a Group of Farmers Leaving a Community," in Christian Farm Crisis Action Committee *Brief to the Saskatchewan Government on the Subject of a Proposed Moratorium on Farm Foreclosures*, 23 January 1989.

14. Saskatchewan Agriculture and Food, *Farm Income Forecast*, September 1989.

15. Saskatchewan Agriculture and Food, "1990 Net Farm Income Outlook," *Statistical Facts*, 7 December 1989.

16. Dishaw, "Farm Depression Hurts Saskatchewan Economy."

17. "The numbers tell what's happened to farming," *The Western Producer*, 4 January 1990.

18. Auer, *Prairie Farming*.

19. Ibid.

20. "Lending Institutions hold estimated 1.5 million acres of farmland in west," *Union Farmer*, November 1989.

21. Dishaw, "Farm Depression Hurts."

22. Farm Debt Review Board, *Percent Net Farmers Through Federal and Provincial Financial Review Processes*, July 1989.

CHAPTER 5

1. Economic Council of Canada, *Minding the Public's Business* (Ottawa: Economic Council of Canada, 1986); J. Vickers and G. Yarrow, *Privatization, An Economic Analysis* (Cambridge: MIT Press, 1988).

2. G. MacLean, *Public Enterprise in Saskatchewan*, Regina: Crown Investments Corporation of Saskatchewan, 1981.

3. P. Starr, "The Limits of Privatization," in S. Hanke, ed., *Prospects for Privatization,* (New York: The Academy of Political Science, 1987), p. 125.

4. M. Ignatieff, "The Myth of Citizenship," *Queen's Quarterly* 94(4) (Winter 1987), pp. 966–985; H. Hardin, *The Privatization Putsch* (Halifax: The Institute for Research on Public Policy, 1989).

5. M. Pirie, "Principles of Privatization," in M. Walker, ed., *Privatization: Tactics and Techniques* (Vancouver: The Fraser Institute, 1988), p. 5.

6. C. Thatcher, *Backrooms* (Saskatoon: Western Producer Prairie Books, 1985), p. 203.

7. Thatcher had nothing but contempt for this approach. He comments that Devine "was a great believer that talk makes it appear as though something is happening if there is enough of it." Thatcher, *Backrooms*, p. 203.

8. Saskatchewan, Legislative Assembly, *Debates and Proceedings*, 26(21B), 18 April 1983, p. 1144.
9. M. Stobbe, "Saskatchewan's Heritage: Going once . . . going twice . . . ," *Briarpatch* 13(5) (June 1984).
10. M. Nemeth and F. Orr, "Too Sweet? Devine's PAPCO deal is blasted by the NDP," *Alberta Report*, 7 July 1986; P. Prebble, 'Selling off Saskatchewan," *Briarpatch* 16(4) (May 1987).
11. "Weyerhaeuser expects good year for pulp," *Star Phoenix* (Saskatoon), 23 January 1988.
12. O. Letwin, "International Experiences in the Politics of Privatization," in M. Walker, *Privatization*, p. 66.
13. G. Lane, *Economic and Financial Statement, 1987*, Regina: Department of Finance, 1987.
14. E. Smillie, "Dental Plan Dropped," *Briarpatch* 16(10) (December 1987/January 1988).
15. The Fraser Institute, *List of Conference Participants*. Distributed to participants of the International Symposium on Privatization, Vancouver, 22–24 July 1987.
16. Pirie, "Principles of Privatization," p. 16.
17. The proceedings of the conference are published in Walker, *Privatization*. A journalistic account can be found in M. Stobbe, "Allies in Plunderland," *Briarpatch* 16(7) (September 1987).
18. Saskatchewan, Legislative Assembly, *Debates and Proceedings*, 31(68B), 27 June 1988, p. 2606.
19. D. Eisler, *Leader Post* (Regina), 8 April 1989.
20. N. Scott, "Taylor gets cabinet's 'privatization' job," *Leader Post* (Regina), 18 January 1988.
21. "Taylor looks forward to privatization role," *Leader Post* (Regina), 25 January 1988.
22. "Different meetings, towns but same photos, quotes," *Leader Post* (Regina), 18 February 1989.
23. D. Eisler, *Leader Post* (Regina), 3 September 1988.
24. Union Graduate School, *Doctoral Program: General Information*, Cincinnati: Union Graduate School, 1987.
25. R. Burton, "Privatization conference to revive sensitive issue," *Star Phoenix* (Saskatoon), 12 December 1989.
26. V. Northcott, "The last of Devine's privateers," *Briarpatch* 19(6) (July/August 1990).
27. D. Traynor, "Employees will purchase Crown Printing Company," *Star Phoenix* (Saskatoon), 7 December 1988.
28. J. Sutherland, "Westbridge! Ho!" *Saskatchewan Business* (July/August 1990).
29. D. Eisler, "Tories have vested interest in ensuring success," *Star Phoenix* (Saskatoon), 8 July 1989.
30. *Report of the Provincial Auditor to the Legislative Assembly for the Year Ended March 31, 1988* (Regina: Queen's Printer, 1989), pp. 20–21.
31. Eisler, "Tories have vested interest."
32. "Westbridge president tired of controversies," *Star Phoenix* (Saskatoon), 21 June 1990.
33. Sutherland, "Westbridge! Ho!" p. 26; P. Martin, "Westbridge dumps Superior, predicts decline in profits," *Star Phoenix* (Saskatoon), 30 January 1990.
34. Saskatchewan, Legislative Assembly, *Debates and Proceedings*, 33(35A), 8 May 1990, pp. 1193–1195; 33(37A), 10 May 1990, pp. 1247–1251; 33(38A), 11 May 1990, pp. 1300–1302.
35. "Chaplain residents resigned to sale," *Leader Post* (Regina), 25 March 1988.

36. N. Scott, "Province sells Sask Minerals," *Leader Post* (Regina), 28 March 1988; D. Traynor, "Peat plant deal angers Atkinson," *Star Phoenix* (Saskatoon), 31 March 1988; R. Burton, "Sask Minerals: Sold far too cheaply, NDP claims," *Star Phoenix* (Saskatoon), 6 April 1989; "Price was lower," *Leader Post* (Regina), 18 April 1989; D. Traynor, "Sask Minerals fetched good price: Devine," *Star Phoenix* (Saskatoon), 7 April 1989.

37. M. Marud, "Meadow Lake gets chopsticks factory; sawmills privatized," *Star Phoenix* (Saskatoon), 16 June 1988; R. Burton, "Mill sale 'classic example' of privatization," *Star Phoenix* (Saskatoon), 17 June 1989; R. Burton, "Meadow Lake pulp mill planned," *Star Phoenix* (Saskatoon), 17 June 1988.

38. R. Bothwell, *Eldorado: Canada's National Uranium Company* (Toronto: University of Toronto Press, 1984).

39. J. Schnurr, "Mega merger: SMDC and Eldorado form a uranium supercorp," *Saskatchewan Business* 9(3) (April/May 1988); "Ottawa, Sask. negotiate merging Eldorado, SMDC," *Northern Miner* 73(48) (8 February 1988); "Merger leaves Ottawa with Eldorado's debts," *Financial Post* 82(9) (27 February 1988).

40. Saskatchewan Mining Development Corporation, *Annual Report*, 1987.

41. *Summary of Letter of Intent Respecting Proposed Merger of Eldorado Nuclear Limited and Saskatchewan Mining Development Corporation*. Released by Premier Grant Devine and the Honourable Barbara McDougall, 22 February 1988.

42. B. Johnstone, "Poor conditions may delay Cameco share offering," *Leader Post* (Regina), 14 June 1989.

43. D. Traynor, "Sask Power sells gas reserves for $325 million," *Star Phoenix* (Saskatoon), 23 April 1988.

44. B. Johnstone, "Bond deal said good for investors," *Leader Post* (Regina), 26 April 1988.

45. D. Traynor, "Sask Power bond issue over the top," *Star Phoenix* (Saskatoon), 9 July 1988.

46. M. Mandryk, "NDP says reported 'holiday' worrisome," *Leader Post* (Regina), 23 February 1989.

47. M. Mandryk, "Devine says future of PCS undecided," *Leader Post* (Regina), 27 February 1989.

48. Bruce Johnstone, *Leader Post* (Regina), 18 March 1989.

49. G. York, "Saskatchewan selling firms worth $2 billion," *The Globe and Mail* (Toronto), 9 March 1989.

50. For the best outline of these issues, see L. Pratt and J. Richards, *Prairie Capitalism: Power and Influence in the New West* (Toronto: McClelland and Stewart, 1979), pp. 250–303.

51. N.D. Olewiler, *The Potash Corporation of Saskatchewan: An Assessment of the creation and performance of a Crown Corporation* (Ottawa: Economic Council of Canada, 1986) (discussion paper 303).

52. J. Warnock and S. Checkley, "The potash rip-off," *Briarpatch* 18(10) (December 1989/January 1990).

53. "Potash Corp. profit fuels debate on sale," *The Globe and Mail* (Toronto), 22 April 1989.

54. D. Traynor, "Safeguards will keep control of PCS in province: Lane," *Star Phoenix* (Saskatoon), 15 April 1989.

55. Bruce Johnstone, *Leader Post* (Regina), 30 September 1989.

56. P. Martin, "Privatization: Potash bond sale finishes strong," *Star Phoenix* (Saskatoon), 8 November 1989.

57. P. Martin, "Greed driving force in PCS bond popularity," *Star Phoenix* (Saskatoon), 4 November 1989.

58. D. Eisler, "PCS shares create little interest in Europe," *Star Phoenix* (Saskatoon), 10 January 1989.

59. "PCS sale comes in soft market; government thinks price is right," *Star Phoenix* (Saskatoon), 29 September 1989.

60. C. White, *Power for a Province—A History of Saskatchewan Power* (Regina: Canadian Plains Research Center, 1976).

61. Saskatchewan, Legislative Assembly, *Debates and Proceedings*, 32(32A), 9 May 1988, p. 1160.

62. N. Scott, "Sask Power to be split," *Leader Post* (Regina), 10 May 1988.

63. SaskPower, *Annual Report*, 1987.

64. D. Eisler, "Romanow, NDP stake future on SaskEnergy stance," *Star Phoenix* (Saskatoon), 22 April 1989.

65. G. York, "Standoff over SaskEnergy keeps legislature empty," *The Globe and Mail* (Toronto), 25 April 1989.

66. M. Mandryk, "Privatization opposed; Tories trailing in poll," *Leader Post* (Regina), 3 May 1989.

67. M. Mandryk, "SaskEnergy privatization meetings poorly attended," *Leader Post* (Regina), 31 May 1989.

68. "Government pitch to sell SaskEnergy stretches law on marketing securities," *The Globe and Mail* (Toronto), 24 May 1989.

69. M. Mandryk, "Gov't yanks ads on privatization," *Leader Post* (Regina), 27 May 1989.

70. L. Barber, *Report,* Saskatchewan Commission on SaskEnergy (Regina: Government of Saskatchewan, 1989), p. A3–1.

71. SaskEnergy, *Brief to the Barber Commission on Sask Energy Public Participation*, Regina: SaskEnergy, 1989; SaskPower, *Brief to the Barber Commission on Sask Energy Public Participation*, Regina: SaskPower, 1989.

72. SaskEnergy, *Brief to the Barber Commission,* pp. 41–42.

73. Barber, *Report.*

74. D. Eisler, "Conciliatory Devine reconsiders policies," *Leader Post* (Regina), 13 October 1989.

75. M. Wyatt, "Report isn't seen as approval," *Leader Post* (Regina), 10 November 1989.

76. R. Burton, "SGI move rekindles privatization debate," *Star Phoenix* (Saskatoon), 17 July 1990.

77. D. Traynor, "SGI sale illegal, appeal court rules," *Star Phoenix* (Saskatoon), 4 December 1990.

78. G. Brock, "Province re-thinking privatization issue," *Leader Post* (Regina), 7 December 1989.

79. G. York, "NDP attacks Devine's privatization plan," *The Globe and Mail* (Toronto), 20 March 1989.

80. M. Wyatt, "Tory support falls sharply: Poll," *Leader Post* (Regina), 12 July 1990.

81. R. Burton, "Prominent Saskatonians join Reform party," *Star Phoenix* (Saskatoon), 11 July 1990.

CHAPTER 6

1. Saskatchewan, Churchill River Board of Inquiry, A.H. MacDonald, *Report*, June 1978.
2. Saskatchewan, Department of Finance, *Budget Estimates*, 1980–81, 1981–82, 1982–83.
3. Saskatchewan, Department of Finance, *Budget Speech*, 5 March 1981, p. 40.
4. Environment Minister Neil Byers to Saskatoon Sutherland MLA Peter Prebble, 18 December 1978; Alfred Moore, regional coordinator of the National Farmers Union, to Premier Allan Blakeney, 28 November 1978.
5. *Why People Say No*, Regina: Regina Group for a Non-Nuclear Society, April 1980. See also the testimony of Dr. Alan Anderson, sociology professor at the University of Saskatchewan, and submissions by the Warman and District Concerned Citizens Group, recorded in: Saskatchewan, Warman Refinery Hearing, *Transcripts*, 1980, p. 1522.
6. The meetings were held under the auspices of the Federal Environmental Review.
7. The inquiry was established by Order in Council 222/77. Saskatchewan, Cluff Lake Board of Inquiry, Hon. Mr. Justice E.D. Bayda, *Report*, 31 May 1978.
8. The intention of the surface lease was to make provisions for environmental monitoring and protection, occupational health, and northern employment as part of the contractual obligations agreed to by the mining developer. The onus was on the Government of Saskatchewan to enforce the contractual commitments.
9. US Natural Resources Defence Council. T. Cochran, "Atoms for War/Atoms for Peace," a paper presented at St. Thomas More College, University of Saskatchewan, 13–15 February 1981; G. Edwards, "The Myth of the Peaceful Atom," in E. Regehr and S. Rosenblum, eds., *Canada and the Arms Race* (Toronto: James Lorimer and Co., 1983); "Nuclear Wastes: What Me Worry?" A Critique of Energy, Mines, and Resources' Report: The Management of Canada's Nuclear Wastes," Canadian Coalition for Nuclear Responsibility, 1978 (revised and updated, 1987).
10. Saskatchewan, Legislative Assembly, *Debates and Proceedings*, 12 April 1979, p. 1672.
11. See Saskatchewan, Warman Refinery Hearing, *Transcripts*, p. 552. At the hearing, Mr. Katzman also released the results of an opinion survey that he conducted in his constituency: he asked, "Are you in favour of a uranium refinery in the Warman area?" He found that 224 were in favour while 803 were opposed.
12. *Environmental Magna Carta Act*, (Bill No. 96), cited in Saskatchewan, Legislative Assembly, *Debates and Proceedings*, 12 May 1981, pp. 3246–52.
13. Saskatchewan, Legislative Assembly, *Debates and Proceedings*, 1981, pp. 3246–52.
14. Interview with Joan Harrison and Terry Hartley, former coordinators of the Energy Conservation Information Centre in Saskatoon, 27 November 1990.
15. Saskatchewan, *Public Accounts*, 2, 1981–82, pp. 151–161; *Public Accounts*, 2, 1983–84, pp. 124–127. The actual figure cited in the 1981–82 Public Accounts for the Saskatchewan Department of Environment is $9,683,177. However, $409,980 of this is for Treaty Indian Land Entitlements and Policy Development and grants to various Indian bands in Saskatchewan. This item was thus deleted to make the expenditures in the two fiscal years more comparable.
16. "Cigar Lake Test Mine Environmental Impact Statement: Executive Summary," Cigar Lake Mining Corporation: August 1987, p.1.
17. "Uranium: the Most Strategic Mineral of All," *Multinational Monitor*, April 1981, p. 19.
18. "Cigar Lake Test Mine," sec. 1.9, "Mining Concepts."

19. Ibid.
20. Eagle Point is actually two deposits, Eagle Point North and Eagle Point South. CAMECO owns 100% of Eagle Point South and 66.7% of Eagle Point North. See CAMECO, *Annual Report*, Saskatoon, 1989; Saskatchewan, Energy and Mines Mineral Development Branch, A. J. Gracie and P. L. Schwann, "Saskatchewan Exploration and Development Highlights," November 1989, p. 7.
21. Environmental Impact Statement, Collins Bay A-Zone, D-Zone, and Eagle Point Development, Executive Summary, Eldorado: August 1989.
22. Saskatchewan, Information Services, "Environment Approval Granted for Uranium Mine Expansion," 6 January 1988.
23. Saskatchewan, Environment and Public Safety, "Technical Review Comments on the Environmental Impact Statement for the Proposed Meadow Lake Pulp Mill," February 1990.
24. Ibid, pp. 2–3.
25. "Environmental Hearings Won't be Held for Mills," *Star Phoenix* (Saskatoon), 2 February 1990.
26. "Millar Western 'Comfortable' with Mill Terms," *Star Phoenix* (Saskatoon), 21 March 1990.
27. Saskatchewan, Legislative Assembly, *Debates and Proceedings* (Budget Estimates for Saskatchewan Environment and Public Safety), 20 June 1990, p. 2311.
28. "Saskatchewan, CARGILL say they're determined to build new fertilizer plant," *The Western Producer*, 15 February 1990, p. 5.
29. "Hodgins won't release report of review panel," *Star Phoenix* (Saskatoon), 9 May 1990.
30. "Saferco offering details," *Times-Herald* (Moose Jaw), 7 June 1990.
31. Press release by G. McKinney, "Rafferty Dam project a potential environmental disaster," 2 June 1986; "Letter expresses concerns about environmental impact," *Leader Post* (Regina), 22 September 1987.
32. B. Weichel, "Squandering Rafferty," *NeWest Review* 14(3) (February/March), pp. 26–29.
33. The Newsletter: Saskatchewan Environmental Association, January/February 1990.
34. The Newsletter: Saskatchewan Environmental Society, March/April 1989.
35. "New Dam political trade-off: ex-aide," *The Gazette* (Montreal), 12 September 1988.
36. "Court ruling sets back dam project," *Star Phoenix* (Saskatoon), 11 April 1989.
37. "Dam go-ahead sell-out: SCRAP," *Star Phoenix* (Saskatoon), 1 September 1989.
38. "New Review Panel into Rafferty ordered," *Star Phoenix* (Saskatoon), 29 December 1989.
39. "Rafferty Dam Construction Suspended," *Star Phoenix* (Saskatoon), 27 January 1990.
40. "Lyons suspects secret deal lets Rafferty work continue," *Leader Post* (Regina), 30 March 1990.
41. "Rafferty work will rumble on while panel deliberates its fate," *Leader Post* (Regina), 28 April 1990.
42. "Rafferty 80 per-cent complete by fall," *Star Phoenix* (Saskatoon), 28 April 1990.
43. "Rafferty work will rumble on."
44. "Bouchard warns Sask.," *Leader Post* (Regina), 11 May 1990.
45. Vern Greenshields, "Environment Lost in Rafferty Suit," *Leader Post* (Regina), 23 October 1990.
46. "Devine's Affidavit Indicates Rafferty Deal with de Cotret," *Star Phoenix* (Saskatoon) 2 November 1990.

47. "De Cotret files rebuttal affidavit," *Star Phoenix* (Saskatoon), 3 November 1990.
48. "Minister Accepts Resignation of Rafferty-Alameda Review Panel," Minister news release issued by Environment Canada, 12 October 1990.
49. "De Cotret counters with affidavit," *Leader Post* (Regina), 3 November 1990.
50. "Suit may hobble Ottawa's case," *Leader Post* (Regina), 20 October 1990; "SaskPower seeks license assurance," *Leader Post* (Regina), 31 October 1990.
51. "Pro-dam broadcast slammed," *Leader Post* (Regina), 30 October 1990; "Dam show stirs up balanced t.v. issue," *Star Phoenix* (Saskatoon), 31 October 1990.
52. "Bid to stop dams rejected," *Star Phoenix* (Saskatoon), 16 November 1990, p. A1; "Ottawa loses Rafferty fight," *Leader Post* (Regina), 17 November 1990.
53. "SCRAP puts blame on Ottawa," *Leader Post* (Regina), 16 November 1990.
54. "Dam supporters jubilant at court victory," *Star Phoenix* (Saskatoon), 16 November 1990, p. A12.
55. "Provincial lawyers argue dam agreement invalid," *Leader Post* (Regina), 8 November 1990; "Ottawa loses Rafferty fight," *Leader Post* (Regina), 17 November 1990.
56. "Environmental review process said flawed," *Star Phoenix* (Saskatoon), 7 November 1990, p. A9; "SCRAP puts blame on Ottawa," *Leader Post* (Regina), 16 November 1990.
57. "Review 'too late' for dam," *Leader Post* (Regina), 28 May 1990.
58. David Orchard and Marjaleena Repo, "More than environment at stake in Rafferty-Alameda," *Star Phoenix* (Saskatoon), 2 November 1990.
59. "Brothers still fighting Rafferty-Alameda dam project," *Leader Post* (Regina), 23 October 1990; "Fight continues on dam project," *Leader Post* (Regina), 22 November 1990.
60. "Review 'too late' for dam," *Leader Post* (Regina), 28 May 1990.
61. "Hills cited for saving," *Leader Post* (Regina), 17 April 1990.
62. Cited in "Great Sand Hills residents leery about drilling plans," *Leader Post* (Regina), 2 May 1989.
63. *Star Phoenix* (Saskatoon), 25 July 1990.
64. "15 Key Lake spills recorded since April 1st," *Star Phoenix* (Saskatoon), 14 January 1984.
65. Ibid.
66. "Second spill handled safely," *Star Phoenix* (Saskatoon), 10 January 1984.
67. Under the Blakeney government, surface lease agreements were signed with the operators of the Cluff Lake and Key Lake mines. The contract between Key Lake Mining Corporation and the government helped avoid questions about the provincial government's jurisdictional right to regulate health and safety in uranium mines. The lease agreement specifically spelled out the province's right to do so.
68. Saskatchewan, Department of the Environment and Public Safety, *Budget Estimates*, 1982–83, 1983–4.
69. "Quick cleanup of spill key to saving river," *Star Phoenix* (Saskatoon), 9 January 1984.
70. "Radioactive water leaks from mine," *Star Phoenix* (Saskatoon), 9 November 1989.
71. "Radioactive spill raises fears for fish," *Star Phoenix* (Saskatoon), 9 November 1989; "Rabbit Lake spill–chronology of events," Star Phoenix, 22 November 1990.
72. "Uranium mine spills total 153," *Star Phoenix* (Saskatoon), 10 November 1989.
73. "Radioactive water leaks from mine," *Star Phoenix* (Saskatoon), 9 November 1989; "Snow slows work on radioactive spill," *Leader Post* (Regina), 11 November 1989; P. Shuttle, "Gap Between Nuclear Safeguard Theories and Practice," *Star Phoenix* (Saskatoon), 3 January 1990.

74. "Spilled Water Exceeded Allowable Radium Levels," *Star Phoenix* (Saskatoon), 16 November 1989.
75. "Band Leader Calls Meeting to Discuss Uranium Spill," *Star Phoenix* (Saskatoon), 11 November 1989.
76. "Second spill at Rabbit Lake sparks new call for inquiry," *Star Phoenix* (Saskatoon), 11 January 1990.
77. "90,000 litre Collins Bay spill quickly contained," *Star Phoenix* (Saskatoon), 10 January 1990.
78. "Crown seeking $50,000 fine against CAMECO," *Star Phoenix* (Saskatoon), 22 November 1990; "CAMECO fined $50,000 for spill," *Star Phoenix* (Saskatoon), 28 November 1990.
79. "Contamination after spill compared to city's water," *Star Phoenix* (Saskatoon), 22 November 1990.
80. "CAMECO fined $50,000 for spill," *Star Phoenix* (Saskatoon), 28 November 1990.
81. Saskatchewan, Department of Finance, G. Lane, *Budget Address*, March 1989, p. 10.
82. Ibid., supplementary brochures.
83. Saskatchewan, Legislative Assembly, *Debates and Proceedings*, 9 June 1989, pp. 1966–67.
84. "Cruise test cancelled in mid-flight," *Star Phoenix* (Saskatoon), 8 November 1990.
85. Saskatchewan, Legislative Assembly, *Debates and Proceedings*, 1 September 1987, p. 2229.
86. Ibid, p. 2233.
87. The W-5 program aired on Sunday, 29 September 1985.
88. Proceedings of Saskatchewan Crown Corporations Committee, 26 May 1988.
89. The 1955 Atoms for Peace Treaty was amended on 28 April 1980 by the Agreement for Co-operation of Civil Uses of Atomic Energy Between the US and Canada. Article 14 of the 1980 agreement amends article 12 of the original agreement to read: "designated nuclear technology, material, equipment and devices, major or critical components and components subject to this agreement and source or special material [i.e., uranium and highly-enriched uranium, respectively] used in or produced through the use of any components subject to this agreement, and over which the party has jurisdiction, shall not be used for any military purpose."
90. CBC Radio program "It's a Matter of Survival," program 2, 23 July 1989. Comments by Dr. Mick Kelly, atmospheric scientist at the University of East Anglia in England.
91. Lecture by David Eyre of the Saskatchewan Research Council at the Saskatoon Unitarian Centre, 30 September 1989.
92. Saskatchewan, Legislative Assembly, *Debates and Proceedings*, 18 June 1990, p. 2188.
93. The provincial government's slow pace may be overridden by action at the federal level. On 2 November 1990 federal Environment Minister Robert de Cotret announced his commitment to fully phase out CFCs by 1997. (New Bans on CFC Use in Canada Will Step Up Domestic Phase Out Program; news release issued 2 November 1990 by Environment Canada.)

CHAPTER 7

1. The "numbered" treaties are Treaties no. 1–11.
2. The Natural Resource Transfer Agreement R.S.C. 1985, Appendix 11, No. 26, provides that "the Province will from time to time on the request of the Superintendent General of Indian Affairs set aside, out of unoccupied Crown lands hereby transferred to its administration, such further areas as the said Superintendent General may, in agreement with the Minister of Natural Resources of the Province, select as necessary to enable Canada to fulfil its obligation under the treaties with the Indians of the Province . . ."

3. Supreme Court Reports [1973], p. 313.
4. For the purposes of this chapter, the current name, FSIN, will be used.
5. Memo from J.L. Tobias, minister of Indian affairs, to W. Gordon, 19 April 1973. Tobias suggested entitlement for only five bands in the south and 13 throughout the remainder of the province. See also letter and attachments from J. Buchanan, minister of Indian affairs, to A. Blakeney, premier of Saskatchewan, 18 August 1975.
6. T. Bowerman, paper presented to F.S.I. in Regina, 4 December 1974.
7. Appendix to letter from T. Bowerman to D. Ahenakew, representative for F.S.I., 23 August 1976. The appendix is the basis for the "Saskatchewan formula."
8. Meeting with minister of Indian affairs and Ted Bowerman et al., Ottawa, 31 January 1977.
9. Allmand to Bowerman, 14 April 1977.
10. Faulkner to Bowerman, 27 February 1979.
11. Bowerman to Sanderson, 25 March 1981.
12. Munro to Lane, 7 July 1982.
13. Munro to Lane, 31 August 1982.
14. The federal government agreed to a freeze on transfers during the review except for the transfer of federal Indian student residences at Prince Albert and Lebret. These transfers had already been promised and only awaited an Order in Council. See letters from Munro to Lane, 31 August 1982; Munro to Lane, 26 November 1982; Munro to Sanderson, 5 January 1983.
15. Munro to Dutchak, 11 January 1984.
16. Revised Statutes of Canada, Appendix 11, No. 21, 1985.
17. Cabinet submission on Indian Treaty Land Entitlement, 13 June 1984.
18. Crombie to Sanderson, March 1985.
19. Order in Council 808/85. *The Saskatchewan Gazette*, 30 August 1985; Order in Council 1310/85. *The Saskatchewan Gazette*, 3 January 1986.
20. McKnight to H. Nicotine, Chief of the Red Pheasant Band, 17 December 1986.
21. Ibid.
22. Hodgins to McKnight, 18 March 1988.
23. Saskatchewan, Legislative Assembly, *Debates and Proceedings*, 21st Legislature, 2nd Session, 22 June 1988, p. 2355.
24. Ibid., p. 2359.
25. Crowe to McKnight, 25 March 1988.

CHAPTER 8

1. R. Mahon, "Canadian public policy: the unequal structure of representation," in Leo Panitch, ed., *The Canadian State: Political Economy and Political Power* (Toronto: University of Toronto Press, 1977), p. 183.
2. J. Barbash, "The New Industrial Relations in the US: Phase II," *Relations Industrielles* 43(1) (1988), p. 34.
3. R. Sass, "The Saskatchewan Trade Union Amendment Act, 1983: The Public Battle," *Relations Industrielles* 40 (1985), pp. 591–622.
4. Saskatchewan Labour Relations Board certification order, 6 April 1973.
5. Sass, "Trade Union Amendment Act," p. 594.

6. Ibid.

7. "McLaren Defends Labour Chairman's Pay," *Star Phoenix* (Saskatoon), 22 November 1983.

8. *The Saskatchewan Trade Union Act*, R.S.S. 1978, c. T-17, ss. 11(1)(m).

9. *Retail, Wholesale, and Department Store Union, Locals 454 and 480 and Canada Safeway Limited, Regina, Saskatchewan*, S.L.R.B. File No. 392–85, 10 January 1986.

10. *The Saskatchewan Trade Union Act*, R.S.S. 1978, c. T-17, ss. 33(4).

11. *Communication Workers of Canada and Northern Telecom Canada Ltd.*, S.L.R.B. File No. 062–85, 27 August 1985.

12. *Linda Heckel of Saskatoon and Revelstoke Companies Ltd and Construction and General Labourers Local Union 890*, S.L.R.B. File No. 071–84, 13 August 1984.

13. Saskatchewan Department of Human Resources, Employment, and Labour, *Annual Report*, 1989.

14. Saskatchewan Department of Human Resources, Employment, and Labour, *Annual Report*, 1982–88.

15. Calculated from Saskatchewan Department of Human Resources, Employment, and Labour, *Annual Report*, 1982–89.

16. D. McConachie, "Unions Fear Falling Membership," *Star Phoenix* (Saskatoon), 15 February 1984.

17. C. Boese, "Bill 88 Repealed," *Saskatchewan Business Journal*, January 1984, p. 17.

18. Letter to "All Member Firms" by the Saskatchewan Construction Labour Relations Council, 12 December 1983. The letter was sent out to members of the council on 1 March 1984.

19. Letter of the Saskatchewan Construction Labour Relations Council, 22 February 1984. This letter was circulated as a "legal opinion."

20. Bob Sass from Kerry Westcott, 14 March 1984.

21. "Building Firms Pressure Unions," *Star Phoenix* (Saskatoon), 14 February 1984.

22. *The Saskatchewan Trade Union Act*, S.S. 1983, s.37.

23. *United Brotherhood of Carpenters and Joiners of America, Locals 1805 and 1990 and Cana Construction Ltd*, S.L.R.B. File No. 99–84–20–85, December 1984, pp. 20–21.

24. D. McConachie, "Saskatchewan Unions Fighting For Survival," *Star Phoenix* (Saskatoon), 13 February 1984.

25. Interview with John Hart by Bob Sass, 21 March 1984.

26. Reported to New Democratic Party Task Force on Social Justice, Saskatoon, Spring 1984.

27. Interview with Bob Todd, Secretary of the Carpenter's Provincial Council of Saskatchewan, by Bob Sass, 15 March 1985.

28. Saskatchewan Bureau of Statistics, *Economic Review*, 1986, p. 13; and 1989, p. 13.

29. Quoted in H. J. Michelmann and J. S. Steeves, "The 1982 transition in power in Saskatchewan: the Progressive Conservatives and the public service," *Canadian Public Administration* 28(1) (1983), p. 6.

30. Ibid., p. 9.

31. M. d'Entremont, "Job Insecurity: Concession Bargaining Comes to Saskatchewan," *Briarpatch* 15(1) (February 1986).

32. G. Lane, *Saskatchewan Economic and Financial Report*, March 1987, p. 14.

33. Earnings figures from Saskatchewan Medical Care Insurance Commission, *Annual Report*, 1982 and 1988. Adjustment to 1981 dollars calculated from Saskatchewan *Monthly Statistical Review*, May 1982 and January 1989.
34. Calculated from *Monthly Statistical Review*, 1982–1990.
35. Saskatchewan Department of Human Resources, Employment, and Labour, *Annual Report*, 1987–88, p. 5.
36. Saskatchewan, Legislative Assembly, *Debates and Proceedings*, Vol. 31(53B), 6 June 1988, p. 1877.
37. B. Sass, "Bill 73 Employment Benefits Act: A Bill of Rights for Saskatchewan Employees or a Step Backwards?" *Canadian Review of Social Policy* 23 (1989).
38. G.B. Reschenthaler, *Occupational Health and Safety in Canada: The economics and three case studies* (Montreal: Institute for Research on Public Policy, 1979), pp. 101–106.
39. P. Manga, R. Broyles, and G. Reschenthaler, *Occupational Health and Safety: Issues and Alternatives*, Technical Report No. 6 (Ottawa: Economic Council of Canada, 1981), pp. 224–225.
40. Quoted in R. Sentes, "Labour Department remodels OH+S Policy," *Canadian Occupational Health and Safety News*, 28 March 1983, pp. 3–4.
41. Saskatchewan, Legislative Assembly, *Debates and Proceedings*, 25(39A), 16 December 1982, pp. 1795–1797.
42. Interview with John Alderman, director of the Occupational Health and Safety Branch, 7 August 1985, by Mark Stobbe.
43. Saskatchewan, Department of Labour, *Annual Reports*, 1982–84.
44. Alderman interview by Stobbe.
45. Ibid.
46. T. Craig, "Pulp mill workers ordered back to job," *Star Phoenix* (Saskatoon), 31 May 1985, p. A3.
47. Alderman interview by Stobbe.
48. *Occupational Health and General Regulations*, s. 42(2).
49. R. Sass, "As Darkness Falls," *Briarpatch* 18(9) (November 1989), pp. 22–23.
50. Memorandum from Hugh Miller to Myles Morin, 14 August 1989.
51. Saskatchewan Workers' Compensation Board, *Annual Reports*, 1984–89.
52. Workers' Compensation Act Review Committee, *Report of the Workers' Compensation Act Review Committee*, September 1986, p. 21.
53. Saskatchewan Workers' Compensation Board, "Directive of the Workers' Compensation Board: Earnings Replacement Policy," 28 June 1988.

CHAPTER 9

1. For an overview of the history of health insurance, see M. G. Taylor, *Health Insurance and Canadian Policy: The Seven Decisions that created the Canadian Health Insurance System* (Kingston: McGill-Queen's University Press, 1978). See also C. D. Naylor, *Private Practice, Public Payment: Canadian Medicine and the Politics of Health Insurance, 1911–1966* (Kingston: McGill-Queen's University Press, 1986).
2. Interview with Herman Rolfes.
3. Saskatchewan, Department of Finance, *Budget Estimates*, 1983–84.

4. C. Stephan, "Health, social services to cost $1.3 billion," *Leader Post* (Regina), 20 March 1983.

5. C. Dundas, "Health Department budget over $1 billion mark," *Leader Post* (Regina), 22 March 1984.

6. "Hospital Projects," *Leader Post* (Regina), 16 April 1985.

7. Stephan, "Health, social services."

8. Dundas, "Health Department budget."

9. L. Johnsrude, "Health takes back seat to budget promotion: NDP," *Star Phoenix* (Saskatoon), 31 May 1985.

10. Ibid.

11. Ibid.

12. Editorial, "Expensive Exercise," *Star Phoenix* (Saskatoon), 5 December 1985.

13. "Health care spending said cut," *Leader Post* (Regina), 20 February 1985.

14. D. Yanko, "St. Paul's anesthetists protest budget shortfalls," *Star Phoenix* (Saskatoon), 7 June 1986.

15. M. Mandryk, "NDP accuses health minister of 'misusing' health funds," *Leader Post* (Regina), 29 November 1985.

16. D. Herman, "Hospitals await C-T scanners," *Leader Post* (Regina), 29 November 1985.

17. J. Crockatt, "Sask. health care understaffed: Liberals," *Star Phoenix* (Saskatoon), 17 February 1986.

18. N. Scott, "Health care gets big shot in the arm," *Leader Post* (Regina), 26 February 1986.

19. E.H. Baergen, SMA Executive Director, letter to the editor: "When will government stop breaking its provinces," *Star Phoenix* (Saskatoon), 3 December 1987.

20. Ibid.

21. B. Allan, "Striking Interns win a limited victory," *Leader Post* (Regina), 18 June 1985.

22. A. Clay, "P.A. Anesthetists will strike Tuesday," *Herald* (Prince Albert), 7 April 1986.

23. D. Eisler, *Leader Post* (Regina), 29 September 1987.

24. D. Eisler, "P.C. Resolution calls for user fees for medicare," *Leader Post* (Regina), 22 December 1987.

25. "Sask. residents satisfied with health care: Taylor," *Star Phoenix* (Saskatoon), 23 October 1986.

26. For example, Graham Taylor visited former Saskatchewan Conservative leader, Dick Collver, who offers a pre-authorized type of medical insurance called Q-Care. Q-Care gives a computerized number to each client so that the costs of health care services can be monitored. For more detail, see D. Eisler, *Leader Post* (Regina), 13 March 1985.

27. B. Spencer, "McLeod wants innovative solutions to funding problem," *Leader Post* (Regina), 25 November 1986.

28. SPHA, C. Brown, *Profile of Reductions in Health in Saskatchewan*, 21 November 1987, p. 2.

29. For an overview of the cutbacks, see B. Spencer, "Lane intends to change health system's priorities," *Leader Post* (Regina), 18 June 1987.

30. Ibid.

31. Ibid.

32. SPHA, C. Brown, *Profile of Reductions*.

33. "McLeod mum on inquest, leaked health care report," *Leader Post* (Regina), 21 September 1988.

34. SPHA, C. Brown, *Profile of Reductions,* p. 10.
35. Ibid., p. 11.
36. Ibid., p. 14.
37. Saskatchewan, Department of Finance, *Budget Address,* June 1987.
38. R. Burton, "812 charges allege abuse of prescriptions," *Star Phoenix* (Saskatoon), 22 December 1987.
39. D. Eisler, *Leader Post* (Regina), 13 June 1987.
40. E. Fowler, "Petition tabling 'childish antics' premier says," *Star Phoenix* (Saskatoon), 21 October 1987.
41. A. Kyle, "New health care cards will eliminate rebate process," *Leader Post* (Regina), 3 November 1988.
42. Editorial, "Public Wants Medicare," *Star Phoenix* (Saskatoon), 30 June 1987.
43. Saskatchewan, Health Services Utilization Review Committee, *Study into Growth in Use of Health Services,* January 1989.
44. Saskatchewan, Department of Health, *Annual Report,* 1987–88.
45. Review Committee on Health Services, *Study into the Growth in Use of Health Services,* January 1989.
46. Saskatchewan, Department of Health, Medical Care Insurance Commission, *Annual Report,* 1985–86.
47. According to the Review Committee on Health Services' *Study,* "the percentage figures do not add to the 'Total' increase due to the multiplicative impact of fees and volume on total expenditures. The increase in fees and volume compound to the total increase of 152.9 percent," p. 12.
48. Review Committee on Health Services.
49. Saskatchewan, Department of Health, *Annual Report,* 1987–88.
50. Rural residents have the highest rate of hospital utilization for noncoded procedures. (Noncoded procedures refer to all other procedures excluding diagnostic and surgical procedures.) Consequently, Saskatchewan has one of the highest rates of hospital procedures in the country.
51. Saskatchewan, Department of Health, *Annual Report,* 1982–83 to 1987–88.
52. C. Dundas, "Health Department budget over $1 billion mark," *Leader Post* (Regina), 22 March 1984.
53. D. Herman, "Saskatoon hospitals meet summer goals for cutting costs," *Star Phoenix* (Saskatoon), 28 July 1987.
54. D. Left, "Local hospitals cut to the bone," *Herald* (Prince Albert), 16 May 1987.
55. "McLeod says hospital waiting lists not a serious problem," *Leader Post* (Regina), 17 September 1987.
56. N. Scott, "Hospital waiting lists still hot topic," *Leader Post* (Regina), 23 September 1987.
57. P. Jackson, "Hospitals to cut operating backlog," *Star Phoenix* (Saskatoon), 13 October 1987.
58. D. Yanko, "City Hospital's waiting list slashed," *Star Phoenix* (Saskatoon), 29 November 1989.
59. Saskatchewan, Department of Health, *Saskatchewan Hospital Services Plan, Statistical Tables Supplementing the Annual Report,* 1987–88.
60. Saskatchewan, Department of Labour, *Saskatchewan Labour Report,* 1982–83 to 1989–90.

61. Saskatchewan, Department of Finance, *Budget Estimates*, 1988–89.
62. "Hospitals could soon face more strike disruption," *Leader Post* (Regina), 22 October 1988.
63. L. Orosz, "Striking nursing-home workers demand halt to privatization," *Leader Post* (Regina), 1 November 1988.
64. N. Scott, "Nursing supervisors leery about changes," *Leader Post* (Regina), 24 September 1988.
65. D. Herman, "MDs not consulted on abolition of MCIC," *Star Phoenix* (Saskatoon), 5 November 1987.
66. D. Eisler, *Leader Post* (Regina), May 1987.
67. Z. Olijnk, "Limit put on payments to doctors," *Leader Post* (Regina), November 1987.
68. R. Wilkins, and O. B. Adams. *Healthfulness of Life* (Montreal: Institute for Research on Public Policy, 1983).
69. Statistics are collected only for Natives with treaty status. Metis, Inuit, and other groups are excluded.
70. Statistics cited in D. Hay, "Mortality and Health Status Trends in Canada," in S. Bolaria and H. Dickinson, eds., *Sociology of Health Care in Canada* (Toronto: Harcourt Brace Jovanovich, 1988).
71. V. Greenshields, "Budget Hikes Health Care Funds by 11%," *Star Phoenix* (Saskatoon), 31 March 1989.
72. N. Scott, "Health Money was Top Priority," *Leader Post* (Regina), 10 April 1989.
73. E. I. Schwartz, *Report on Enhancement of Regional Hospitals*, December 1987.
74. Ibid., p. 24.
75. "Heavy Dose of Money Kicks Off Campaign," *Star Phoenix* (Saskatoon), 27 June 1988.
76. "New chiropractic limits hurt chronic sufferers," *Star Phoenix* (Saskatoon), 30 May 1987.
77. D. Traynor, "Underfunding said costing interns," *Star Phoenix* (Saskatoon), 4 August 1989.
78. D. Eisler, "Dental Plan savings far below prediction," *Leader Post* (Regina), 16 June 1987.
79. M. Mandryk, "Unemployed dental therapists blast Devine," *Leader Post* (Regina), 11 June 1988.
80. "Government Dental Gear gathers Dust," *Leader Post* (Regina), 27 May 1989.
81. "Leftover dental equipment said headed for scrap heap," *Leader Post* (Regina), 13 June 1989.
82. B. Doskoch, "Dental Workers win partial court victory," *Leader Post* (Regina), 3 March 1990.
83. M. Ommanney, "Major surgery proposed for health care system," *Star Phoenix* (Saskatoon), 2 May 1990.
84. "Hospital Plan Criticized," *Leader Post* (Regina), 24 February 1989.
85. J.W. Atkinson, J. MacKay, and R. Coombs, *Future Direction for Saskatoon's Hospitals: A Plan for the Consolidation of Acute Care Services*. A Study for the Saskatchewan Commission on Directions in Health Care, 31 July 1990.
86. G. Struthers, "Murray hospital plan could duplicate costs," *Star Phoenix* (Saskatoon), 14 July 1990.
87. M. Ommanney, "McLeod promises quick action on hospital report," *Star Phoenix* (Saskatoon), 11 August 1990.
88. Editorial, "Hospital Board proves leader," *Star Phoenix* (Saskatoon), 10 September 1990.

89. G. Klein, "Doctors want hospital proposal slowed down," *Star Phoenix* (Saskatoon), 14 September 1990; B. Braden, "Family physicians balk at proposed amalgamation of hospitals," *Star Phoenix* (Saskatoon), 22 September 1990.
90. Atkinson et al., *Future Directions,* p. 62.
91. M. Ommanney, "Atkinson report for decision: McLeod," *Star Phoenix* (Saskatoon), 11 September 1990.
92. N. Scott, "New Board for Hospitals," *Leader Post* (Regina), 26 October 1990.
93. For a description of the College of Medicine's problems, see Atkinson et al., *Future Directions,* and K. White, *Towards a New Beginning, Review of the College of Medicine,* University of Saskatchewan, March 1989.
94. E. Freidson, *Professional Powers* (Chicago: University of Chicago Press, 1986).

CHAPTER 10

1. Letter, "NDP to blame for problems at U of R," *Leader Post* (Regina), 23 February 1985.
2. "Demand for 'quality' education on horizon says new report," *University Affairs* 30(3) (October 1989), p. 11.
3. "Task force report endorsed," *Leader Post* (Regina), 5 January 1983.
4. L. Thoner, "Maxwell hints math, science to be compulsory," *Star Phoenix* (Saskatoon), 8 November 1983.
5. D. Oshanek, "Literacy campaign begins next year," *Star Phoenix* (Saskatoon), 19 December 1983.
6. Thoner, "Maxwell hints."
7. "Student places increased 3,100 in technical training expansion," *Leader Post* (Regina), 29 June 1983.
8. L. Thoner, "Kelsey staff cuts hurt program," *Star Phoenix* (Saskatoon), 16 June 1984.
9. D. Oshanek, "Northern technical institute opens in P.A.," *Star Phoenix* (Saskatoon), 3 September 1986.
10. "NIT gives city $10.5 million shot in the arm," *Herald* (Prince Albert), 13 September 1986.
11. A. Clay, "Educational centre promised by Tories," *Herald* (Prince Albert), 22 September 1986.
12. R. Suave, "Graduates praise technical institutes," *Leader Post* (Regina), 19 March 1987.
13. "Education talks get under way," *Leader Post* (Regina), 18 February 1987.
14. P. Jackson, "Province plans major educational initiatives," *Star Phoenix* (Saskatoon), 2 April 1987.
15. D. McMillan, "STI adjusts to budget cuts," *Leader Post* (Regina), 5 April 1986.
16. D. Oshanek, "New Kelsey postings 'don't make sense,'" *Star Phoenix* (Saskatoon), 15 May 1987; D. Oshanek, "Odds of being accepted at Kelsey poor," *Star Phoenix* (Saskatoon), 20 May 1987.
17. "At last, technical schools are updated," *Star Phoenix* (Saskatoon), 16 May 1987.
18. D. Oshanek, "Axed courses may find new homes," *Star Phoenix* (Saskatoon), 21 May 1987.
19. J. Parker, "Student drops course in disgust," *Star Phoenix* (Saskatoon), 16 June 1989.
20. G. Klein, "College workers claim revolt cost jobs," *Star Phoenix* (Saskatoon), 16 June 1989; J. Parker, "Bridge City College under investigation," *Star Phoenix* (Saskatoon), 17 June 1989; "Bridge City students got $1 million," *Star Phoenix* (Saskatoon), 26 June 1989.

21. "STI students set to 'go forth' with college," *Times-Herald* (Moose Jaw), 6 May 1987.

22. "Autonomy for tech, schools very popular says NDP survey," *Herald* (Prince Albert), 7 May 1987.

23. "College board refuses to help," *Times-Herald* (Moose Jaw), 6 May 1987; "Resignations called 'unfortunate glitch,'" *Star Phoenix* (Saskatoon), 9 July 1987; T. Kirkpatrick, "'Unfortunate . . . sour grapes' says minister of resignations," *Herald* (Prince Albert), 10 July 1987.

24. "Unfortunate glitch," *Star Phoenix* (Saskatoon); D. Lett, "Adult education moves defended by Hepworth," *Herald* (Prince Albert), 14 May 1987.

25. D. Oshanek, "More independence for technical schools urged," *Star Phoenix* (Saskatoon), 18 October 1986.

26. A. Kyle, "SIAST workers set up pickets as contract talks at impasse," *Leader Post* (Regina), 7 March 1989.

27. M. Laforest, "SIAST attacks seniority: union," *Star Phoenix* (Saskatoon), 8 March 1989.

28. L. Sheppard, "Union applauds decision by Labour Relations Board," *Times-Herald* (Moose Jaw), 3 April 1989.

29. Barber cited in Z. Olijnyk, "U of R unveils $42.3 million plan," *Leader Post* (Regina), 14 March 1986; "U of R accounts for $93 million," *Leader Post* (Regina), 4 November 1987.

30. E. Schroeter, "Provincial government gives universities more money," *Leader Post* (Regina), 30 August 1984.

31. "U of S won't drop 'lesser' courses," *Star Phoenix* (Saskatoon), 19 March 1987.

32. "University budget squeezed," *Leader Post* (Regina), 17 July 1982.

33. "Universities to get grants," *Leader Post* (Regina), 6 April 1984.

34. Z. Olijnyk, "University enrolment up 12.5%," *Leader Post* (Regina), 13 January 1987.

35. D. Eisler, "Economic reality must be faced, Hepworth tells student protestors," *Leader Post* (Regina), 30 January 1987.

36. N. Scott, "U of R management said inefficient, unwieldy," *Leader Post* (Regina), 27 February 1987.

37. Z. Olijnyk, "Cost summary irks U of R students," *Leader Post* (Regina), 5 March 1987; editorial, "University of Regina report card: is it a fair accounting?" *Leader Post* (Regina), 5 March 1987.

38. Z. Olijnyk, "Grant freeze said likely to close doors to students," *Leader Post* (Regina), 13 March 1987.

39. L. Johnsrude, "Hepworth gives U of R four years to eliminate deficit," *Star Phoenix* (Saskatoon), 19 March 1987.

40. L. Behm, "Students devastated by university closure," *Herald* (Prince Albert), 16 April 1987.

41. "U of R cuts protested," *Leader Post* (Regina), 16 April 1987.

42. K. O'Connor, "Donated grain will help library grow," *Leader Post* (Regina), 14 April 1988.

43. "Barber blasts Ottawa for halting U of R deal," *Star Phoenix* (Saskatoon), 9 June 1988.

44. "U of S to cut clerical staff," *Star Phoenix* (Saskatoon), 19 May 1983.

45. K. Humphries, "Home economics profs return to learn college's fate sealed," *Star Phoenix* (Saskatoon), 10 July 1987.

46. L. Thoner, "U of S may turn down students unless funds hiked," *Star Phoenix* (Saskatoon), 23 April 1983; L. Thoner, "U of S rejects quota on college enrolments," *Star Phoenix* (Saskatoon), 11 May 1983.

47. D. Oshanek, "Arts college considers limiting enrolment," *Star Phoenix* (Saskatoon), 9 April 1985.

48. R. Piche, "U of S will protect core facilities," *Star Phoenix* (Saskatoon), 25 April 1987.

49. P. Mackinnon, *Governing the University of Saskatchewan: Tentative Proposals for Change, Issues and Options, July 1987.*

50. Viewpoint, S. Federoff, "Saskatchewan universities need long-term planning," *Star Phoenix* (Saskatoon), 21 April 1988.

51. B. Fairbairn, "The prof motive. Radical conservatism at the University of Saskatchewan," *NeWest Review* 14(1) (October/November 1988), p. 22.

52. Mackinnon, *Governing the University of Saskatchewan.*

53. G. Struthers, "U of S faculty vote immediately on full walkout," *Star Phoenix* (Saskatoon), 23 March 1988.

54. A. Ehman, "Impasse at U of S remains despite talks," *Star Phoenix* (Saskatoon), 31 March 1988.

55. A. Ehman, "Increase to U of S decline in real terms, Kristjanson says," *Star Phoenix* (Saskatoon), 2 April 1988.

56. Letter, M. Hayden, "False information colors faculty strike," *Star Phoenix* (Saskatoon), 4 April 1988.

57. "Talks set in U of S profs strike," *Leader Post* (Regina), 29 March 1988.

58. Letter, J. Hope, "Faculty had no choice to withdraw services," *Star Phoenix* (Saskatoon), 13 April 1988.

59. "U of S faculty calls for resignation of the president," *Leader Post* (Regina), 29 May 1988.

60. "Some faculty members want outside president," *Star Phoenix* (Saskatoon), 7 July 1988.

61. Letter, F. Langford, "Both faculty, students seek quality education," *Star Phoenix* (Saskatoon), 9 August 1989.

62. D. Collie, "Immediate back-to-work bill for faculty unlikely," *Star Phoenix* (Saskatoon), 4 April 1988; "U of S students used as pawns: Hepworth," *Star Phoenix* (Saskatoon), 31 March 1988; "Next few days critical to U of S exam situation," *Star Phoenix* (Saskatoon), April 1988.

63. M. Mandryk, "Unhappy profs will heed back-to-work bill," *Leader Post* (Regina), 7 April 1988.

64. M. Ommanney, "U of S mediator pushes 11.5% hike," *Star Phoenix* (Saskatoon), 30 August 1988.

65. Editorial, "Ivory tower demands need tuning to reality," *Leader Post* (Regina), 7 April 1988.

66. R. Piche, "U of S will protect core facilities," *Star Phoenix* (Saskatoon), 25 April 1987; L. Kristjanson, *Report to Senate*, Fall 1988.

67. "U of S to get more money: Andrew," *Star Phoenix* (Saskatoon), 2 February 1989.

68. Z. Olijnyk, "Adult-education funds sought," *Leader Post* (Regina), 20 November 1986.

69. P. Jackson, "Province plans major educational initiatives," *Star Phoenix* (Saskatoon), 2 April 1987.

70. Z. Olijnyk, "Expanded role for community colleges," *Leader Post* (Regina), 30 July 1987.

71. Brief from the City of Melfort to Saskatchewan Cabinet, "Proposal for a Saskatchewan Junior College system," 17 January 1989; D. Oshanek, "Rural university colleges proposed," *Star Phoenix* (Saskatoon), 23 December 1987.

72. "College official calls for standard courses," *Leader Post* (Regina), 3 March 1988; Oshanek, "Rural university colleges proposed"; M. O'Brien, writing in the *Leader Post* (Regina), 3 March 1989.

CHAPTER 11

1. Saskatchewan, Department of Social Services, *Summary of Day Care Regulations*, July 1979. As this article goes to print (November 1990) new child care regulations have just been implemented in Saskatchewan. See *The Child Care Act*, Section 27, Order in Council 948/90, *The Saskatchewan Gazette*, 24 October 1990.

2. For more detail, see J. A. Martin, "The Continuing Struggle for Universal Day Care," in J. Harding, ed., *The Politics of Social Policy: The Blakeney Years in Saskatchewan 1971–82* (in progress).

3. Saskatchewan NDP, *New Deal for People*, February 1971, p. 14.

4. This policy was contained in The Family Services Act, Regulation 213/75. Approved by Order in Council, 1239/75.

5. Saskatchewan, Department of Finance, *Budget Estimates*, 1981–82, 1982–83.

6. K. Cooke, Status of Women of Canada, *Report of the Task Force on Child Care* (Ottawa: Department of Supply and Services, 1986). See chapter 13.

7. Canada, Special Committee on Child Care, S. Martin, *Sharing the Responsibility* (Ottawa: Department of Supply and Services, 1987).

8. J. Martin, *Childcare in Saskatchewan: What We Have, What We Want* (Saskatoon: Action Child Care, 1988).

9. Sample Survey and Data Bank Unit, *Day Care Needs in Saskatchewan*, University of Regina, 1978.

10. Saskatchewan Child Care Association, *The Child Care Story: The Struggle, the Reality, the Vision,* October 1989.

11. "Day care centres face lack of funds," *Star Phoenix* (Saskatoon), 7 September 1984.

12. These programs are described in: Saskatchewan, Department of Social Services, *Annual Reports*, 1975–1988.

13. There is no mechanism specified in the regulations which allows for regular adjustments in the subsidy.

14. National Council of Welfare, *Child Care: A Better Alternative*, Ottawa 1988.

15. These figures do not correspond directly because in 1984 child care spaces under the jurisdiction of the former Department of Northern Services were transferred to the Department of Social Services. Eight centres and "some" family day care homes were transferred according to government officials.

16. The move toward family day care also reflects the attitude that what's good for business is good for everyone. As a member of the Minister's Advisory Committee on Child Care in 1983, I inquired about the origins of the "demand" for family day care spaces. I was informed that the long lists for family day care were names of individuals who wanted to set up a family day care business rather than parents requesting this form of care.

17. National Council of Welfare, *Child Care.*

18. See note 1.
19. Personal interview with M. Bokshowan, president, Saskatchewan Child Care Association, 14 September 1989.
20. In general, day care workers across Canada are shamefully underpaid. For more detail, see Kargo Communications (Vancouver), *The Bottom Line: A Study of Wages and Working Conditions of Workers in the Formal Day Care Market* (Ottawa: Status of Women, 1988).
21. See for example: Sharon West, *A Study on Compliance with the Day Nurseries Act at Full-Day Child Care Centres in Metropolitan Toronto* (Toronto: Ontario, Ministry of Community and Social Services, 1988).
22. Gordon Dirks to Dawn Shark, chairperson, Daycare Advisory Board, 19 December 1983. This letter was copied to members of the Advisory Board. Author's personal files.
23. As a member of the Minister's Advisory Board, I was shocked by the minister's apparent change in opinion and tried to convince him that the possibility of lower quality care was equally possible in "mom and pop" day care centres as in the large corporate centres. Later, a 1986 study commissioned by Brian Mulroney's Parliamentary Task Force on Child Care found that the lowest quality of care was in the "small-profit" sector. For more detail, see SPR Associate Inc./National Mail Surveys Inc. *An Exploratory Review of Selected Issues in For-Profit Versus Not-For-Profit Child Care* (Toronto: October 1988).
24. "Care For-Profit Not Dead, Activist Reveals: Judith Martin resigned from the Minister's Advisory Board and made a public statement," *Star Phoenix* (Saskatoon), 2 February 1984.
25. Saskatchewan, Department of Social Services, J. Zazelenchuk, *Directions for Child Care in Saskatchewan: A Report*, 1984.
26. Ibid., p. 20.
27. G. Dirks, minister of social services, Saskatchewan, to R. Hnatyshyn, MP, 11 September 1985. Author's personal files.
28. J. Epp, minister of health and welfare Canada, *Federal Government's Child Care Strategy*, 3 December 1987.
29. Saskatchewan, *Speech from the Throne*, 21 March 1988.
30. A commercial centre, "Lots for Tots" opened in Estevan (Premier Devine's constituency) almost a full year before the legislation was passed. In October 1988, a commercial centre for infants was opened in Saskatoon. Although it was completely illegal given the legislation at the time, the government turned a blind eye.
31. At first glance, the delivery of child care services in Canada appears to be protected from free trade because it was excluded from the "service" section of the agreement. However, it was not excluded from the section related to investment. American individuals and corporations not only could argue that they have the right to set up day care centres in Saskatchewan, but they could also demand public assistance for which nonprofit groups are eligible.
32. See note 1.
33. "Budget Highlights," *The Globe and Mail* (Toronto), 27 April 1989.
34. West, *A Study on Compliance.*
35. S. Prentice, *The Politics of Care: Child Care in Ontario.* A major paper in partial fulfilment of the Master of Environmental Studies, Toronto: York University, 1987.

CHAPTER 12

1. T. Rofuth, "Moving Clients into Jobs," *Public Welfare* 10 (Spring 1987), p. 12.
2. C. Leman, *The Collapse of Welfare Reform: Political Institutions, Policy, and the Poor in Canada and the United States* (Cambridge: MIT Press, 1980), p. xiii.
3. Compiled Statutes of Canada, *Canada Assistance Plan Act*, 1966, C. 45, S.1.
4. Saskatchewan Finance, *Budget Estimates*, 1990–91, p. 10.
5. D. Guest, *The Emergence of Social Security in Canada,* 2nd ed. (Vancouver: UBC Press, 1985), p. 155.
6. A. Moscovitch, "The Canada Assistance Plan: A Twenty Year Assessment 1966–1986," in K. Graham, ed., *How Ottawa Spends Your Tax Dollar* (Toronto: Lorimer, 1988), p. 274.
7. D. Adams, *A Productive Welfare System for the Eighties: A Review of the Saskatchewan Assistance Plan* (Regina: Saskatchewan Social Services, 1983), p. vi.
8. Department of Indian Affairs and Northern Development, Personal communication to author, 1987.
9. Saskatchewan Social Services, *Annual Report*, 1984; Saskatchewan Finance, *Budget Address*, 1987.
10. B. Jeffery and A. Shadrack, *Living Without Power,* Working Paper Series No. 2, Regina: Social Administration Research Unit, University of Regina, 1986, pp. 31–33.
11. J. Struthers, *Through No Fault of Their Own: Unemployment and the Canadian Welfare State, 1914–45* (Toronto: University of Toronto Press, 1983), p. 6.
12. G. Riches, and L. Manning, *Welfare Reform and the Canada Assistance Plan: The Breakdown of Public Welfare in Saskatchewan 1981–1989,* Working Paper Series No. 4, Regina: Social Administration Research Unit, University of Regina, 1989, Table 10, p. 14. Note that the average Canadian income for a single-parent family is below the poverty line.
13. Ibid., p. 15.
14. Ibid.
15. Ibid., p. 16.
16. Ibid.
17. "Welfare payment ruling could be costly for Sask.," *Star Phoenix* (Saskatoon), 27 January 1989.
18. Federal Court of Canada, *Finlay R. vs. Canada*, Mr. Justice Teitelbaum, Trial Division, T–3666–82, 24 January 1989, p. 19.
19. G. Riches, *Food Banks and the Welfare Crisis* (Ottawa: Canadian Council on Social Development, 1986).
20. Monthly records, Regina food bank, 1989.
21. Riches and Manning, *Welfare Reform*, pp. 21–23.
22. Saskatchewan Department of Human Resources, Labour, and Employment, *The Saskatchewan Labour Market*, December 1988.
23. Saskatchewan Finance, *Budget Papers*, 1989, p.c.10.
24. Saskatchewan Social Services, *Monthly Bulletin of Statistics*, Table 3, p. 9.
25. Saskatchewan Social Services, *Monthly Bulletin of Statistics*, 1985–1987; *Quarterly Statistics*, 1988.
26. Rofuth, "Moving Clients," p. 20; M. Morris and J. B. Williamson, "Workfare: The Poverty/Dependency Trade Off," *Social Policy* 18(1) (Summer 1987), pp. 49–50; H. J. Karger and D. Stoesz, "Welfare Reform: Maximum Feasible Exaggeration," *Tikkun* 4(2) (March/April 1989), pp. 118–122. See also Saskatchewan Social Services, Saskatchewan Employment Development Program, 31 March 1986 (6).

27. Canada/Saskatchewan, *Canada/Saskatchewan Memorandum of Agreement re: Canada Assistance Plan*, 1967, sec. 2(b)(ii).
28. Ibid., sec. 2(c).
29. Saskatchewan Social Services, *Saskatchewan Assistance Plan Regulations*, sec. 4; Saskatchewan Social Services, *Saskatchewan Assistance Plan Manual*, chap. 2, sect. 1, p. 2.
30. Saskatchewan Social Services, *Saskatchewan Assistance Plan Regulations*, sec. 6.1.
31. Ibid., sec. 6(b).
32. Canada/Saskatchewan, *Accord on Employability Enhancement for Social Assistance Recipients*, 4 July 1986, sec. A1.
33. *Canada Assistance Plan Act*, part iii, sec. 15(3)(a).

CHAPTER 13

1. V. Greenshields, "20% fail to pick up April Welfare cheques," *Star Phoenix* (Saskatoon), 28 May 1988.
2. Saskatchewan Legislative Assembly, *Debates and Proceedings*, 32(103B), 22 August 1989, pp. 4368–4369.
3. V. Greenshields, "New measures cut welfare overpayments," *Star Phoenix* (Saskatoon), 15 June 1988; and "Social Services Minister Grant Schmidt estimates one in 10 on welfare cheats," *Star Phoenix*, 30 April 1989.
4. Saskatchewan Legislative Assembly, *Debates and Proceedings*, 32(103B), 22 August 1989, pp. 4352–4353.
5. E. Fowler, "Fraud Squad skulker upsets victim," *Star Phoenix*, 15 May 1987. Personal communications with members of Equal Justice for All.
6. Saskatchewan Legislative Assembly, *Debates and Proceedings*, 32(77A), 14 July 1989, p. 2661.
7. Henry Kutarna, assistant deputy minister of social services, to Valerie Stubbs, President of the Saskatoon Self-Help Council, 30 May 1988.
8. D. Yanko, "Closure of Self-Help Council deplored," *Star Phoenix*, 2 June 1988.
9. The Honourable Bill Neudorf, MLA, minister of social services, to Peter Prebble, MLA, 23 March 1990.
10. Ibid.
11. G. Riches and L. Manning, *Welfare Reform and the Canada Assistance Plan: The Breakdown of Public Welfare in Saskatchewan, 1981–1989* (Regina: Social Administration Research Unit, 1989), p. 31.
12. Saskatchewan Social Services, *Saskatchewan Assistance Plan Manual* (Regina: Saskatchewan Social Services, 1988), chap. 2, sec. 1, p. 2.
13. Greenshields, "New measures"; T. Herriot, "When the Welfare Inspector Makes House Calls . . ," *Briarpatch* 15(8) (October 1986); descriptions of incidents told to the authors by assistance recipients.
14. These examples are from cases in which the authors have served as advocates.
15. Saskatchewan Social Services, *Saskatchewan Assistance Plan Regulations*, sec. 6.1.
16. Ibid., sec. 6(b).
17. P. Elliott, "Wage Slaves: The Tory government of Grant Devine decided to put Saskatchewan's welfare recipients to work," *Saturday Night* 104(10) (October 1989).

18. Canada/Saskatchewan, *Accord on Employability Enhancement for Social Assistance Recipients*, 4 July 1986.
19. M. Stobbe, "Social Services forces cruel choice," *The Commonwealth* 49(4) (April 1989).
20. Elliott, "Wage slaves."
21. Saskatchewan Legislative Assembly, *Debates and Proceedings*, 32(103B), 22 August 1989, pp. 4368–4369.
22. Riches and Manning, *Welfare Reform*, p. 27.
23. *The Canada Assistance Plan Act*, part iii, sec. 15(3)(a).
24. Z. Olijnyk, "Welfare will be cut off for skipping job course," *Leader Post* (Regina), 18 April 1988.
25. Saskatchewan Legislative Assembly, *Debates and Proceedings*, 32(103B), 22 August 1989, p. 4370.
26. D. Greschner, *The Horror of Chambers: Why Chambers is Wrong–A Purposive Interpretation of "Offered to the Public"* (unpublished paper) (Saskatoon: University of Saskatchewan College of Law, 1987); and A. Jevcak, "Licence to discriminate," *Briarpatch* 16(5) (June 1987).
27. A. Paavo, "Chambers case nears conclusion," *Briarpatch* 16(1) (February 1988).
28. G. Taljit, "Welfare recipient told to find job," *Star Phoenix* (Saskatoon), 8 April 1987.
29. D. Traynor, "Province 'hasn't money' for welfare back pay," *Star Phoenix* (Saskatoon), 28 June 1988.
30. Saskatchewan Social Services, *Saskatchewan Assistance Plan Manual*, chap. 12, sec. 2.
31. W. Lutz, *Report of the Provincial Auditor to the Legislative Assembly for the Year Ended March 31, 1988* (Regina: Queens Printer, 1989), p. 71.
32. M. Stobbe, "Red tape and you," *The Commonwealth* 49(9) (October 1989).
33. This description is based on numerous cases in which the authors served as advocates for recipients.
34. Federal Court of Canada, *R. Finlay vs. Canada*, Mr. Justice Teiltelbaum, Trial Division, T–3666–82, 24 January 1989.
35. Saskatchewan Legislative Assembly, *Debates and Proceedings*, 33(58B), 11 June 1990, p. 1976.
36. G. York, "Transfer payments ruled illegal when welfare cheques cut," *The Globe and Mail* (Toronto), 7 July 1990.
37. Saskatchewan Social Services, *Assistance Plan Manual*, chap. 12, sec. 2, p. 5.
38. R. Burton, "Ruling curbs flexibility for aid: Neudorf," *Star Phoenix* (Saskatoon), 16 July 1990.

CHAPTER 14

1. M. Crozier, S. P. Huntington, and J. Watanuki, *The Crisis of Democracy: Report on the Governability of Democracies to the Trilateral Commission* (New York: New York University Press, 1975).
2. See Warren Magnusson et al., eds., *The New Reality; the Politics of Restraint in British Columbia* (Vancouver: New Star Books, 1984).
3. A. Paavo, "With a little help from their friends," *Briarpatch* 18(6) (1989), pp. 6–13.
4. A. Smith, *An Inquiry into the Nature and Courses of the Wealth of Nations*, rev. ed. (New York: Oxford University Press, 1976).

5. "Stocking capital regardless of price," *The Economist*, 298(7432), 8 February 1986, p. 63.

6. B. Harrison and B. Bluestone, *The Great U-Turn; Corporate Restructuring and the Polarizing of America* (New York: Basic Books, 1988).

7. Canada, House of Commons, *Hansard*, 6 June 1989.

8. *The Saskatchewan Promise*, Regina: Ministry of Economic Development and Trade, 15 August 1984, p.1.

9. Canada, The Royal Commission on Dominion-Provincial Relations, *Report* (Ottawa: The King's Printer, 1939).

10. Canada, Royal Commission on the Economic Union and Development Prospects for Canada, D. S. Macdonald, *Report*, 3 vols. (Toronto: University of Toronto Press, 1985).

11. Ibid., vol. 2, p. 157.

12. E. Carmichael, W. Dobson, and R. Lipsey, "The Macdonald Report: Signpost or Shopping Basket?," *Canadian Public Policy* XII (February 1986), pp. 23–39.

13. Macdonald, *Report*, vol. 3, p. 219.

14. R. Seymour, "Devine yens for Asian funds," *Times-Herald* (Moose Jaw), 4 March 1989.

15. P. Prebble, "Selling off Saskatchewan," *Briarpatch* 16 (May 1987), pp. 27–28.

16. "Lloyd still waiting for heavy oil plant," *Leader Post* (Regina), 28 November 1989, p. C–11.

17. B. Johnstone, "Questionable economics for fertilizer plant," *Leader Post* (Regina), 10 February 1990.

18. J. Warnock and S. Checkley, "The potash rip-off," *Briarpatch* 18 (December 1989), pp. 11–13.

19. T. Pugh, "Peter Pocklington gets handouts," *Union Farmer* 38 (March 1987).

20. R. Sass, "Blowing the whistle on Intercon," *Briarpatch* 13 (January/February 1984), pp. 14–16.

21. J. Warnock, "The Shand-Rafferty-Alameda Project," *Briarpatch* 19 (June 1990), pp. 8–19.

22. M. Stobbe, "Saskatchewan's Heritage: Going once . . . going twice . . ." *Briarpatch* 13 (June 1984), pp. 7–9.

23. Saskatchewan Government Employees Union, *Privatizing our Parks: Not in the Public Interest*, Regina, April 1988.

24. Warnock, "The Shand-Rafferty-Alameda Project."

25. "Western Free Trade," *Buy Saskatchewan Bulletin* 32 (July 1989), p. 1.

26. Cited in T. Corcoran, "Interprovincial trade barriers entrenched within beer industries," *The Globe and Mail* (Toronto), 3 March 1990.

CONTRIBUTORS

RICHARD BARTLETT is a Professor of Law at the University of Saskatchewan. He has published extensively in the areas of aboriginal law and natural resources law, and has acted as counsel on many matters in those areas.

LESLEY BIGGS is an Assistant Professor in the Department of Sociology, University of Saskatchewan. She has published a number of articles on the history of health care in Canada.

BRETT FAIRBAIRN is a historian at the University of Saskatchewan. He is the author of reports on accessibility and extension at the University of Saskatchewan. His other publications concern cooperatives and German history.

HOWARD LEESON is an Associate Professor of Political Science and department head of the University of Regina. From 1978–1982 he was Deputy Minister for Intergovernmental Affairs. He is the author of books and articles on Canadian politics and federalism.

IAN MCCUAIG is studying economics at the University of Saskatchewan.

LORALEE MANNING is a qualified social worker and until recently worked as welfare rights advocate at the Regina Welfare Rights Centre. She is now Executive Director of the Council on Social Development Regina Inc.

JUDITH MARTIN is the administrator of the Saskatoon Community Clinic. She is the founding chairperson of the Saskatchewan child care advocacy group Action Childcare and the founding chairperson of the Canadian Day Care Advocacy Association.

PETER MILLARD was born in Wales but has lived in Saskatchewan for a large part of his life. He has an active interest in human rights, and has been president of the Saskatchewan Association on Human Rights. He is head of the English Department at the University of Saskatchewan, and apart from his scholarly work in literature has written extensively on art.

TERRY PUGH is editor of the *Union Farmer*, a monthly newspaper published by the National Farmers Union. He has served on the editorial boards of *NeWest Review* and *Briarpatch* magazines, and has contributed articles and photographs to *Canadian Dimension*, *This Magazine*, *Prairie Messenger*, the *New York Guardian*, the *Western Producer*, and other periodicals. In 1987 he edited *Fighting the Farm Crisis* (Saskatoon: Fifth House).

PETER PREBBLE is a New Democratic Party member of the Saskatchewan legislature. He has a long involvement with the province's environmental movement.

DIANA RALPH is an Associate Professor in the faculty of Social Work at Carleton University (since 1988) and was formerly a faculty member in the School of Social Work at the University of Regina (1980–1988). She has been an activist in Saskatchewan welfare rights, women's, Native, and popular coalition groups.

MERRILEE RASMUSSEN is a Regina lawyer and a sessional lecturer at the College of Law in Saskatoon. For 12 years she was Saskatchewan's Legislative Counsel and Law Clerk. Now a Master's student in Political Science at the University of Regina, she was the recipient of the Queen Elizabeth II Scholarship in Parliamentary Studies in 1989.

GRAHAM RICHES is Professor of Social Work and Director of the Social Administration Research Unit at the University of Regina. He is author of *Food Banks and the Welfare Crisis* (Ottawa: CCSD, 1986), and co-editor with Gordon Ternowetsky of *Unemployment and Welfare: Social Policy and the Work of Social Work* (Toronto: Garamond Press, 1990). He also co-edits the *Canadian Review of Social Policy/Revue canadienne de politique sociale*.

ROBERT SASS is presently Associate Professor of Industrial Relations and Organizational Behaviour at the University of Saskatchewan. He was formerly Associate Deputy Minister of Labour and Executive Director of the Occupational Health and Safety Branch in the Saskatchewan Department of Labour from 1972–1982.

MARK STOBBE works as a constituency office manager for two New Democratic Party members of the Saskatchewan legislature. He has written numerous articles on privatization, social services policy, and occupational health and safety issues.

JOHN W. WARNOCK has authored four books on political economy and lectures at the University of Regina. He is a member of the editorial collective of *Briarpatch Magazine*.

Printed in Canada